LOFOTEN
◆
Page 16 -53

NORDFJORD
◆
Page 54 - 71

SOGNEFJORD ◆ *Page 72 - 81*

HORDALAND ◆ *82 - 89*

KARMØY ◆ *Page 90 - 99*

JÆREN ◆ *Page 100 - 119*

LISTA ◆ *Page 120 - 131*

Norway

Sweden

BOHUSLÄN - GOTALAND
◆
Page 138 - 143

HALLAND
Page 144 - 161

JUTLAND
◆
Page 218 - 243

Denmark

SJÆL-LAND
◆
Page 194 -217

SKÅNE
◆
Page 162 -187

SYLT ◆ *Page 250 - 263*

WADDEN ISLANDS   **NORDERNEY**
◆   ◆
Page 280 - 297   *Page 264 - 273*

Holland

NOORD-HOLLAND ◆ *Page 298 - 315*

ZUID-HOLLAND ◆ *Page 316 - 337*

ZEELAND ◆ *Page 338 - 351*

WEST-VLAANDEREN ◆ *Page 358 - 371*

Belgium

Germany

NORMANDY
Page 378 - 395

France

CONTENTS

♦

8 - 131 ♦ NORWAY

16 - 53 ♦ LOFOTEN
In and around Svolvær, Leknes, Flakstad, Moskenes & Surf

54 - 71 ♦ NORDFJORD
In and around Selje, Stryn & Surf

72 - 81 ♦ SOGNEFJORD
In and around Sogndal and Aurland

82 - 89 ♦ HORDALAND
In and around Voss

90 - 99 ♦ KARMØY - ROGALAND
In and around Skudeneshavn & Surf

100 - 119 ♦ JÆREN – ROGALAND
In and around Stavanger, Orrestranden & Surf

120 - 131 ♦ LISTA
In and around Farsund & Surf

132 - 187 ♦ SWEDEN

138 - 143 ♦ BOHUSLÄN - GOTALAND
In and around Grebbestad

144 - 161 ♦ HALLAND
In and around Åsa, Varberg & Surf

162 - 187 ♦ SKÅNE
In and around Mölle, Malmö, Ystad & Surf

188 - 243 ♦ DENMARK

194 - 217 ♦ SJÆLLAND
In and around Hornbæk, Gilleleje, Hundested, Copenhagen & Surf

218 - 243 ♦ JUTLAND
In and around Løkken, Klitmøller, Nørre Vorupør, Hvide Sande & Surf

GERMANY ♦ 244 - 273

SYLT ♦ 250 - 263
In and around Westerland & Surf

NORDERNEY ♦ 264 - 273
In and around Norderney & Surf

HOLLAND ♦ 274 - 351

WADDEN ISLANDS ♦ 280 - 297
Ameland, Terschelling, Vlieland, Texel & Surf

NOORD-HOLLAND ♦ 298 - 315
In and around Wijk aan Zee & Surf

ZUID-HOLLAND ♦ 316 - 337
In and around Scheveningen & Surf

ZEELAND ♦ 338 - 351
In and around Domburg & Surf

BELGIUM ♦ 352 - 371

WEST-VLAANDEREN ♦ 358 - 371
In and around Oostende & Surf

FRANCE ♦ 372 - 395

NORMANDY ♦ 378 - 395
In and around Dieppe, the D-Day beaches, Cotentin & Surf

Photo: Melchior van Nigtevecht

A WORD FROM US

After travelling the shores of southwest Europe for many years, we thought it was about time to broaden our horizons and head north. Moreover, we also thought it was about time to share with you the beauty of our own front yard; the North Sea!

We started as far north as the Lofoten archipelago and moved, slowly, steadily, down towards the north of France. Along the way we met up with, bumped into, started talking to and sharing waves with, inspiring, funny, knowledgeable and friendly seaside people. Whether they were fellow travellers, surfers, entrepreneurs, fishermen or women, artists, photographers, dog walkers or simply passing by, all helped to create this new surf and travel guide.

Needless to say, this book is about the seaside. It's about every aspect of it, because that's what we love. It's about travelling, about surfing, about people.
And we hope you love it too, and enjoy the NW Europe edition of the I Love the Seaside guide as much as we've enjoyed creating it.

We want you to get into the feeling of a trip before you're even going. We want you to remember that awesome adventure. We want you to have a lovely tool in hand and use it over and over again.

We're here to inspire, so you can go and explore.

HOW TO USE THIS GUIDE

◆

This guide takes you from the Lofoten Islands, in the north of Norway, down the west coast, the shores of Sweden and Denmark, hops to a couple of Germany's islands, and then follows Holland and Belgium's coastlines south before a last hurrah along to Normandy's peninsula. Of course, we expect that you'll travel your own route; dropping in and out wherever suits, using a chapter, skipping to your next destination, or curled up at home on the sofa, flicking through the guide and dreaming of adventures to come. Our aim, and greatest hope, is to guide you along and inspire you on your journey, whether you're a surfer, a seaside lover or simply a traveller who admires the great outdoors!

We don't stop at each spot, or list every place we've been, but if you follow the coast from one area to the next, you'll find each place we pinpoint is a central location from which you can go and explore; it's essentially the surfbreaks, the beaches, and the ocean of course, that take the place of your compass. All the things we recommend for you to discover are within a day's reach of the seaside.

PRICES

◆

Due to seasonal price changes, especially for hotels and campsites, we've chosen to use symbols which give you an indication of price ranges. Note that it's all relative, the ◆€◆ or ◆€€◆ range in Norway, for example, suits Norwegian standards.

◆

◆€◆ Cheap as chips
◆€€◆ Pretty reasonable
◆€€€◆ Affordable treat
◆€€€€◆ Luxurious extravagance

SURF SCHOOLS AND SHOPS

◆

Big thing in this guide, of course. The schools and shops mentioned within are either approved and loved by us, or recommended by trusted partners. Those that we don't mention: it doesn't mean they're inferior, malfunctioning or what-not. Certainly not. In some surfing areas there are so many, with so little difference between them, that in those areas we were very picky and chose those we feel offer special character or atmosphere, that add a twist to the definition of surf shop. In the areas where schools and shops are scarce, we mention any in the area, because they can be useful if in need of wax, leash, repair, etc.

SURF SPOTS

◆

On our travels along the coast of Europe we meet so many friendly locals, surfers and saltwater addicts. Most of them are happy to share waves and even take us out to their favourite local - but sometimes secret - surf spot. We respect that, and them, and therefore try to avoid misusing those warm and welcoming gestures. None of the surf spots mentioned in our guide are secret, they're known to many. While we only list the well-known, that doesn't mean there aren't many more spots to discover for yourself. So, since we're huge fans of exploring and meeting new people to learn, share, and make friends, we encourage you to do a little exploring yourself, with that same respect in mind. We sincerely hope you understand our choice.

◆

Not all who wander are lost.

◆

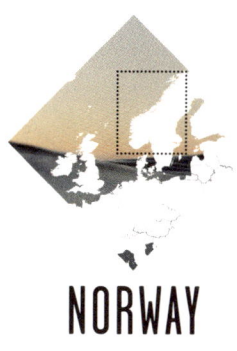

NORWAY

With close to a quarter of a million kilometres of coastline, Norway's shape makes for meandering lengths of outstanding beauty. It's intriguing, to say the least. Even the land takes on a fluid feeling as the surrounding seas - North Atlantic meets Norwegian & North Sea, add a drop of Barents, a tap on the top from the Greenland and a tickle of the Skagerrak from below - create constant coastal change. There are thousands of islands (and those are just the saltwater ones, not even counting the freshwater islands), which makes it quite some challenge to try travelling mainly along the seaside. We tried. And we failed. But what's to love is that both coast and inland provide a playground for anyone that adores to be outdoors; offering mind-bending views, lakes as big as seas with the blues of Andalusian skies, straight to the stars cliff faces and mammoth mountains.

There are only 5 million people in this big, big country, so there will be times you travel for hours, or days, and meet no one at all; come prepared, and cherish it, the uncrowded spaces to explore. When you're in the mood for faces, you'll find towns feel uncomplicated, villages friendly. Indoor places, as in: coffee bar, café, brewery, guesthouse and, of course, saunas abound; all are as attractive as a fireplace and hot chocolate on a cold day. Just don't count on a last minute late night tipple takeout, since you can't buy alcohol from shops after 18:00 hrs. And yes, Norway is an expensive country, even for northern European standards. But then again, there's the 'allemannsretten'; the right to roam all unfenced and uncultivated land, put up your tent for the night, fish for your supper (sea only - freshwater requires a permit), and pick berries, wild herbs and mushrooms. You'll find signs in most parks with specified dos and don'ts: please read them carefully, they're very user-friendly, with more do-ing than don't-ing. Needless to say, but saying it anyway: never, ever, leave your rubbish.

And say what about the weather? Well, it's a much-heard cliché but oh so true: in Norway they say there's no such thing as bad weather, only inadequate clothing. They love to spend time outdoors: camping, picnicking, hiking, whatevering, as long as it's not inside. So, yes, take that hipster raincoat, add an extra sweater, and make sure your shoes can keep your feet dry while all else is wet. Summers can get warm, sunny, misty, showery and everything in between. You'll be surprised how enjoyable being outside all day can get; even in relentless rain, when you pass a 700 metre high waterfall, picking hands full of blueberries and raspberries on the path, and hear the distant sound of crackle-snapping glacier ice.

SURFER-TRAVELLER TYPE NORWAY

♦

You love a bit of arctic vibe and are keen on seeing greenish-purplish lights dancing in the night sky, you know how to handle a camera, or get frustrated you don't. Remote areas don't scare you, you can get used to tunnels, and not using your fifth gear for weeks – let alone the sixth! Foraging berries and herbs and chanterelle mushrooms from the forest is your idea of a wild party. You're the next level outdoorsy type, or a newbie who loves to hang out in hot tubs and can add a bit of swagger to wearing active wear.

WORDS AND CONCEPTS THAT MIGHT COME IN HANDY

♦

God dag! Meaning hello, good day! Sounds like *'goo dagh'*.

Or just say *Morn!* as in a more informal 'Hi/Good Morning!'

Vi sees = See you later

Takk = Thank you

Vær så god! Literal translation 'Here it is' but used as *'You're welcome!'*
(Usually to a food offering.)

God tur = Have a nice trip

Det regner = It's raining

FOOD FACTS

BRUNOST

A brown-coloured block of substance with a sweet taste, made from the whey of goat cheese. Expect a bit of caramel flavour mixed with a slight something savoury, the texture of cheese. And have it in slices on bread, maybe topped off with jam.

RØKT LAKS

Smoked salmon. Of course you know the taste of smoked salmon. But it's said that Norwegian salmon's deep rich flavour is the result of the cold waters, which causes the fish to grow more slowly.

AKEVITT

You should also try Akvavitt, a sturdy Scandinavian spirit, in Norway distilled from potatoes instead of grain, flavoured with spices and herbs such as coriander, caraway and dill, matured in oak casks, and said to aid the digestion. (also called Akvavit or Aquavit - 'Water of Life'). Skål!

Photo: Melchior van Nigtevecht

A BIT ON SURF IN NORWAY

Little is documented, as such, but according to well-informed sources (aka surfers of a certain age and stature we met in surf shops, car parks, or in the water) surfing in Norway started in the 1980s in Jæren, in the southwest, during the heyday of wind-surfing. Local Roar Berge and some American oil workers recognised the potential and started exploring the many beaches.

Others claim it started during the 1960s in the northerly Lofoten Islands. The story goes a few guys saw the surfboard photo on a Beach Boys album cover and built themselves a board, filled with insulation from a fridge. Others say considering the fact that they had no wetsuits and the sea reaches a max of 16°c in summer, that the probability of this story being true, although very romantic, is pretty low. But, at the Unstad Arctic Surf Camp in Lofoten, we saw the evidence: the surfboard and an accompanying photo of the album. Apparently Thor Frantzen, (whose daughter now runs Unstad Arctic Surfcamp), and his friend, Hans Egil Krane, worked on ships when they were young boys. While sailing the world, they had their first surf experience in Sydney, Australia. Back home, the board on the '62 Beach Boys album 'Surfin' Safari' inspired them to make their own.

The second wave of surfers came in the 1990s, as surfing became a big hit in northern European countries; contests kicked off, films, magazines, and a wider range of boards became available. These surfers, and their kids, are now part of a fast growing surf community, which even Norway's Crown Prince Haakon is a member of. Actually, it's quite a royal affair: his wife Mette-Marit and their 2 kids surf too. You can well imagine a 'Gone Surfing' sign on the door of the Royal Palace - highly cool huh! They all attended the Eurosurf 2017 contest, hosted by Norway for the first time in Borestranden, Jæren.

SO WHEN AND WHERE'S YOUR BEST BET FOR CONSISTENT SURF IN NORWAY?

♦

Although spring, autumn, and especially winter, bring the most powerful waves and consistent swells, the cold and lack of daylight tend to hold back the masses. But even in summer the most popular spots will never be as crowded as the south of France, or Portugal, so you'll have your fair share of waves.

The Lofoten Islands in the north are well explored, especially by those with an eye for arctic beauty and no fear of neoprene. (Thick layers of it.) Further north are numerous remote islands and inlets, peninsulas and pristine bays which are less well-travelled. Or head south a bit to the west coast breaks around Nordfjord, some two hours up from the city of Bergen, which get more popular every year. As with most of Norway's coast, the beautiful backdrop of cliffs, hills and lakes will blow you away.

A couple of hours down from Bergen, we explored Karmøy in the southwest, and Lista down south, both bountifully blessed with empty line-ups and beautiful beaches. In between the two, the more consistent and most popular spot is Jæren: here the North Sea provides easy rollers at beachbreaks and more demanding slabs at boulder rock points, with a backdrop of dunes and grasslands, oodles of charming little towns, and the surprisingly contemporary and smart city Stavanger.

LOFOTEN

While the Nordic countries are pretty well known for fish, the chain of islands that make the Lofoten archipelago have been the centre of Europe's cod fisheries for more than a thousand years. And what calls the cod to Lofoten, as well as what follows the cod - fishermen, orcas, dolphins, sea eagles - is a great big bit of what makes Lofoten so attractive to seaside lovers and surfers.

Due to the warming effect of the Gulf Stream, the climate's not as cold as you'd expect within the Arctic Circle, which makes for stable conditions. Add some solid shelter from the great 'Lofoten Wall', and the vestfjorden expanse of water has all the ingredients to make it a cod's dream spawning ground. (Keep that 5/4/3 wetsuit at hand though - it's not exactly the tropics. Save your boardshorts and bikinis for the hot tub, you'll find plenty of those around.) And that great wall we mentioned - Lofotveggen - is a formidable sight; a range of mountain peaks that rose from the sea during the last ice age, sheltering the bays and inlets to the south and making quite the impression as you arrive, whether by sea, road or air.

Other things you'll notice; colourful fisherman's cabins, lots of ocean inspired arts and crafts, genuinely friendly locals, and a salty sea smell with more than a hint of fish; especially from February to May, when stockfish production is in full swing and the hjell - wooden hanging racks - are full of cod drying in the cold air and wind.
But how to decide when to visit... winter means a good chance of seeing the Northern Lights, while summer's midnight sun makes for some extra special surf sessions. Perhaps the big decision is how long to stay...

TRAVEL INFO

◆

Depending from where you travel, Lofoten isn't quite around the corner. It's a long leg coming from the south by car or campervan. So you could consider the option of flying in and either rent a car or campervan, or use public transport. Travelling by public transport is excellent, but requires some planning, so check the timetables carefully. Lots of companies rent out cars, from Evenes airport you can try Rent-A-Wreck for good prices (**w.** rent-a-wreck.no - select Harstad/Evenes). Campervans can be rented from Arctic Campers, with rental stations in Leknes and Tromsø (**w.** arcticcampers.no - see Sleep section for info).

BY AIR
◆

From most countries there are flights to Oslo. Via Oslo there are flights to the main airport Evenes (EVE) near Narvik/Harstad, or the smaller airports of Svolvær or Leknes. From the airports at Leknes, Svolvær and Røst it's necessary to use a taxi, there are no buses. From Evenes Airport (Narvik/Harstad) there's a twice-daily Lofotekspressen (Lofoten Express).

w. norwegian.com, flysas.com & wideroe.no

BY BOAT
◆

Regular ferries and express boats sail between Moskenes to the mainland Bodø in 3-4 hrs, and between Svolvær to the mainland Skutvik via Skrova in 2,5 hrs.

w. torghatten-nord.no

PUBLIC TRANSPORT
◆

Between Å and Svolvær there are usually 4-6 buses per day, (Sundays can be an exception). There are bus connections to many parts of Lofoten. Coming from Narvik: You can travel on the daily bus service across Lofoten on the E10 all the way to Å. The bus stops en route include Svolvær and Leknes. Info bus schedule:

t. +47 7577 2410 / 9947 3999
w. 77nordland.no

FOOD FACT

♦

COD, CAVIAR AND LIQUID GOLD

♦

The archipelago's climate not only creates the ideal breeding ground for cod, it's also perfect for stockfish production. Traditional cod harvesting takes place during the best time to dry the fish, when the weather maintains a stable temperature just above freezing, with not too much rain. Too much frost will spoil the fish, as ice destroys the fibres in the flesh, so that biting chill wind early in the year is something to celebrate: it's what gives the stockfish of Lofoten and Vesterålen the reputation of being the very best. Must try?

During the intense weeks of cod harvest, Lofoten also waves farewell to tons of fish shipped away to be salted, cod-roes exported to Sweden for caviar, and then there's the cod liver oil to be sorted out too: "It's our liquid gold," as one of the locals said.

IN AND AROUND SVOLVÆR

•

Svolvær is the municipal centre of Vågan, and the biggest town in the Lofoten Islands. Relatively big though: what with its population of about five thousand. But if you're in need of a bit of city vibe, and wanting to leave the active wear at home for a day, this is your chance. It's not exactly Paris-a-go-go, but there's a shopping mall, a cinema, there are art galleries and an international art festival every September, and you'll have a choice of restaurants. You can even chill out and have a beer at the freezing cold bar, Magic Ice, while admiring their display of ice sculptures. And there's cod, hung up in racks, of course.

If you want to get up close and intimate with the spectacular walls of the Trollfjord, here's your starting point. Several companies offer boat or kayak tours up and down the narrow fjord, and it's quite a spectacle to see the big cruise ships navigating their way in and out of the really very narrow entrance. If you'd rather take to the heights; overlooking the town and all around stands the iconic granite pinnacle, Svolværgeita, patiently waiting for you to climb its summits (once you've changed back into your active wear that is).

Tourist office (Svolvær Turistinformasjon) **a.** Torget 18, 8300 Svolvær

TO DO
•

From Svolvær starts the **132 km scenic road E-10**, which runs all the way to Å - the last letter of the Norwegian alphabet is Å, hence the name, since the village Å sits at the southern end of the archipelago.

Only 5 km southwest of Svolvær sits the quaint village of **Kabelvåg (1)** with its large wooden church, Vågan Kirke, and a little row of houses cuddled up to the harbour's shore. As far back as the 12th century people built their settlement here, as they followed the retreating ice cap and moved north.

Some 25 km east from Svolvær you'll find the Venice of the North, **Henningsvær (2)**. This town, with around 400 inhabitants, is as close to a traditional Norwegian fishing village as you can get in this part of Lofoten. Lining the harbour are rorbu cabins, reflecting their colours in the glassy water. This, and the dramatic backdrop of granite mountains make you want to take up painting and shout 'Bob Ross, eat your heart out'.

The northern lights, or Aurora Borealis, must be one of the most magical phenomena you could ever witness. A gigantic must-see - at least once in your life. Spend a week in Lofoten in late September, and you may even get bored with yet another night of dancing green lights in the sky, there're so many! Nah, you won't get bored, promise. The Northern Lights appear when electrically charged particles from the sun collide with gaseous

particles in the earth's atmosphere. Your best chance of seeing it's between the beginning of September and April. The Aurora Borealis is still there the rest of the year, but the nights aren't dark enough to see it in the summer. If you want to be sure you're not missing out, deepen your knowledge, see it from different perspectives or want to learn how to photograph the phenomenon perfectly, there are plenty of options to join the Aurora Borealis party, here are our picks:

Steven Henriksen is a passionate photographer of everything Lofoten, from the spectacular landscape to the Northern Lights. Originally from Denmark, he moved to the archipelago at a young age, and he's not planning to head back to his place of birth any time soon: 'I feel I have everything I need up here in the arctic, just outside my doorstep.' Some 3,5 years ago he started helping people find the Northern Lights and the best spots to take good shots from, thus **Lofoten Arctic Photography** (3) was born. Besides making the most amazing photos of his beloved environment, he offers customised guided tours and workshops on landscape and night photography. Of these tours the most popular is, not surprisingly, the Northern Lights tour; an adventure all in itself, where you find yourself chasing the Aurora, even in tough conditions. Aurora season starts at the end of August and ends in mid-April. A tour can last between 4 to 8 hours, during which you'll learn about camera settings, composition, use of filters, local specialities, and you can request specific hikes or locations. The landscape tour (covering all of Lofoten) can be booked all year, with up to 2-day tours available. The midnight sun tour is from end of May to mid-July.

t. +47 9017 4250
fb. lofotenarcticphotography

The Polarlightcenter (4) on the northern island Austvågøy is your best option to learn everything there is to know about the Northern Lights. Dutch couple, Rob and Therese, moved to Lofoten in 2007 and started the business, where they share their passion for the Northern Lights. With a presentation of photos and animations, and of course live action when it's on, they'll explain all you want to know about this phenomenal light show. After the presentation you go outside for a night walk to witness the auroras. The Polarlightcenter provides accommodation too, with ocean view and, of course, the Northern Lights dancing above, behind and at the sides.

a. Midnattsolveien 1706, Straumnes, 8315 Laukvik
t. +47 9112 4668
w. polarlightcenter.com

Chilling out's your idea of fun? Don't miss the ice bar and gallery **Magic Ice** (5) in Svolvær. But no need to worry about getting too cold, the admission fee includes a drink and use of a warm coat to wear while you refresh yourself. This is a bar where it's appropriate to bring your children along. And they'll love it! Besides admiring the ice sculptures you'll learn about coastal culture, traditions and nature. And of course the bar's stocked with all kinds of refreshments. Open all year.

a. Fiskergata 36, 8300 Svolvær
t. +47 7607 4011
w. magicice.no/locations/svolvaer

Northern Alpine Guides (6) offer climbing and mountaineering courses and guiding for all levels. Whether alpine or rock, whether you're old, young, travelling by yourself or with your family, whatever height or difficulty you fancy, they'll tailor the instructing or guiding to make your wish come true. All guides are qualified and certified, with years of experience. If you've never climbed anything but a ladder, you can choose their introduction course to rock climbing and learn from the start during two days outdoors in beautiful surroundings.

a. Kalleveien 23, 8310 Kabelvåg
t. +47 9424 9110
w. alpineguides.no

All this outdoor activity of surfing, hiking, climbing or just hours in the car tired your muscles? Try **Nakken Naturterapi** (7) for a good massage, reflexology or cupping therapy.

a. Nakkenveien 22, 8310 Kabelvåg
t. +47 7630 0731

Some fine northern Norwegian art is on show at **Galleri Lille Kabelvåg** (8) by artists and owners, Thor Erdahl and Inger Anne Nyaas. Since their aim's to be part of the local community's cultural events, there are regular exhibits of work from guest artists, directors and musicians. Open all summer; in autumn and winter open only on Saturday from 12:00 to 15:00 hrs and Sunday from 16:00 to 19:00 hrs.

a. Torget, 8310 Kabelvåg
t. +47 4165 3207
w. lillekabelvaag.no

The Kaviar Factory (9) is a venue for both local and international contemporary art. The owner, Miss Venke Hoff, and her husband Rolf Hoff have assembled, with passion and a deep love

of art, a large collection over some 30-odd years. Besides their collection you'll find art books, designer pieces, and original items for children in their shop. The Kaviar Factory's building used to be a real factory where 'Lofoten Paste', caviar, was produced in the 1950s.

a. Henningsværveien 13, 8312 Henningsvær
t. +47 9073 4743
w. kaviarfactory.com

Dance, try locally brewed Lofotpils, and see some of Norway's best known artists perform at this (as yet) small-scale festival. And after the concerts you can go clubbing inside. It's all part of **Trevarefest (10)**, a yearly pop music festival, held in summer, at the end of July/beginning of August. Not only a perfect way to get a feel for Norway's pop scene, but also to meet up with young Lofoten. Although you'll find an audience of all ages overall it's a late 20s to early 30s kinda party. Tickets sell out fast, so move quickly if you decide to go!

a. Dreyers Gate 72, 8312 Henningsvær
w. trevarefest.no

Take your climbing to the next level with **Nord Norsk Klatreskole (11)**. The school's been running courses since 1973, so they've proved pretty professional, we'd say! They offer climbing courses for all levels and guide you to 'splendid routes and magnificent peaks', as they say themselves. And it's so true, what can we say; they rock! The crew are a passionate and knowledgeable bunch of outdoor people. They also rent out fisherman's cabins to stay. Find them at the Klatrekafeen - the rock-climbers café. Open all year.

a. Misværveien 10, 8312 Henningsvær
t. +47 9057 4208
w. nordnorskklatreskole.no

Kayak along Henningsvær's coast to discover spectacular scenery with **Kayak Lofoten (12)**. The nickname 'Venice of the North' makes a lot of sense, but we think it's even better than that. You'll explore the rugged coastline, paddle into hidden beaches, spot sea eagles and otters, and if you're lucky even whales. In July you can join the midnight-sun tours. From March to October they have guided kayak tours every day around Henningsvær, which include a visit to the historic town and some interesting troll stories! All tours take up to 3 hrs. If you're not the paddling type, or the weather isn't that kayak friendly, you can also join their hiking trips around the Henningsvær mountains.

a. Gammelveien 6, 8312 Henningsvaer
t. +47 4680 5648
w. kayaklofoten.com

If the stunning beauty of Lofoten hasn't already quietened your mind, **Norlandia** (13) arranges meditation events and holds silent retreats at different locations - but mostly at the scenic Dreamcatcher retreat in Laukvika, in the southeast of the archipelago. For information on their programme and events you can check their website or send them an email.

t. +47 9806 7716
e. ingvild.austgulen@gmail.com
w. silentlofoten.weebly.com
w. visitdreamcatcherretreat.com

EAT/DRINK/HANG OUT
♦

Is it a bar, a restaurant? **Bacalao** (14) is big and busy, that's for sure. Overlooking the harbour of Svolvær, the restaurant that feels like a large pub transforms into a bar after the kitchen closes. There are regular live music events and DJs playing. Before the party hour they serve, obviously, bacalao (cod) and fish burgers among other things. Open every day. ♦€€♦

a. Havnepromenaden 2, 8300 Svolvær
t. +47 7607 9400
w. bacalaobar.no

Finding wholesome and freshly baked bread throughout our travels in Norway became a bit of a quest: our Dutch bakery standards weren't easily met, or even topped as they were in Germany and Denmark. So you can imagine our 'yeah, baby, yeah!' upon finding the organic **Bakeri Unseld** (15) in Kabelvåg. This little bakery uses organic ingredients, bakes a wide range of delicious pastries and breads, made from various sorts of wheat and grains, like spelt, or rye. They serve tasteful sourdough or gluten-free bread, and variations with walnuts, pumpkin and raisins. You can even order a locally roasted organic coffee with that. They serve lunch and take-away, they also have a little stand selling organic items, varying from juices and tea to healthy food for your dog! Open all year. ♦€♦ ♦€€♦

a. Torggata 11, 8310 Kabelvåg
t. +47 9813 0320
fb. baeckereilofoten (Bakeriet i Kabelvåg)

Eat, drink, listen to some music, and enjoy the view of Kabelvåg's harbour from the restaurant and bar **Praestengbrygga** (16). Either in the sun on their dockside terrace, or inside where the use of dark wood on the floor and walls, and the staff of course, give the place a warm and cosy vibe. Open all year. ♦€♦ ♦€€♦

a. Torget 9, 8310 Kabelvåg
t. +47 7607 8060
w. prestengbrygga.no

Our favourite by far is **Trevare Fabrikken** (17). The old woodwork

factory now turned into cultural house serves food and their locally brewed Lofotpils, holds events, and offers yoga classes. As well as putting on the earlier mentioned annual music festival, Trevarefest. A perfect place to chat and meet up with locals and tourists alike, or open up your laptop and consider this your office for the day, have a bite to eat, listen to some live music and above all, admire how they've done the place up. It's a perfect combination of rustic and industrial, creativity and originality. And it comes with very friendly staff and a smashing view of the ocean and mountains. Accommodation will be on offer as well, from summer 2018. Open all year. ♦€€♦

a. Dreyers Gate 72, 8312 Henningsvær
w. trevarefabrikken.no

The colourful and cosy **Henningsvær Lysstøperi & Café** (18) serves a choice of sandwiches, pizzas and cakes. See if you can resist their sweet treats at the counter, seducing you with their luscious looks and smell. The Lysstøperi's not just a café and lunchroom, they make their own candles too. Lots of them: in a wide range of colours and sizes, decorating and adding to the cheerful atmosphere of the place. Open all year till 17:00 hrs. ♦€€♦

a. Gammelveien 2, 8312 Henningsvær
t. +47 9055 1877 / 7607 7040
w. henningsvarlys.no

Lofotmat (19) serves local seafood dishes. It's a very pleasant restaurant in the small fishing village Henningsvaer.

Sometimes it's a plus not to have an overwhelming choice on the menu, this is exactly what Lofotmat offers; catch of the day and seasonal food. They also have a small selection of local - and not so local - delicacies for sale, such as Italian sausages and olive oil and French cheese. ◆€€◆

a. Dreyers Gate 56, 8312 Henningsvær
t. +47 9771 7059
fb. lofotmat

The **Klatrekafeen** (**20**) is the local rock climbers' café. It's décor's an eclectic mix of Nepalese, hipster, urban, outdoor, vintage, and Nordic furniture and design. It represents perfectly its clientele: besides local and visiting climbers you'll find yourself in the company of surfers, runners, fishermen, local workers and office people in their free time. Anything and everything goes, whether you're into climbing or not, you will feel right at home to grab a bite to eat, share a warm or cold drink, meet up with fellow travellers, or find a climbing buddy and for climbing gear. They also have places to sleep on offer. ◆€€◆

a. Misværveien 10, 8312 Henningsvær
t. +47 9095 4619
w. nordnorskklatreskole.no/klatrekafeen

SHOP
◆

Rundt & Rundt (**21**) is an eco-friendly gift shop with a bonus: to see the artist and owner at work, Sylvia Henriksen. She uses recycled textiles to make sustainable design items. Some are even labelled 'zero waste', like the washable make-up pads in a bag. You'll find colourful bracelets made out of tablecloth, washable lunch bags, gifts for children and interior products. Sylvia uses found objects, and makes us think twice about consumption and pollution and the change we can make. The shop also sells products from local farms such as wool, herbs, spices and natural skin products. Open all year.

a. Torggata 10, 8310 Kabelvåg
t. +47 9589 9723
w. rundtogrundt.no

If you're anything like us, still reading paper, printed books, old, new, second-hand, exchanged on the way, you should definitely check out **Kabelvåg Micro Library** (**22**). It's in Kabelvåg's town square, and is open 24 hours.

You may exchange or take a book for free. We like, like, like it a lot!

You'll need to keep your head and ears warm at times up here in the north, so you might as well do it in style. Mind your hat and check out **Cod and Haddock (23)** in Henningsvær. Amongst other woollen stuff they sell their famous woollen hats: 'Designed in Lofoten, made in the Himalayas, used worldwide'. Maybe throw in a pair of socks while you're there?

a. Misværveien 10, 8312 Henningsvær
w. haddock.no

SLEEP
♦

Campervan: There are plenty of campsites in the area, but if you're just looking for services like disposal points to empty your chemical toilets, you can use the following locations: Akkarvikodden picnic area, Sandsletta Camping in Laukvik (€ - closed in winter), Purkholmen Bobil Camping in Solvaer (€), Lofoten Turist Rorbusenter (€) and Kabelvåg Feriehus & Camping (€). More info on septic tank stations, waste disposal and WC locations, check:

w. cleanuplofoten.no/map

Our definite recommendation and preferred means to make your way round the archipelago is to rent a campervan from **Arctic Campers (24)**. We should know, because we used this way of transportation! They have (super) models ranging from a basic VW Caddy to

a VW Transporter 4x4 cabin camper. Their absolute rock star must be the Aurora Dome Camper, which gives you a 360° view of the sky from inside the van, so there's no need to leave the camper to check for Aurora activity, how cool is that! Watch the starry night, or midnight summer sky from the warmth and comfort of your bed: it's a five star experience within the confines of your own house on wheels. All their campers include bedding, gas stove, fridge, sink and water tanks, kitchen utensils and cleaning kit, heater, and on-board wifi. Arctic Campers have rental stations in Leknes, Tromsø and Oslo. Available all year. ♦€€♦

t. +47 4101 7430
w. arcticcampers.no

Hammerstad camping (25) has pitches right next to a fishing spot. There are cabins that sleep up to nine persons. And the biggest perk? If you're into fishing you can rent a small fishing boat for your daily fresh catch. The campsite's located at the Austnesfjord, which is considered one of Europe's richest fishing fjords. Open all year. ♦€♦

a. Austnesfjordveien 720, 8300 Svolvær
t. + 47 9162 7025
w. hammerstadcamping.no

Kabelvåg Feriehus & Camping (26) is surrounded by green hills and mountains, has lakeside pitches for tents, space for campervans, there're cottages for rent and is popular with both hiker and biker community. Open all year. ♦€♦

a. Mølnosveien 19, 8310 Kabelvåg
t. +47 7607 8620
w. kabelvag.com

Taking centre stage in Henningsvær's harbour, the white wooden sea houses of fish giant **John H. Giæver (27)** (say again?). They're actually part of the fish farm of the Giæver company that has fishing factories all over Norway. Workers at the factory use the houses in the busy months that hundreds of tons of cod need to be processed. In summer though, Giæver rents out six rooms for reasonable prices. The kitchen, showers and living room are shared with the other guests. They also have a few newly restored fishermen's 'shacks' and apartments for rent at the quay, all have a private bathroom and kitchen. The reception is situated at the fishing factory of John H Giæver at the end of the harbour. Available in summer. ♦€♦ ♦€€♦

a. Hellandsgt 79, 8312 Henningsvær
t. +47 7607 4719
w. giaever-rorbuer.no

The **Dreamcatcher Retreat**'s **(28)** biggest attraction must be its amazing view. Although the house, which used to be a homestead, is cosy enough and very nicely decorated, you'll still be staring outside a lot. It's so beautiful, no matter what season, the ocean and mountain view, with its ever changing lights, it never grows old. The old sheep and haybarn (fjøs) has been restored into a comfortable guesthouse. Located near the fishing village of Laukvik, the Dreamcatcher Retreat is for up to seven persons, but can house up to twelve persons for group bookings, workshops and retreats. Open all year. ♦ €€ ♦

a. Midnattsolveien 1778, 8315 Laukvik
t. +47 9082 8103
w. visitdreamcatcherretreat.com

IN AND AROUND LEKNES

Because of its situation, on the island Vestvågøya, bang in the middle of the archipelago, it's easy for us to make Leknes the centre of all the activities you can do, all the sights you can see and all the lovely places to eat, sleep or drink in the area. Leknes itself is not the quaint fishing village you maybe expect to find. In fact, it's not a fishing village at all – which in itself is quite remarkable in this area. The boats you'll see in the harbour don't bring fish but tourists; it's one of the biggest hubs for cruise ships. In town you'll find supermarkets and a shopping mall, and Leknes airport has daily scheduled national flights (to Bodø). The surroundings, however, are don't-forget-to-breathe beautiful. So we're very happy to guide you out of town; to go hiking, climbing, fishing, horse riding, maybe even snowboarding or skiing, surfing, of course, or… err… hula-hoop?!

Tourist office inside the library at Storgata 31, 8370 Leknes.

TO DO

Follow the Viking Trail across the Gimsøy Nature Reserve. On a horse, of course, an Icelandic horse no less, under the guidance of **Hov Gård Riding Centre** (**29**). The Hov farm's hundreds of years old and has been run by the same family, Hov, generation after generation. Its grounds hold some of the oldest monuments of Scandinavia, such as Viking graves and temples. You might be riding under the dancing northern lights, will certainly be listening to fascinating Viking stories and admiring the landscape of the Gimsøy island. Choose a private tour, tailored to your wishes, a Northern Lights tour, or a 2 to 4 day trip with accommodation and food included.

a. Thore Hjorts vei 471, 8314 Gimsøysand
t. +47 9755 9501
w. hovgard.no

The clear waters surrounding the Lofoten islands appear deceptively tropical. And you can actually do exactly the same things you would do in tropical waters, like snorkelling and scuba diving. You just need a much thicker wetsuit. **Lofoten Diving** (**30**) will provide you with that, and take you for your ocean adventure from their RIB boat. They promise you'll see spectacular underwater beauties: starfish, kelp forests, all kinds of little and large fish, crabs and much more. Lofoten Diving offers day tours and PADI courses, for all ages and skills. In winter they offer orca and cod-spawning tours, in summer we recommend you book in advance. Open all year.

a. Sjømannsgata 5, 8300 Svolvær
   and Skarsjyveien 67, 8373 Ballstad
t. +47 4004 8554 and +47 4005 1852
w. lofoten-diving.com

Lofoten Yogastudio (**31**) in Stamsund teaches beginner and advanced

classes. They offer dynamic, calm and acro yoga, and mindfulness workshops. All classes include meditation and Pranayama (breath work). Drop-in classes are available, as are private classes with teacher Mona Sveum. They also offer retreats with a combination of yoga, mindfulness, hiking, and exploring the outdoor possibilities of Lofoten. Open all year, but opening hours and schedule vary depending on season.

- **a.** J.M. Johansens vei 99, 8340 Stamsund (entrance near the NOR theatre)
- **t.** +47 9015 0523
- **w.** lofotenyogastudio.no

One of the very special attractions for this area is that you can surf and ski in one day. Depending on the season and snow conditions you can check out the **Lofoten Snowboard and Ski Resort (32)** in Stamsund. It's a state of the art, modern facility with a 1700 metre downward slope.

- **a.** Alpinhytta Stamsund, 8340 Stamsund
- **t.** +47 7608 9411
- **w.** lofotenalpinsenter.com

At Vikten, in a conspicuous-looking wooden building, covered with green and facing the ocean, you'll find **Glashytta (33)**; the workshop of glass-blower Åsvar Tangrand. Why'd we recommend this place? Glassblowing is a very special, and unique kind of craftsmanship, and if you have the chance to witness the process, especially in such an environment as this, it's just something we wouldn't want you to miss. And you'll get warm just watching, that's a bonus. There's a coffee shop and unique pieces of glass and pottery displayed for sale. Open all year.

- **a.** Vikten, 8373 Ballstad
- **t.** +47 9771 6023
- **w.** glasshyttavikten.no

Yet again an option to go horse riding, with the pioneers of horse riding tours in Lofoten no less! The local guides from **LofotHest (34)** take you out on mountain rides or a midnight sun expedition in the surroundings of Rolvsfjord (northeast of Leknes, near Valberg). They take a maximum of four persons on tours, so lots of personal attention and lots of love for the horses. Also note that the longer tours, like the Farm Trail that crosses the mountains and follows an ancient path, are for skilled riders only. A short tour (1,5 hrs) can be adjusted to the riders' skills. Open all year.

- **a.** Valbergsveien 966, 8357 Valberg
- **t.** +47 9059 0309
- **w.** lofothest.no

Get the Viking vibe by seeing, smelling and tasting what Viking life was like back then. **The Lofotr Viking Museum (35)** is especially nice for children, because there are lots of interactive activities: you can shoot with a bow and arrow, row a Viking ship and eat Viking food. There's an almost 80 metre long reconstructed Viking house, people running around with Viking clothes on, and you can dress up as one yourself. Bet you always wanted to do that. Go on then. Open all year.

- **a.** Prestegårdsveien 59, 8360 Bøstad
- **t.** +47 7615 4000
- **w.** lofotr.no

Okay, this must be one of our most interesting activities in the area: who can resist a jolly Hula Hoop! We met hula-lady Elisabeth Færøy Lund in the bay of Unstad, hooping an arctic hoop-dance with a hula gang. And they seemed to have heaps of fun. **Hoop 'n Hike (36)**, that's Elisabeth and her team of local and international hula teachers, offers year round workshops in Lofoten, teaching you to hoop those hips, and thus introducing you to the global hoop community. Every September she takes hula-hoopers (newbies and advanced) on a four-day arctic hoop and hike experience. You'll be exploring your hoop skills, indoor and outdoor, making new friends, and in the process, enjoying the arctic nature.

t. +47 9429 2322
w. hoopnhike.no

Unstad bay is by far the most photographed and surfed coldwater spot in the north – and claimed to be the first ever surfed in Norway. The break gets pretty busy when the **Lofoten Masters (37)** is on: the world's northernmost international surfing competition. The event's popularity has increased every year since it started in 2007. The event began as a fun get-together for the handful of Nordic surfers in the area, then over the years became more serious than just a surfers' gathering. But even now the international competitors have joined the fun, the aim remains: that all ocean-loving people feel welcome, no matter what level, age, gender or nationality. And it's much more than 'just' surfing; expect a movie night, beach clean, live music, party (of course), food and drinks (obviously) and an awesome vibe - arctic aloha all over the place! The four-day event's organised by Lofoten Ekstremsportklubb and hosted by Unstad Arctic Surf, held every year in September at Unstad, and includes competitions for men and women.

w. lofotenmasters.com

Lofotensea (38) organises several sea trips, whether you want to go fishing or sightseeing, you can view the surroundings from a different perspective, at a slow or fast pace. The latter's a trip on a RIB with a choice of routes and sights, one of which is a spot where you can watch grey seals and eagles. The fishing tour guides you through the whole business of catching and preparing fish. Lofotensea only takes small groups and family trips. Open all year.

a. J.M. Johansens Vei 135,
   8340 Stamsund
t. +47 4750 7399
w. lofotensea.no

Make sure you stop at **Haukland beach (39)**, whether to hike, wander about, have a picnic on the white sands, or just check if that clear blue water is as tropical in temperature as its appearance. (Waddayathink...). There's a walking path, along the headland to the north, connecting Haukland beach with the next beach, Uttakleiv. If you want to explore the picturesque Haukland bay, the most perfect option; rent a SUP or kayak. **Experience Lofoten Islands** rents out all the gear, including wetsuits if needed. There are single kayaks (where you can bring your fishing gear) or kayaks with room for two persons + a child. The rental station is at Haukland beach, just off the E10, near Leknes. Open during the summer season.

t. +47 4151 0255
w. experiencelofoten.no

With a livestock of some 200 goats, the organic cheese farm, **Aalan Gård (40)**, in Bøstad produces all sorts of tasty goats' cheese. You can visit the

farm, which has a mighty fine garden full of herbs and other animals too. Everything's made and produced in a natural way, thanks to a strong belief (we agree!) that farming must benefit nature. In addition, taking good care of the animals, and considering the health of consumers when producing goods. You can taste and purchase a selection of cheese and other fabulous products in the garden shop and their recently opened farm café.

a. Lauvdalen, 8360 Bøstad
t. +47 7608 4534
w. aalan.no

Board the taxiboat **M/S Øysprinten (41)** and sail alongside the steep Lofotveggen cliffs. Try counting the many inlets, islands and beaches you pass. Dream an endless dream staring at the horizon or imagine what you would do with your own private island

up here. You'll be hopping islands all the way up to Stamsund and return to Ballstad. This taxi ride takes about three hours, and, oh, they serve fish soup before you leave. Let's just hope the weather stays calm. Open all year.

a. 8376 Ballstad harbour
t. +47 9009 7601
fb. oysprinten

EAT/DRINK/HANG OUT
◆

Freshly baked cinnamon buns, great cakes and a perfect coffee, what else? Maybe two floors filled with stuff your (young) children can horse around with so you can deeply, calmly and truly enjoy your cinnamon bun and coffee? **Gamle Skola's** (**42**) just your place.

The characterful décor includes art and reminders of your early school days. The café's a haven of peace, while the 'Lekeland', the indoor playground, is what it should be: a fun-filled fool-around-and-make-lots-of-noise-who-cares area. Also perfect for those - oh so rare - rainy days. Open all year. ◆€◆ ◆€€◆

a. Grundstadveien 454, 8360 Bøstad
t. +47 7608 4264 / 4010 2666
w. gamleskola.com

Now that you have a taste for cinnamon buns, you must, (we implore - you must!) go and try the buns at **Lill Gunn's Gårdsbakeri** (**43**) in Bostad. The lovely and welcoming Lill Gunn Markussen (who had a little cameo in our crowdfunder film) serves the best we tasted. And we tasted a lot! She and her daughter busy themselves making all kind of pastries, like their speciality 'rømmelefse', a creamy sweet pancake. The shop also sells local handcrafted items, such as warm socks and hats, chocolate, jams, juices and soap. Open all year, weekdays only. ◆€◆ ◆€€◆

a. Vikingveien 36, 8360 Bostad
(just off the E10, in a little farmhouse)
t. +47 9083 0537
fb. lillgunnsgaardsbakeri

How a hydroelectric power station can have a second life as an art hub is demonstrated very nicely at **Art Café Kraftstasjonen** (**44**), located right at the beach of Haukland. The little power station once used running water from the nearby river to provide electricity for the area. As a silent but obvious reminder of its former life, there's a large switchboard behind the counter, which fits in perfectly with the artistic décor at Kraftstajonen. It's not just a gallery; it's a proper café, and a very nice one we'd say, with a sunny terrace and lots of local art and handcrafted items on show and for sale. (The two kids portrayed in the mural at the side of the building are the owners' children). Kraftstajonen is one of those places we feel really excited about, and we just love to bring it to your attention; the reason we started this guide in the first place! Open from June to August. ♦€♦ ♦€€♦

a. Haukland 22, 8370 Haukland
t. +47 4151 0255
fb. Kraftstasjonen Haukland

Sans og Samling (45) is a bit hidden, but once you're there you'll be glad you found it. And apparently you won't be the only one, because it's a really quite

popular place. Maybe we just think it's a bit hidden, because we didn't find it right away, but anyway, it sits in the same building as the city's library and tourist office. Tastefully decorated and a homely place, you can enjoy their daily fresh soups and pastries, and if you're lucky a live concert. ♦€€♦

a. Storgata 29, 8370 Leknes
t. +74 9417 8208

And yet another one of our favourites and a must-visit: restaurant **Himmel og Havn (46)** in Ballstad. The restaurant's located a little away from

the road (Moloveien), at the pier of Solsiden-Brygge. There's a small sign, but ask around and people gladly show you the way - it's a bit of a local hotspot. In what appears to be an old boatshed they've created an extremely cool and cosy place, furnished with vintage chairs and tables and adorned with a collection of stuff-from-seemingly-all-over-everywhere. There's also a small shop, they organise summer concerts, and some evenings they serve a varied local tapas buffet. You're welcome for breakfast, lunch and dinner and everything in between and after, Himmel og Havn is a very easy-going place. Sit inside, or watch the lively harbour scenes outside from the deck. Open in summer, in winter only weekends. ♦€€♦

a. Moloveien 45, 8373 Ballstad
t. +47 9047 0004
w. himmeloghavn.no

Kræmmarvika Havn (47) is located at the south end of Ballstad and serves more traditional meals. The interior is in tune with the rich fishing history of the area. ♦€€♦

a. Kræmmervika 36, 8373 Ballstad
t. +47 9166 1330
w. kremmervikahavn.no

SHOP
♦

Since 1995 Kristian Breivik, one of the first local surfers, has been designing his own boards, under the apt name 'Frost Surfboards'. In 2013 he established the **Lofoten Surfsenter (48)**, the northernmost surf shop in the world. You can usually find Kristian in the shop, and needless to say he's a great source of info on surf in the area, and surfboards for that matter. The shop has a wide range of boards, including his own brand, all your surf essentials and a small collection of clothes. Besides surf lessons, rental of boards and surf gear you can test their high performance Frost and Firewire boards. The Surfsenter also organises the yearly Lofoten Surf Festival, usually held in the middle of August: a festive day celebrating the fun of surfing with contests (but nothing too serious), music, and surf clinics. The shop's located at Unstad bay. Open all year, closed in January.

a. Unstadsjøveien 39, 8360 Bøstad
t. +47 9533 2292 / 4561 7114
w. lofotensurfsenter.com

The biodynamic farm and cheese factory **Lofoten-Gardsysteri (49)** is run by Dutch couple Marielle and Hugo Vink. After their studies in the Netherlands they worked for a month in Norway and fell in love with the farming life. Fast forward 17 years and here they are; on their large plot of land, beautifully located between hilly slopes, successfully producing goats' cheese and other

products, supplying delis and markets in Lofoten - and even one in Paris! Their 155 goats roam free all day on the land, the 'utmark', which is a communally owned plot, shared with other farmers. The goats hop happily off to the utmark in the morning after milking, and at the end of the day they come back for another session. Marielle and Hugo sell their many sorts of cheese and sausages in the 'gårdsbutikk', farm shop, amongst other local products. You can have a drink and taste cheese, join them in a mini-cheese-making workshop, walk around in their school garden project and have a chat with the goats. They offer a Norwegian 'matpakke', a picnic pack which comes with a map + guide to a mountain hiking route that surrounds the farm. We like a lot. The Gårdsbutikk opens daily in June, July and August, the rest of the year only at weekends.

a. Saupstad, 8360 Bøstad
(on the road to Unstad beach)
t. +47 9508 2958 / 9527 7106
w. lofoten-gardsysteri.no

SLEEP

♦

Campervans can use the disposal points at Torvdalshalsen picnic area, Brustranda Sjø Camping (€), the Esso service station in Leknes, the Hagskaret picnic area (May 15 - Oct 1) or at the Utakleiv beach to empty chemical toilets. Up to date info and addresses:

w. cleanuplofoten.no/map

Near the Hov Hestegård Riding Centre and horse farm you'll find the **Hov Camping** (50). Beautifully located right by the beach with an ocean view to the north (midnight sun direction, in case you never thought about where it hangs out). As you may have noticed, there are a lot of 'northernmost' things in Lofoten. And as it so happens, next to the campsite and Hov farmland there's the world's northernmost golf course - Lofoten Links. No need to worry about low flying golf balls though, it's still some 700 metres away. The campsite has pitches on grassland and is pretty basic, but has all the facilities such as showers, toilet and communal kitchen. Open all year. ♦€♦

a. Hov, 8314 Gimsøysand
t. +47 9755 9501
w. hovcamping.no

You're allowed to stay overnight at the surf spot in **Unstad** with a **tent or van**, if you donate the right amount in a special box. (Tent 100 NOK - Campervan 150 NOK). There are no facilities.

Unstad Arctic Surf's **(51)** located right at one of the best surf spots of the archipelago and it's been around for a while. From a campsite with a few cabins in 2003, it grew organically into what it is today: one of the nicest places to stay and hang out for surfers

visiting Lofoten. Unstad Arctic Surf's run by Tommy Olsen and his wife, local Marion Frantzen, whose parents opened the campsite in the early days. Tommy moved up and began surfing the local spots in 2000 and hosts the Lofoten Masters each September. As per our little story in the surf history of Norway section, there's some evidence, or should we say artefacts, to be found at Unstad Arctic Surf. If you want to find out about the first surfers in Norway, truth or myth, check out the surfboard and photo that inspired them to build the famous board in the first place. They're both here! Unstad Arctic Surf consists of a main building with a restaurant, bar and rooftop lounge. Then there are big cabins that sleep up to eight people (one of them has its own sauna), some smaller cabins for two people, a campsite with use of all facilities in the main building (showers, toilets and wifi – also a great plus, hot tub and sauna, AND free use of fat bikes). The restaurant's open from breakfast to dinner, and there's a small skate ramp in the garden. ◆€◆ ◆€€◆

a. Unstadveien 105, 8363 Unstad
t. +47 9706 1201
w. unstadarcticsurf.com

The spacious, traditional **Mærvoll Sjøhus (52)** - seahouse - located between Tangstad and Unstad is a perfect option if you're travelling with a group of people or are on a tight budget. The view of the fjord and mountain's to die for! The house is where workers of the Mærvoll Produksjonslag, former cod fishery, used to live during the busiest work season. The crew of each fishing vessel had their own so called 'rorbu'. Most of the rorbu - rooms - sleep up to six people, with shared showers, toilet and kitchen. There's also the possibility to rent the very cute, 120-year-old grass-roofed house. Open all year. ◆€◆

a. Maervollveien 205, 8360 Bøstad
   (Seahouses Joh.L.Unstad Sjøhus)
t. +47 7608 5427
w. bobasen.com/view-493.php

If you're into mountains, ocean and outdoor sports and longing for a remote place to combine getting your work done with a little Lofoten lifestyling, the **Arctic Coworking Lodge (53)** must be your paradise found. Their motto is 'work, stay and play with like-minded people', and it's likely one of the most beautiful co-working and co-living environments in the world. Whether you're a digital nomad, designer, working on your thesis, or even writing a book, if you need a space to concentrate but also the synergy, knowledge and inspiration of other people working (and playing) around you, a co-work place might just be the thing for you. In June 2018 the Arctic Co-work Lodge opened its doors in a tiny place called Tangstad, only five minutes away from the main surf spot, Unstad. Offering a choice of private room or shared room where you have the privacy of a little wooden cubicle, with wifi in all rooms, a shared workspace, living room and a private phone booth. Open all year.
◆€€◆

a. Tangstad 190, 8360 Bøstad
t. +47 4004 4606 (Rolf) / 9860 3234
w. arcticcoworking.com

'Life is beautiful'. It's written, oh so delicate and subtle, on one of the walls of **Ludvigbua (54)** cabin. The fisherman's cabin is located in a quiet bay near Stamsund. As subtle as the statement on the wall, the cabin is light, white and minimalistic, yet decorated cosily enough to make you feel right at home. There's everything you need and it sleeps up to 6 people, so a perfect option if you're with a small group and want to save money. And since saving money in Norway is a bit of a challenge, it's good to have options, right? Open all year. ◆€◆ ◆€€◆

a. Buøyveien 19, 8340 Stamsund
t. +47 9055 2710
w. ludvigbua.net

A stay at the **Hattvika Lodge (55)** or one of their cottages feels like a holiday all on its own. The lodge, a typical Scandinavian villa, and the authentic fisherman's cottages from the 1880s, were recently renovated. They now cater perfectly to guests who want to come home and indulge in a bit of comfort after a day filled with kayaking, fishing, diving, kiting, skiing, surfing, hiking, or all of the above. Since

Hattvika collaborates closely with local providers of such activities, there won't be a day in your stay to get bored. As if you could! The interiors are beautifully decorated; with white, natural and dark wood, and Scandinavian design, and most have underfloor heating - yay! And that's just inside. Outside you can relax while you warm up in the Finnish sauna, or gaze at either the stars, the sun that never sets or the northern lights from the wood-fired hot tub. There are mountain bikes, SUPs and kayaks available. All apartments are located right beside, or close to the water and have terraces, whether you stay in the luxurious lodge or the comfy 'fisherman's nest', a six-bed dormitory. From some you can see Mount Skottinden, rising above Ballstad. They are all self-catering – which is a good thing, since you maybe won't want to leave the place once you get comfortable after an outdoorsy day. Or, and here's the best part, owner Kristian prepares a super delicious tailor-made dinner at your request! Open all year.
♦€€♦ ♦€€€♦

a. Hattvikveien, 8373 Ballstad
t. +47 9302 8887
w. hattvikalodge.no

On the same pier and in the same building as restaurant Himmel og Havn you'll find the cabin apartments of **Solsiden Brygge (56)**. From designer suites to studio apartments, they all have great views of either the harbour or surrounding countryside: gloriously green hills and backdrop of mountains. The reception is one of their biggest assets, where you can hang out amidst a collection of groovy, odd and fishy memorabilia or warm up at the woodstove. Open all year. ♦€€♦ ♦€€€♦

a. Moloveien 41, 8373 Ballstad
t. +47 4046 3333
w. solsiden-brygge.no

THE ARCTIC
SURF EXPERIENCE

UNSTAD ARCTIC SURF
UNSTADARCTICSURF.COM

Photo: Melchior van Nigtevecht

IN AND AROUND FLAKSTAD AND MOSKENES

If you check a satellite view of the Lofoten archipelago and zoom in, you could mistake it for really old cheese: a bit coarse, full of holes - the holes being lakes and fjords and ocean inlets. When you see it in real life, this dramatic landscape is so staggeringly beautiful it can make you lose your sense of direction, even more so when you reach the southern tip, the island of Moskenesøy, with its granite peaks rising up over the Vestfjorden. Best you experience this overwhelmingly incredible freaking gift of nature on foot, bike, SUP, kayak or boat. But do be aware of how easy it is to lose your bearings and plan your route when you take a hike or rent a kayak or a bike. Being surrounded by ocean, lakes and mountains can do that, so don't worry that your internal GPS is going haywire – it's to be expected that you'll feel at a loss; not only for where you are, but for words, for where you put your keys, phone, car, compass, camera, kids... Camera! Well, we suggest strapping that securely round your neck; because we totally expect you - and don't blame you for it - to feel a sudden compulsion for taking endless photographs of the many red-coloured rorbuer, the old fishermen's cabins dotted around inlets, and their bright reflections looking back at you from the water. Just try to resist.

On your map of where to stop off: on the island of Moskenesøya, most of which is in the Moskenes municipality, we hold a whole lot of love for villages like Sørvagen, Å (the end of the road, and last letter of the Norwegian alphabet) and the jaw-droppingly gorgeous Reine. As you explore further north you'll find (to help confuse you a little further) the northern tip of Moskenesøya, including the Solbjørnvatnet lake, actually belongs to the Flakstad municipality, along with the island Flakstadøya. Make sure to strap a map round your neck with that camera if you're not exploring with a guide.

Tourist information centre Moskenes, on Sørvagen main road, open May to September.
Tourist office Flakstad, Flakstadveien 459, 8380 Ramberg.

TO DO

♦

Biking's relatively easy-breezy if you stick to the main roads, since the main roads follow the coastline and are therefore fairly flat. Mountain biking on the other hand... well, biking along mountains and hills is not easy per definition. The Allemansretten, the right to roam, allows you to follow any and all trails (but strictly the trails, riding on open land is prohibited). Above the treelines, though, you're allowed to bike on open land. Reine Adventure offer outdoor tours; bike, hike, kayak, ski. They also rent out bikes, and camping equipment too.

w. reineadventure.com

Locally known as Moskstraumen, the **Moskenes Maelstrom (57)** is what gave powerful whirlpools their name. Caused by strong tidal currents meeting in the Vestfjorden, made swirlier due to the 'underwater spine' of Lofoten's mountains, and intensified by the pull of the moon, this complicated system of whirlpools and eddies in the open sea has been written about by Edgar Allen Poe and Jules Verne, among others. It's also another factor as to why Lofoten's such a cod magnet: because of the many microorganisms that are sucked in, it's like an all-you-can-eat restaurant for fish. Of course, where there's (lots of) fish, there are fishermen (and women). The effects of this phenomenon are one of the main reasons people settled here for thousands of years, and you can visit some of the original settlements from those days. Organised boat trips pass the Moskstraumen - at a safe distance! - a seal colony, a number of long-abandoned settlements and the famous Refsvika sea cave, **Kollhellaren**, where you can see the 3000-4000 year-old cave paintings. Don't expect one of those trips where you just sit on your butt, take photos and wait till it's over. This trip's about long hikes and getting wet and/or cold, so you need to be relatively fit and dressed for the occasion. You can book this, or a less active trip at the tourist information centre in Sørvagen, about 5 minutes from Reine. Daily boat trips also depart from the jetty of Å between May and October.

Do take the narrow road of the E10 towards **Nusfjord (58)**, coming from Leknes towards Flakstad. Described as an 'authentic fishing village' by every other tourist official, Nusfjord is definitely not just another tourist trap. It's exceptionally pretty, and fairly interesting too – a village turned into museum. Nusfjord's one of the oldest fishing settlements of Lofoten, located in a naturally sheltered harbour. You'll see old loading cranes, the Landhandel - the town's shop - of which the interior is preserved beautifully, and the storage hall with black and white photos of yesteryears. Almost all of the rorbuer, the fishermen's cabins, are now rented out to tourists. Of course that's the case all over Lofoten, but the rorbuer of Nusfjord are indeed authentic as can be. Built at the end of the 19th century, now restored to accommodate visitors that appreciate 21st century comfort. To get there take the 807 off the E10 between Napp and Ramberg.

Kari Schibevaag is one of those incredible human beings who chooses to live exactly the life and lifestyle that fits her best. The former world champion at kiteboarding is an ocean-loving adventurer pur sang, pure and uncomplicated, and she happily shares all of her outdoor experience. She'll take you on SUP, kite, surf, snorkel or kayak adventures to show you her beloved Lofoten. And if you're not into any of that (no! really?), check out her lovely little very cosy shop where she sells beanies, ponchos, surf-related clothes and gear. If she's not in her shop, out exploring or walking her dog, you can find her at the **Lofoten Activity Center/Sakrisøy Rorbuer (59)** in Sakrisøy. Here you can also rent a SUP, book a guided SUP trip, or take a yoga class. Kari's an enthusiastic, athletic and active lady, to say the least (that's why we've featured her in our Seaside Locals series) and one of your best bets for a first-rate guided adventure.

a. Skagen Camping Flakstadstranda, 8380 Ramberg
t. +47 9207 1722
w. schibevaagadventure.com

Here's a challenge. You're off to a white sand beach with turquoise water situated in between steep vertical cliffs, only reachable by foot (at least 1 hour walk), known for its perfect waves. Do you bring your surfboard? There may be surf. There may be not. You don't want to miss out, right? What if after hiking steep uphill and steep downhill for an hour and a half or so, you reach the beach and see peeling peaks, but you didn't bring your board?! The beach we love to walk to without a longboard underarm is **Kvalvika (60)**. Maybe you've seen the docu-film North of the Sun (Nordfor Sola), by two young Norwegian filmmakers, Inge and Jørn, who spent nine months of a cold arctic winter on an isolated Norwegian beach.

If not, why not? Go see it! They took only their boards and suits and warm clothes, and ate food that was past the sell-by date and therefore free. They built a hut from driftwood and washed up on the beach stuff, and passed their time beach cleaning when not surfing. (A helicopter later picked up the 3 tonnes of rubbish they cleared over the months.) So, it's well worth the hike to this paradisiacal beach, if not to imagine how Inge and Jørn lived here all those months, then for the sheer beauty of it: the views, the changing perspectives, the shifts in light, and clouds lingering around mountaintops. There are several routes to choose from: the easiest way (still no walk in the park) is to drive to Fredvang, continue for about 3 km until you reach the small parking area, where the trail starts. Going up (170 m) feels relatively easy, but then you face a steep descent.

Reine Adventure (61) has quite a bit of (environmentally-friendly) adventure to offer. Whether you want to use their years of experience and expertise on guided expeditions, or prefer to go on your own. There's the Bike and Camp: you're provided with bike, tent, camping gear and maps, and the staff help you plan your own tour.

Or how about a day or a week of camping and kayaking; guided or individual, paddling along the deep fjords and camping on remote beaches. In winter there's the **All-in-one Ski and Boat tour**: transport and accommodation is an old fishing boat, a zodiac drops you at the most perfect skiing spots, fishing and cooking will be done on board and for 'free time' they'll bring kayaks along! Open all year.

a. just off the E10, Sakrisøy, 8390 Reine
t. +47 9077 9814
w. reineadventure.com

If you fancy a bit of fishing with the local fishermen, check in at **Aqua Lofoten Coast Adventure (62)**. They also offer boat safaris to visit bird colonies, the Kollhellaren cave paintings at Refsvika, and the Moskenes Maelstrom, or will take you diving and snorkelling.

a. Reine Ytre Havn 1, 8390 Reine
t. +47 9901 9042
w. aqualofoten.no

Bunesstranda (63) (Bunes beach), yet another breathtakingly beautiful isolated beach, can only be reached by boat and a 1 hour walk. To get there take the ferry from Reine to Vindstad - a scenic trip all in itself, crossing the Reinefjorden. From the tiny village of Vindstad, a far from demanding trail (± 2,5 km) leads to the beach. There are no facilities or shops in the village or at the beach, so best to bring your own snacks and drinks. And maybe your tent - it's permitted to camp overnight. Before you go: check the weather forecast and the timetable for the ferry. And remember, the joy is in the journey!

Maybe a museum of fishing doesn't sound all too sexy or appealing, or the least bit exciting, but since you're in Lofoten and fishery seems to run in the DNA, the **Norwegian Fishing Village Museum (64)** in Å should be on your list. It gives you a superb insight into Lofoten's fishing industry over the centuries, and therefore Lofoten and its inhabitants too. There's a boathouse with the traditional wooden Nordland boats, a cod liver oil factory, an old grocery shop and you'll see how a typical fisherman's family lived. Also activities for children, exhibitions, demonstrations and guided tours to learn all there is to know about the day-to-day life of the Lofoten fisherman.

a. E10 120, Å, 8392 Sørvågen
t. +47 7609 1488
w. museumnord.no/en/norwegian-fishing-village-museum

EAT/DRINK/HANG OUT

Smell something fishy? Some restaurants in Lofoten have whale meat on the menu. It's not even rare. Whale steaks… oh? That's food for discussion all by itself. Some local folks see it as eating just another fish, where others consider it not done, in most countries even by law. What to do? Let your conscience speak, try to inform yourself by asking the owners how and where the whales are caught, and how common it is to eat whale. And try to figure out which fish species are local and abundant and therefore a safe choice. You might decide that a non-native predator that can harm the native eco-system can be on your list of okay–to-eat marine species. You might not. Most locals care about the marine life and are well aware of their importance to the region. So, no one will hold it against you if you want to know what, exactly, is on your plate.

Enjoy an unpretentious but tasty dish at Nusfjord's quaint little tavern, **Oriana** (**65**). The building's original purpose was to store food and brandy in the late 1800s. The name stems from a cargo ship named Oriana, and the owner of it being a big boss of Nusfjord in the old days. The figurehead of the Oriana is still on display in the tavern. ♦€♦ ♦€€♦

a. Nusfjord (it's small, you'll find it)
t. +47 7609 3020
w. nusfjord.no

Home-made stews, cakes and local dishes with some vegetarian options are served at the roadside restaurant **Kafe Friisgården** (**66**). Sit either inside or in the garden of their century-old log house. They also have rooms available. Closed in winter. ♦€€♦

a. Flakstadveien 422, 8380 Ramberg
t. +47 4156 2581

Anita's Sjømatt (**67**) sells what must be some of the finest fish burgers you've tasted, among a lot of other things fishy, as in cod, salmon, prawns, shellfish and wolf fish. You'll find the shop - where else - at the fish docks in Sakrisøy. Open in summer. ♦€♦ ♦€€♦

a. 8390 Sakrisøy (on the E10 roadside)
t. +47 9006 1566

Krambua Restaurant (**68**) has seafood dishes on the menu, mostly local ingredients with a tat of Italian and a pinch of Swedish soul. The chef's Swedish, his wife's Italian, and they both adore the archipelago, that's why they moved here long ago. What'll be on your plate depends on the catch of the day, seasonal herbs and veggies and the chef's inspiration. Krambua's interior is relaxed and intimate with lots of wood and natural materials, set in an antique building, lots of little touches that add to the loving vibe of the place, the food and the owners. Closed in November and December. ♦€€♦

a. 8390 Hamnøy
t. +47 4863 6772
w. krambuarestaurant.no

Of course you'll find excellent fish restaurants in Reine, but if you're up for something else tonight, or would like some vegetarian options for a change, try the restaurant and café **Lanternen** (**69**). It's a friendly and easy-going place, which serves some really nice pizzas and a generous buffet on Sundays, sometimes accompanied with live music. Lanternen's also a perfect place for a snack and a beer after a hefty hike. Open all year. ♦€♦ ♦€€♦

a. In the main square, 8390 Reine
t. +47 9413 3793
w. lanternen-reine.com

At kaffebar and interior décor shop, **Bringen** (**70**) in Reine you can feast your eyes on a delicious array of cakes, chocolate mousses, brownies, more cakes, wraps and of course, coffee. Have a bit of a sweet tooth? You'll love this place! Open all year. ♦€€♦

a. In the main square, 8390 Reine
t. +47 7609 1300

Restaurant **Maren Anna** (**71**) is in the tiny harbour of Sørvågen, in a former cod liver oil factory. It's an uncomplicated place serving traditional and fresh local food, its unique selling point being the amazing view of the harbour and boats, the fjord and mountains. In summer you can hang out till dark… (which, um, is not going to happen is it). The bar doesn't close until 02:30 hrs, so for night owls or those who suffer insomnia from the never setting sun, this is your go-to bar. Regular live music and small concerts are held, at least once a month. Open all year. ♦€€♦

- **a.** Sørvågen 8392
- **t.** +47 7609 2050
- **w.** marenanna.com

SHOP

Landhandel (**72**), in museum-village Nusfjord, is part of the museum scenery, but it's still a shop as well. The grocery store dates back to 1907, and although they now sell mostly souvenirs, woollen hats and jumpers and stockfish, the shop retains the style of the early 1900s in all its looks, shelves and cupboards included. Open all year.

- **fb.** nusfjord-landhandel

If your wish is not to leave Lofoten without a proper souvenir, make sure to check out Sakrisøy's **Bric 'A' Brac** (**73**). The shop, right above the Lofoten Toy Museum, sells some remarkable stuff. There's old furniture, vintage cutlery, some tools - need a gaff anyone? A rusted teapot or coffee grinder perhaps? Open all year.

- **a.** Sakrisøy, 8390 Reine
- **t.** +47 9003 5419
- **w.** lofoten-info.no/bric

Bakeriet på Å (**74**) is the place to be for your morning coffee and fresh bread. The bakery's part of the Norwegian Fishing Village Museum in Å, the oven from the 1800s still in use, and you can witness fresh cinnamon buns being made. And then eat them of course. Open all year.

- **a.** 880 E10, Å, 8392 Sørvågen
- **t.** +47 7609 1488

If you're anything of a fishing geek, and have big or small fishing plans, make sure you stock up at **Lofotsport Bua** (**75**). Not just for fishing gear, bait and the right clothing, but even more so for information and chit chat about fishing. Open all year.

a. In the main square, Leira, 8390 Reine
t. +47 9545 9610
fb. lofotsportbua

SLEEP
♦

Campervans can use the disposal point in the harbour of Reine to empty their chemical toilet. At the parking area in Nusfjord you're allowed to stay overnight with your campervan (NOK 150). More info on:

w. cleanuplofoten.no/map

Either stay in one of the little cabins, the beach house, or pitch your tent, or park your van on the large piece of land close to the beach at **Skagen Camping** (**76**). Camping facilities are basic but the atmosphere's friendly and it's a beautiful spot. Open from mid May to early September. ♦€♦

a. along the E10, 8380 Ramberg
t. +47 9503 5283
w. skagencampinglofoten.com

Ramberg Gjestegård (**77**) is situated near the beach of Ramberg. It has nine cabins that sleep up to four people. The smaller cabins (two person) all have a great view of the beach. Their campsite has all the facilities you need and they rent out bikes. If you don't feel like preparing your own dinner, there's a restaurant too. You can book the cabins in advance, but in summer you can't make reservations to stay at the campsite. Just show up or call to find out if there's space. Open all year. ♦€♦ ♦€€♦

a. Flakstadveien 361, 8380 Ramberg
t. +47 7609 3500
w. ramberg-gjestegard.no

The nostalgic **rorbuer**, the fishermen's cabins you find in fishing villages along the entire archipelago, were used by seasonal workers at the fish factories and boats during the busiest fishing season. Since modern fishing boats have cabins on board there's no use for them any more. But they make a great place to stay for your holiday. All along the E10 you'll find rorbuer for rent. We selected a few we think are worth checking, amongst many others: Rorbuer in Hamnøy (**w.** rorbuer.no) / Sakrisoy Rorobuer in Sakrisøy (**w.** sakrisoyrorbuer.no).

Lofoten Bed and Breakfast (**78**) rents out rooms, apartments and rorbuer. You'll find them on the main street, driving into Reine. The apartments are in a renovated house from the 1940s and are the only bed and breakfast deal in the area. Open all year. ♦€€♦

a. 8390 Reine
t. +47 4822 8334
w. lofotenbedandbreakfast.no

And last, but certainly not least, our favourite rorbuer in this area, located at the end of the E10 in Å: **Å Feskarbrygga** (**79**), run by a local fisherman and his family. You'll feel right at home here and they're a great source of information on the area. They have bikes and boats for rent. Open all year. ♦€♦ ♦€€♦

a. 8392 Å, Sørvågen
t. +47 9116 1999
w. aafeskarbrygga.no

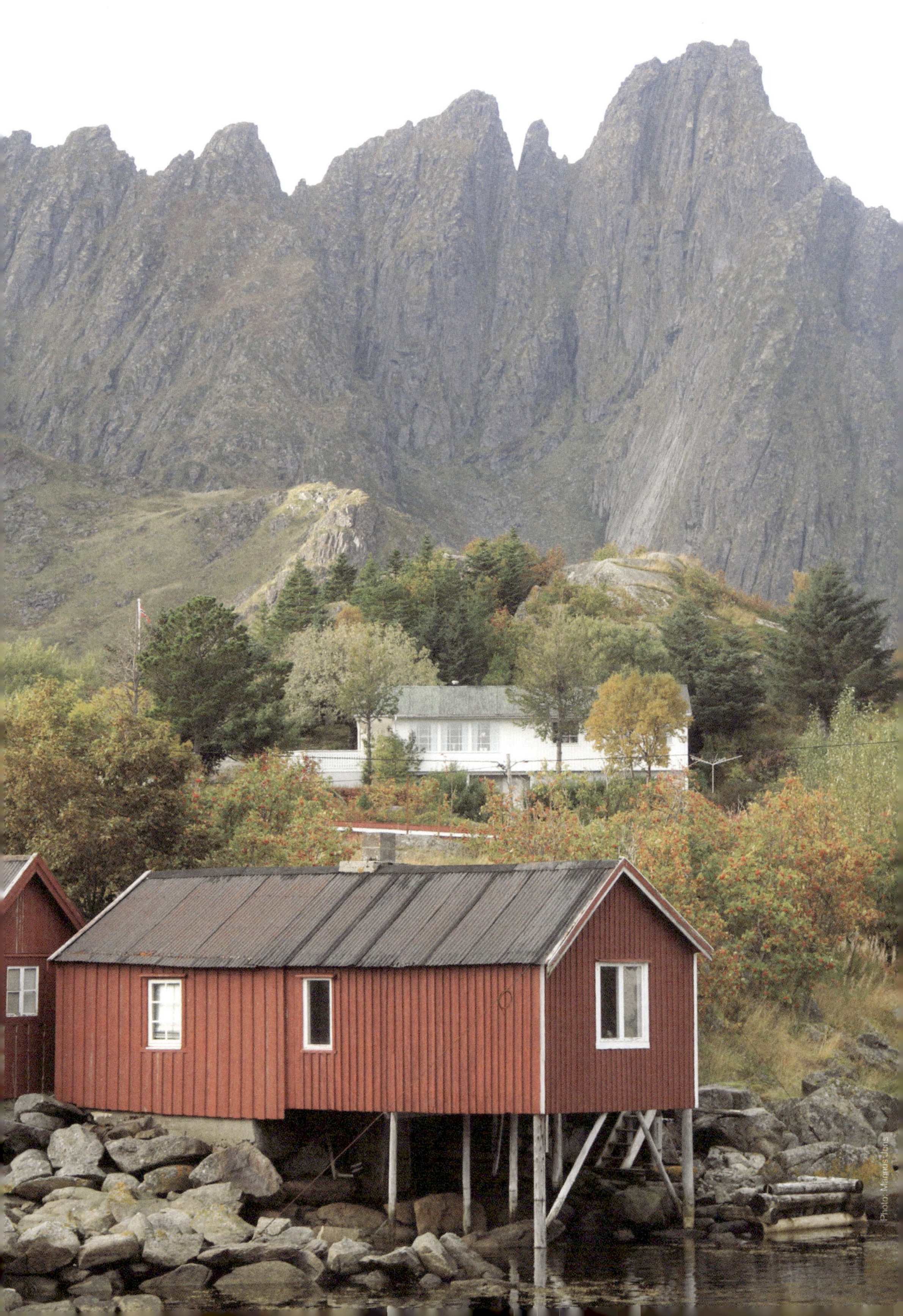

SURF

The Lofoten archipelago is becoming increasingly popular, partly due to its photogenic and dramatic backdrop. Search the net using hashtag Lofoten and you'll see why it attracts photographers and filmmakers, and why magazines want to cover the area. And why surfers want to go here, despite it being inside the Arctic Circle? Well, what surfer would go to a place just because of its backdrop. The surf can be epic, with powerful swells that build up from Greenland. Actually, the surf can be anything between choppy, cold mush and epic. Summers are perfect for learning, with occasional days of epic. Autumn's probably the most crowded period, since the waves are making better shapes, it's not too cold and there're still enough daylight hours to squeeze in two sessions a day. The bonus? Witnessing the Northern Lights. They start being visible from early September. Winter swells, however, are the most consistent for epic deliveries. Epic waves, empty line-ups with epic backdrop, but the hours of daylight are epically short. Unless you've got Nordic blood running through your veins you'll want to be in your 4/3 and probably booties in summer, start wearing gloves in autumn, and be fully suited in 5/4/3 (or higher numbers) with a good hood for winter and spring.

Delp (I), situated between Laukvik and Grunnfør, is a small northwest-facing bay with stones and boulders over sand. Some say it's for experts only, but it can have its days of rideable waves for intermediates. Best at mid-tide, needs a proper WNW swell.
◆ *Intermediate to advanced/sand, boulders and stones/parking near road/no facilities.* ◆

Unstad (II) is Lofoten's best known and most consistent surf spot. It picks up all available swell, and therefore you'll never be alone. But even if it can get crowded at times, the vibe's pretty chilled out (no pun intended). Unstad is a large bay, exposed to both wind and swell, and works best at mid to high tide with a NW swell. Surfing wise, the bay's divided into three spots: the right is one of Norway's best pointbreaks, fast and hollow, no beginner's spot; the beach is the perfect beginner's spot, but watch out for hidden boulders; the left point works better with a SW-W swell, picks up more swell than the right, and is definitely not a beginner's spot. Watch out for currents at all three. ♦ *All levels for beach/intermediate-advanced for points)/sand, boulders and stones/ easy parking both sides of the bay/ small picnic area/toilets/campsite/surf school/surf shop/restaurant.* ♦

Uttakleiv & Haukland (III). A headland divides the beaches of Uttakleiv and Haukland. Uttakleiv is a big beach near the fishing village of the same name. It works best at mid-tide and needs a big SW or medium to big NW swell. Haukland needs a big W swell. Both spots come to life in winter. In summer they're popular with holiday folks and weekenders. ♦ *All levels/ sand, stones/easy parking/summer restaurant and kayak rental at Haukland/picnic area.* ♦

Flakstad (IV) is an exposed NW-facing sandy beach, popular with both kite and wind surfers. Works best at mid tide with a small to medium NW swell. Flakstad's a perfect bay for beginners. ♦ *All levels/sand/easy parking/campsite/surf school/small surf shop.* ♦

Kvalvika (V) is only reached after a long (but beautiful) hike, so don't expect any crowds. But then again: you never know what to expect after one and half hour hiking to a surf spot. The NW facing beach is protected by steep cliffs and needs small to medium NW swell. ♦ *All levels/sand/isolated/no facilities.* ♦

SCHOOL RENTAL REPAIR

◆

The **Lofoten Surfsenter** (**80**) at Unstad Bay sells all your surf essentials; leashes, wetsuits, boards, wax etc. You can test out their own brand of performance boards (Frost), rent boards, and book surf lessons. Broken board or dings? The Surfsenter also does repairs.

a. Unstadsjøveien 39, 8360 Bøstad
t. +47 9533 2292 / 4561 7114
w. lofotensurfsenter.com

Unstad Arctic Surf (**81**) has a little shop where you can get your wax and other surf essentials, they rent out boards and give surf lessons. They're located right on Unstad Bay.

a. Unstadveien 105, 8363 Bøstad
t. +47 9706 1201
w. unstadarcticsurf.com

Kari Schibevaag rents out SUPs and organises guided SUP tours from **Lofoten Activity Center / Sakrisøy Rorbuer** (**82**) in Sakrisøy (Reine). You can also book kite or surf lessons. Best to give a call first to see where she's at, surf lessons are usually at Flakstad beach.

t. +47 9207 1722
w. schibevaagadventure.com

Photo: Marinus Jeiss

SEASIDE LOCAL: KARI SCHIBEVAAG

♦

There's something about this woman. She's not famous in a celebrity sense but everybody seems to know her. She's not rich, but she has the most fulfilling life one could wish for. She doesn't do one thing. No, no. She does a lot of things, most of them involving the ocean.

"I'm not a rich girl where money's concerned, but I have everything I need for a super life."

Although at one time she did excel at one thing, very much: kiteboarding. She's won the world title seven times. And twelve times she's won the World Snowkite Masters. She loved it then, the life of competition and world titles. Now she loves travelling and making expeditions. She loves surfing, she loves exploring the ocean and lakes on a SUP, with her dog as companion and orcas passing by. She loves freediving, running, hiking. And she loves Lofoten. It was during the shoot of a boat trip in Lofoten for television, back when she was still competing in the World Tour, that she fell in love with the archipelago. Originally from Stavanger, in the south of Norway, she soon realised in Lofoten that she'd found her place, and so moved up north and started her own company: Schibevaag Adventure.

Kari is still a passionate and mind-blowingly amazing kitesurfer, spending most of her time in Lofoten, although in winter she likes to travel abroad; taking pictures, writing for magazines, blogging, or go on expeditions further north. "I'm not a rich girl where money's concerned, but I have everything I need for a super life. I have a house, a car and a tent." And a business to run. She's made a life for herself doing what she loves and passing it on. She's using the sea and fjords as playground, wind and waves as energy, and kites, surfboards, SUPs and kayaks as toys and tools. Letting everyone in on the joy of being on the water, letting your body work, float, and fly. "The ocean means everything to me. I need the ocean and the mountains around me to feel free." Her house is tiny. She's put a lot of effort into getting her perfect-sized container house at exactly the spot where it is now, with a view of fjord and ocean. She loves small things. "My house is a perfect and free place for me. I sometimes live in my car, and in a tent, or borrowed van. I love this life because I can travel and see even more of Norway. I can change my view every morning." Not living a very conventional life, in a conventional house in a conventional place reflects her philosophy on life - to be yourself and do what you love. "Don't care what people say about you. It can be hard, but if you can manage it, you'll like it better this way." Any advice on where to go to in Lofoten, Kari? "My advice to visitors is to go see the amazing beach at Flakstad and fjords inside Sakrisøy." That's where you're likely to find her too. But if you don't, she's probably hiding in the mountains: "I sometimes need my time away from people and phone…"

♦

Find Kari online:
w. schibevaagadventure.com / schibevaag.com

♦

NORWAY

Photo: Malinus Jons

51

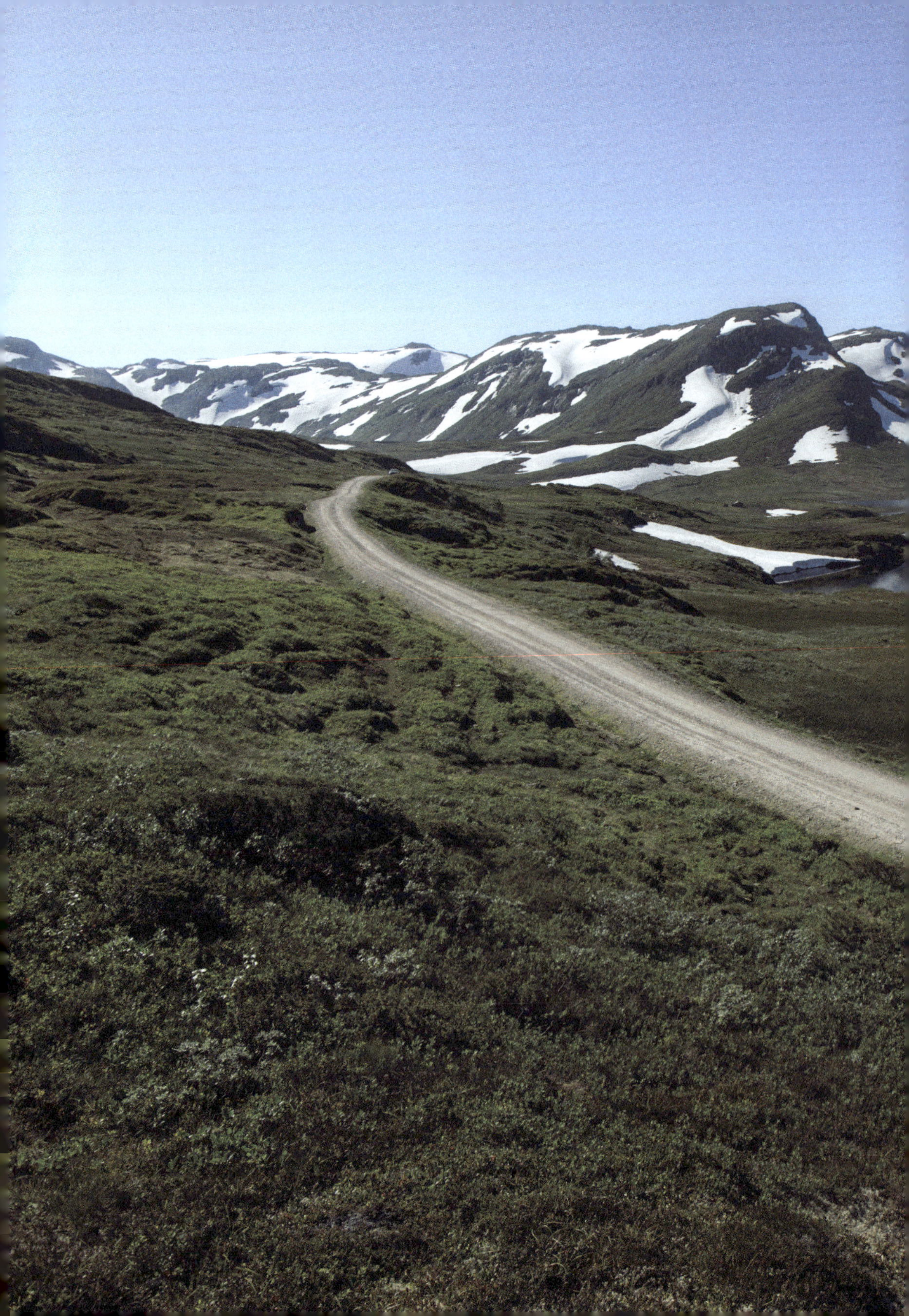

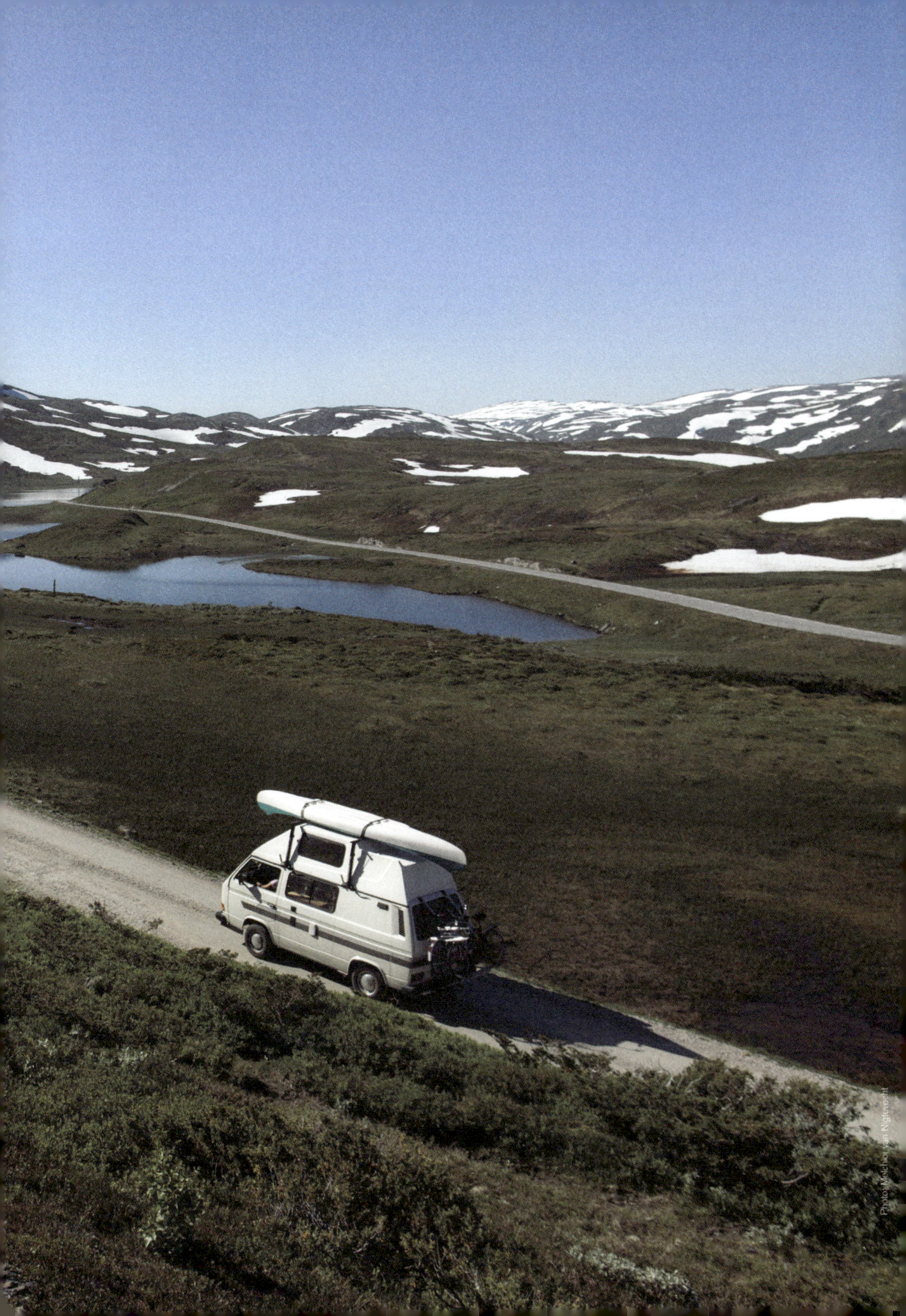
Photo: Melchior van Nigtevecht

Nordfjord

- ERVIK (II) ◆ 1
- ◆ 2, 6-8
  ERVIK
- HODDEVIK (I) ◆ 4, 11-14
  HODDEVIK
- ◆ 3, 9, 10
  STADLANDET
- ◆ 5
  SELJE
- ◆ 17
- ◆ 16
- ◆ 15
- ◆ MÅLØY
- ◆ 22
  NORDFJORDEID
- ◆ STRYN/LOE
- ◆ SANDA
- ◆ FLORØ
- ◆ 29

NORDFJORD

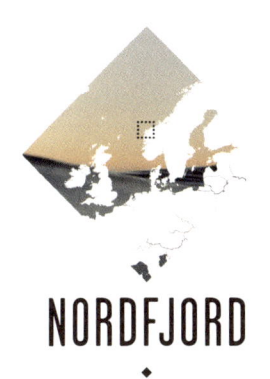

The Nordfjord district, in the north of Sogn og Fjordane county, is called the 'all in one fjord' by its own tourist board. Well, of course, if you had to describe it in one sentence, that's just what you'd come up with. Let's see; there's the 106 km long fjord, Europe's largest mainland glacier - Jostedalsbreen, Europe's deepest lake - Hornindalsvatnet, some impressive mountains, and the wild and wonderful seaside landscape along the Norwegian Sea, with countless inlets and islands. The options for outdoor sports and recreation are, as in most parts of Norway, overwhelming. So much to do and see! There's a good chance you'll miss a surf session because checking spots is a very different affair from what you're used to: it can easily take up half your day to drive from one spot to the other. Or you're just too busy doing other stuff, like taking a day's hike, biking downhill, listening to the roar of a waterfall, or photographing a glacier in the last light. You do know it takes forever in summer before the sun sets? If it sets at all...

Driving alongside the endless Nordfjord is dreamlike, but before you get all meditative, a route between fjord and mountain range or a narrow tunnel will demand your focus on the road and oncoming traffic. Also, there are only a few fishing communities and lakeside villages where you can find a supermarket, restaurant or gas station, so if you need any of those services, better not wait until the next town. There might not be another, you see.

One thing you'll notice is the grass-topped roofs on countless houses and huts. When asked if those roofs require a lot of maintenance, a local shrugged: 'We use goats for that.' We've never seen it, and hope you'll forgive us if the quote's untrue, but imagining the scene of goats on a roof is far better than to actually check this fact... If you happen to see some and get a pic, please send it to us!

TRAVEL INFO

Travelling by car? Roads are scenic, that's for sure. And it gets even more scenic further north. But sometimes narrow and you need to slow your pace, which isn't necessarily a bad thing. Make sure you have your camera at hand. Especially if you see those roof-goats munching. From Oslo or Trondheim it takes about 8 hours to the Stad peninsula, or a 6 hour drive from Bergen.

BY AIR

There are flights from Oslo to Ålesund, Ørsta/Volda and Sandane, run by national flight company Wideroe. SAS, Norwegian, KLM and other international flight companies have flights to Ålesund.

w. wideroe.no

BY BOAT

Ah yes, boats, ever so convenient in a country blessed with fjords and mountain ranges! The ferries are your shortcuts from one peninsula to the other, crossing fjords little and large. There's an express boat from Bergen to Selje, departing twice every day (5 hrs). The trip itself is a beautiful experience.

w. norled.no

The coastal steamers of Hurtigruten travel along the coast of Nordfjord.

w. hurtigruten.com

BY BUS

There are buses to Maurstad, approx 30 km south of Selje, from Oslo. And several other places in Norway.

w. nettbuss.no

To Stryn and Loen: catch the UNESCO Fjord Bus Tour from the 10th of June to the 13th of August, between Geiranger/Sogndal and Stryn/Loen. Hop on and off, stay overnight along the route or choose a one-day round trip. You can start in any of the four cities.

w. fjordtours.com

Photo: Medflex van Nigtevecht

IN AND AROUND SELJE

This area, Stadlandet - the Stad peninsula - holds a few of Norway's best-known surf spots, and the most photographed road towards one of them: Hoddevik. The winding road is a sight for sore eyes, for sure, even on the most grey, windswept and rainy days. But there's more to it, here, than just the surf. If it was just surfing you were after, you'd be in the south of France or Portugal, right? But since you came all this way, we're sure you can appreciate not only the surfing bays of Ervik and Hoddevik, but also the countless other less visited little bays and inlets, the grand cliffs towering over the water, the winding roads, and everything in between. And enjoy it all, even if there's not a wave in sight.

Selje is the name of the municipality but also the name of the main town. Before you set off to anywhere remote, this is the place to do your shopping, fill up your tank or ask at the tourist office for maps and information. A grocery shop can also be found in Leikanger, a half hour drive from Hoddevik.

Tourist office in Sunnivahuset, Selje (next door to the Selje pastor estate). **t.** + 47 4044 6011

TO DO

Norway's Scenic Routes. Although you could easily say that every other road or route you take in the north is scenic, there are actually a few drives in Norway specially selected for their outstanding beauty. Not only do they showcase the country's breath-taking scenery, the unique charm of each of the chosen routes has been very carefully enhanced with a combination of art, architecture and design. With great attention to detail and consideration for the natural environment, the 18 Scenic Routes use features such as rest stops and public toilets, viewpoints and footpaths, and outdoor art to make a statement or highlight a detail, or at times simply for aesthetic pleasure. The choice of materials used, like steel, glass, cement and wood, not only withstand extreme weather conditions, but also look oh so perfectly suited to their settings.

Not marked on our map, but just north of the Nordfjord area you'll find one of the Scenic Routes: the **Trollstigen**, Troll's Road. Well worth the drive up. This 104 km route in the Romsdalen area includes fjords, roads carved into steep mountainsides, some hair-raising bends, a bridge across a waterfall, and a ferry crossing. Also lip-smackingly impressive the **Atlanterhavsvegen**, Atlantic Road, has been named the 'world's most beautiful drive'. It curves around the coast and crosses the ocean via small islands and bridges. If you're getting a thirst for roadtripping (forget the surf?) there are many more amazing drives throughout the guide.

Drive up to **VestKapp (1)**, the West Cape, to get a 360° view of the area from the top of this 496 m high sea cliff on the northwest side of the peninsula. The best hour is around sunset, which, yes, can be as late as eleven or never at night in summer. Park your car, walk around, talk to the many, many sheep, shout against the wind, try to count the islands you see, look down from the cliffs to realise how tiny you are. The narrow road up to the cape's easy to find, follow the signs for Stadlandet/ Vestkapp. There's a small kiosk, supposed to be open in the summer season, although it's not very clear if and when. Don't worry. Enjoy the view. Careful to not step in sheep shit. The road's closed during winter.

The bay of Ervik is a treat, with its backdrop of green hills and cliffs. You can take a short hike up to the **cave** (**2**), right above the little fishing harbour. To get there you walk towards the harbour, then just before the road descends to the harbour take the path on your left. The network of tunnels you'll find is a leftover from WWII. You can take a wander through to have a spectacular view from the other end. One of them leads to a ladder, which in turn leads up to someone's garden, bit odd, but apparently you can enter, walk through the gate and get back on the trail.

At the far end of the bay there are large stone crosses from an ancient **graveyard** (**2**) overlooking the ocean. The graves date back as far as 1550, and most are from sailors who lost their lives at sea. The white brick chapel was built as a memorial for the victims of the steamship SS Sanct Svithun, which was bombed in 1943. The ship bell is used in the chapel, engraved with an appreciation message for the heroic local people who helped rescue the survivors.

If you want to learn about the ins and outs of the Stad peninsula, its nature and stories, join the knowledgeable guides from **Stadt Nature Guiding** (**3**). They offer guided hikes and outdoor experiences. Available all year.

a. Ytre Leikanger, 6750 Stadlandet
t. +47 4151 3473
w. stadtnaturguiding.no

Bygda Yoga Skule (**4**) is run by yogi Gry Hansen. Gry has over 18 years of yoga experience and is a passionate surfer. In summer lessons are held in a barn-turned-studio in Hoddevik bay, where she works and tries to live in harmony with the tide and waves. You can also join her classes in the studio located in Årvik, a tiny settlement tucked away at the far west point of the peninsula. The Årvik studio is open all year, has a view over the Atlantic and, ah yes, a heated floor!

You can also hold your own yoga retreat here, up to a max of 6 people. Gry suggests it's possibly the smallest yoga retreat in the world. The Hoddevik studio is located opposite Stad Surfing hostel: open from June to September, daily drop-in yoga classes available, usually at 10:00, or 18:00 hrs, depending on the waves... Contact Gry for details and class times.

a. Årvik, 6750 Stadlandet
t. +47 9155 0407
w. bygdayogaskule.com le

Hikes: There are numerous hike and bike trails on the peninsula, like the path following the ancient **Dragseid road**, between Drage in the south and Leikanger in the north. In the old days people used the road to avoid having to sail the rough waters around the West Cape and the Stad peninsula. It's said that during really bad weather boats were dragged along it to cross the peninsula. Nowadays it's only used for hiking and is preserved as a national monument. A few hikes, following this trail roughly, start opposite a small car park and memorial cross, along the Fv632 road towards Hoddevik.

From **Hoddevik** you can also take a steep and hefty hike up the mountain. The trail starts right behind the Stad Surfing hostel. Although it's a challenging hike, you'll be rewarded with an indelible view of the bay and valley.

On the **island of Selja** (5), just 1 km off the coast from the town of Selje, you'll find the ruins of **Selja Monastery**. One of the oldest religious buildings in Norway, here's where people came to pray as far back as a thousand years ago, and it's still a popular pilgrimage place. The monastery, built by Benedictine monks in the early 1100s may be in ruins, but the tower's still intact. In the days before roads were made, the locals travelled mainly by boat and so the island's central location made it an ideal spot to gather. You can learn all about the island, its history and culture, with a guided tour during the summer months. Points of interest include Viking graves and the remains of a traditional Viking farm, remnants from the Middles Ages, Iron Ages, really all the Ages. You can easily walk the 3 km length of the island, or take a round trip, which takes about 2 hrs and includes a walk up a 200 m high hill to get to the monastery. To reach the island, take the ferry from Selje, there are regular services in summer, tickets are available from the tourist office.

Enjoy a **SUP tour** (6) on the lakes and waterways of the Stad peninsula with Ervik Surf Shop. Depending on the weather, of course, they'll take you out to the most beautiful spots, paddling through the bluest water, a pristine landscape and alongside giant cliffs. Available during summer months, if weather allows.

a. Morkadalen, 6750 Stadlandet
t. +47 4053 9920
w. erviksurfshop.com

If you feel a bit 'city-deprived' after an overload of nature and outdoor activities, visit the surprisingly nice city of **Ålesund**, 125 km to the north of Selje. It's close to the Geiranger fjord and Trollstigen, one of Norway's Scenic Routes. But bugger that, if you're here for a bit of city life, right? Ålesund's built on a row of islands, so it's one of the things we love most - a seaside city. A fire destroyed almost the entire city in 1904, and it's been rebuilt. Since those years were the glorious era of Art Nouveau architecture, you'll find an abundance of the typical natural forms, curved lines and ornate details on the coloured houses, buildings, doors and windows.

EAT/DRINK/HANG OUT

A lot of guesthouses and hotels in the area also serve a good meal, and welcome you to have a coffee, beer or snack. Like **Stad Surfing** in Hoddevik, who serve a tasty homemade meal and you don't need to be a guest at their surfcamp. And there's **Furebuda Lodge** in Leikanger that has a pub, and a restaurant - Stormfast - serving freshly caught fish and meat from free-roaming cattle. The pub - Njord - is where guests and visitors meet locals and vice versa. A perfect place to get insider tips and hear local stories since you sit together at long tables. See Sleep section for more details.

SHOP

For your basic **shopping needs** there's a grocery store in Leikanger, as well as some traditional cafés like Cornerstone and Korsen, for snacks, drinks or a simple meal.

The friendly **Ervik Surf Shop** (7) is the only surf shop in this area, so, your go-to place if in need of wax, leashes, boards, info and whatnots. The lovely couple, Calle and Julia, run the cosy shop, set in an old sheep shed. Both originally from Sweden, but living and surfing happily-ever-after in this remote part of Norway. The shop's conveniently situated between the surf breaks of Hoddevik and Ervik, and is a bit of a meeting point for the small surfing community of the Stad peninsula. They have a broad range of surfboards, their own surfboard brand OCK that's made specially for the Scandinavian waters, as well as all your coldwater surf accessories. You can also rent surf equipment, snorkel gear, go on a guided SUP tour or arrange surf lessons from their experienced and ISA qualified instructors. Even if you don't really need anything, do visit the shop: hang around, take in the surroundings, you may feel a bit jealous of their picture perfect renovated country house, big garden, complete with adorable toddler. And do look into Calle's inspirational photo book full of Norwegian outdoor people, it's beautiful and impressive and gives you an idea of what's possible in the sometimes unforgiving and extreme climate of this country. Man of all trades, Calle's also a professional guide to the historic monastery on Selja island. Closed during winter from November to February.

a. Morkadalen, 6750 Stadlandet
t. +47 4053 9920
w. erviksurfshop.com

SLEEP
♦

The **guesthouse of Ervik Surfshop** (**7**) has the best view at Stadt and it is fully equipped for 2-6 persons. Fishing straight from the balcony… Closed in winter. ♦€♦ ♦€€♦

a. Morkadalen, 6750 Stadlandet
t. +47 4053 9920
w. erviksurfshop.com

The word 'camping' in **Erviksanden camping** (**8**) is a bit rich. The location couldn't be better, but it's just a field. There's a shack with a shower and a toilet at the other side of the road near the entrance, and there's one pole for electricity. Although far from expensive, it's not cheap either, considering what you get. But there's no other option, and, as said; the location is perfect, right behind the beach, a skip-hop away from the surf. ♦€♦

a. Ervik, 6750 Stadlandet
t. +47 9750 9943
fb. Erviksanden camping

Furebuda Lodge (**9**) offers basic but sleekly decorated accommodation. The building was fully renovated in 2017 and the view from the bathrooms is a treat. All rooms have double beds, can be changed to twin if you don't want to get too intimate with your travel buddy. Every room has a huge aerial photo of the surroundings, so you'll be inspired to go out and explore the minute you wake up. They also rent out houses in the area, and a big plus are their restaurant and pub where visitors and locals alike love to hang out. ♦€€♦

a. Leikanger, 6750 Standlandet
t. +47 9971 4098
w. furebuda.no

Youth Hostel **Dragebu** (**10**) is your cheapest option to stay, situated close to Hoddevik beach. The hostel is open all year. ♦€♦

a. Det Grønne Husset i Drage, 6750 Stadlandet
t. +47 9514 8353
f. dragebu overnatting

Hoddevik Beach Camping (**11**) is not much more than a field, with a perfect view of the beach and surf. There's no free camping allowed in Hoddevik, so if you want to sleep in tent or van, this is your only option. Basic facilities, like toilets and sinks; you pay extra for a shower and electricity. It's relatively cheap, although not quite value for money, except for the view. ♦€♦

a. Hoddevik, 6750 Stadlandet
t. +47 5785 7481
w. hoddevikstrandcamp.no

Stad Surfing (12) is a surf hostel right on the beautiful beach of Hoddevik, only a few steps from the surf, which has been there for over 20 years. It started with the owner living here and more and more surfers would pass by, so he offered visiting surfers a room to rent. He bought some more boards for visitors to use and rent, and slowly his house started to become the surf hostel it is today. There are nicely decorated shared and private rooms, you can rent surf gear or book lessons, and daily yoga classes (by Gry Hansen) are on offer. You get the good vibes and homely atmosphere for free. The best surf around here is in winter, so for that, and for all the other cold days, luckily there's a hot tub in the garden. The hostel has a little shop in the reception, and their restaurant's a delight; both guests and visitors are welcome to enjoy a tasty home-made meal. Open all year. ◆€€◆

a. Hoddevik, 6750 Stadlandet
   (at far end of road
   towards beach, on right hand side)
t. +47 5785 6944
w. stadsurfing.com

The little surf hostel **Akka Surf (13)** has room for up to 8 persons, and it's like staying at your favourite aunt's house. The favourite aunt would be Anne, who runs Akka, and is known to be a bit of a 'surf mama' around here. All local surfers know her. She's around the house most of the time or if not, you'll find her in the garden opposite the house, picking herbs, edible flowers and tending to the fruits and vegetables. (As a guest you're allowed to tuck in.)

Other times she'll be in the shed next to the house working on her artwork called 'Under Water', made from waste and trash picked up from the beach and countryside. It's part of The Plastic Project: a cooperation between the surfcamps of Hoddevik to keep the beach clean and make people, especially children, aware of the use of plastic and its consequences. The space where all the trash is collected and sorted feels like a greenhouse, except it's not veggies, but a second life for waste that's cultivated here. Anne's house feels like a museum. "Everything gets a second life in my house, I never buy anything new." she states. Every wall, nook and cranny's filled with little treasures, a painted object or photo that makes you curious about when and where it is and who took it. We fell in love with the view from 'The Chillroom' upstairs; it overlooks the bay, and you can just sit there all day staring at the ocean, the altering light, birds flying by, and, who knows, daydreaming of living here. Open all year. ◆€€◆

a. Hoddevik, 6750 Stadlandet
t. +47 5785 6609 / 9118 2382
fb. akkasurf

Stay for free: There's a perk for travellers/visitors who participate in at least two hours of beachcleaning, thus taking part in The Plastic Project: you can stay for free in one of the Heimplanet tents at Anne's little campsite opposite Akka Surf house! Ask Anne for details.

With **La Point Surfcamps (14)** you can choose between two options to stay in Hoddevik, either at Villa Utsikten, or Villa Innsikten.

The more secluded Villa Utsikten has four bedrooms and is situated further up the valley. It comes with sauna, a clear view of the bay, valley and cliffs, and a relaxed vibe. Suited to people who like to meet other travellers, but appreciate a bit of tranquility. Villa Innsikten houses up to 20 people, in dorms for 3-4 people and double rooms. It's a short walk from the beach and you'll feel the energy of the other guests busy doing fun stuff like slacklining, skating on the mini-ramp, if not surfing or chilling out. Perfect for solo travellers or groups of friends. Open from March to November. ♦€♦ ♦€€♦

a. Hoddevik, 6750 Stadlandet
t. +47 4663 9742
w. lapointcamps.com/surfcamp/norway

Always dreamed of **sleeping in a lighthouse**? The Vågsøy municipality, the headland just south of Selje, has four lighthouses, with three of them available for overnight stays. As lighthouses have a tendency of sitting either far out, or high up and away from urbanisation, and as close to sea as foaming waves can spit, it's sure to be an experience that will bring you closer to the elements. Watch the sun set or the sun rise, see the tides change at these deliciously weather-beaten places:

Ships pass by at **Ulvesund Fyr (15)**, built in 1870, at the land's end just northeast of Vågsøy, You can enjoy the view of the Stad peninsula. There's a café, a shop and a permanent photo exhibition. It's a perfect family getaway. Open from June to August. ♦€€♦

a. along the Fv603 road, nr 20, 6718 Deknepollen
t. +47 5785 1777 / 9524 0487
w. ulvesundfyr.no

Skongenes Fyr (16) is an automatic lighthouse with no road access, which makes it all the more adventurous and romantic. It's an hour's (easy) walk from Halsør. You can also visit this lighthouse as a daytrip. It's run by Ytre Nordfjord Turlag, which is a partner of the Norwegian Mountain Touring Association. Open all year. ♦€€€♦

a. along the Fv602, Halsør, 6710 Raudeberg
t. +47 4895 5867
w. ut.no/hytte/10253/skongenes-fyr

Kråkenes Fyr (17) is located at the far west point of the Vågsøy headland. It has five double rooms and one bridal suite, which goes by the name of Storm Suite… Bring your own food, maybe book a massage, and enjoy the view. The rooms are decorated in a homely style, and the friendly host, Bettina, will be happy to help you out and give all the info you need. The Storm Suite is open all year, double rooms are available from May to October. ♦€€€♦

a. Kråkenes Fyr, 6710 Raudeberg
t. +47 9502 3668
w. krakenesfyr.com

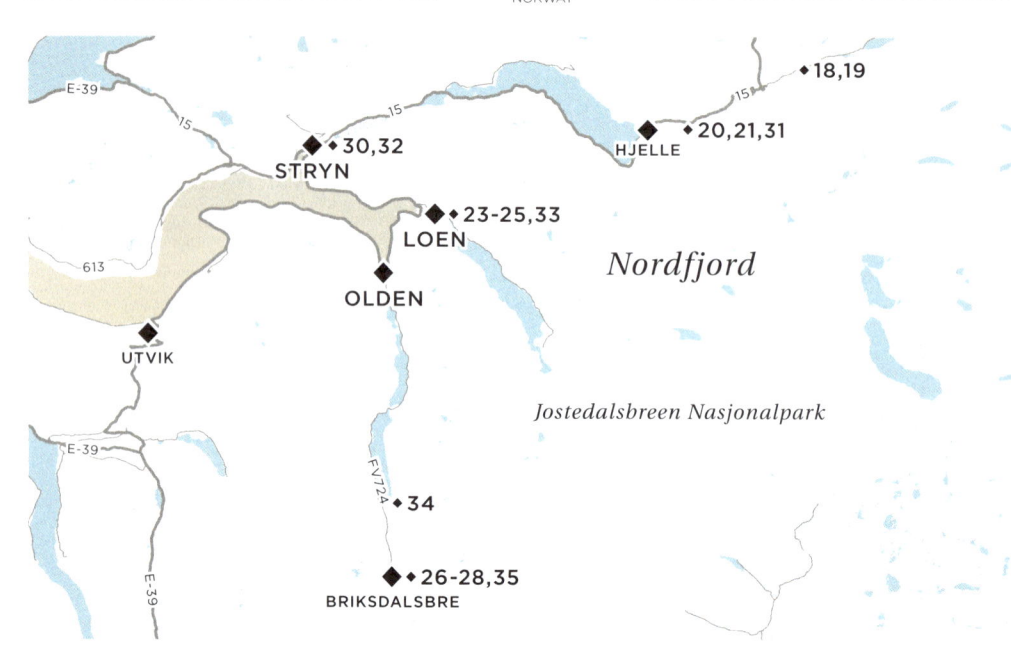

IN AND AROUND STRYN

◆

Stryn's a little way inland, surrounded by mountains, valleys and lakes. It's where you'll find the Jostedalsbreen National Park, and glacier tongues spilling thick white carpets of ice and snow. Not exactly the seaside, we know, but travelling down south from the Stad peninsula, the area has so much to offer we wouldn't want you to miss out. Even if not the ocean, you'll have enough water surrounding you, that's for sure. Parts of it are frozen, or pour down from great heights in vast quantities. (Really, try having a conversation near one of these grand waterfalls!) The road following the fjord is an attraction in itself. The water's azure, the green hills and mountains rise straight up from the water. The Stryn municipality, including the village of the same name and Loen, Innvik and Utvik, is the centre for year-round skiing and all things icy and snow. Stryn's also the spot to stock up on groceries, fuel, or maybe some socks and a raincoat before heading off to a glacier or national park.

Tourist office at Perhusvegen 24.

TO DO

◆

Paradoxically enough, there's a ski centre that only opens in summer, just an hour's drive from the village Stryn. The **Stryn Summer Ski Centre** (**18**) is situated on the Tystigbreen glacier at 1065 m and offers a pretty unique experience of skiing/snowboarding in the midst of summer. No need to wear six layers of clothes or a technical snow jacket, which you probably didn't bring anyway. There's a ski shop where you can rent gear and buy a lift pass, and a café for snacks and drinks. Open from end of May to end of July. The road's closed from October to May.

a. along the National Tourist Route Gamle Strynefjellsvegen (Rv258), 6783 Stryn
t. +47 4583 7077
w. strynsommerski.com

Another great way to explore the Tystigbreen glacier is to take a **glacier walk** at Strynefjellet, near Stryn Sommerski. The knowledgeable guides of **Briksdal Adventure** (**19**) take you up the glacier to a spot where you can enjoy your lunch while you take it all in – the view that is, not just lunch. The trip will take around 5-6 hours, and safety is assured. You'll need some hiking experience for this trip. Your starting point's at the Stryn Sommerski station, where you take a chairlift up. Helmets, harness, ice axe, ropes and other necessities are provided. You have to pack your own lunch though, and wear appropriate clothing for the weather. If you don't have suitable shoes you can rent their mountain boots. Open in July and August.

a. Meeting Point at the Stryn Sommerski car park
t. +47 9013 8308
w. briksdaladventure.com

Stryn Festival (**20**) is all about celebrating the great outdoors. Think kayaking, biking, bouldering, summer skiing, mountain biking, climbing. And après ski, of course! And concerts and eating, and drinking and more music. The festival takes place at and around Folven Camping, also known as the Ibiza of Scandinavia, and the Stryne festival's home ground. There are guided tours, a river race, climbing courses, SUP safaris, you can test gear, the skate park's open all day to play, and you don't need to be a pro at anything to participate. In fact, now's your time to learn new outdoor stuff!

If you like the great outdoors in the daytime, but prefer to spend the night sleeping, you can check in at next door's campsite, Nygård. The festival takes place every year on the second weekend of June, and you'll need a festival ticket to enter, and to stay at the campsite.

a. Folven Camping, 6798 Hjelledalen (on the Rv15)
w. strynefestivalen.no

Finding a place to go skating is easy; there are several ramps and parks in the area, including a **skateboard park (21)** at the Stryn Stadium, the skate park with mini ramp and some street obstacles in front of Folven Camping, and a skate park in the centre of Sandane.

Do you want to get friendly with some good-natured natives? Learn all about the Fjord Horse, that has its origins in this very place, the Nordfjord. They're known for their sweet character: not too moody and demanding, thus were used as workhorses in the olden countryside days. (Not complaining about work hours or organising a workers' union whatsoever, good horsies). Nowadays, you can take a leisurely ride on them through the mountains. A good place to start is the **Norwegian Fjord Horse Centre (22)**, in Nordfjordeid, since they're the national centre for this breed. You're not just jumping on the back of a horse, you learn about their character, how to communicate and cooperate with these beautiful animals. In summer they organise weeklong riding camps for children, but they also offer 1 hour rides and day trips through the mountains. Open all year.

a. Rådhusvegen 6E, 6770 Nordfjordeid
t. +47 5786 4800
w. norsk-fjordhestsenter.no

The **Skåla mountain (23)** towers to the east above Loen, with its summit just over 1840 m above sea level. You can hike all the way to the top. And although you need to be in good condition, it's an easy trail that ascends gradually, so you can even take older kids, if they're used to a long hike. Consider it a day trip (16 km round-trip, approximately 8 hrs), so pack snacks, drinks and appropriate clothing, and start early. You'll notice the vistas changing constantly, passing a waterfall, an old farm, glacier-carved valleys, the Skåla lake, and the final reward: the 360° view from the round tower on top. The tower, Kloumanstornet, was built in 1891 from surrounding stones, and you can stay overnight in one of the 22 beds, or in the recently built Skålabu cabin. From the top you can see Jostedalsbreen glacier and the Sunnmøre Alps. The walk starts in Tjugen (2 km from Loen) at a dirt road near Lovatnet lake.

A Via Ferrata (Italian for Iron Road) or Klettersteig is the name for a climbing route that's equipped with climbing aids, such as steel cable and/or rail and ladders, fixed to the rocks. Climbers secure themselves to the cable for a (relatively) safe ascent or traverse, without the need for ropes. The **Via Ferrata Loen (24)** is a well-kept route that goes all the way up to Hoven mountain's summit, towering 1011 m above the Nordfjord. If you're a first-timer at this you can take a guided climb all the way up. You'll be secured with a harness, and if it's perhaps something you thought you'd never dare do; this must be the safest way to try. Imagine looking down from the steep mountain down to the fjord, oh my, we're talking super selfie opportunity! And if it feels daunting at times, remember, you'll not only be rewarded with amazing views, but the biggest pat on the back from yourself. At 750 m high, the Gjolmunnebrua suspension bridge, the longest in Europe, connects you to the next part of the climb. It's a whole experience in itself, walking lightly as you can from one end to the other, feeling like a cord dancer, crossing a deep canyon. You'll continue up, climbing and hiking. At the top you can sit back and relax, maybe pat your back again, at the Hoven restaurant - with a view to die for - then take the easiest way down with the Loen Skylift cable car. (Aha, there's a cable car! Now you tell me…) Experienced climbers can rent ferrata equipment at the Loen Active shop. In winter you can take up cross-country skiing, or book a guided ski tour on the mountain. The Via Ferrata is open from May to October.

a. 6789 Loen (in the centre of Loen between Hotel Alexandra and Hotel Loenfjord)
t. +47 5787 5800
w. loenactive.no

The aforementioned **Loen Skylift (25)** takes you from the fjord to the top of Mt. Hoven (1011 m) in only five minutes. So, it's either that or climbing five hours… The panorama restaurant on top offers a spectacular view over the mountains. Open all year.

a. 6789 Loen (you'll spot it, coming from Stryn, just before entering Loen)
t. +47 5787 5900
w. loenskylift.com

The **Briksdal Glacier** (**26**) is an arm, or tongue, whatever you want to call it, of the Jostedal Glacier, the largest glacier in continental Europe. Part of the Jostedalsbreen National Park, the glacier's easily reached by foot along a 3 km mellow trail, starting either from the parking area right after campsite Melkevoll, or the Briksdalsbre Mountain Lodge. If you're not up for the walk, you can take a ride on a motorised 'Troll Car' (buggy). The trail ends as close as you can get to the glacier, which is not so close you can touch it, by far, but enough to be impressed. You'll see the incredible image of water frozen still as it drops from 1200 m, and can imagine the roar of the melting ice at its edges as it descends to the fjord. It's not just the glacier: it's the milky-ish blue ice water of the lake and the steep mountains and fierce waterfalls that are all part of the experience. In summer it can get pretty busy! Go early to beat the buses dropping off cruise ship passengers. To get there: follow the road of the Oldedalen Valley from Olden towards the Briksdal Glacier.

Around the glacier are a few beautiful **hikes** (**27**), some considerably vigorous, others less demanding:

The very first part of the **Kattanakken (the cat's neck) trail**, up until the viewing point, is easy enough for everyone. After Sauskärholten, the viewing point, it's time to head back if you have a fear of heights or are not an experienced hiker. The trail continues along steep ridges, and although it's fairly easy walking terrain, it's not exactly a walk in the park considering the heights. But we guess by now you know the rewards… stunning views, to say the least. You'll see Briksdal Glacier in its full glory. The hike takes you up to 1458 m above sea level and takes around 4 hours. To get there you start walking towards the glacier, then take a path right (you'll see the sign), just before crossing the bridge at the waterfall.

The **Oldeskaret trail** follows a former livestock trail that's been used by travellers over the centuries. Some parts are pretty steep, especially at the beginning of the trail, and can be slippery after rain, but there are rope safeguards along the steepest sections. On top you'll be rewarded with views over the Oldedalen valley. The whole hike takes around 5 hours. At the end of summer you'll find loads and loads of berries to pick at the beginning/end of the trail. The start (and end) is behind the Melkevoll Bretun campsite, passing the waterfall.

A very **tranquil hike**, not too demanding at all, is the path through a lush, green valley at the northern side of the glacier. You can follow the entire route, which takes approx 4 hours, or just walk until you've had enough and return. You'll probably meet a goat or two, but not many people. There's a hikers' hut where you can spend the night, or, if you're curious like us, leaf through the journal to see who's been sleeping there. The entrance to the path starts from the small parking area near Aabrekk Farm, some 2 km back down the main road from the parking for the glacier.

If you're into **sport climbing and bouldering**, check out the many marked routes between Stryn and Loen. Any information about bouldering, routes and guides can best be gathered at the reception of Melkevoll Bretun camping (see Sleep section). They're very active and enthusiastic about climbing and bouldering, and there are bouldering areas at the campsite too. They also rent out mats/crash pads.

One of the most enjoyable yoga classes we had was by teacher Johanne Melkevoll at Melkevoll Bretun camping. You can get sweaty, yes, but it's definitely relaxing. She, and all other teachers here, cater for all levels in the same class, giving each and every person the attention they need, so no worries if you're an absolute beginner. Classes are held in their nature shala, **Blue Mountain Hall (28)**, which has a perfect view of the surrounding mountains and valley. If you plan to stay a bit longer you can also join one of the retreats on offer, like a week of yoga and hiking. In between, there's time for a sauna and cooling down in the ice-cold stream, and all sorts of outdoor activities. You can also opt for one of the relaxing and therapeutic massages and treatments. Classes are available from May to September, for info and dates for the retreats check the website.

a. at the end of the road of Oldedalen Valley, towards the Briksdal glacier, 6791 Oldedalen
t. +47 5787 3864
w. bluemountainyoga.no

Have a challenging river experience and go rafting or riverboarding in the Jølstra. This river is considered to be one of the best white water adrenaline-enhancing rivers of Northern Europe. If riverboarding's new to you, **Jølster Rafting (29)** has very skilled instructors to introduce and guide you to this extreme and intense way to flow with the forces of the river. Open from May to September.

a. Tangane 22, 6800 Førde
t. +47 9006 7070
w. jolster-rafting.no

EAT/DRINK/HANG OUT

Stryn Kaffebar & Vertshus (30) is one of the oldest houses in Stryn, built in the late 1800s. Saved from destruction the house is now in good use as a café and bed & breakfast. Its characteristic, cosy lived-in atmosphere definitely complements enjoying your coffee, cake or lunch. Open all year. ◆€€◆

a. Tonningsgata 19, 6783 Stryn
t. +47 5787 0530
w. strynvertshus.no

SLEEP
◆

As mentioned before, **Folven Camping (31)** in Hjelledalen - some 30 min drive from Stryn - is nicknamed the Ibiza of Scandinavia. Not sure if it's the right nickname, because it doesn't have any of the hippie-chic vibe, but it's definitely happening-with-an-outdoorsy-flair. There's a skate park with mini ramp and street obstacles, a pumptrack for BMX, and a slackline park. Then there's its location at the foot of Strynefjellet (the Stryn pass, connecting fjords and mountains), close to all the options for activities us outdoor folks love: climbing and bike tracks, summer skiing and boarding, hiking and kayaking. The friendly staff can advise you about all sorts of activities in the area. The site has pitches for tents, campervans and caravans, and there are cabins for rent. Open April to October. ◆€◆ ◆€€◆

a. Folven, 6798 Hjelledalen
   (along the Rv15)
t. +47 4766 6900
w. folven.no

10 km west of Stryn you'll find the **Robjørgane Farm Houses (32)**. These wooden cabins all have picture-perfect views of the Nordfjord and hills and mountains surrounding the lake. The cabins sleep up to five people, and they all have fireplaces, yay! The site, with buildings dating back as far as 1850, is an ecologically run farm with sheep and chickens. The owners happily show you around. From here you can easily go on hikes, or fishing quests in the nearby mountain lakes (you usually need a permit for freshwater fishing, but we were told there's no need for a permit here. To be on the safe side: check with the owners first). Open from May to October. ◆€€◆

a. Robjørgane, 6783 Stryn
t. +47 5787 6414 / 9159 0890
w. robjorgane-panorama.no

Situated at Lovatnet lake (Loen lake), **Sande Camping (33)** obviously has perfect views. There are pitches and facilities for tents, caravans and campervans, they have grass-roofed wooden cabins and houses for rent. Besides being in the right spot for outdoor activities and a daytrip to the Bødal glacier, you can easily spend a day inside their sauna, get a massage or participate in a lesson of Qigong. (Get your body's energy lines fired up!). Open all year. ◆€◆ ◆€€◆

a. Lodalsvegen, 6789 Loen
   (along the Fv723)
t. +47 4166 9192 / 9795 4513
w. sande-camping.no

Staying at the **Aabrekk Gard (34)** (farm) has a few perks, besides being nicely situated in a green valley close to a hiking trail: you can order all sorts of yummy sweet and hearty pancakes from the farm. The recently restored houses cluster around the farm, at the foot of a hill, just off the road towards Briksdal glacier. Open all year. ◆€€◆

a. 6791 Oldedalen (along the Fv724)
t. +47 9138 2569
w. aabrekk-gard.no

Our absolute favourite is camping **Melkevoll Bretun (35)**. Within walking distance from the Briksdalbreen, you'll have the glacier in sight at one side, and a roaring waterfall at the other. The terraced site has pitches for tents, campervans and caravans and a few characteristic wooden lodges and cabins. It's all set up in perfect harmony with the surrounding nature. From the campsite a challenging hike starts up from the valley, or an easy track takes you to the Briksdal glacier. A shared living space is used by all visitors to cook, barbecue, or just have a drink sitting around a big fireplace. There's a small sauna in each the men's and the women's sanitary blocks. From the sauna you can jump straight in to the icy cold little river that runs straight through the site. Large rocks are great to practise bouldering, and you can join daily yoga classes. The reception area also serves as a small place to hang out, check your mail, chat with the very friendly and knowledgeable staff, or have a coffee and a homemade cake. If you don't want to stay at the campsite, but do want to use all the facilities, you can buy a day pass. Open from April to October. ◆€◆ ◆€€◆

a. 6791 Oldedalen (at the end of the Fv724
   towards the Briksdal glacier)
t. +47 5787 3864 / 9131 9832
w. melkevoll.no

SURF

With all this open ocean, combined with a plethora of west-facing bays, you might be surprised we only mention two surf spots here. There must be others, surely. The thing is: checking one spot, then deciding it's not good enough or it doesn't work and heading to the next can take up half the day, what with the tiny winding roads, waiting for oncoming traffic to pass at a wider section, goats crossing, mountains and fjords to hurdle. We made the mistake once of taking a wrong turn to a town with a very similar name as a surf spot. There was no place to turn and nothing else to do than just go on, and on, till almost the end of the road. The road got smaller and the canyon at one side deeper, the cliffs at the other side steeper. We couldn't turn until just before the end of the road, where someone had left the gate open to his house. No need to tell you we never made it in time for a surf session that day. Tide had gone up and down again by the time we got back. Point is: there's a lot to explore, and the journey is the - breath-taking - mission in these latitudes. Enjoy the ride.

Hoddevik is a small but largely surf-minded community in a valley at the end of a hair-pinned road. A very photogenic road we might add. Steep mountains flank the valley and the half-moon shaped bay of **Hoddevik (I)**, and do a mighty job of protecting the bay from strong winds. This consistent beach break works best at a medium SW-W swell from low to mid tide. All surf schools in the area teach at Hoddevik. ◆ *All levels/sand and some stones/few parking spots and paid parking at campsite/surf school/campsite/restaurant.* ◆

Ervik (II) is on the other side of the mountains, and picks up more swell than Hoddevik. Hence it's not so protected, so the wind can be a spoilsport. The waves are more powerful and hollow but hold perfectly in the right clean conditions. There's a gentlemen's agreement between surf schools not to teach at Ervik, so you won't find any lessons here. It's not a beginners bay

SCHOOL RENTAL REPAIR

♦

anyway, there are many rocks, a fast take-off at a right hand pointbreak, and you won't want to compete with the few-but-very-dedicated locals when it's on. Can get pretty busy in summer, in winter you'll be happy to see another surfer joining the line-up. Works best with small to medium W-NW swell from low to mid tide. ♦ *Intermediate/sand, rocks and boulders/easy parking/campsite.* ♦

You'll pass **Ervik Surf Shop (6)** on your way towards Ervik bay, there's a small sign at the side of the road. You'll find all your surf necessities and a friendly chat. You can book surf lessons and SUP tours, rent surf gear, and if you're in need of a repair, this is your best bet to get it fixed. You can even arrange a fishing permit at the shop. Closed during winter from November to February.

a. Morkadalen, 6750 Stadlandet
t. +47 4053 9920
w. erviksurfshop.com

Stad Surfing (12) in Hoddevik offer private and group surf lessons and courses, rent out surfboards, wetsuits and SUPs, and provide guided SUP tours. Open all year.

a. Hoddevik, 6750 Stadlandet
   (at far end of road
   towards beach, on right hand side)
t. + 47 5785 6944
w. stadsurfing.com

La Point Surf Camps (14) in Hoddevik offer surf courses from 2 to 7 days for different levels. Open from March to November.

a. Hoddevik, 6750 Stadlandet
t. + 47 4663 9742
w. lapointcamps.com/surfcamp/Norway

Jostedalsbreen Nasjonalpark

◆ 1,2,16,17
JOSTEDAL

◆ SKEI

◆ 5,10
SKJOLDEN

◆ 11
LUSTER

◆ 3
FJÆRLAND

◆ 4
GAUPNE

◆ 6
ØVRE ÅRDA

◆ 18

◆ 20

◆ 12,13,19
SOGNDALSFJØRA

◆ LEIKANGER

◆ LÆRDALSØYRI

Sognefjord

◆ 7

◆ 8,21
AURLANDSVANGEN

◆ 9,14,15
FLÅM

SOGNEFJORD

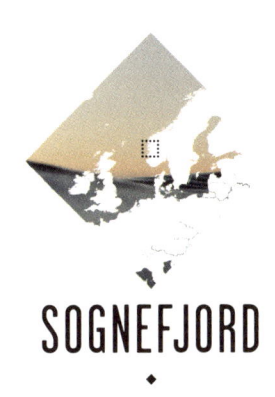

Travelling to Sognefjord, whether you're coming from north or south, you'll cross the heart of Fjord Norway. Everything and everyone who boasts about having the longest this, the largest that, you may diss, but in the case of Sognefjord's surroundings, you might just want to check it all out. The longest (of Norway) would be Sognefjord itself, whose arms reach out and wind their way between mountains, beckoning you to kayak, sail or raft. It's also the deepest, by the way. From the sea it stretches a little over 200 kilometres inland. The largest is Jostedal glacier – almost 500 square kilometres of ice. You'll see its impressive branches reaching down into valleys from all angles while driving through the area, even when checking the rearview mirror. Driving through the many tunnels, or choosing passes if weather permits it, witnessing the landscape changing from lush to barren, from enchanting to imposing, you'll probably make more stops than you might have planned. Of all the destinations in Norway, this is one of the most year-round friendly places to visit.

TRAVEL INFO

Driving through, or getting to this area you'll want to hop on a ferry or boat at some point. Express boats run daily from Bergen to Sogndal, making stops along the fjord at Vik, Balestrand and Leikanger. A daily boat service from Bergen to Flåm runs from the 1st of May to the 30th of September. The boat to Flåm also connects with ferries to Gudvangen, Kaupanger and Lærdal. No need to say that a ferry ride is a little holiday all in itself. More info on schedules and timetables: **w.** norled.no / fjord1.no

BY AIR

Sogndal Airport is situated on a mountaintop – you'd almost want to book a flight just for that! Widerøe has several direct daily flights from Oslo and Bergen to Sogndal Airport.

w. wideroe.no / avinor.no

BY BUS

Direct buses from Oslo, Bergen and Trondheim to Sogndal run several times a day.

w. kringom.no

BY TRAIN

Bergen Railway run daily services between Bergen and Oslo. An exciting journey is taking the Flåm Railway from Myrdal's mountain station all the way down to Flåm station at Aurlandsfjord. It's the steepest (on standard gauge tracks) in the world, and stops at scenic spots. Check the Norges Statsbaner for timetables.

w. nsb.no

IN AND AROUND SOGNDAL AND AURLAND

◆

The municipalities of Sogndal sit conveniently along the shores of the fjords, at the centre of all things outdoor, between some of the most beautiful panorama routes. We'll continue with the superlatives, because this is the area where you find the world's longest tunnel and world's steepest railway. The Lærdalstunnelen connects Lærdal with Aurland and has a dizzying length of 24,5 kms. In summer you can choose to take the pass, Aurlandsvegen, instead of the tunnel. It's a welcome alternative for those who don't enjoy the very many tunnels in the first place. Prefer a slow, sit-down-and-take-it-all-in way of travelling? The Flåm Railway train choo-choos its way down from the mountain at Myrdal to the fjord in Aurland.

Although you'd think all of Norway is pretty green, Lærdal (in between Sogndal and Aurland) is designated as one (out of four) of Norway's certified sustainable destinations because of its local engagement, and in terms of lasting commitment. Besides managing things like water use and waste disposal, and preserving their cultural heritage, for you as a visitor it means that most of the tourist businesses you deal with will do their utmost to work in environmentally friendly ways.

Tourist offices: Parkvegen 5 (Sogndal, in the Mix Kiosk Parkbygget) / Vangen 1 (Aurland, in the 'Heradshuset'). In Flåm you'll find a tourist information centre at the railway station.

TO DO

◆

We do hope you like **hiking**, or otherwise, take up hiking as your new hobby. Walking is the best way to fully take in the landscape, and there are many paths for all levels available. Since Sognefjord is home to two large national parks, Jotunheimen and Jostedalsbreen, the options are numerous. Some start conveniently at car parks along the main roads, and panoramic routes.

Combine **kayaking and glacier walking** with the knowledgeable guides of **Icetroll** (**1**). You'll be crossing Nigardsbrevatnet lake in a kayak before taking a hike to the glacier. The guides can tell you everything and absolutely all about glaciers, how they form, where they used to be and what (maybe) will be their future. After a leisurely walk, rope and crampons will be used to explore the glacier. Children can also join this 3 to 4 hour tour, which is possible only in May and June. From July on the Styggevatnet snowshoe tour is available; first kayaking the lake and then using a narrow, frozen gorge to reach the glacier. Bit more demanding and adventurous this one.

a. Breheimsenteret, 6871 Jostedal (along road 604)
t. +47 9701 4370
w. icetroll.com

During winter it's safe to explore the stilled world of the **blue-ice caves** (**2**) under the Nigardsbreen glacier with the guides from **Jostedal Signatur**. You'll start at Jostedalen hotel and put on skis or snowshoes to start the hour-long journey towards the glacier. From there on you'll explore the caves. The tour takes up to 6 hours and is for small groups. Available from December to April, bookings must be made at least 3 days in advance.

a. Breheimsenteret, 6871 Jostedal
t. +47 9592 3689
w. jostedalsignatur.no

If you want to really get into the science of glaciers, visit **The Norwegian Glacier Museum** (**3**). Set in a futuristic building, just after you leave the tunnel coming from Fjærland, heading south, on your right hand side. Find out why ice seems blue, why a fjord gets its

75

greenish colour, how fjords, and glaciers are formed, how a glacier's energy is used. See ice sculptures, a Siberian mammoth (thirty thousand years old and as dead as a… erm… mammoth). And, last but not the least interesting: learn about the fragility of our climate, the melting of glaciers and effects. Open daily from April to October.

a. Fjærlandsfjorden 13, 6848 Fjærland
t. +47 5769 3288
w. bre.museum.no

Some family fun's to be had at the Leirdøla river: either **body-rafting**, or **canyoning** with **Fjord Active** (**4**). There are cliff jumps, natural water slides, swimming and climbing involved. The guides provide you with all safety equipment such as helmets, lifejackets and wetsuits. It's suitable for kids 10 years and over. First make your reservation, then follow their directions to the meeting point: Take road 55 to Gaupne, take road 604 in the direction of Jostedal. After 10 km you're there.

a. Leirdalen, 6868 Gaupne
t. +47 4702 7878 / 9176 3754
w. fjordactive.com

Maybe you brought your own, and we don't need to tell you where to go paddle your **SUP**, what with so many lakes. If not, and you want to explore a bit of one of the branches of the Nordfjord on a SUP, you can rent them at **Adventure Tours** (**5**), situated at the Lustrafjord in Skjolden.

a. Skjolden Brygge, 6876 Skjolden (next to 'Bryggjehuset' café & pub)
t. +47 9691 3130 / 9576 6385
w. adventuretours.no

Kayak your way through the magical, mystical and secluded area of the Sognefjord in the valley of Utladalen, under the guidance of **Bulder Og Brak** (**6**). Every season has something to offer, and their experienced staff will happily share a cold air route in winter as well as a late summer tour. Besides paddling, they like hiking, so you can either book a guided kayak or hiking trip. Bulder Og Brak's located at the northern end of the Årdalsvatnet lake. Open all year.

a. Strandvegen, 6884 Øvre Årdal
t. +47 9521 1657 / 9752 2139
w. bulderogbrak.no

Instead of taking the longest tunnel (24,5 km) to get from Lærdal to Aurland (or the other way round), you can choose to drive the **Aurlandsvegen** (**7**) – if the weather allows it. It's also called 'the snow route'. You'll be driving a stunner of a scenic route, with its highest point at 1300 m. So, yes, there'll be snow. The first part, coming from Lærdal, is pretty steep and has sharp turns, passing green hills and wetlands. You can stop at the sign with a little backpacker painted on. There's a hiking path running through heathland, along a little river. It's an easy hike but you need shoes that don't mind getting wet. (Nobody else saw it, but I swear I saw a little troll here.) If you're travelling in a van or with a tent, try staying overnight at the parking on top. It's just something else waking up in a barren and snowy landscape in the middle of summer. You can make some hikes up here too.

At the very end of the pass, just before making your descent, stop for a killer view at the **Stegastein viewpoint** (**8**). A state-of-the-art wooden platform's jutting 30 metres out from a mountain, hovering 650 metres above the majestic Aurland fjord. And if you need to go, do go - take the ladies toilet at the back and enjoy the view from up there! The Aurlandsvegen usually opens from 1st of June to 15th October, (depending on the weather). The road from Aurland to the viewpoint (7,5 km) is open all year.

If you want to do a kayak tour for several days, combined with hiking, join the expeditions of **Njord Kayak Centre** (**9**). They offer adventurous tours up to 10 days, staying overnight in tents at the water's edge. They always start from Flåm and explore the near or far surroundings, depending on your chosen duration. They only travel in small groups, and we love their 'leave no trace, only ripples' philosophy. Their kayak season runs from May to September.

a. Flåm Beach, 5741 Flåm
t. +47 9132 6628
w. seakayaknorway.com

EAT/DRINK/HANG OUT

◆

Get your cabbage stew or cheesecake after a hard day's work at playing outdoors at **Eide Farm** (**10**) in Skjolden. It has a very cosy Scandinavian feel to it, the food's good and it's set in a pretty idyllic surrounding. Open all year.
◆€◆ ◆€€◆

a.   Lustravegen 4405, 6876 Skjolden
t.   +47 9510 9643
w. eidegard.com

Lustrabui bakery (**11**) bakes its bread in an old wood-fired oven. Hei, hei! That sounds deilig! And it is damn tasty, you should try some raisin or cinnamon buns too, to go with your coffee. Find the bakery just off the 55 road in Luster, between Skjoldne and Gaupne. Open all year. ◆€◆

a.   Bringebakkane 2, 6872 Luster
t.   +47 4694 8845
w. lustrabui.no

In Sogndal, at the fjord, you'll find **Dampskipskaien** (**12**) 'the steamliner quay'. This small pub with a great view serves home-made soup and locally cured ham, along with other snacks. It's a bit of a hang out for all of those who love to play outside, whether kayaking, skiing or mountain biking. And guess what: you can also rent bikes, kayaks and canoes here. Open all year.
◆€◆ ◆€€◆

a.   Bryggjegota 6, 6856 Sogndal
t.   +47 9776 8862
fb. dampskipskaien Sogndal

Inside the Quality Hotel Sogndal, a modern building in the centre of the village, you'll find the **Vågal Burger and Gin** (**13**). The restaurant serves all kind of burgers, from vegetarian and fish to regular burgers, gourmet style. You can also order them as take-away if you feel a bit out of place. Open all year. ◆€€◆ ◆€€€◆

a.   Gravensteinsgata 5, 6856 Sogndal
t.   +47 5762 7700
w. qualityhotelsogndal.no/vagal-burger-gin

Driftwood walls, a big fireplace and craft beer. Make sure to visit the **Ægir BrewPub** (**14**) in Flåm. Ægir's been brewing ales and lagers since 2007 and their beers are sold throughout Norway. Maybe you'll have come across one or two of the Ægir beers in a bar, restaurant or shop somewhere on your journey. In 2011 they added a distillery where they produce aquavit. Since Ægir's a giant and the master of the ocean in Norse mythology, you have our interest… Nah, it's the craft beer of course! But Ægir the giant is certainly an inspiration to the brewery: according to the myth, he has the biggest brewing kettle and brews the best beer. You can visit the brewpub to have a drink, or eat lunch or dinner. Their chef doesn't only serve beer with your food, there's beer in your food too. Marinades and sauces are spiced with hops, herbs and of course Ægir beer. If you'd like a souvenir (beer or schnapps perhaps?) you can get some tasteful ones from their outlet. Ægir's brewery offers beer and aquavit tastings on reservation. In the afternoons in June, July and August at 16:00 hrs, they'll tell you about the brewer's craft and the brewing process. Open all year. ♦€♦ ♦€€♦

a. A-feltsvegen 25, 5743 Flåm
   (in Flåmsbrygga, the cluster of buildings at the Aurlandsfjord)
t. +47 5763 2050
w. flamsbrygga.no/en/aegir-brewpub

The large terrace at **Furukroa Kafè** (15) is a perfect spot to have your lunch and enjoy the view of the harbour. The café serves traditional Norwegian food and some vegetarian dishes too. Open all year. ♦€♦ ♦€€♦

a. A-feltsvegen 25, 5743 Flåm
t. +47 5763 2050
w. flamsbrygga.no/en/hotel/furukroa-cafe

SLEEP
♦

The Sognefjord is a camping area par excellence. There are so many nice sites, almost all situated at picture perfect locations; we could fill another guide with them. So here's a small selection of those we like:

The quiet **Nigardsbreen Camping** (16) sits at the edge of the Nigardsbreen valley, convenient for planning day trips in and around the National Park and glacier (4 km). It's small, basic, and its location is a grand plus. The camping is close to the Breheimsenteret Visitor Centre, where you'll find all sorts of info on the national park. Besides pitches for camping there are chalets for rent. Open in the summer season. ♦€♦

a. Gjerde 4, 6871 Jostedal
   (just off the Fv 334)
t. +47 5768 3135

Family-friendly **Jostedal Camping** (17) is also situated in the valley, near the Jostedalsbreen glacier and Breheimen National Park. Bit bigger and there are a lot of activities on offer, like rafting and kayaking trips. Besides pitches for camping there are small and bigger cabins for rent. The cosy cabins sleep up to 6 people, they all have a wood-burner stove. Open from May to October. Cabins are available all year. ♦€♦ ♦€€♦

a. Jostedalsvegen 3041 Gjerde, 6871 Jostedal
t. +47 9775 6789
w. jostedalcamping.no

Uteplassen (18) at Selseng in the Sogndalsdalen valley has cabins, apartments and a campsite. It's a small, magical and tranquil place surrounded by mountains and green fields and is open all year. ♦€♦

a. close to the E5 at Svidalen
   - follow directions from the website
t. +47 4691 0456
w. ute-plassen.com

Kjørnes Camping & Cabins (19) is situated at Sognefjord, some 3 km from Sogndal centre. They have pitches and cabins, and there's a small playground for toddlers. Open all year. ♦€♦ ♦€€♦

a. Kjørnes, 6856 Sogndal
t. +47 9754 4156
w. kjornes.no

Near Balestrand you'll find the friendly family-run **Veganeset Camping** (20), also situated at Sognefjord, offering pitches for camping and cabins. Open from mid-May till mid-September. ♦€♦

a. Dragsvik 15, 6899 Balestrand
t. +47 5769 1612 / 9112 8133
w. veganesetcamping.no

Looking for something a bit more upscale and special than a campsite or a cabin? You will like the characteristic and singular **29|2 Aurland** (21). It's an old farm refurbished into a sweet little hotel. They're big on sustainable tourism, and wherever possible they limit their footprint, recycle and use recycled materials, serve mainly local and organic food (some from their own garden), and promote hiking. As a guest you can use their bicycles for free, they have a wood-fired hot tub and offer guided nature and local culture tours. In short: a lot of likeable stuff going on here! You can see in every little detail the owners, Tone and Bjorn, have put their heart and souls into their business. After travelling around the world, Tone, who used to be a journalist, and Bjorn, still using his skills as a master builder, couldn't find a better place to live with their children than the mountains and fjords of Aurland. The name, 29|2, refers to the property number and municipality. Their main season is from the last weekend of April to September, but they're open all year on request (except Christmas and Easter). ♦€€♦ ♦€€€♦

a. Tokvamsvegen 12, 5745 Aurland
t. +47 9002 6156
w. 292aurland.com

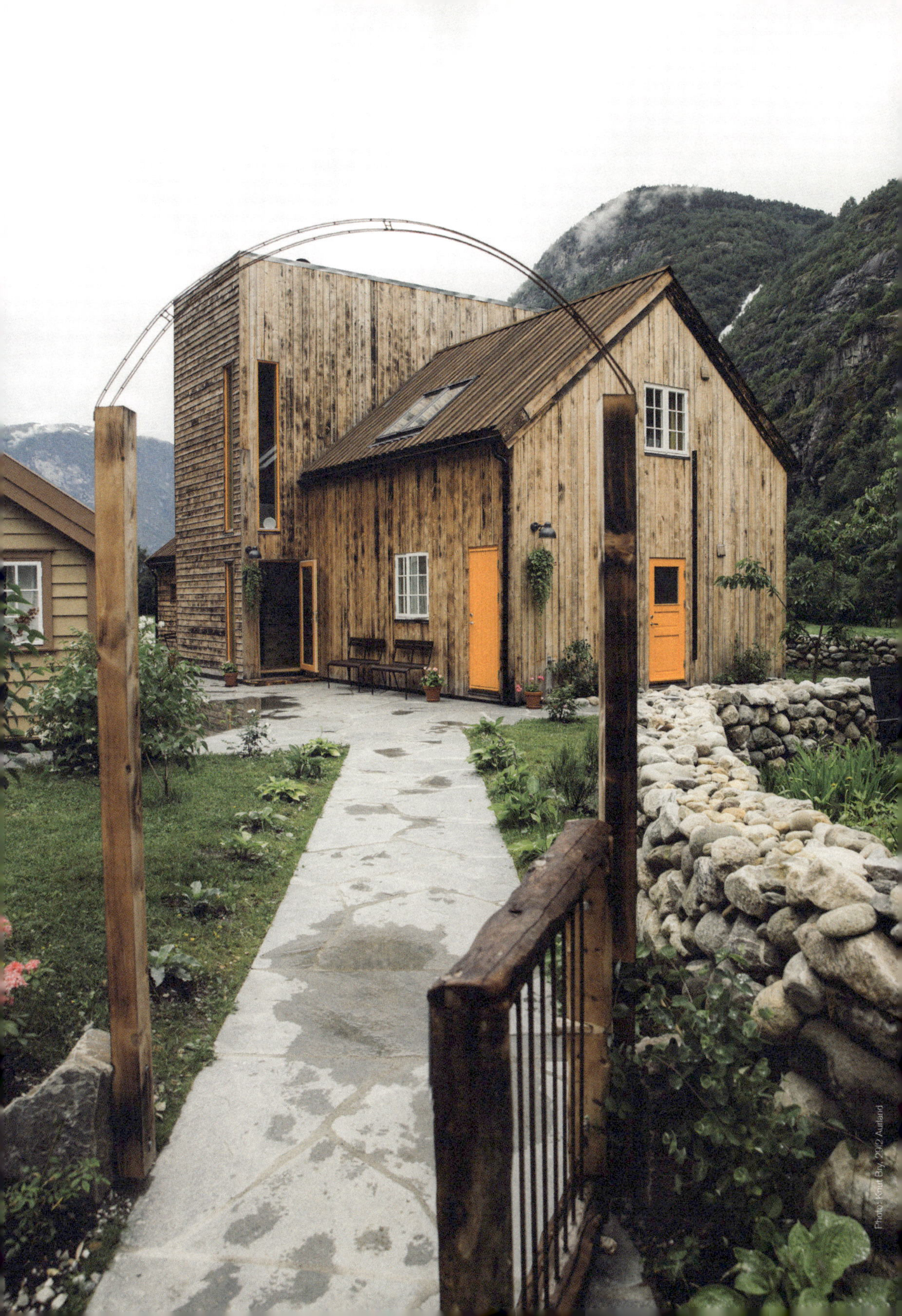
Photo: Knut Bry, 2012 Aurland

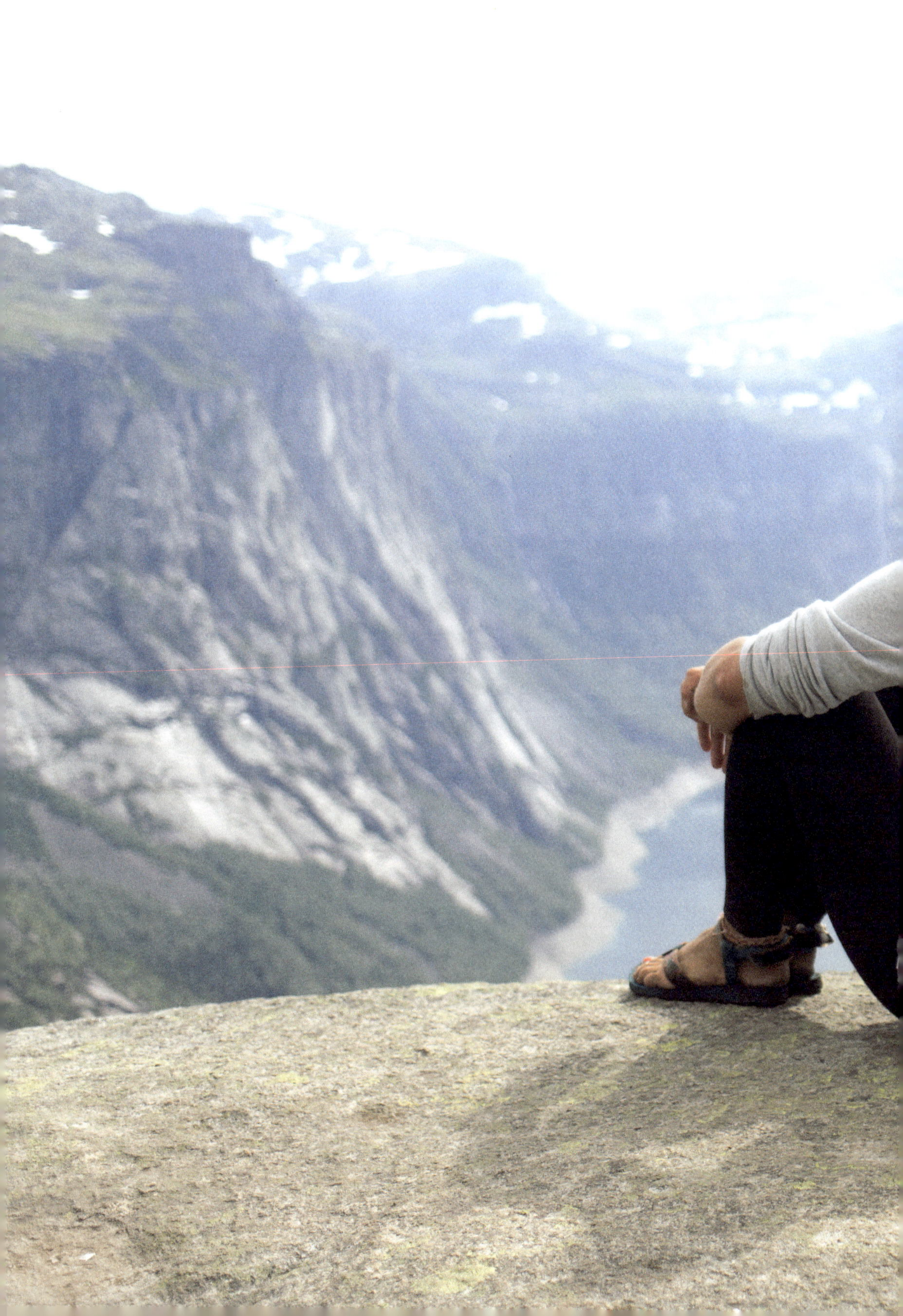

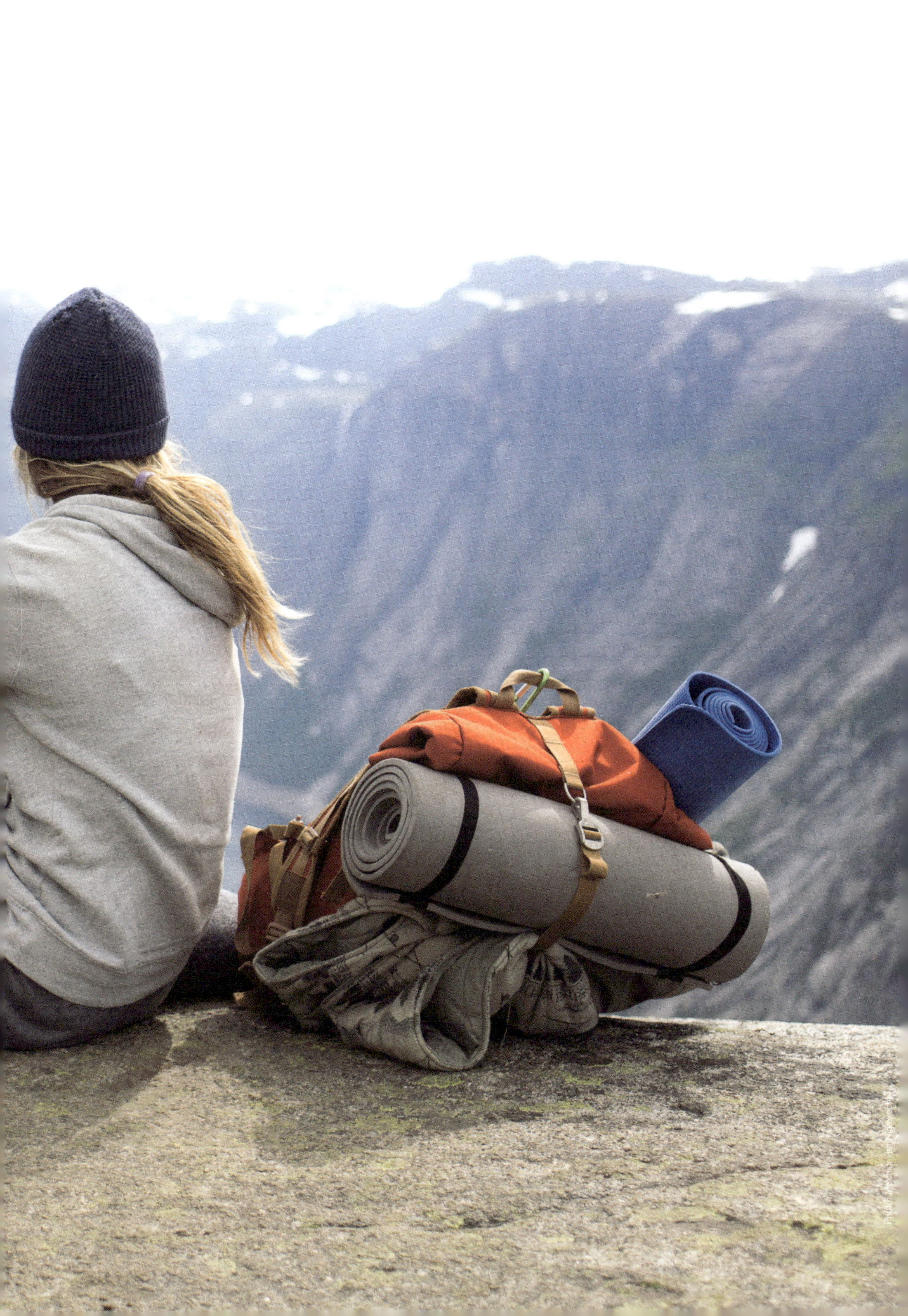

HORDALAND

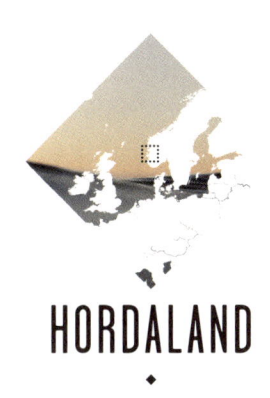

Water. Water everywhere. Salty, from the North Sea, and fresh, from the fjords. Frozen at glaciers and in masses from waterfalls. They're all connected, and no better way to see, feel and experience their connection than in this part of Norway. The waterfalls are loud, large, and - sorry, can't help ourselves - ludicrously luscious. Driving past them, with screen wipers on full speed, hearing a roaring thunder, you'll be twisting your neck trying to measure them up from the window. So you can only imagine how impressive they are to hike past, or turn into an abseil adventure park, or the wild-whitewater-fun they produce once channelled into a river. Literally thousands of islands are scattered around the mouth of the Hardangerfjord and coastline, and at some point or other you'll need one of the many ferries crossing the fjord, or you'll be driving forever to get anywhere. But the crossings are part of the experience. Time to be still and see, observe how the water continuously forms the landscape.

TRAVEL INFO

To give you an idea of time when travelling by car, it's about a 5 to 6 hour drive from Oslo to Voss. From Bergen it takes 1 to 1,5 hours. Even if you drive a fast car, once you arrive in this mountainous area, and with the 80 kmph speed limit, you're forced to slow your pace.

BY AIR

The closest international airport is Flesland in Bergen. The airport has flights to several cities in Norway and many European destinations.

w. avinor.no/flyplass/bergen

BY BOAT

Several ferries run between islands and connecting headlands. Their schedules can vary by season, but are usually quite frequent since they're so essential to the infrastructure. There's an international ferry connection with Denmark. For the shorter stretches it's best to just show up and wait in line. Most ferries are operated by Tide.

w. tide.no

BY BUS & TRAIN

Trains on the Bergen Railway run between Oslo and Bergen regularly, and have stops in between throughout Hordaland (Voss and Dale, amongst others). Infrequent local bus lines run from Bergen to smaller communities and are managed by Skyss (**w.** skyss.no). National buses between bigger cities are operated by Norway Bussekspress.

w. nsb.no / nor-way.no

IN AND AROUND VOSS

Voss and its surroundings are a mecca for the outdoor and extreme sports lover. Unsurprisingly, this area's brought forth dozens of skiing and biathlon Olympic games athletes and world cup medallists. It even has a river (very, very hush, hush secret) surf spot, somewhere… The town itself is pretty nice and has some laid-back places to enjoy a beer, or shop for your outdoor gear. Voss hosts the world's largest extreme sports festival, Ekstremsportveko, each year and it seems that the festival vibrates its energy long after the base jumpers have packed up and music stages are gone. The old wooden centre was completely destroyed after a German bombing in WWII, so the city doesn't have much of an old feeling to it, except for the 13th century Voss church. But the vibe and surrounding forests, rivers, fjords and snow-capped mountains make up for it in a wonderful way.

Tourist office at Skulegata 14.

TO DO

Festival Ekstremsportveko in Voss is said to be the largest extreme sports festival in the world. The event started in 1998 with a few sports; rafting, skydiving and paragliding. With its increasing popularity, other sports, like skating and wakeboarding, were added every year. And with its growing number of sports, (international) athletes and audience, in came the music! The festival now has a 3-day music event spicing up the sporty vibe with pop, rock, funk and reggae. With most activities so reliant on the weather, the organisation specialised itself - by learning the hard way - in the art of accepting challenges, creating alternatives, solutions and plan Bs. That's why the festival is such an exhilarating success, bursting with positivity, no matter the circumstances. So, what can you expect? A festive week, that's for sure, with parties, movie nights, and extreme sports from bouldering to base jumping, skydiving to speed flying, and all in between. There are several festival areas and free shuttle buses run between them. You can participate actively as an athlete, or book activities and try them out. Or, completely free, watch in awe. And party - extremely of course. The festival's held annually at end of June to beginning of July.

w. ekstremsportveko.com

Bicycling: you can rent bicycles at Endeve Sport (see Shop section) or Voss Hostel (see Sleep section).
In the land of the Vikings it turns out to be a strenuous quest to find some serious and in-depth history, true and factual stories of the blonde, horn-helmeted (maybe?), sea-faring folk. But for fun, entertainment, and an uncomplicated romanticised idea of being somewhat close to the truth there are plenty museums, theme parks and experiences. **Viking Valley (1)** is amongst the latter; a 'Viking experience' that is absolutely satisfactory for the whole family. The recreated Viking village of Njardarheimr, complete with smells and sounds and dressed-up men and women acting out all kind of daily Viking activities and plays you can participate in. Want to learn the art of archery, or fancy a bit of axe throwing? Anyone? Open from May to October.

a. Njardarheimr, 5747 Gudvangen. Next to the E16
t. +47 4624 5462
w. vikingvalley.no

Voss Active (2) is active in all sorts of, err, activities. Amongst a lot of other things, they offer high rope and zipline courses. If you're more of a water-adept, try their white water rafting, or river boarding. The Stranda and Raundal rivers are their playground, with Stranda having a multitude of spectacular rapids over a stretch of 8 kms. And when there's too little water for rafting and such, usually late summer, try canyoning: slipping, sliding, jumping (a 3 metre cliff!), climbing and swimming in clear pools, caves and natural water slides. Since all surrounding nature is their terrain, they also use the grand Skjervossen waterfall for rappelling. You'll descend down the side of the waterfall, of course equipped with a harness, wetsuit and helmet, and looked after by experienced staff. Ah, and then they've just what you need as an after-raft, after-descent, or after-anything really. At their Elvatun Restaurant & Outdoor Spa you can eat, obviously, and choose either one of the hot tubs or wood-fired sauna (or both) ending with a cooling dip in the river.

a. Vossestrandvegen, 5713 Vossestrand
a. Nedkvitnesvegen 25, 5710 Skulestadmo (Rafting Senter, 5 km north of Voss centre)
t. +47 5651 0525
w. vossactive.no

If you're not into all the extreme stuff, but do want to explore the surroundings in a bit of a sporty fashion, you can **rent a SUP** at **Outdoor Norway (3)** and paddle the tranquil Vangsvatnet lake from the centre of Voss. Outdoor Norway's located close to Fleischer's Hotel and the Kulturhus. Open from June to October.

a. Evangvegen 14, 5700 Voss
t. +47 9708 7318
w. outdoornorway.com/sup-rentals-2

Whether you're a beginner or an experienced white water kayaker wanting to work on your techniques, **Kayak Voss (4)** offers half and full day guided kayak tours and courses. If you want to dive right into the adrenaline-enhancing rush of white water kayaking without prior experience, try a tandem trip. An experienced instructor will guide you through the rapids from the back of the kayak. They also rent out kayaks so you can explore on your own. Open from April to October.

a. Bjørkemoen, 5700 Voss
t. +47 9015 0859 / 9111 1356
w. kayakvoss.net

The hike towards **Trolltunga rock** (**5**) (Troll's Tongue) is long and pretty demanding. It's 12 km on uneven terrain. But the reward: you 1100 metres high on a cliff that sticks out 700 m over Ringedalsvatnet lake. This hike is only recommendable if you're in good condition, and it's best to stay overnight in your own tent. Starting point is near the small village of Odda, there's a pay car park and info point (follow signs to Skjeggedal), or leave your car in Odda and take the shuttle bus to the start point. Follow the ascending road Måglivegen up until you reach relatively flat terrain, then continue till you reach the rock (that being some 4 hours later). The roundtrip, 24 km, can take 6 to 8 hours. Come prepared: camping gear, warm dry clothes, drinks, food, compass, headlamp and camera. By all means, bring your camera! The walk can be done from mid-June to mid-September.

Aaaah, sore muscles from hiking, climbing, kayaking... Or the lack of surfing? **Toves Muskelterapi** (**6**) (Tove's Muscle Therapy) offer classic massages, like sports massage and Thai massage. Or maybe you're in need for some foot care, a waxing job perhaps? Forgot all about those hairy legs while wearing your long raincoat, didn't you!

a. Vangsgata 38, 5700 Voss
t. +47 9157 6625
w. tovesmuskelterapi.no

Different bodywork on offer, but just as intense as biking uphill or running downhill - same sweaty results - the Bikram yoga series by instructor Lis Wortman of **Voss Yoga and Bodywork** (**7**). Beside 90-minute Bikram yoga classes, she gives private yoga classes, therapeutic bodywork and massages at the Myrkdalen Hotel in Voss. Open all year.

a. Uttrågata 27, 5700 Voss
t. +47 9854 2794
w. vossyogaandbodywork.com

Here's your chance to realise at least one of your life's dreams ('cause who doesn't dream of flying?) in the wind tunnel of **Voss Vind** (**8**). Your body will be weightless and you can do the bird thing, or the Superman thing, free fall or flip a somersault, or four. All within the safe confines of the vertical wind tunnel in Voss. Best of all the things to do if the weather's not inviting for outdoor adventures.

a. Oberst Bulls veg 28, 5705 Voss
t. +47 4010 5999
w. vossvind.no

The **Bordalsgjelet Gorge** (**9**) reveals 50 shades of green within walking distance from Voss centre. You'll see the effects that water and ice have on the earth, over a period of thousands of years. To get there, follow the path along the Vangsvatnet lake towards the bridge, at the end of the wooded Prestegardsmoen nature reserve. Cross the bridge and from there follow the signs to Bordalsgjelet. It's a 5 km, easy walk, takes about 1,5 hours (return trip to Voss). The walk can be done between May and November, in winter it's likely snow-covered.

Paragliding (**10**) is a big, big thing in Voss. Paragliders from all over the world come here to fly because of the many starting places, in all directions, and the strong thermal activity. There's a peak in summer, but you can give it a go all year round. If you're into the airborne idea, try **Vossa Tandem** for a flight with an instructor (pilot).

t. +47 4577 5703 (Vossa Tandem)
w. vossatandem.no

Or maybe you want to go even higher. **Skydive Voss** (**11**) offer tandem skydives and courses for first-time jumpers. Of course experienced skydivers are very welcome too. If you're with a family and only one of you decides to jump, the others can entertain themselves at the site: there's a climbing tower, playground, trampolines, slackline, café and a sundeck to watch the skydivers land. Open from late April to September.

a. Flyplassvegen 135, 5705 Voss
   (drop zone at Bømoen Airport)
t. +47 5651 1000
w. skydivevoss.no

Driving along the Rv13 (the beautiful hairpin route along Skjervet), you'll come across the **Skjervsfossen Waterfall** (**12**) at several points. An impressive waterfall, Skjervsfossen drops 150 metres. You can hike along some parts of it. And it's not the first time we implore you to visit a toilet: at the parking on top the restrooms have a glass wall looking down over the river rapids. You've got to love the Norwegians, and what they do with their National Tourist Routes restrooms!

Paddle under Hardanger Bridge, Norway's longest suspension bridge, through the Hardangerfjord. Not guaranteed, but there's a chance of seeing small dolphins or seals popping up next to or in front of your kayak.

Hardangerfjord Active (**13**) rent out kayaks, rowboats and bicycles, and offer guided kayak tours, from Hardanger and Lofthus. They're situated 7 km south of Kinsarvak in a small settlement, Lutro (3 km north of Lofthus).

a. Ullensvangvegen 583, 5781 Lofthus
t. +47 9201 6887
w. hardangerfjordactive.com

Get a bit of the city vibe by planning a trip to **Bergen** (**14**). It's doesn't have the small-scale charm of Stavanger in the south, or the liveliness of Oslo to the west, but it's a city with unexpected character. You're often warned that it's always raining in Norway, and even more often in Bergen. But then again, you're in a city and there's no need to stay outdoors all the time (do bring an umbrella along, and wear it as your hottest, most elegant accessory). To start you can hop on the Floibanen Funicular up the Floyen mountain, to get an overview of the city. Then there's the obligatory Bryggen with its wooden houses along the harbour. Less well known is the thriving street art scene, with the greatest respect for facades, your best shot at seeing some old and fresh pieces is in Skostredet, between the centre and the fishing harbour. And for more established and contemporary art you can go gallery/museum hopping along the Lille Lungegårdsvann lakeside, in the centre of town. There's also an interesting children's art museum, KunstLab. What else? Cafés are beyond hip, restaurants are doing their Nordic cuisine thing, and shops come in abundance. The tourist office is located in Torget Fish Market. Travelling with a campervan? You can park and stay overnight at Bergenshallen parking (see Sleep section) and take the Light Rail to the centre.

Some 2 kms north of Skare, driving along the Rv13 from Odda, you can't miss **Låtefossen waterfall** (**15**). First of all, you think it's started raining (again!?), secondly, you wonder why the traffic's slowing down, then third, you hear the thundering sound of tons of water tumbling down from a great height. It's said to be a little over 160 metres, but you could have fooled us - although born from the river Austdølo and fed by several lakes, with the two streams coming down it looks like it was formed in heaven. This is certainly not the only, or the most, impressive waterfall in the area, but it just has such an exciting feel to it, being so close to the road, with tourists from all over the world taking selfies dressed in raincoats and under umbrellas. And it has its very own souvenir shop and restaurant. There are some small car parks just before crossing the old stone bridge.

EAT/DRINK/HANG OUT
◆

After you're all amped up from kayaking rapids, downhilling steep slopes or maybe jumping out of a plane, THE place to chill out, grab a craft beer, watch some live music, dance, hang out, or just have a fresh roasted coffee and a snack is **Tre Brør** (**16**) café and bar. In the daytime their friendly staff serve coffee, cakes, lunch and dinner - mainly based on seasonal produce - in the café, garden or terrace. At night the small but über-cosy bar below focuses on music (concerts, DJs, jam-nights) and beer. The local craft beer from Voss Brewery, and on tap almost two dozen different beers from small Norwegian breweries, alongside an incredible choice of bottled beer from around the world. Start saving up, a night out is going to cost you, but it's definitely one of the best and most atmospheric bars in Norway. Situated in the main square, near the church, in one of the prettier older buildings of Voss, the shop is a 5 minute walk from here (see Shop section). Open all year. ◆€€◆

a. Vangsgata 28, 5700 Voss
t. +47 9570 3832
fb. Tre Brør Kafé, Voss

SHOP
◆

Tre Brør Leskebutikk (**17**) is where you can stock up on all the goodies that the café at the main square serves, and more. You can fill up large bottles with locally brewed beer, (they sometimes have tastings), organic juices and lemonades, and get a freshly roasted coffee and all the accessories to make your own. We think the place is a breath of fresh air. Not that you're short of it in these surroundings, but metaphorically speaking, we'd expected to see more of these distinctive, warm and characterful places. So, all in all, let's hear it for Tre Brør! Open all year.

a. Vangsgata 43, 5700 Voss
t. +47 9510 3832
fb. Tre Brør Kafé, Voss

Outdoor sport shop **Endeve** (**18**) has it all: the right footwear, active wear in all sorts and sizes, fishing gear, bike stuff, and frankly, it's pretty neat! But foremost: pretty practical. Open all year.

a. Vangsgata 47, 5700 Voss
t. +47 5651 1119
w. endevesport.no

This area of the Hardanger fjord, especially around Ulvik and Ullensvang, is famed for **fruit** produce. It's the relatively mild climate and protection from the mountains in combination with long summer days making the soil fruitfully happy, even at this high altitude. In late summer you'll find little market stalls along the fjordside roads selling their fruit, usually with the help of an honesty box. You'll find cherries, pears, plums and apples. Along the fruit and cider route, on the hillside of Ulvik, there are three farms where you can join a cider tasting.

SLEEP

◆

Campervans can park and stay at Bergenshallen, 10 minutes from the centre of Bergen (and take the Light Rail into town). Emptying of wastewater and toilets, fresh water available, 150 NOK.

a. Vilhelm Bjerknes' vei 24, 5081 Bergen

At **Voss Camping** you can park your camper (only weekends!) between the campsite and the swimming pool, and use all their facilities for reduced prices.

a. Idrottsvegen 5, 5700 Voss
t. +47 5651 1597
w. vosscamping.no

Near Voss you can stay for free at a small parking site at the lake, approx. 5 km from the town centre. There's a toilet and a bakery.

a. Kvallsvegen 3, 5700 Voss (southwest from town, along the E16 to Bergen)

Tvinde Camping (19) sits right next to Tvindefossen waterfall. From here it's easy to go fishing, rafting or on a hiking expedition. They have pitches with a lot of room to roam, cabins and apartments for rent. Open from mid of April to September. ◆€◆ ◆€€◆

a. Tvinde, 5700 Voss (12 km north of Voss, near the E16)
t. +47 5651 6919
w. tvinde.no

Stay in a renovated farmhouse or cabin at **Eenstunet (20)**. There are several accommodations to choose from, with the largest sleeping up to 9 persons. The rooms are minimalistic but warm and have homely decor. You get the feeling you're staying at your stylish Scandinavian grandmother's (who has a great eye for detail). It's a family friendly place with a big garden, a communal room with a fireplace in one of their renovated barns, and another farmhouse is used for brewing beer (!). Open all year. ◆€€◆

a. Ænsmoen 47, 5710 Skulestadmo (6 km north of Voss, near the E16)
t. +47 5651 6834 / 9959 7419
w. eenstunet.no

Boutique hotel and restaurant **Store Ringheim (21)** near the centre of Voss is a traditional family farm transformed into a modern but distinctive Nordic-style stay. The owners are the tenth generation working and living on the Ringheim farm. The hotel has 14 comfortable rooms, all uniquely decorated, with its original details - alcove beds and pitched roofs - as the leading theme. Open all year. ◆€€◆ ◆€€€◆

a. Mølstervegen 44, 5705 Voss
t. +47 9540 6135
w. storeringheim.no

Voss Camping (22) is conveniently situated near Voss' centre. Green, shaded and right beside the lake. They have pitches and some basic cabins for rent. Open all year. ◆€◆

a. Idrottsvegen 5, 5700 Voss
t. +47 5651 1597
w. vosscamping.no

Voss Hostel (23) is your best option for a nice stay with a tighter budget, and perfectly suited for solo travellers or groups of friends. The hostel sleeps up to 180 people, with private rooms (lake view!) and shared rooms with bunkbeds available. There's a communal kitchen and room where guests meet, with a fireplace and terrace. You can rent a SUP or canoe to tour the lake, they serve coffee, organic ice-cream and locally brewed beer. The hostel's got a sublime vista of Gråsida mountain. Open all year. ◆€◆ ◆€€◆

a. Evangervegen 68, 5700 Voss
t. +47 5651 2017
w. vosshostel.com

HAUGESUND

♦ 2
AVALDSNES

♦ 11

FOSEN

◆ UTSIRA ♦ 1

KOPERVIK

♦ 5,12
ÅKREHAMN

ÅKRASANDEN
(I)

Karmøy

FERKINGSTAD
(II)
♦ 13
FERKINGSTAD

♦ 3
SANDVE

SANDVESANDEN
(III)

♦ 4, 6–10, 14–16
SKUDENESHAVN

KARMØY

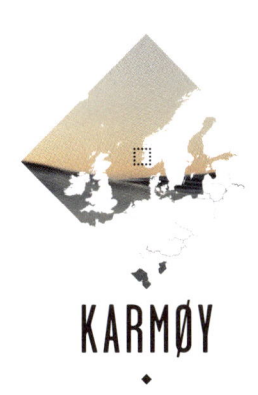

Being on a quest for surf and the great outdoors we could easily have skipped this island, based on the flimsy bits of info found on both subjects before we left. But, we do like to explore the unknown. And after we befriended an enthusiastic young man from Karmøy during our trip up north - who happened to be a stoked surfer of the little known Karmøy breaks - luckily we decided we would indeed travel to the island between Hordaland and Jæren to see what's what. Known as a seaside escape for many Norwegians, Karmøy is yet to be discovered by holidaymakers from abroad. It has all the white sandy beaches you find in the southwest, the islands and inlets you see in the northwest, AND the seductive mountains and fjords. Being surrounded by water, the light's still bright even on the less sunny days. Reflections in the ocean, lakes and marshland puddles over the heather moorland create dreamed-up purple and red skies at sunset. It's the kind of place that very pleasantly surprises with its unpretentious and subtle beauty. Oh, and they don't mind if you do a little beach barbecue, as long as you take care, clean up after, and use the designated barbecue bin.

TRAVEL INFO

Karmøy's a large island in comparison to smaller ones, but not that large; from Haugesund Airport up in the north it's only 30 kms to Skudeneshavn on the south of the island. Connected to the mainland by 2 bridges, there's no need to take a ferry. If you happen to get lost, you'll easily find your way back to one of the main roads that run along the coast. You're always close to the sea, and most villages are situated on the coast.

BY AIR

National and international flights frequent Haugesund Airport, towards the northern end of the island. Buses and taxis run to and from the city centre.

w. avinor.no/flyplass/haugesund

BY BUS

The express coach service Kystbussen runs along Norway's west coast, between Bergen and Stavanger (w. kystbussen.no). The easiest and most environmentally friendly way to travel in the region is with the green Kolumbus buses.

w. kolumbus.no / tide.no

IN AND AROUND SKUDENESHAVN

Skudeneshavn sits on the south of the island. The well-preserved old town, with all 225 wooden houses and boathouses painted white, is easy on the eye, and even easier to portray. Just point your camera, click, and there you have it: quaint little seaside town! Lively in summer, somewhat desolate in winter, the 18th century town built around a harbour has few year-round inhabitants. But you won't find many for sale signs; most of the houses here are second homes to people whose families have owned a house here since forever. And it's no biggie to see why you'd never want to sell your property here. It's a lovely, lovable and much loved place. If you like curious old stuff, do visit the tiny museum in one of the wooden houses: it's got century-old ice skates, sixties washing powder boxes, funny looking repair kits, ancient looking socks and pre-war-coffee packages. Art seems to be in vogue; every other corner you turn you'll find a small, but usually contemporary art gallery. The people of Skudeneshavn welcome tourists, and love to share their history and stories, as long as you respect their privacy (hard to do while peeping over their hedges and looking into their adorable gardens). A short drive from town away are the beautiful North Sea beaches like Sandvesanden, Hebnes and Ferkingstad. To the east the narrow coastal road runs through thick pine forest all the way up to the larger town of Kopervik. Most likely the only traffic you'll have to stop for are sheep crossing.

Tourist office at Kaigt 5.

TO DO

◆

Biking: No hills to speak of on Karmøy but it has got some nice trails. And because of its size, you can bike around the island in a day! A very nice round trip is to start at Skudeneshavn, follow the narrow winding road 511 towards Kopervik, passing purple heather, pine forests and lots of beehives - many flowers a thriving bee community makes. Take a left turn at the dirt road, Burmavegen, crossing the island on fairytale-like marshland and more heather moors. You'll end up at Ferkingstad, on the west side of the island. From here return to Skudenshaven along the coast. You can also follow this route by car. But so much nicer to take in slow, slowly pedalling along. The tourist office in Skudeneshavn has bicycles for rent.

Utsira (1), the little island 18 kms west of Karmøy, is called the street art island without streets. The UTSIRART project started in 2014 with the initiative of a few creative minds and the help of islanders and other volunteers. In one week, artists from the UK, Norway and Spain came to spice up the island with colours, drawings, messages and paintings. And new work keeps appearing. Although more famously known for its many birds, and a tradition in lobster fishing, surprisingly enough the island's barns, windmills and turbines, silos and other buildings and rocks are a living, breathing canvas for international street art and graffiti artists. The small community of just over 200 inhabitants have embraced the UTSIRART phenomenon, the artists and their work, and seeing more people coming to the island to admire the open-air gallery in a windblown landscape, they happily offered their barn doors and house walls to be painted on. For sure, this is one of the most unique places to do a street art tour, biking through fields, seeing rocks painted on, windmills telling the story of Norse mythology figures Frigg and Frøya, silos turned into giant boxes of lobster soup, or a big red heart on the mayor's wall. Bristol born artist JPS (short for Jamie Paul Skenlon) left humorous messages and fantasy figures, and created a Street Art Gallery in the basement of an old school. There's a small street art café and an artist residence in the lighthouse area. You can reach Utsira by ferry from Haugesund. The ferry trip (4 times a day) to Utsira takes about 1 hour.

w. utsira.net

'And now for something completely different' as the Monty Python people used to say… The **Nordvegen History Centre and Viking Farm** (**2**) is another attempt to let us in on the mysterious Viking history. Although the History Centre has many artefacts and is all very neatly organised, with headphone guiding telling you the stories and dates behind the artefacts and paintings, it seems all a bit too theatrical. Especially the movie, telling the story of Harald Fairhair, shown before you enter the exhibition. Maybe he did unite Norway into a kingdom, and had some tough fiends and semi-gods to conquer, but when we were there a young girl left the room crying because of the scary characters shown in the film! The bit we liked way better was the Viking Farm, connected to the centre with a footpath towards a forested island. This is where you do learn how the 'North Way' ancestors lived. There are reconstructed buildings; a farm with a longhouse, fireplace, roundhouse, and a huge boathouse. In summer friendly young people dressed up as Vikings do their Viking things as if it's the Viking Age. A girl knitting, a man telling stories around the fireplace, any questions you want to ask are answered and a small tour is available. The History Centre is open all year, the Viking Farm opens June, July and August.

a. Kong Augvalds veg 103, 4262 Avaldsnes
t. +47 5281 2400
w. avaldsnes.info

Ole Morten of **Oppkoma** (**3**) offers kayak rental and guided sea or river kayak trips. He also has the necessary equipment for snorkelling and coasteering. Oppkoma's on the west coast of Karmøy, and the weather and waves play a big part in the activities offered at sea. There are sheltered places if the waves are too big or the wind too strong. Closed in winter.

a. Søre Ferkingstadveg 113, 4274 Stol
t. +47 9118 0570
fb. Oppkoma

The Jungle (**4**), or Tarzan Park, or the more prosaic, but official name 'Skudenes School and Recreational Park' is a go-to for children that need to use up a bit of energy and like a challenge. They can take a Tarzan leap, swinging from rope to rope, or try their hut building skills. Creative challenges are built from ropes, car tyres and wood, there are swings in trees and much more.

a. Dr. Jensens vei 24, 4280 Skudeneshavn

EAT/DRINK/HANG OUT

◆

According to Norse mythology Vili and Vé are the two brothers of Odin that helped shape the cosmos. The café **Vili & Vé** (**5**) in Åkrehamn is a 'koselig' cosmos, very cosy, very friendly indeed. Old, young, locals and tourists alike sit around the tables, enjoying their sandwiches, salads, cakes and coffee, chatting away with each other, or the staff with their brilliantly contagious big smiles. Open all year. ◆€◆

a. Klæhaugvegen 20, 4270 Åkrehamn
t. +47 5204 4055
fb. Vili&Ve

Woi! Talking locally brewed beer, by now you may have noticed we like that stuff. Or the Norwegians do? Even in a small town like Skudeneshavn they've got their own brewery! **Skudenes Bryggeri** (**6**) brews seven varieties of craft beer. And luckily they have regular tastings: every Saturday between 10:00 and 14:00 hrs. There's a small shop too, where you can buy their beers. Or a t-shirt. Open all year. ◆€€◆

a. Storamyr 20, 4280 Skudeneshavn
t. +47 4064 1075
w. skudenesbryggeri.no

Café **Holmen Brygge** (**7**) in the old town of Skudeneshavn is the perfect place for a coffee and a Belgian waffle in the sun. The café sits right by the water. It's also a bit of a cultural gathering place where small festivals, jazz concerts and other cultural events are held. Good atmosphere, no doubt about it. Open all year. ♦€♦ ♦€€♦

a. Holmen 9, 4280 Skudeneshavn
t. +47 9262 4880
fb. HolmenBrygge

Bistro and pianobar **Smiå** (**8**) is the place to meet the local sailor folks, fishermen or the odd surfer. Perfect for when the sun's out. And when the wind's howling; you're sheltered on their terrace. Open all year. ♦€♦ ♦€€♦

a. Søragadå 4, 4280 Skudeneshavn
t. +47 5285 3615
w. smiaabistro.no

Café and restaurant **Lanternen** (**9**) is where the summer residents and boat people gather. Located smack in the middle of Skudeneshavn, you can't miss it. A warm décor and tasty food makes you feel right at home, even if you're not wearing your boat shoes today. Open all year. ♦€€♦

a. Torget 4, 4297 Skudeneshavn
t. +47 5282 8200
w. restaurantlanternen.no

Ah, this little cute café - so small we couldn't find a name, but apparently called **Verdens Minste Kafè** (**10**), world's smallest café. Besides a good strong espresso, pancakes and organically produced home-made food, they have their delicious baked goods for sale, along with a small collection of books and magazines and clothing. The café, the tiny museum and some more initiatives are part of Gamle Skudeneshavn, an association of local people who like to share and preserve Skudeneshavn's history and culture. Open all year at the weekends, from Wednesday to Sunday during summer. ♦€♦ ♦€€♦

a. Søragadå 23, 4280 Skudeneshavn
t. +47 9931 4117
fb. "verdens minste" cafè

SLEEP

◆

Campervans: Emptying of toilet and wastewater at Circle K Station in Skudeneshavn, Skudenes Camping, and Esso Station in Avaldsnes.

Fancy having a jacuzzi and sauna in your bathroom? **Tresviken Cabins** (11), on the west coast of Karmøy, facing the sea and surrounded by stone hills, have all that and a lot of privacy on top. Okay, the jacuzzi is a bathtub that produces bubbles, but still! Wake up to the sound of the ocean, heat up the sauna then take a dip in the ocean. The cabins sleep up to 9 people. Open all year. ◆€€◆

a. Tresvikvegen 41, 4264 Kvalavåg
t. +47 5284 0246
w. tresviken-feriehytter.no

Bed and Breakfast **Dugneberg** (12) is a peaceful and quiet place, set in a farm, located about 2,5 kms from Åkrehamn. There are a lot of hiking opportunities from the farm and the location is a big asset. They have unassuming, but big and bright single and double rooms. Open all year. ◆€€◆

a. Vestre Karmøyveg 435, 4270 Åkrehamn (look out for the sign 'Rom' driving on the main road 47)
t. +47 4815 0787
w. dugneberg.com

Sandhåland camping (13) is within walking distance from the beach. The site has camping pitches and cottages for rent that sleep up to 5 people. All cottages have ocean view. Closed in winter. ◆€◆ ◆€€◆

a. Sandhålandsveien 36, 4272 Sandve
t. +47 4767 2227
w. sandhaaland.no

Skudenes Camping (14) is a 4-star and indeed very nice campsite - although there seem to be a lot of rules to obey, bit of a bummer and almost makes you want to misbehave… but their staff are friendly enough. The pitches have enough space and privacy, there's protection from the wind with lots of green hillsides. Besides pitches they have cabins, apartments and bikes for rent. Open all year. ◆€◆ ◆€€◆

a. Postvegen 129, 4280 Skudeneshavn
t. +47 9209 8565
w. skudenescamping.no

Reinertsen House (15) is part of the Gamle Skudeneshavn, the association of local people with a heart for preserving the history and art of the old centre of Skudeneshavn. The Reinertsen house dates back to 1842 and used to be a bakery. Some details, like the bread shelves, still show. You can either book a room, or rent the whole house if you're with a larger group or family. The house sleeps up to 10 people. ◆€€◆

a. Søragadå 23, 4280 Skudeneshavn
t. +47 9007 9242
fb. reinertsenhuset overnatting

It's possible to spend a night in the 1875 **Vikeholmen Lightkeeper's House** (16). The lighthouse was built in 1875 and stands on an island at the entrance of the Skudeneshavn harbour, and is only accessible by boat. Conveniently enough, with staying at the house comes a boat. The house sleeps up to 12 persons, you'll have to bring your own sleeping bags, sheets or duvet though. But it'll be a blast! The house is rented out by the Skudeneshavn Seamen's Association and rental is per week only. Open from April to October. ◆€€◆

a. Vikeholmen, 4280 Skudeneshavn
t. +47 9707 2948 / 4810 4654
w. skudenes-sjomannsforening.com

SURF

Although Karmøy's known as a kite and windsurf destination, it does have its days when you don't need a sail, and the island has a lot more potential than you'd think. The strong winds can be a party pooper (that's why we've added extra info as to which winds what spots are protected from). And the perk? No crowds! And a super-friendly vibe! It's not the Atlantic, it's the North Sea. But, as every North Sea surfer knows, there are more surfable waves than you'd expect when looking at forecasts that show strong sideshores and the smallest of swell periods.

Åkrasanden (I) consists of several white sand bays with some small islands dotted out front. The backdrop of sloping hills and dunes, wooden huts and coloured beach chairs brings to mind the beaches of northern Brittany. Works best (and only) on a big W-SW swell and is protected from north winds. ♦ *All levels/beachbreak/easy parking/ picnic area/toilets/showers/restaurant.* ♦

The wide open bay of **Ferkingstad (II)** is your best option when it's small. You'll have a clear view of the surf from the parking spot at the north end of the beach. There's some protection from southwest winds thanks to the green hills and big boulders surrounding the bay. Works best at mid-tide with a small to medium NW-W swell. ♦ *All levels/ beachbreak and stones/easy parking/ no facilities.* ♦

Sandvesanden (III) is a beauty of a bay, protected by hills, huge boulders and dunes. So it needs a bigger swell to work. When we were there we saw its potential as what may be the best surf spot of Karmøy. Works best with medium to big W-SW swell and is protected from north winds. ♦ *All levels/beachbreak/easy parking/toilets/shower.* ♦

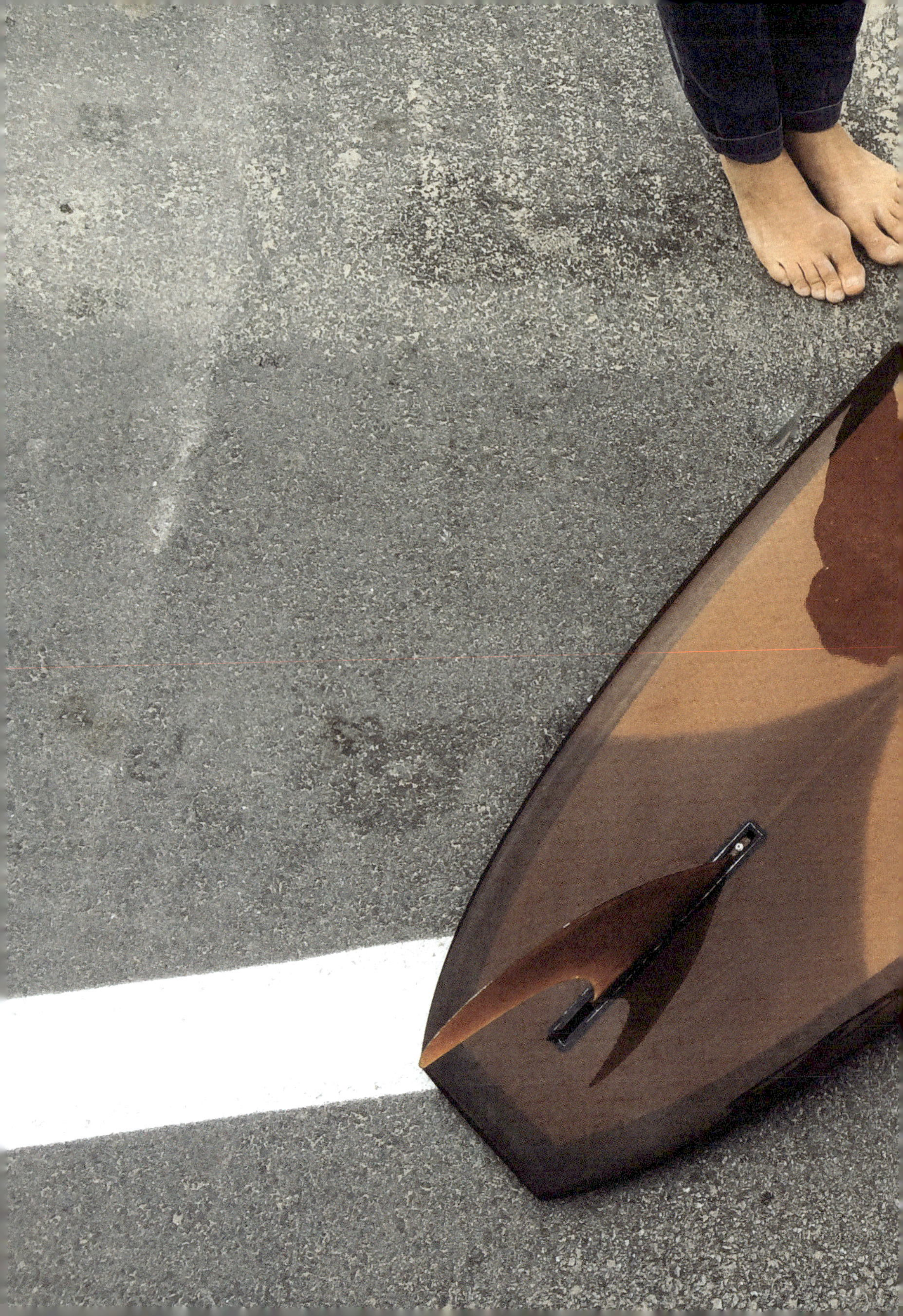

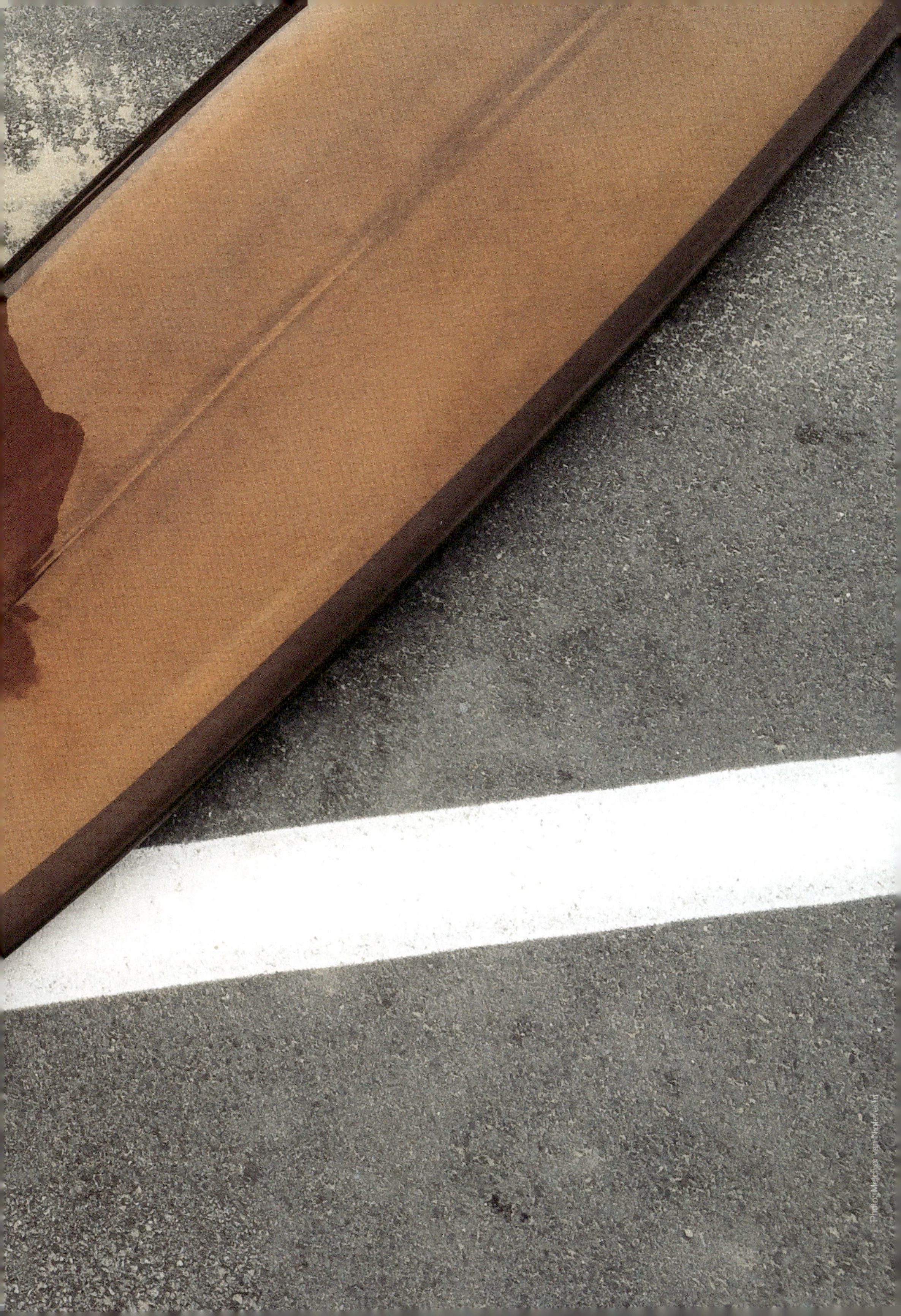

TAU

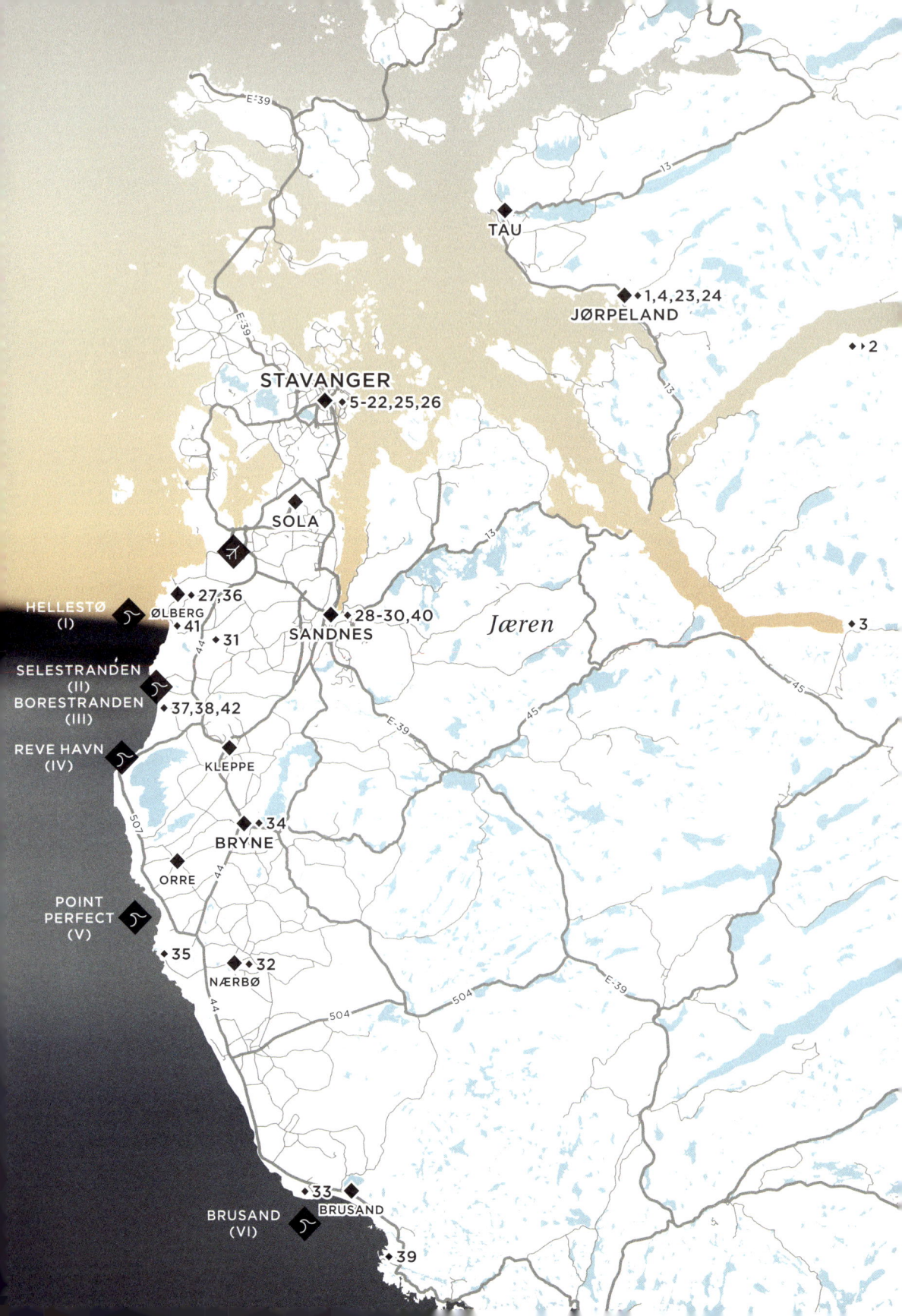

♦ 1,4,23,24
JØRPELAND

♦ 2

STAVANGER
♦ 5-22,25,26

SOLA

HELLESTØ
(I)

♦ 27,36
ØLBERG
♦ 41
♦ 31
SANDNES
♦ 28-30,40

Jæren

♦ 3

SELESTRANDEN
(II)
BORESTRANDEN
(III)
♦ 37,38,42

REVE HAVN
(IV)
KLEPPE

♦ 34
BRYNE

ORRE

POINT
PERFECT
(V)

♦ 35
♦ 32
NÆRBØ

♦ 33 BRUSAND
BRUSAND
(VI)

♦ 39

JÆREN

Jæren is completely different from the north of Norway. In that it's flat. However, in place of mountains it has lagoons, salmon rivers, sloping hills, dunes, woods, farmland and a long winding coastal road. And surf spots. Surf spots galore. But before heading straight for the 60 km coastline in search for surf, don't miss out on the city of Stavanger. It's funky, easy going and pretty diverse; but we'll talk more about that later.

In summer, driving alongside farm fields bordered with dry stone walls, you'll see neat rows of round hay bales everywhere. Packed in white, blue and pink plastic, it looks like a landscape artist thought it would be a funny idea to put large rolls of toilet paper in farmers' fields. Besides being home to all the heavies in the petroleum industry such as Exxon, Shell and Norway's own oil company, Statoil, Jæren holds Norway's largest agricultural industry; not just crops and livestock but agricultural machinery manufacturing too.

To the east of Stavanger you'll find the famous Preikestolen - the Pulpit Rock - towering above the enormous Lysefjord. Moving south from the Stavanger peninsula, along your highway to swell - Road 507, or Route 44 - it's mostly farmland up until Brusand. Here the scenery slowly transforms into a more rugged hillsides-and-forests landscape.

TRAVEL INFO

◆

Driving along the coast from Stavanger, you'll undoubtedly notice a change in landscape between Bore and Ogna. This part of the road (41 km) is one of the Norwegian Scenic Routes.

BY AIR
◆

Norway's second largest airport is Sola International Airport in Stavanger. Both national and international flight companies have direct flights to/from Stavanger.

w. avinor.no/flyplass/stavanger

BY TRAIN
◆

Trains run between Stavanger and Oslo (via Kristiansand), Bergen, and the south of Norway. They're impressive train rides, especially the 75 km stretch between Stavanger and Egersund, called the Seaview Rail or Jæren Railway Line.

w. nsb.no

BY BUS
◆

The Express coach runs between the Trolltunga, the Preikestolen, and Stavanger.

w. tide.no / kolumbus.no

Photo: Melchior van Nigtevecht

IN AND AROUND STAVANGER

We love Stavanger to bits! And we're not even that keen on cities. But we do like surprises and that's what Stavanger offers. Yes, the old part is lovely with all its coloured houses and shops and koselige cafés. The cruise ships - as big as extraterrestrial motherships - look otherworldly huge in front of the small harbour buildings. And if you want to learn how oil and gas production has influenced Norwegian society you should definitely check out the Petroleum museum near the cruise terminal. But then move on, to the outskirts of the old centre. It's just bursting with creative and entrepreneurial energy, spitting out art and music venues, health and food bars and cultural gatherings. All initiatives seem to be set up with a funky urban vibe but in a fresh and inherently Scandinavian? Norwegian? Stavanger-ish? style. You'll slowly pick up the vibe, walking from the city centre past whitewashed wooden houses towards Stavanger Øst, East Stavanger. Here's a thing happening: that thing where a neighbourhood everyone turned their backs on transforms itself into a creative hub. Usually involving abandoned warehouses and large industrial buildings. And people with more ideas than money. In Stavanger Øst the streets seem deceivingly empty, especially coming from the busy centre. But in truth they're a breath of fresh air, the walls of houses, buildings and shops spiced up with street art and graffiti - lots of it - and every other corner holding a yoga studio, brewery, gallery, photo studio or wine bar.

Tourist office at Strandkaien 61 (next to harbour, between cruise ships and historic centre).

TO DO

♦

'Glad mat' literally means 'happy food'. It's exactly what you can expect at the **Gladmat Food Festival**. Well, actually, you'll be the happy one, the food making sure of that. The annual festival is the biggest food fest in Scandinavia; a four-day celebration of local and traditional food. There are tastings, food fusions with global influences, theme dinners, and chefs getting together, sharing knowledge and finding inspiration. The festival's usually held at the end of July, with many restaurants taking part. The festival terrain, filled with food stalls, is mainly set up around the harbour.

w. gladmat.no

During the **Nuart Festival** national and international artists are invited to show their talents. Both indoor and outdoor, since the festival facilitates non-traditional art being taken to the streets, where walls and buildings will display, and be used as, canvases. This pioneering annual festival is usually held at the beginning of September, with the art exhibition ongoing till October. During the festival there are also workshops, debates (about art, of course, and especially about the notion of what art is or can be), art tours and performances.

w. nuartfestival.no

Biking: Cycling your way through Stavanger is one of the best ways to go about the city. At PaaHjul you can rent city and all-terrain bikes. Or if you have your own bicycle that needs fixing, this is the place to go. They're located right next to the main train station. Open all year (from very early in the morning).

t. +47 4797 5994
fb. Paahjul Sykkelverksted Stavanger

One of the most distinctive images of Norway you'll see in folders, travel guides and travel photos is the **Preikestolen (1)**, the Pulpit Rock. The cliff towers an impressive 604 metres above the Lysefjord, and resembles a giant pulpit. Want to hike to the top and experience the view? Get the same photo for yourself? The hike starts at the Preikestolen Fjellstue Mountain Lodge. It's pretty demanding, with an ascent of 350 m, but doable for most hikers who have a little experience. A roundtrip takes 4 to 5 hours - but that's if you hike and hike with hardly a stop. So, leave real early, or to avoid having to share the picture of you on the pulpit with many others, start at midnight. Wearing a headlamp, of course, and walk until you see the sun rise, adding a touch of magic to your hike. Want to descend real quickly? A steel wire zip line was added in 2017 to boost the fun. The zipline's available from May to September, with the start point just off the trail, zipping down to the mountain lodge. It promises views of the fjord and Stavanger peninsula. Or if you just can't be bothered with walking at all, a short helicopter sightseeing flight might be your thing; in collaboration with Pegasus AS, Preikestolen Camping offers flights twice a week - for camping guests only though (w. preikestolen-camping.com).

a. Preikestolvegen 521, 4100 Jørpeland
t. +47 5174 2074
w. preikestolenfjellstue.no

If you haven't noticed yet, you're unlikely to be missing the gym on your journey through Norway - if you are, perhaps try the 4444 steps (yes, four thousand four hundred & forty four steps) up the mountain at **Flørli (2)**. It may not come as a surprise: this is the longest wooden stairway in the world. It takes around 3 hours to walk up and down again, or - and this is strongly advised - for the route down, take the trail back to Flørli. Although now mainly an active tourist attraction, both stairs and trail were used in building and maintaining the waterways that run alongside the stairs, leading from the dam to the hydroelectric power station. Flørli itself is a little village on the banks of the Lysefjord, only accessible by boat. It's a hub for all things active, like canoeing, hiking and, err, stairway walking!

a. 4128 Flørli
w. florli.no

Hit the (flat) water and go on a SUP Safari with **Frafjord SUP & Kayak Center (3)**. The Frafjord, an inlet of the Høgsfjord, is about an hour's drive from Stavanger. The SUP & Kayak Center is located next to the Frafjord pier. When the sea's calm enough, they also offer tours at and around the beaches of Jæren - for a sea trip either inquire or keep track of their Facebook and Instagram updates. Open daily from June to August.

a. Frafjord, 4335 Dirdal
t. +47 4058 8283
w. frafjordsup.com

The studio of **Solvik Yoga (4)** is located next to the water, about 10 minutes drive from the Preikestolen. But who wants to practise yoga in a studio, when there's the chance to combine going for a hike and doing yoga at some of the most amazing places you've ever done (and maybe ever will do) yoga, surrounded by the stunning scenery.

And to top that, Solvik Yoga teaches - on demand - yoga to you and your friends right on top of the Preikestolen! They offer yoga courses, workshops, festivals, healthy lifestyle events, and retreats. Drop-in classes are also available. Hiking and yoga outdoors combo is within a 4-day retreat, where everything's provided for, including a yoga mat. The asanas, however, you have to practise yourself. Check their website for timetables and upcoming events.

a. Tveitavikvegen 1, 4100 Jorpeland
t. +47 4124 9281
w. solvikyoga.no

Okay, so there's SUP, there's yoga. Why not combine the two with **SUP Stavanger (5)**, who organise classes at different locations, such as Revsvatnet Lake, and regular classes near Solvik Camping in Jørpeland. Check out their Facebook page for daily SUP courses, as well as for SUP Yoga classes.

a. Lupinveien 9, 4022 Stavanger
t. +47 4176 0200
fb. SUP Stavanger

Stavanger Sentrum Street Art Tours (6) guide you through the street art history of Stavanger. In a 90-minute walk you'll be shown and taught about the hidden art works and great murals of the city, and the past Nuart Festival's themes that sometimes led to the creation of the pieces. There's a tour every Saturday from May to October, starting at 13:00 hrs from just outside the tourist office at Strandkaien 61 (by the harbour).

w. streetarttours.no

The Geopark (**7**) is a fun playground next to the Norwegian Petroleum Museum, based on the offshore Troll oil and gas field. It was built using recycled materials from the industry, with large pipes to climb and crawl through, big buoys to skippy on. Young and older kids can skate, climb, play ball, or try their hands at graffiti.. Open all year.

a. Kjerringholmen, 4001 Stavanger

There's **Hot Yoga** and **yoga** (**8**) is hot in Stavanger, here are just a few of the many options, all have drop-in classes available:

Sweat your pants off during the Bikram yoga classes at the studio of **Hot Yoga**. Open all week.

a. Soltunvegen 1, 4050 Sola
t. +47 9747 9933
w. hotyoga.no

Satya Yogahus offers yin and hatha yoga classes. They have 3 studios in Jæren: in Stavanger, Sandnes and Kleppe. Open all year.

a. Badehusgata 33, 4014 Stavanger
t. +47 9075 8494
w. satyayoga.no

House of Movement offers yoga and pilates classes.

a. St. Svithunsgate 12, 4008 Stavanger
t. +47 9070 0994
w. houseofmovement.no

Skating (**9**): conveniently enough, Stavanger offers skate options outdoor and indoor - they're well aware of their own weather conditions.

The indoor and outdoor skate pool of **Stavanger Skate Klubb** is open all year. Call or send them a message to ask if you can join the party.

a. Paradisveien 21, 4012 Stavanger
t. +47 4502 8171
fb. StavangerSkateKlubb

Outdoor **Tasta Skatepark** is bright, big and has different sizes of pools and obstacles. It's one of the many skate parks that Betongpark have built throughout the country. Open all year.

a. Gjerdeveien 81, 4028 Stavanger
w. betongpark.no

In the heart of Stavanger you can't miss **Fargegata** (**10**). This street is lined with wooden houses all painted in bright and pastel colours of green, yellow, red, blue and purple. It's a shopping street that also houses lots of cafés and restaurants. Always busy as you can guess, and yes, touristy, but none the less pretty cool and very hyggelig.

EAT/DRINK/HANG OUT
◆

Since we fell in love with Øst Stavanger, and there's a lot going on, we share our picks, but probably by the time you're there, some new places will have popped up!

Almost every other person from Stavanger, or that knows it well, will advise checking out **Tou Scene** (**11**). And for good reason. It's well known for its independent and distinguishing policy of promoting everything artistic, cultural or musical. Set in an abandoned brewery, and all the terrain around it, it's the place to go see a concert, a performance, art, music, film, or go dancing. In the same place you'll find the bar ØST in a small cabin. This was the place to be for workers of the brewery after they finished their shifts. Bet they were drinking their own brew. Open all year. ◆€◆

a. Kvitsøygata 25, 4014 Stavanger
t. +47 9300 4217
w. touscene.com

Get the freshest and most delicious nutritious bread from **Jakob's Brød og Kafé** (**12**). The bakery, now on its own two feet since separating from Fermenten café (see nr 14), is also a snug hangout on drizzly days. Because the 'og Kafé' in the name means there's more pleasure to be obtained: coffee, yes, and salads, soups, pizzas. You can even learn how to bake your own pizzas and bread. Well, not on a daily basis, but there are baking courses offered every now and then. Better learn from the best! Open all year. ◆€€◆

a. Kvitsøygata 30, 4014 Stavanger
t. +47 4587 0007
w. jakobsbrod.com

Hverdagsgodt (**13**) means 'everyday good'. So, that's what's on the menu here, good stuff, every day! Homemade and healthy breakfast and lunch, smoothies and juices. They make everything from scratch: their own bread, their own pesto, their own cake. The girls from Hverdagsgodt would not want you feeling stuffed and unhealthy, but feeling fulfilled and happy. You can also order snacks and take-away. Wholesome and healthy of course! Open all year.

◆€◆ ◆€€◆

a. Pedersgata 23, 4013 Stavanger
t. +47 9190 5229
w. hverdagsgodt.no

Aussie Craig Norman came to Stavanger to work in the oil and gas industry, met a lovely lady, decided to stay and look for adventure. This is how **Fermenten** (**14**) and brewing company **Yeastside** were born. They're the brainchildren of his wild but insightful imagination, and not the least of his adventurous and happy-go-lucky mentality. Craig's a bit of a fermenting freak, if such a thing exists. Showing his many pots and pans and breweries at the back of Fermenten café, he explained to us that it's just doing what people have been doing for ages to conserve food without using unnatural additives. Not to mention the health benefits of food that's preserved this way, like creating probiotics, b-vitamins, and beneficial enzymes. Since it's a time consuming process, you won't find many fermented foods in today's supermarkets, except for good old sauerkraut, or plain yoghurt. Besides a fair choice of fermented goodies like kombucha, kimchi, pots of fermented veggies, there's an instore bakery, a cheesemaker - the Stavanger Ysteri - and Craig's passion project: the Yeastside brewing company. A perfect place to hang out, read a book (on fermenting perhaps?), let the kids play in the large area full of stuff kids like to play with, enjoy a freshly brewed coffee or craft beer. As Craig says himself, Fermenten is an arena, or venue for makers and creators. Go see for yourself, just don't miss this one on your visit to town! Open all year. ◆€€◆

a. Ryfylkegata 13, 4014 Stavanger
t. +47 9944 6630
w. fermenten.no

Cobblestoned Øvre Holmegate, or Fargegata - the colourful street - and its surrounding streets, in the centre of Stavanger, are home to some fine shops, cafés and coffee bars:

We love the friendly and welcoming vibe of **Kokko Kokko (15)**, as much as their coffee, home-made cakes and soups. You can sit for hours, reading, working, chatting, or browsing their selection of books and magazines on sale, either downstairs, upstairs, or outside on their small terrace. Open all year. ♦€€♦

w. kokkokokko.no

Bøker & Børst (16) is a cosy café, always lively inside, and outside on the terrace. A place you can go in the daytime, as well as at night, with a Vinyl DJ party every Saturday, a large selection of Scandinavian beer, and good times all round created by a mix of locals, expats and tourists alike. Open all year. ♦€♦ ♦€€♦

w. bokerogborst.no

Grab a beer, do a little dance or talk skate, surf, music, art and meet up with the young creatives of Stavagner in **Hanekam (17)**. They've got regular music events and quizzes. And a quirky stairway done up with skate decks! Open all year. ♦€♦ ♦€€♦

w. hanekam.no

Just off Fargegata, near the cinema (Kino Stavanger) you'll find **EGGET (18)**. Recommended on several occasions, by locals and expats, we agree this is one of the finer and nicest restaurants of Stavanger. They don't have a traditional card, but offer a menu based on what they have available - the availability depending on the season and the chef's choice of the day. Vegetarians: you will love to know they have meatless and even vegan options on their menu. Open all year. ♦€€♦ ♦€€€♦

a. Steinkargata 23, 4006 Stavanger
t. +47 9840 7700
fb. eggetstavanger

SHOP
♦

The funny looking bookshop **Løvås Bruktbu (19)** in Stavanger Øst is absolutely stuffed to the brink with books (new and second-hand), comic strips, magazines and DVDs. It's over 40 years old, so chances are you'll find a long sought-after treasure, somewhere between the shelves upon shelves of all things print and paper. Open all year.

a. Pedersgata 25, 4013 Stavanger
t. +47 5189 3554
fb. Løvås Bruktbu

The **Fevang Brothers Barbershop** (**20**) is a strictly gentlemen-only affair. Get a clean-cut shiny hairdo, a razor sharp shave, or a new beard-do. You definitely won't mind waiting your turn whilst admiring the shop's artefacts and photos, or the heavily tattooed arms of the barbers. It's a super friendly place, run by the sharply dressed Fevang brothers. You'll sense their strong and proud family connection. Having lost one of their brothers, their bond's stronger than ever, as is expressed by their identical tattoo of a cross, right under the eye. Girlfriends and wives be aware, you're really not allowed to go any further than a peek inside from the doorstep! Open all year.

a. Øvre Holmegate 7, 4006 Stavanger
t. +47 5186 1950
w. fevangsbarberstue.com

Kant (**21**) is yet another gem, sat in the middle of Fargegata. The shop, owned by designer Froda Goa, an avid surfer of the Jæren breaks, is the place to get your hands on some uniquely designed t-shirts, caps, hats, sweaters and mugs. Living right at one of Jæren's best breaks, overlooking the never-ending ocean every day, you can only imagine his inspiration coming from that very sea. Shells, fishing rope, lighthouses and abstract lines representing the sea, it's all there. He set himself to have a new design almost every month, so it's not very likely you'll see the shirt you just bought on somebody else, ever. Froda's a passionate and easy-going local who loves his surroundings, his work, the ocean and will fill you in if you have any questions on any of these subjects.

a. Øvre Holmegt. 9, 4006 Stavanger
t. +47 9183 6557
w. kant.no

SrfSnoSk8 (**22**) is Norway's oldest surf shop (since 1978). They have a wide range of surf essentials, and if you need to talk surf, surf history, boards or fins, this is your go-to place. It pays to go see them before you head for the breaks. Set in a bit of an odd spot just outside the city centre - a big building, shared with a gym and some other companies.

a. Hillevågsveien 70, 4016 Stavanger
t. +47 9286 7030
w. srfsnosk8.no

SLEEP

♦

At **Preikestolen Fjellstue** (**23**), the mountain lodge located at the start of the Preikestolen trail, you can rent dorm rooms, private rooms, cabins and even a hammock. They also rent out equipment for hiking or ice climbing and offer guided hikes to Preikestolen and Trolltunga, up north. If you want to start early, this is the perfect place to stay the night before you set off. There's also a restaurant, if you just want to rest and eat after the hike, and move on afterwards. Open all year. ♦€♦ ♦€€♦

a. Preikestolvegen 521, 4100 Jorpeland
t. +47 5184 0200
w. preikestolenfjellstue.no

Also located near the base of the trail is **Preikestolen Camping** (**24**). The site has pitches only, no cabins. There's a restaurant, a tourist information stand, and from June to September they offer guided kayak tours. Short but affordable helicopter flights can be arranged from the campsite, for guests only. Open all year. ♦€♦

a. Preikestolvegen 97, Jossang,
   4100 Jorpeland
t. +47 4819 3950
w. preikestolencamping.com

If you prefer to stay in town, maybe go out, or just linger a bit longer, the Stavanger city camping and Stavanger youth hostel **Mosvangen** (**25**) are perfect options, especially if you're on a tight budget. Smack in the middle of town, next to the Mosvatnet lake. The campsite has pitches and simple cabins. The youth hostel is located at the camping. There's a public swimming pool that you can pay to use. Open all year. ♦€♦

a. Henrik Ibsens Gate 21, 4021 Stavanger
t. +47 5153 2971 (camping) /
   +47 5154 3636 (hostel)
w. stavangercamping.no / hihostels.no

Sleep in a typical whitewashed wooden Stavanger house at **Bed, Books & Breakfast** (**26**). Located in a quiet area of town, but within walking distance of the centre. Bring a book - you can swap! Open all year. ♦€€♦

a. Byfoged Christensens Gate 12,
   4011 Stavanger
t. +47 5152 5050 / 9082 3526

I LOVE
THE SEASIDE

THE SURF & TRAVELGUIDE

IN AND AROUND ORRESTRANDEN

♦

The long sand beach (3 km) of Orre is protected landscape, as are all Jæren's beaches. At Orre the flora and fauna are protected as well. Even surfing is prohibited during nesting season at some parts; catching waves is believed to disturb the birds. Most likely this law wasn't drawn up by a surfer… But this fact aside, it pays to visit the Orre Recreation Centre (Friluftshuset på Orre) in Klepp to find out all there is to know about birds, plants, flowers, their local habitat and other nature reserves in the area. The wetlands of Jæren attract thousands of migrating birds in spring and autumn, using it as a resting place before moving on.

The small communities along the coast; Orre, Bore, Sola, Brusand, and cities Klepp and Sandnes, are mostly famed for their beaches, lagoons, rivers and sand dunes. That's exactly the attraction and it's all made so easy to play outside, whether it's hiking, surfing or horse riding. There are car parks, trails, toilets, but no restaurants or cafés at the beach, so tourism here is a low-key, bring-your-own and enjoy the simple things kind of vibe.

Klepp tourist office at Rädhuset, Solavegen 1.

TO DO

♦

At the end of May the village of Bryne turns into a festival ground. **Jærdagen** & **Jærnåttå** are actually two festivals, one morphing into the next. Jærdagen is a 3-day event with local and international food and market stalls; there's entertainment, a fairground and a couple of thousand people filling up the town square. On Friday and Saturday nights during Jærnåttå, the square turns into a large open-air music hall with live music, dancing, eating and just having a good time. The festival is annually held in the centre of Bryne.

w. jaerdagen.no / jaernatta.no

You can't get your **crab (27)** any fresher than to buy it off the fishermen at Ølberg. Mayonnaise, some salad and sandwiches, et voila, you're all set to prepare a 3-star meal.

Tryggvi (28) is an Icelandic horse farm offering guided rides on Icelandic horses. The trips can take from 1 to 3 hours, depending on your experience. If you're a beginner, you'll learn some basics first, with time for you and the horse to get acquainted a with eachother. Besides their 40 horses, the farm has chickens, rabbits, beehives, and cats and dogs running around. Open all year, but guided rides are only at weekends and during holidays.

a. Kvernelandsveien 117, 4323 Sandnes
t. +47 9187 1497
w. tryggvi.no

A perfect option for a rainy day is visiting the **Vitenfabrikken (29)**, The Science Factory, in the centre of Sandnes. The modern building houses several floors full of science and technology, and in the process you'll learn more about the surroundings of Sandnes as well. But the best part is the way it is presented in an interactive and playful way. Children won't get bored, they can try their hands at breaking glass with their voice, or playing games to find out how energy works.

a. Storgata 28, 4307 Sandnes
t. +47 4777 6020
w. vitenfabrikken.no

Get a full stretch of your body, heart and soul at **Atha Yoga (30)**. Their studio at Sandnes is open to drop-in classes for all levels. They teach Jivamukti yoga, a vigorous form of yoga with as much emphasis on physical practice as mental and spiritual. Open all year, check their site for class times.

a. Langgata 7, 4300 Sandnes
t. +47 5153 0392
w. jivamuktiyoga.no

If you're anything of a vintage car freak, pay a visit to the **TS Museum (31)** at Tjelta, in Sola municipality. TS are tractor builders, but also have a large collection of old cars, trucks, motorbikes, and of course, tractors! Quite unexpectedly, they all still run, even some that are almost a century old. Open all year, entrance is free.

a. Vigdelsvegen 637B, 4054 Tjelta
t. +47 5144 4000
w. tsmaskin.no

Another great interactive technology museum is the **Jærmuseet Vitengarden (32)** (the Science Farm) in Nærbø, municipality Hå. The building itself is interesting from an architectural point of view, but more importantly - kids and grown-ups alike will enjoy and learn from a visit. Vitengarden focuses on the green sciences, exploring possibilities and showing development concerning food, agriculture and culture. Their philosophy is 'learning by doing'. Open all year.

a. Kviavegen 99, 4365 Hå / Nærbø
t. +47 4777 6020
w. jaermuseet.no

Kvassheim Lighthouse (33) and surrounding buildings in Brusand are today used as museum, café and historical information centre. In this area rescue operations at sea are part of the coastal history. Exhibitions on the rescues, the surrounding wetlands, or the changes from ice-age to present, a photo gallery, and a telescope are just a few of the many things you can see, do or experience at the lighthouse. The café serves some pretty tasty home-baked goodies. Open all year on Sundays, and daily between 25 June to 17 August.

a. Kvassheim, 4363 Brusand
t. +47 5166 7170
w. jarenfri.no/no/steder/
friluftsfyret-kvassheim

EAT/DRINK/HANG OUT

◆

From daily fresh bread from the in-house Jærbakeren bakery, to vegetarian burgers with rhubarb sauce, go get it at burger restaurant **Rabalder** (**34**). Rabalder means 'making a fuss'. But, hopefully, your burger isn't too much fussed around with. The restaurant is known for its good burgers (with Angus beef), made from fresh and local ingredients. So, what the fuss is about we're not sure, it's pretty clear to us. This makes for a perfect after-surf dinner. Open all year. ◆€◆ ◆€€◆

a. Jærvegen 270, 4352 Bryne
t. +47 5162 6060
w. rabalderburger.no

The old vicarage **Hå Gamle Prestegard** (**35**) in Nærbø has been used throughout the years as a priests' house, residence of a senior civil servant, and an administrative centre. Today it's a cultural centre with permanent and temporary exhibitions, always with a leading theme. Around the theme there are books, sculptures, paintings, fashion, and modern design on display, some of which are for sale. There's a gallery and a restaurant in 2 separate buildings. The restaurant is extremely koselig, with a distinctive Scandinavian and homely atmosphere. A bit north of the Prestegard is an ancient burial ground, and next to the vicarage you'll find the remains of a settlement. Open all year. ◆€€◆

a. Håvegen 347, 4365 Nærbø
t. +47 5179 1660
w. hagamleprestegard.no

SLEEP

◆

The nicest places to stay in this area are the campsites either at, or within walking distance of the beach. Almost all campsites have cabins for rent.

Ølberg Camping (**36**) is located right at the beach. They have pitches in the sand dunes and cabins for rent. Open from May to August. ◆€◆

a. Ølberg Havnevei, 4054 Tjelta (close to airport)
t. +47 5165 4375

Bore Strandcamping (**37**) is within walking distance of the most consistent surf spot of Jæren - Borestranden. Spread out over a large area are pitches and a choice of cabins for rent. Open all year. ◆€◆

a. Nordsjøvegen 123, 4352 Kleppe
t. +47 9761 6623
w. borestrand.no

It's all good, it's all lovable. The wooden containers of **Boretunet** (**38**) are enjoying their third life; originally used as accommodation for workers, they were then part of a housing project in nearby Stavanger, and now (third time lucky) they've found a home right on the beach, backed by farmland. The best thing; you can stay here, as comfortable as can be, in this very different place with a hostel vibe and the smart looks of a tiny house. Open all year. ◆€€◆

a. Borestranda 481, 4354 Klepp
t. +47 4803 9906
w. boretunet.no

At the other side of the bay is the smaller campsite **Ogna Camping** (**39**), with pitches and cabins for rent, sleeping up to 8 persons. Open in summer. ◆€◆

a. Nordsjøvegen 4061, 4364 Sirevåg
t. +47 5143 8242
w. ognacamping.no

SURF

Jæren is known for the best and most consistent surf of 'Norwaii'. The North Sea does indeed deliver, you'll see! There are beachbreaks and boulder rock points, some popular and easily accessible, some less well known, some secret and a bit of a search. During migratory times, and wintering or nesting periods some spots are no-go areas, pay attention to the signs or ask the locals! If you venture into a protected area you risk not only a guilty conscience but also a hefty fine, much to the frustration of local surfers. Jæren's beaches are wave magnets, due to their different positions. There's usually some break working somewhere, even with a southerly swell. The tidal difference is very small, which can be either a blessing or a disadvantage; you can surf at almost all tides, but miss the strong push of high tide. Summer surf is not uncommon, although the other seasons bring the best waves.

The beach of **Hellestø (I)** is a wide and open beach backed by sand dunes, and therefore a bit of protection from northern winds. Works best with small to medium W-NW swell, usually works at all tides, depending on the sandbanks.
• *All levels/beachbreak/easy parking/toilets/surf school and rentals.* •

The beachbreak and rivermouth at **Selestranden (II)** is popular with kiters, windsurfers and surfers alike. To the north side a right point breaks over boulders. The middle beachbreak is best for beginners. Works best with small to medium SW-W-NW swell, all tides. There's a hiking path all the way up to Vigdel beach following the coastline. • *All levels/beachbreak and boulders/easy parking/toilets at the small Sele harbour to north side.* •

Just south of Sele starts the endless stretch of beach, **Borestranden (III)**; Jæren's most popular surf spot. It's hardly world class but does pick up any available swell. Bore works best with small to medium SW-W-NW swell, at all tides. There's a small skate ramp

between the campsite and the car park.
* *All levels/beachbreak/easy parking/ toilets/surf school & rentals/campsite.* ♦

Reve Havn (IV) produces some perfect waves and holds up well in a strong offshore wind. You need to be an experienced surfer for this one and be very, very aware of your role as a visiting surfer. You can either try to enter and leave over the boulders or paddle out from the harbour. Works best with medium to big NW swell, on higher tide.
* *Advanced level/stones and boulders/ only few parking places available/no facilities.* ♦

Between Bore and Reve are several pretty good reefbreaks and breaks over stones and boulders that all need a medium or big NW swell. Befriend a local to find out where, and act with the utmost respect to farmers' land. Best to park along the R507 road and walk to the surf. ♦ *Advanced level/stones and boulders/no parking/no facilities.* ♦

Near to the (very small) Skeie Airport and Bore you'll find (or not, it's not that easy to find) **Point Perfect (V)**. Although the name suggests otherwise, this is a slow wave, but depending on your choice of board you could consider it a perfect point. Works best, or perfect so you will, with a small to medium and clean SW-W-NW swell, at all tides. ♦ *All levels/stones and sand bottom/paid parking/no facilities.* ♦

The stunner of a bay at **Brusand (VI)** doesn't work that often due to its south facing position. At its best with S swells at all tides, sometimes bigger W-NW swells can wrap around and reach the bay. ♦ *All levels/sand bottom/small parking at north end, or a bit further next to the soccer field/campsites.* ♦

SCHOOL RENTAL REPAIR

◆

If you need any board repairs your go-to person is **Roar Berge** (**40**), one of the first surfers and pioneers in discovering the Jæren breaks. He's also the founder of the Norway Surf Association (Norges Surf Forbund). Besides being probably the best source of information on surfing in the area, he'll fix any ding in your board, mend your kayak, or if you need anything else repaired he'll do that too - as Roar says: it just takes a little longer and costs a little more. Open all year.

- **a.** Roviksveien 60, 4328 Sandnes (in Norwaii, as he calls it)
- **t.** +47 4503 6432
- **w.** roarberge.no

Local salty, Viking Rune of **Surfschool.no** (**41**), mainly uses Hellestø Beach. Besides lessons you can rent boards. Open from March to November.

- **t.** +47 9112 6489
- **w.** surfschool.no

At Bore beach you'll find Terje from **SrfSnoSk8** (**42**) and his mobile truck. He offers surf and SUP courses and rents out boards. Closed in winter.

- **t.** +47 9988 4320
- **w.** srfsnosk8.no

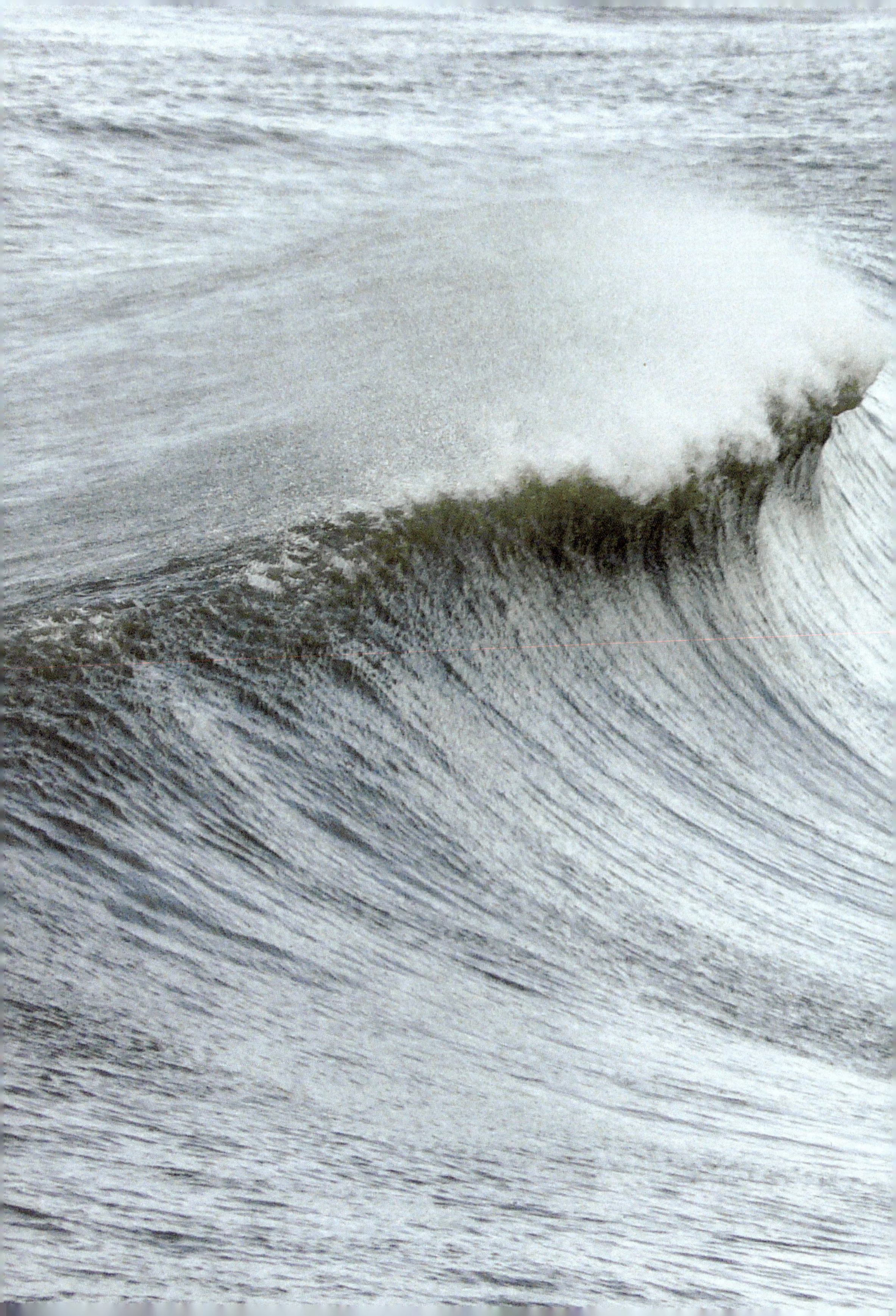

Lista

- 1
- BORHAUG ♦ 2, 9, 12, 15
- ♦ 5
- VESTBYGD
- GRETTESTØ (I)
- TJØRVENESET (II)
- KVILJO (III)
- VANSE ♦ 13, 16
- ♦ 3, 4, 6
- STORE HAVIKA (IV)
- LILLE HAVIKA (V)
- HUSEBYSANDEN (VI)
- ÅPTA
- FARSUND ♦ 7, 8, 10, 11, 17, 18
- LYNGDA ♦ 14
- SALSTE (VII)

LISTA

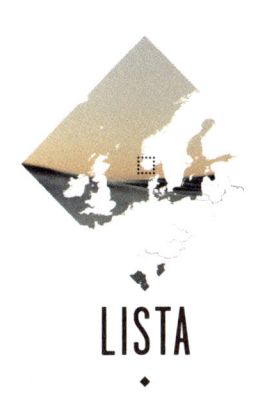

What makes Lista - the large peninsula in the southwest corner of Norway - worth exploring, you might ask... To check the surf? Yes, amongst other things. Like take long hikes, sail, SUP deserted lakes and bays, climb a lighthouse, sleep in a tiny beach house, meet birds, friendly faces, and alpacas. Alpacas? Well, Ja! In the fields surrounding the Lista lighthouse roams a large herd of alpacas - the furry animals with a look of surprise in their camel-like eyes, resembling llamas.

More than anything else, Lista seems to effortlessly surprise with little things that put a smile on your face. Nosy alpacas, a life-size pop art JFK portrait wrapped around a pillar in a farmer's field, a tiny dream house in the middle of sand dunes, free to enter.

Bird watchers will adore Lista, with the peninsula being a stopover for migratory birds. Its position along the Listafjorden and the many wetlands make the peninsula a perfect nesting place for all kind of bird species, and an ideal wintering spot, or stopover for migrating birds. You'll find hides throughout the Lista wetlands and nature parks where you can eat your smørbrød in silence and observe a feathered friend or two.

TRAVEL INFO

Although there are regular buses between cities and villages, to get to the beaches and basically anywhere you want, a car is by far the preferred option in this area.

BY BUS

Ekspress buses run between Lyngdal and Oslo, Stavanger and Kristiansand. From Lyngdal you can take the local bus to Farsund. Sørlandsruta buses run between Kristiansand and Farsund. For local buses and timetables check:

w. akt.no

BY BOAT

Farsund's known to be one of the most welcoming harbours for people travelling by boat, their own boat that is - if you happen to have one you can park up in the marina. And, quite uniquely, it's free!

IN AND AROUND FARSUND

Farsund's a small town that was once a large shipping hub. Now it's a friendly place that warmly welcomes tourists in summer. Being surrounded by water, the reflecting light emphasises Farsund's cleanliness and brightness. It has a southern USA feel to it, with whitewashed and ecru-coloured wooden 3-storey houses along the water's edge. Lista's towns and settlements do have a strong history of farmers moving to and from the USA, whenever the economy went down or up in Lista's agriculture. In the 1900s especially, a lot of folk from Lista emigrated to New York, some of whom returned in the 1960s. Nowadays, there's even an annual American Festival, celebrating the deeply rooted connection Lista feels with the States. And you'll find some street names in Varse and Farsund sounding not so Norwegian, like Brooklyn Square.

Tourist office is at Torvgata 2, 4550 Farsund.

TO DO

♦

You may feel like a cartoon character, or have a flashback to that scene from The 100-Year-Old Man Who Climbed Out the Window with the 2 men and a corpse pedalling along a rail track. But the 'draisines' - rail bikes - that you pedal along the **Flekkefjordbanen (1)** are the prettiest perfectest way to see the scenery without having to watch out for oncoming traffic, potholes, or people crossing. The railway biking trips take you from Flekkefjord to Bakkekleivi in 2 hours, passing through tunnels and forests and alongside lakes. Open from May to October.

- **a.** Rutebilstasjonen, 4400 Flekkefjord
- **t.** +47 9765 7933
- **w.** flekkefjordbanen.no

We have a weak spot for lighthouses, and much to our delight the **Lista Fyr (2)** is not only open to visit, you can even sleep in the former lighthouse keeper's house. There's a visitor centre with a very friendly and helpful lady patiently answering all your questions and handing out information on the region. In addition there's a café and art gallery exposing work from local, national and international contemporary artists, hence the art objects in the area (like the life-sized pop art portrait of JFK, a little south of the lighthouse). Just outside the gates is a hide for watching birds in the adjoining fields and wetlands. The alpacas grazing in the surrounding fields may seem surreal; they're there solely for their wool, and keeping the grass neat and tidy, not for arts' sake. The lighthouse itself is 34 m high and was built in 1853. Open all year, but from October to April only at weekends.

- **a.** Fyrveien 70, 4563 Borhaug
- **t.** +47 9061 2688
- **w.** listafyr.no

The quaint little cabin **Lyset på Lista (3)**, The Light of Lista, looks like someone's Tiny House wet dream. Smack in the middle of nature, steps away from the beach, with a view of sand dunes and ocean, the cabin's designed to overlook the whole area, sitting high on poles with lots of windows. You can enter, hang out, sit, write, contemplate, or even book a night to stay there on a hanging seat (bring your own mattress and sleeping bag though). The purpose of this little gem is to show the possibilities of eco-friendly tourist facilities, using innovative and architecturally interesting ideas. This very hut is designed and built by 2 Norwegian architects and 14 architectural students.

- **a.** Haviksanden, Lista, Farsund (on the way to Haviksanden beach)
- **t.** +47 3838 2115 (tourist organisation taking care of the cabin)

Haviksanden, or Havik beach, is a popular spot for surfing and windsurfing, and on calmer days it's perfect for SUP. **Lista Aktiv (4)** offers courses in all 3 disciplines, or you can rent a SUP to explore the beautiful big bay by yourself. Open in June, July and August.

a. Haviksanden, 4550 Farsund
t. +47 9545 5544
w. lista-aktiv.no

The indoor **Flipside Skatepark (5)** is a smart option on a rainy or windy day. It houses a 17 metre long by 3 metre deep bowl, jumps, rails, razi pad (plastic jump box with a smooth landing) and a foam pit. Almost anything on wheels is welcome, skateboards, obviously, BMX bikes, and rollerblades. If you didn't bring your own, you can rent equipment such as BMX bikes and skateboards. Open all year.

a. Lista Fly og Næringspark, 4560 Farsund
t. +47 9188 3748
fb. Flipside Skatehall

Yoga Lista (6) offers yoga classes linking asanas, yoga poses, and breath in motion. The classes are on request. You can send a text message or phone yoga teacher Ann Helen. She also organises regular events and workshops (check her Facebook). The studio's location is picture perfect, overlooking the beach at Farsund. In summer she teaches outdoors, if the weather allows it, at the beach. Open all year.

a. Torvet, 4550 Farsund
t. +47 9577 3200
fb. YogaLista

Hiking the **Bøensbakken (7)** route takes you along fjords, forests, mountainsides and old bridges (even a century-old swing bridge) in the surroundings of Farsund. This used to be an old railway between Farsund and Sande, that later was converted into a road. Since 1965 no motor traffic is allowed anymore. The walk starts at the Bøen farm near Kjerringdalen, where you can park your car, and is well signposted. The route's 10 km, but even hiking a part of it is nice.

Warm up, or better yet, turn it up higher and get a sweat at **Farsund Badehus og Sauna (8)**. You can buy a drop-in ticket on their website, get the 4-digit code and use it to open the door.

a. Sundsodden 4, 4550 Farsund
t. +47 4177 3245
w. farsundbadehus.no

EAT/DRINK/HANG OUT

♦

Tarebua (9) music café has an Americano western vibe, so bring your big hat and boots and go for it. They've music nights, pub quizzes and an amazing view over the harbour of Borhaug. Open all year. ♦€♦ ♦€€♦

a. Tjørvehavn, 4563 Borhaug
t. +47 9349 0953
fb. Tarebua

As you might have guessed by now, we love a good bakery. **Edgars Bakeri (10)** fits our bill, meets up to our high expectations, hacks it. You'll find Edgars bread and pastries in several locations throughout Norway, the bakery and coffee shop in Farsund's located on the 2nd floor of the AMFI shopping centre. We just figured you might end up there on a rainy day, or have a good reason to do so. Open all year. ♦€€♦

a. Vestersiden 1, 4550 Farsund
t. +47 3834 1555
w. edgars.no

For the best coffee and pastries, sandwiches, and a genial atmosphere, check out **Parken Kaffebar (11)** in the city park of Farsund. They serve homebrewed coffee from some fine Norwegian roasters and have a large selection of teas. Bring the kids, they can play in the small playground while you enjoy your cuppa. Open all year. ♦€♦ ♦€€♦

a. Byparken, Parkveien 3, 4550 Farsund
t. +47 4834 9713
fb. ParkenKaffebar

SHOP

♦

Your go-to place for a new pair of binoculars, a good working GPS or old fashioned compass and map, a camouflage tent, clothes, and bird catalogues: stop by at the **Natur og Fritid** (12) shop in Borhaug. They have all those and more, like some real good information on anything outdoor, nature, birds, and detailed descriptions of hiking routes. Open all year.

a. Fyrveien 6, 4563 Borhaug
t. +47 3870 6750
w. naturogfritid.no

Forgot your big hat, buckle and boots? No worries, **Trunken** (13), an American inspired shop in Vanse will get you fixed for a night out in town. Even when you don't really need that hat or lumberjack shirt, it's fun or at least a bit surreal browsing through their stuff, from old trunks migrants brought back to peanut butter and candles with a Spirit of America scent. And they're located at Brooklyn square, well, holy moly, wadayaknow! Open all year.

a. Brooklyn Square 10 (Former Abraham Berges vei 4), 4560 Vanse
t. +47 3839 6780
fb. trunken-department-store

Ah, luckily there's also some non-American inspired but purely Norwegian focused place where time doesn't stop in the 1960s. **WannaBe Galleri** (14) in Lyngdal sells and shows jewellery, graphics, paintings and sculptures of Norwegian artists, all tastefully displayed in their gallery and shop.

a. Kirkeveien 7, 4580 Lyngdal
t. +47 9710 7937
w. wannabe-galleri.no

SLEEP

♦

Sleeping with the reassuring light of the **Lista Fyr** (15) lighthouse, guarding you and your family or friends, and get your own private key to the lighthouse? Oh nice! You can rent one of the 2 basic but incredibly spacious apartments in the former lighthouse keeper's house, located right next to the Lista lighthouse. Each apartment has 2 bathrooms. Open all year. ♦€€♦

a. Fyrveien 70, 4563 Borhaug
t. +47 9061 2688
w. listafyr.no

From **The Longhouse at Lista** (16) you won't miss a wave, a change in light, cloud or ray of light passing. This beautiful wooden stay has panoramic windows facing the ocean and beach of Farsund. Whether you're a surfer, nature lover, ocean addict, bird watcher, or all the above, you'll love this place, no doubt about it. The house sleeps up to 12 people, you'll have to like each other though, there's only one bedroom. There are comfy bunk beds, single beds and double beds. Perfect for a big family or group of friends. Open all year. ♦€€♦ ♦€€€♦

a. Vanse, 4560 Farsund
t. +47 9798 0325
w. thelonghouseatlista.com

Family-friendly **Lomsesanden** (17) is set within walking distance of the Lomse beach. A great spot from which to go out fishing, boating, hiking or beaching. The camping has pitches and rents out cabins. Open from May to mid-September. ♦€♦ ♦€€♦

a. Loshavnveien 228, 4550 Farsund
t. +47 3839 0913
w. lomsesanden.no

Campervans can stay at the **Farsund campervan camping** (18), located near the ocean and the park. You can use the service facilities at the Verven marina, the site itself has wifi, water, electricity, and you can empty your wastewater and toilet. Open all year, the water connection's closed off in winter. ♦€♦

a. Farøyveien, 4550 Farsund

SURF

Lista is probably best known for its windsurfing spots, but there are beachbreaks and pointbreaks that suit both surfers and windsurfers. The set-up is there: beautiful long stretches of beach, pebble bays, boulder reefs, and no big tidal differences. And lots to discover, especially when a decent SW-W swell's approaching. Since discovering unknown spots is a pretty rare phenomenon along European coasts, take your advantage and go out and explore. Here's some inspiration.

Grettestø (I) is locally known as **Pisserenna**. This break needs a big NW-W-SW or medium S swell to start working. It's far from a beginner's break: a rocky reef and shallow in places. Since this is all natural park, please tread extra carefully. ◆ *Advanced level/ boulder reef/easy parking near spot/no facilities.* ◆

Tjørveneset (II), a little south from Borshavn is a sandy bay, perfect for beginners. Works best with medium to big W-SW-W swell but is easily blown out. ◆ *All levels/sand/small parking area next to road/no facilities.* ◆

Moving further south you'll pass the long stretch of beach at **Kviljo (III)**. Works best with a medium SW-S swell and preferably northerly winds. The small island at the north end of the beach is Rauna. ◆ *All levels/sand/easy parking/no facilities.* ◆

The main surf beach for Lista is the drop-dead-gorgeous **Haviksanden**. The larger stretch to the north, **Store Havika (IV)**, is actually an extension of Kviljo, and separated by a headland from **Lille Havika (V)**. Backed by sand dunes, Haviksanden resembles southern European beaches with its clear water, white sand and black rocks protruding from the sand and the surface of the water. The big bay works best with a small to medium W-SW-S swell. Lille Havika needs a medium to big S or medium E swell, and has some protection from western winds. Some parts of the beach it's prohibited to surf since they're protected natural park. ◆ *All levels/sand and some rocks/easy parking/toilet/surf school in summer.* ◆

Husebysanden (VI), the next bigger bay to the south of Haviksanden rarely works, and needs a big SW-S swell. It has some protection from easterly winds. ◆ *All levels/sand/easy parking/no facilities.* ◆

Saltstein (VII) isn't in Lista, but halfway between Kristiansand and Oslo. It's a popular spot for surfers from Oslo because it's "relatively" near. We did go and see, and maybe the occasional session works out for Oslo and local surfers, but this guide is subject to our own taste, and we just didn't fall in love with the place. Then again, if you're in the neighbourhood and want to increase your chance of surfing with Norway's crown prince: here's where you might get to literally drop in on royalty. Saltstein works best with a medium to big SW-S-SE swell. Gets busy when it's on. ◆ *All levels/boulder reef/difficult parking (in front of campsite)/campsite.* ◆

To be, live, or act better takes action: I Love the Seaside teamed up with KEEN Footwear to share stories of people who make a positive effort to make a change and/or inspire.

Valerie and Tim work, travel, and live in their hostel on wheels - The Nomads Bus - together with their daugther Fenna, baby Ziggy and dog Lewis.

LIFE ON THE ROAD AS A COUPLE

"Travelling together as a couple, whether it's in a bus, a van, on foot or by bike, is without a doubt the greatest relationship test out there. Every situation or different environment brings out new positive and negative sides. With the bus adventure we definitely had to find our way with each other, but also with running the hostel and the bus in general. Right now I can happily say that after living in the bus for 4,5 years, of which 3,5 years with guests, we definitely found our flow on the bus. And adding a kid to this equation is challenging at times, but most of all they're a little happy bundles of energy hopping around the bus."

AND KIDS ON THE ROAD

"For us, Fenna going to school is the least of our worries. Besides the fact that she is only mandatory to go to school from the age of 6, and we wouldn't mind home schooling if needed, we're sure things will work themselves out. Almost every day she has a new backyard, and like all kids she is very curious about the world. Our situation is definitely not your average lifestyle, but we truly believe that kids will always find happiness on the road as long as they can enjoy the outdoors, have someone who listens to them and joins them on their little adventures and big discoveries in life."

*Love grows best in little houses, with fewer walls to separate.
Where you eat and sleep so close together, you can't help but communicate.
Oh, and if we had more room between us, think of all we'd miss.
Love grows best, in houses just like this.*

DOUG STONE

LIFE YOU DON'T NEED A HOLIDAY FROM

"You should be able to wake up with excitement to start the day. Our simple advice: don't wait until the perfect job comes along, but figure out what you love to do, and persist in finding a way to turn it into income. It could mean taking a risk, to follow your dreams and dare to commit to what makes you happy - even if it doesn't take you to the top of the social ladder or make you rich."

REALITY CHECK

"Following our dreams has never been easy, but struggles have been a big part of the beauty of pursuing our goals. The challenges on the road give such a feeling of connection: the vibe of teamwork, the support of the online community and total strangers showing their unexpected kindness. It's during hard times that we were reminded of our perseverance and to never take the beautiful things for granted. We might live in a bus with 8 adults, kids and a dog, and things might break down from time to time (annoyingly at the most unexpected moments), it never outweighs the unforgettable moments. Thanks to sharing with others, finding solutions, and most of all creating memories together, there'll never be anything in the world that could stop us from making crazy dreams come true!"

Check the full interview AND a spicy Nomads recipe: **w.** ilovetheseaside.com/stories
Learn more about The Nomads Bus: **w.** letsbenomads.com

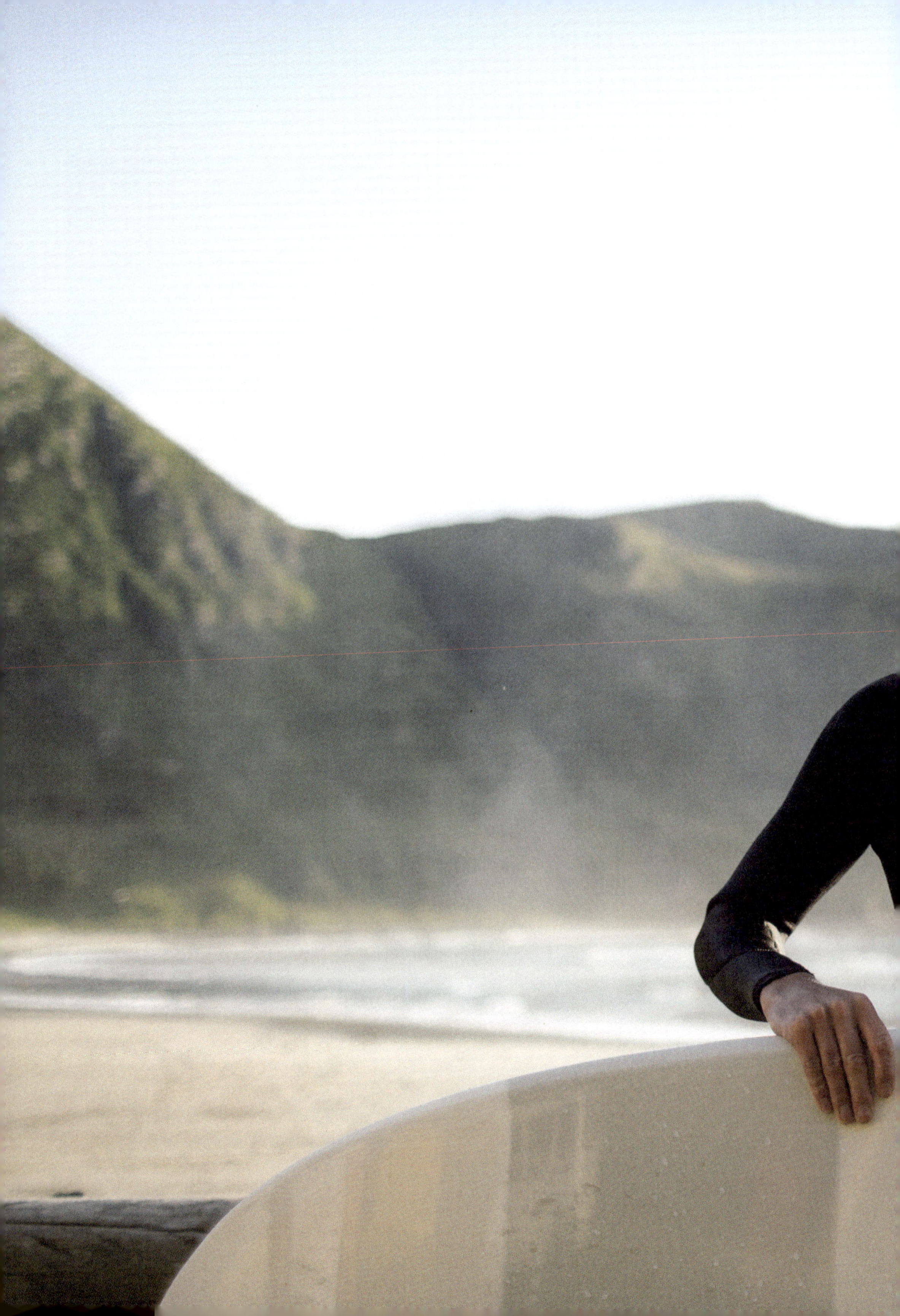

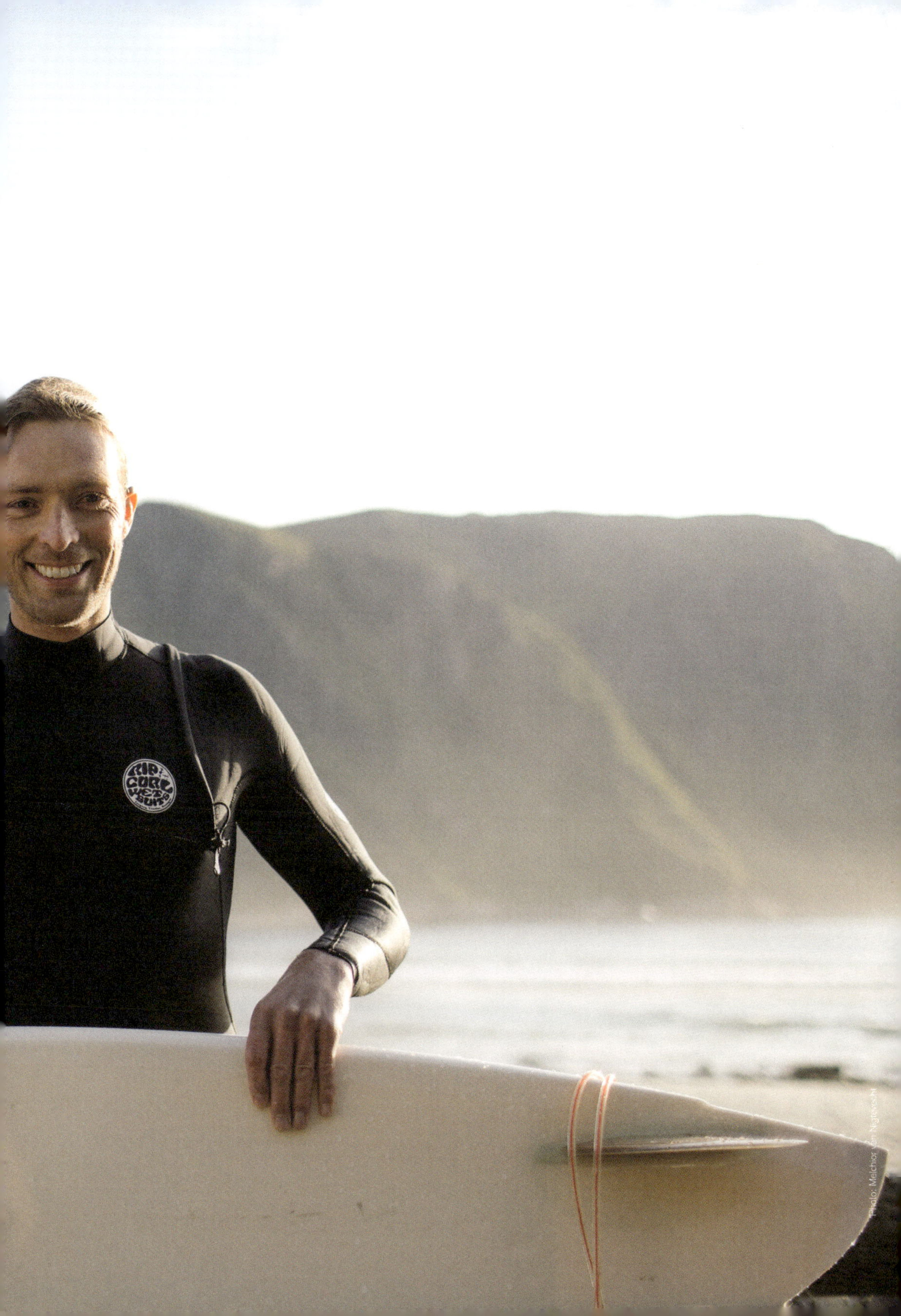

Photo: Melchior van Nigtevecht

Sweden

SWEDEN

Because Swedes tend to refer to the landskap - province - they're from, rather than the county - län - that's what we stick to. There are 25 landskap and we introduce you to only three of them, because surf and seaside, remember? But my my! These three landskap are vast and varied. And as with most things in life, sometimes it helps to limit the options, so as not to drown in them; and take time to discover the places where you know you'll find your favoured options in ripe abundance.

If you weren't aware of it already: Sweden is big, grand, very large. And almost three quarters of its extensive land is covered by thick forest, but inhabited by very few people. The majority of them - almost 85% of 10 million - living in or close to the cities. And the 10 million are doing a mighty fine job of keeping things hip, happening, culturally interesting and fair. Swedes hold freedom of speech, equality and openness pretty highly. As well as taking good care of the environment. They were the first in the world for women to have the right to vote, and to have freedom of the press (since late 18th century). Couples from the same sex can get married and adopt children. All religions are welcome. And howzabout 480 days of parental leave, to be split between the both of you, mum and dad! Sweden's produced the likes of filmmaker Ingmar Bergman, writer Stieg Larsson, and music producer Tim Bergling aka Avicii (R.I.P.). And Skype, and Spotify, and Abba, and Ikea. And Pippi Longstocking! They're big on recycling, being extremely advanced in their knowledge of technologies to use waste for producing energy and heat. So, clean, green and infinite it is, driving through forests, along the coast, rounding another bend.

Please note: We're aware of the surfing possibilities in the Baltic sea, and us picking only spots in the south and south east…there's good reason for that: Baltic surf can be anything from total crap to perfect peeling - but the latter is rare. Breaks are fickle and highly unpredictable. And as we're in the clean green land of Sweden, we think it's better to keep our fuel-guzzling chariots swinging low, our chances of finding waves as high as they can be. Also, on those days the decent waves do arrive further north, do you think maybe the locals deserve them all to themselves after their long wait?

SURFER-TRAVELLER TYPE SWEDEN

♦

You love spending days outdoors, if not in the woods then at least playing games involving wooden sticks like kubb, dancing round a tree, absorbing every ray of sun available, and onshore winds (waves!). You like having endless coffees and baked goods and chats with friends, and cuddling up on the couch on Fridays with the family. You eat everything with pickled herring, love to celebrate the waffle (March 25) and the cinnamon bun (October 4) on their dedicated days, and appreciate the crunching sound when chomping off a piece of your knäckebröt. You simply adore ice-cream, even in the midst of a cold winter, little red houses and, obviously, moose.

WORDS AND CONCEPTS THAT MIGHT COME IN HANDY

♦

Hej - Hello. Sounds informal, but it's justified Hej-ing to old and young, entering a shop or just passing by. When leaving you can say *Hej då,* or *Vi ses.*

Tack - Thank you. Use it more than you're maybe used to.

Lagom - Just enough, about right, this is taken to a cultural level for the Swedes; a lifestyle of being happy with not too much, not too little. Like Scandinavian design: stylish but functional, minimal but sustainable.

Ont i håret - Hung over, literally meaning you drank so much your 'hair hurts'.

Midsommar - The summer solstice. Celebrated in a grand way, which makes sense. Wouldn't you be over the moon, the day the sun only sets for a brief moment after a long, long winter, short of daylight?

Fredagsmys - Cosy Friday. Not to be celebrated at work to end another week at the office, but at home, preferably in PJs, watching a movie, having snacks.

FOOD FACTS

FIKA

A noun and a verb - is done at least a few times a week, spending quality time, meeting up with friends, colleagues, family, and have a coffee with cakes, sweet treats, catching up, chatting, and enjoying each others' company.

RÄKSMÖRGÅS

Open sandwich, high piled with salad, egg, crème fraîche, and shrimp.

RAGGMUNK

A hearty potato pancake, best eaten in winter, preferably fried in butter and served with crunchy fried meat and mashed lingonberries (mountain cranberries).

WRÄNGEBÄCK

The taste of this pale yellow cheese might remind you of cheddar cheese, with a creamy texture. Aged for between 18 and 30 months and washed in salt water, every original cheese wheel bears the robust looking imprint Wrängebäck.

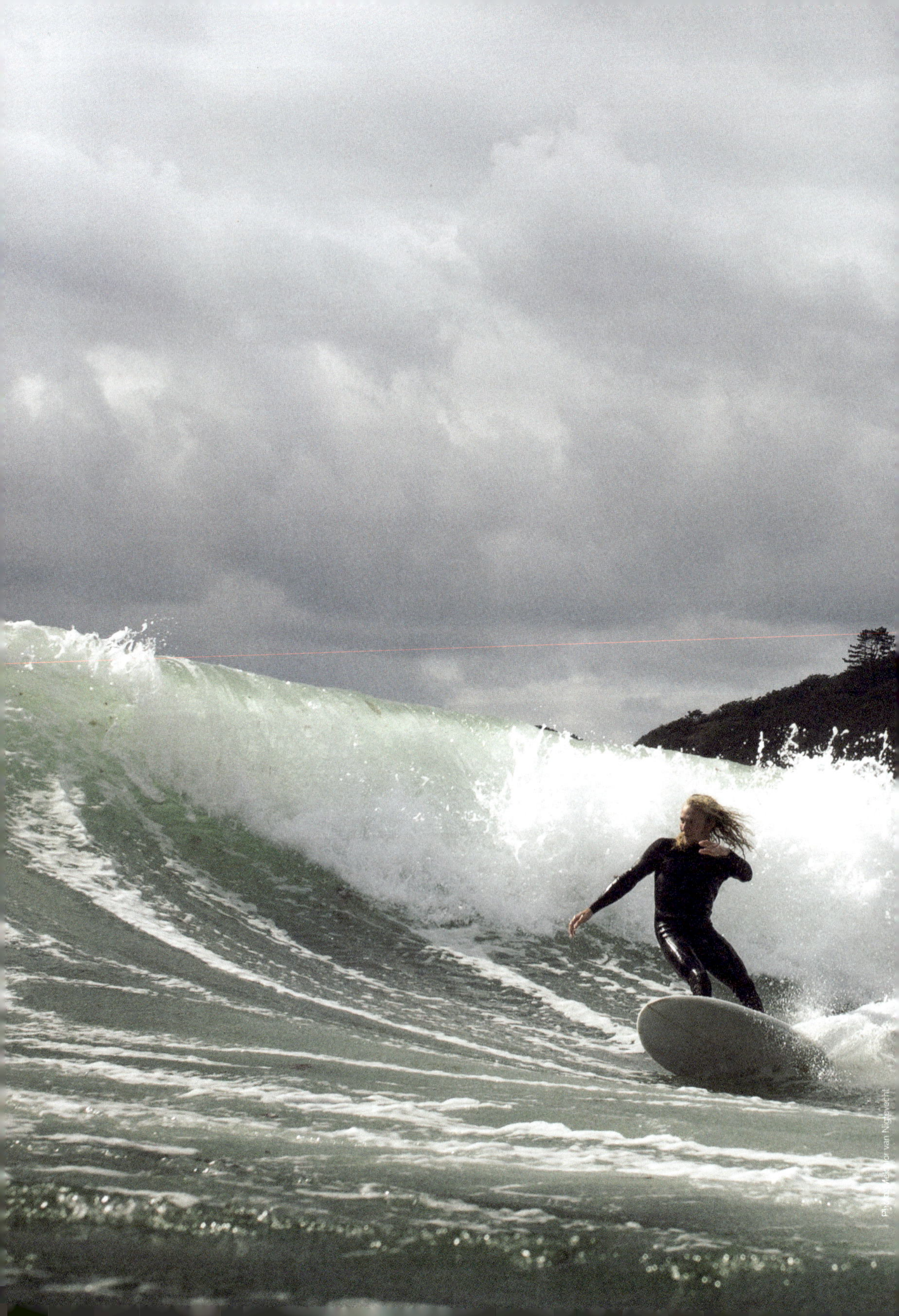
van Nigtevecht

A BIT ON SURF IN SWEDEN

◆

"Our coastline's sick! So many options," assured Markus Boman, owner of one of the oldest surf shops in Sweden - Surfers Paradise in Varberg: "Even if we have no groundswell and are dependent on the wind." It's exactly this stoked attitude that got the Swedes exploring their own coastline for surfable waves, and finding them, against the odds of minimal expectations.

Sweden's surf history is fairly young. In the seventies a small group of avid skateboarders started surfing the breaks south of Halmstad. They didn't mind it being small and windy, but had heaps of fun, especially being the only ones out. Varberg's beaches were probably the first spots where surfing became popular, back in the 1990s. Travelling surfers returned after a surf trip abroad, ignited by the stoke, ready to fire up some Kattegat and Baltic waves, preferring to surf windswell than wait for their next trip. The first pioneers searched maps, roads, headlands, hidden bays and inlets. "We did a lot of walking back then…" says Marcus. With access to weather data and forecasts becoming better, and surfers being surfers, always searching for possibilities, the virus spread. And today, there's no stopping them. Although the whole retro-boards fashion - and the stylish wave gliding that comes along with it - that's spread throughout the rest of Europe has yet to catch on here, there are a (very) few shapers doing their log, longboard and fish things. Of course all this can change in the time it takes you to turn this page; Swedes being Swedes and not far behind on anything really. Surfing, or to be more precise, knowing when to surf, in Sweden, is just not what you think or are used to. Where most surfers wait till the wind dies because it messes up the waves, especially onshore winds, Swedes love strong onshore winds. Makes them drop all and pack in the boards and suits. Here the waves die shortly after the wind does.

You'll find yourself adapting real quick and setting that inner alarm: strong onshore equals waves. There's surf on the whole coast of Sweden, but in some places it's very fickle, unpredictable and rare. In this guide we stick to the west coast (Kattegat) and only a small part of the south and east coast (Baltic Sea) of Sweden. Here you have your best shots at surf, especially in autumn. Don't forget to take your wetsuit: 3/2 or 4/3 will do you fine in summer, in winter you're going to find new love for your 4/5/6, hood, gloves and boots. If you want to learn more about Swedish surf history, the stories of Swedish surfers, and get in to the Nordic and cold water surfing vibe in general, pick up a copy of the beautiful Nordic Surfers Mag. It's in English, so don't worry, you won't get your Å-frames all tangled up. (**w.** nordicsurfersmag.com)

◆ 1
HAVSTENSSUND

◆ 2-9
GREBBESTAD

Bohuslän - Gotaland

GÖTEBORG

◆ 10-12,14-18,20-23,57
ÅSA

◇ 13,19
◆ 24

ÅSA GÅRDA BRYGGA (I)
ÅSA SÖRVIK (II)

Halland

CASTLE (III)
KÅSA (IV)
APELVIKEN (V)
◆ 25-42,44-54,58-61
VARBERG

TRÄSLÖVSLÄGE (VI)
◆ 43,55,56
TVÅÅKER

MELLBYSTRAND (VII)
FALKENBERG

BOHUSLÄN & HALLAND

Oh, Sweden's so big, did we mention that already? We said we'd restrict ourselves to surfing regions, but there you go... Driving along the Bohuslän coast we were so taken by its stunning beauty, we just had to stop and stare and meet people and add it to our guide. I'm sure you won't hold it against us when you go see for yourself. Little and bigger islands are scattered along the coast, fishing communities provide a fresh catch, the light at sunset is simply incredible. You can't resist wanting to paddle, kayak or even swim to one of the many, many islands - a choice of 8000! - having it just for yourself, or maybe you and your friends. So do, please do. We'll advise you on addresses to rent the gear; that's what we're here for. Surfing-wise, you'd need a boat, local knowledge and some luck, but we've been told it's definitely out there!

Halland's smooth coastline on the other hand, and especially Varberg, offers beaches at a wide open North Sea, just ready to provide some waves. Backed by sloping hills, rocky headlands, dunes, farmland and forests; it's all pleasance and peace, and has a happy-go-lucky holiday feel to it.

TRAVEL INFO

If you want to skip a bit of driving, coming from or going to Denmark, there's a twice-daily passenger ferry connecting Grenaa in Denmark with Varberg in Sweden, run by Stena Line. The crossing takes about 4,5 hours.

w. stenaline.com

BY AIR

There are direct flights to and from almost all major European cities from the Göteborg Landvetter Airport.

w. swedavia.se/landvetter

BY BUS

Local and national buses are organised by Västtrafik.

w. vasttrafik.se

BY TRAIN

Varberg train station (in the centre) is a stop for the train service between Gothenburg and Malmö (going on to Copenhagen in Denmark). Tickets and timetables: **w.** oresundstag.se. Local trains are organised by Västtrafik; the nearest station to Grebbestad is Tanum, from here you can take the train to Gothenburg.

w. vasttrafik.se

IN AND AROUND GREBBESTAD

There's a good chance the oysters, prawns or lobster you'll find on menus throughout Sweden were landed in the pretty fishing village of Grebbestad. The vast number of daytrippers, vacationers, seafood lovers and island-hoppers increases the Grebbestad community of some 1500 folks by a zillion-fold in summer, and still its surroundings manage to appear tranquil like a Zen temple. But everyone we spoke to agreed every season offers something special to the place. Marcus Holgersson, owner of outdoor company Skärgårdsidyllen, lives with his family on a sloping seaside hill, with a view over the archipelago. He almost convinced us to stay to witness the magical winter landscape and its silence, paddling a kayak along the many rocky islands. It's just the winter days are oh, so short Marcus… And there's still much to do, still much to see!

Tourist office at Nedre Långgatan 48, 457 72 Grebbestad.

TO DO

◆

Keep an eye out for 'A Taste of Sweden' certificates in restaurants, eateries and farm shops. It ensures you that your chosen place offers sustainable, west Swedish products based on seasonal local produce.

Familiarise yourself with eating seaweed, not only tasty but extremely healthy and wholesome. The Grebbestad archipelago is known for being rich with seaweed. Just north of Grebbestad, Linnea and Jonas of **Catxalot** (**1**) offer workshops and activities related to seaweed. Go on a seaweed safari, learn when and how to harvest it sustainably, and of course, how to cook and prepare the wild-growing sea delicacies. In their shop they have a choice of seaweed for sale. For Linnea and Jonas it's all about 'sea, weed and love', we like! Open all year, in winter one day a week, usually Saturday. No set hours though: "If we're out foraging somewhere then we're closed until we come back."

a. Sjövägen 60, 457 73 Havstendssund
t. +46 709 147 299
w. catxalot.se

The super friendly, and energetic Ingela and Marcus from **Skärgårdsidyllen** (**2**) (meaning idyllic archipelago) offer kayak and SUP rental, and courses. You can either hire a kayak and go on a mini-holiday, hopping from island to island for a few days and camping out on one of them, or book a guided archipelago tour along empty islands, exploring the coastline. All equipment, including a tent, can be rented. The guided tours can be combined with oyster tastings, or maybe you prefer paddling at sunset. Whether you're a first-time paddler or advanced kayaker wanting to take it to the next level, Ingela and Marcus offer courses, such as safety courses, being able to rescue, or work on your roll and paddling technique. Then there's the 'Kayoga': combining kayak and yoga. You paddle out to one of the deserted islands, where you enjoy an open-air yoga class, nice! Ingela and Marcus do offer so much more, like accommodation. They are a great source of information on the area, and work with a lot of other local people offering outdoor activities, like walks. Open all year, just mail or call in advance to make an appointment and all can be arranged.

a. Grönemadsvägen 73, 457 95 Grebbestad
t. +46 702 667 080
w. skargardsidyllen.se

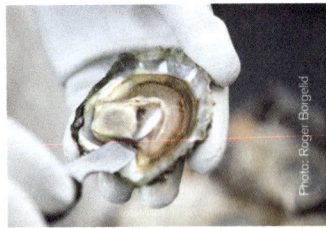

Fishing is on your wish list? There's hardly a better place to do just that than here in the waters surrounding Grebbestad. **Everts Sjöbod (3)** organises fishing trips from Grebbestad. Your catch will depend on the season, and upon return will be cooked at their boathouse. Or you can join an oyster safari. To top it off, you can end your day spent at sea warming up in one of their wood-burning bath barrels. Open all year.

- a. Grönemadsvägen 61,
  457 95 Grebbestad
- t. +46 706 856 363 / 706 725 208
- w. evertssjobod.se

EAT/DRINK/HANG OUT

♦

Restaurang Telegrafen (4) is located in what used to be a telegraph station (for those old enough to remember what a telegraph is). Their chef's not only creating meals and menus, you'll also see his art and furniture displayed throughout the restaurant, together with bits and bobs and collected memorabilia of a travelling life. In summer you can expect live music or art venues. They have a fine selection of wine and like their food to be, as much as possible, locally produced. Open from March to December. ♦€♦ ♦€€♦

- a. Nedre Långgatan 28,
  457 72 Grebbestad
- t. +46 5251 0167
- w. telegrafen.info

Sjögrens i backen (5) is one of those recommendations that we heartily agreed to check out. This café and bakery in Grebbestad's been in the Sjögren family for generations. We bet they tried to outdo each other in baking good, better, best. Today it's Kicki Sjörgen running the baking show. Besides your daily bread the place serves coffee with finger-licking good pastries and sandwiches. Open all year. ♦€♦ ♦€€♦

- a. Nedre Långgatan 34,
  45 772 Grebbestad
- t. +46 5251 4040
- w. sjogrensibacken.se

In the midst of all the green you'll find the red wooden cabin that houses **Falkeröds Trådgärdscafé och Creperié (6)**, the garden café and crêperie. A great place to go with the entire family, especially when it's sunny and warm, since they have a big garden and all sorts of games available. Here's your chance to learn to play Kubb, a traditional game involving wooden blocks that have to be thrown over. Well, that's the very short version of it; the game itself can take well over an hour depending on your, and your opponents', baton throwing skills. On the menu: galettes and -obviously - crepes, waffles, sandwiches and pastries. Open from May to September.

♦€♦ ♦€€♦

a. Falkerödsvägen 8, 457 72 Grebbestad
t. +46 705 513 043
w. falkerod.se

SHOP
♦

Since you're in Scandinavia aka Outdoor Heaven, you might as well go shopping at the gates. One of the largest sports outlet stores of the Nordic regions is right here in Grebbestad. At **Sportshopen (7)** you'll find all the clothes, gear and additional (outdoor) sports items you weren't even dreaming of. Sportshopen must've realised it all can be a bit overwhelming. So they've added a restaurant to settle down, and a bungee trampoline and a skate ramp in order to lose some of that energy that comes with too much excitement. Open all year, activities in summer only.

a. Rörvik 1, 457 95 Grebbestad
t. + 46 5254 4400
w. sportshopen.com

SLEEP
♦

Edsviks (8) is a large family friendly campsite, located at a calm Skagerrak inlet. They have pitches, whitewashed wooden beach cottages and cabins for rent. There's a playground for children.

a. Norra Edsvik 2, 457 95 Grebbestad
t. +46 5251 0394
w. edsvik.nordiccamping.se

From houses to studios or fishermen's cottages, **Skärgårdsidyllen (9)** have a choice of accommodation. They're not the owners of every accommodation but the representatives, and they do a very good job to make sure you're well taken care of. Open all year.

♦€♦ ♦€€♦ ♦€€€♦

a. Grönemadsvägen 73, 457 95 Grebbestad
t. +46 702 667 080
w. skargardsidyllen.se

IN AND AROUND ÅSA

Åsa is not an archetypal kind of town. You know; with a square, church, or at least a city centre. It's more like a settlement, stretched out between forests and beaches, where people like to live with a bit of space surrounding them. "In Åsa, we like the quieter and simpler life," we were told by locals, Göran Sivertsson and Margareth 'Maggie' Engstrom, who were friendly enough to show us around and share their knowledge of this piece of Sweden's coastline. Maggie and Göran are top Swedish SUP racers, who up till recently ran the surf and SUP school 102 (now under the name Surfskjulet). Maggie's competed and won several international races, Göran's also an avid surfer, and partner of a worldwide surf camp company. Between the two of them they know a thing or four about the ocean, boards, waves and determination.

Going around town can take from half an hour up to a day, depending on who you bump into. It seems everyone knows everyone and there's always time to share some news or make inquiries about the family, health or work. What it comes down to, you wouldn't mind hanging around here a bit, and if surf conditions are right, you just might. There are forested areas, quiet beaches and every other shop or restaurant is a good choice. With not many to choose from, that's easy then, isn't it? Activities though, are plenty and the beautiful environment's the perfect place for a bit of athletic exploration.

Tourist office at Stora Badviksvägen 10 (at the Åsa Camping and Havsbad).

TO DO

◆

Surfskjulet (**10**) (formerly known as 102) offers SUP and surf lessons, rental of surf and SUP boards, SUP yoga, SUP down-winders and island tours. So, choose from the many options and afterwards you can sit back and enjoy the sunset from their garden café. Closed in winter.

a. Hamnvägen, 439 52 Åsa
t. +46 300 569 300
w. surfskjulet.se

The biking and kayaking options in and around Åsa are numerous. Jan Ifverström of **Åsa Marint och Fritid** (**11**) wants to share his love for the way cycling through nature or gliding your kayak along the water's surface calms the mind. You see things, discover more, and experience the stillness. He rents out bicycles and kayaks with the option to drive and pick you up at start and end. There's a wide range of bicycles, from touring and mountain bikes to bicycle trolleys and additional children's seats. Open all year.

a. Åsa Stationsväg 24, 439 55 Åsa
t. +46 733 442 433
w. asamarintochfritid.se

The **Kattegattleden** (**12**) is a cycling route that runs 370 km along the coast between Helsingborg and Gothenburg, passing Åsa and Varberg. You don't have to bike the whole 370 kms to experience its beauty: the route's divided into 8 stretches, along which you'll find bicycle rentals and services. And lots to admire, wonder about, amaze, take photos of and enjoy of course! On the kattegattleden website or at local tourist offices you'll find maps, and addresses en route to grab a bite or stay overnight.

w. kattegattleden.se

The island and lighthouses of **Nidingen** (**13**), sit some 70 kms off the coast of Åsa. With its tiny measurements, only 1 km long and about 300 m wide, it's caused grand havoc amongst ships over the years, due to its bigger underwater reefs. The island is a nature reserve and bird sanctuary, and is especially beautiful in spring. You'll find salt-loving plants such as orache and sagebrush, which is a pretty rare find in northern Europe. The island's lighthouses are the oldest of Sweden, lit for the first time as far back as 1624. In 1832 the first was replaced and 2 stone towers were built instead. The 2 lighthouses had no use any more when a third modernised lighthouse was built in 1945. But they're still there and you can visit them. And you can stay in the former lighthouse keeper's house. To get to the island you have to book a daytrip or stay the night at the keeper's house, which now is part of the Gottskär Hotells. A RIB will take you out, while you keep a close eye at sea for seals and tumblers. They're regulars at the waters surrounding the island. Open from May to September.

w. gottskarhotell.se

EAT/DRINK/HANG OUT

◆

Gårda Brygga (14) kiosk and lounge bar is the garden café belonging to the Surfskjulet SUP and surf school. You don't necessarily have to take part in one of their activities; you can just step into the garden and hang out on their big terrace, overlooking the sea, harbour and some islands. There's not a big choice on the menu, but it changes daily and consists of fresh home-made good stuff. They also have tasty shakes and juices. Closed in winter. ◆€◆

a. Hamnvägen, 439 52 Åsa
t. +46 300 569 300
fb. Gårda Brygga Kiosken

Although the competition is small, bakery **Åsa Hembageri (15)** wins with flying colours. Their home-made pastries, cinnamon buns, gluten-free bread, and their speciality: mousse cakes. Mousse as in raspberry, chocolate, strawberry. Yum. Open all year. ◆€◆

a. Stenviksvägen 2, 439 53 Åsa
t. +46 340 651 039
a. asahembageri.se

For such a small place, Åsa has some real gems. **Watson The Corner (16)**, run by a couple of super friendly ladies, serves great salads, juices, vegetarian dishes and sells colourful kitchen and household ware, tea, marmalade, granola, sweets and honey. The food's delicious, which you can also take away, they have cosy corners to sit and admire all the brightly coloured array of art, lamps, and furniture surrounding you. If for any reason you need to uplift your mood, go visit Watson The Corner. Open all year, daily in summer, weekends only in winter. ◆€◆ ◆€€◆

a. Varbergsvägen 1788, 439 54 Åsa
t. +46 709 419 177
w. watsonline.se

Next door to Watson sits another mood enhancing place: the **Åsa Glasscafé (17)** ice parlour. Choose from 36 flavours, either in scoops or a milkshake. Since you usually eat ice-cream on sunny days, luckily the café comes with a terrace. Open from Easter to October. ◆€◆

a. Sörviksvägen 3, 439 54 Åsa
t. +46 729 622 781
w. åsaglasscafe.se

At Åsa's white sand beach Vitasand you'll find **Strandbaren Åsa Vitasand (18)**. With not many other beach bars around, and a campsite as their neighbour, it's a popular place with both locals and tourists. They're famed for their fish and shrimp soups, in summer at weekends they have a BBQ buffet and live music. Even on weekdays, no matter if the weather's a spoilsport, they'll have some entertainment on the menu like music quizzes or singalongs. Open from June to August. ◆€€◆

a. Badviksvägen, 439 54 Åsa
t. +46 705 194 715
w. strandbaren.se

EAT/DRINK/HANG OUT

◆

Campervans: you can park and stay for a small fee in the harbour at Gårda Brygga, with a view over the sea. No facilities, except a toilet. Open all year. ◆€◆

a. Hamnvägen 13, 439 52 Åsa

Stay in the former lighthouse keeper's house on the island of **Nidingen** (**19**). The house-turned-into-hotel and surrounding buildings that were used for storage and workshops sleep up to 22 people. Your stay includes transport by RIB, the accommodations are self-catered. Contact the Gottskär Hotell to book an overnight stay. Open from May to September. ◆€€◆

t. +46 3006 0089
w. gottskarhotell.se

Åsa Camping & Havsbad (**20**) is a large campsite at the Vitasand beach and within walking distance from restaurants, shops and activities. They have pitches and cabins for rent. Open from April to September. ◆€◆

a. Stora Badviksvägen 10, 439 54 Åsa
t. +46 340 219 590
w. asacamping.se

Freadals Trädgårdscafé B&B (**21**) is one of those places you want to stay longer than just a few days. Their enclosed garden is a green oasis, the renovated farm and stables super cosy. And, being Scandinavian, there's a sauna and a jacuzzi. Yay! At the weekends their café is open for snacks and coffee. Open all year. ◆€€◆

a. Näsbergsvägen 22, 439 55 Åsa
t. +46 340 656 652
w. freadalsgard.com

A very nice concept is set up by **Löftadalens Folkhögskola** (**22**). They operate as a residential school for the rest of the year, as a bed & breakfast during the summer holidays. The big glass windows in the communal lounge offer an unspoilt sea view, as do some of the rooms. You can choose private rooms or shared (family) rooms. And a perk for some: the breakfast buffet also has gluten-free and vegetarian options. Open in summer. ◆€◆ ◆€€◆

a. Folkhögskolevägen 19, 430 31 Åsa
t. +46 340 581 800
w. loftadalen.fhsk.se

Rågelund Camping (**23**) is a small campsite right by the sea, just a few kms south of Åsa, at the beach of Rågelund. Rågelund is a long sandy beach, with shallow waters, so safe to go with little children. It's also a popular spot for kitesurfing when the wind's strong. They have pitches and cabins for rent. Open from May to August. ◆€◆

a. Bollebygdsvägen 14, 439 61 Frillesås
t. +46 703 401 134
w. visitkungsbacka.se

IN AND AROUND VARBERG

It took us some time to acknowledge the charm of Varberg. Maybe something to do with the industrial zone and train tracks separating beach from town. But once it settled in (its charm), it settled in. And in the near future the whole city will have a makeover. We were told the train tracks will go underground, the industrial zone be moved and a lot will change for the better. But until then, Varberg's pretty cool as it is. Lots of things happening, especially in summer, great places for coffee, beer, food and shopping, open-minded people and beaches galore.

There's an undeniable surf vibe in Varberg and its near surroundings - surf anything, as in kite, wind, wave. The city's always had a strong connection to the sea. As a shelter against enemies coming from sea, and from the 19th century up until now, it's known for its spas and bathhouses. The two oldest are still in use, the 'hot' bathhouse (1925) and the iconic 'cold' bathhouse Kallbadhuset (1903), sitting on stilts above the sea.

Tourist office at Västra Vallgatan 39 (in the centre near Brunnsparken).

TO DO

Hallifornia is a big, big annual summer festival in Varberg celebrating Halland's seaside culture. Beside all kind of water sports, surfing, SUP, kite and wakeboarding, there's skating, yoga, dance and of course food and music - it's a festival after all! Testing, contests, workshops, demonstrations and more are held at various festival locations at the beach and in the city centre. The festival lasts 3 days and is always held in week 29, so that's usually the third week of July.

w. hallifornia.se

On **Surfer's Day**, every year during the first weekend of July, Surfers Center Varberg lets you test all sorts of surfing gear and boards.

a. Tångkörarvägen 17, 432 54 Varberg
t. +46 725 254 176
w. surferscenter.se / surfers.se

Hiking through the forests surrounding **Borrås Skåra gorge** (**24**) is pretty relaxing, away from the hustle and bustle of town and people, a bit mysterious and gives you a view of all surrounding forest, fields and seaside landscape. The gorge isn't impressively deep with 10 metres, but the big round rock hanging between the walls is quite surreal. Although there are signs leading up to the gorge, you'll hardly meet a soul out there. Directions: drive along the E20 between Åsa and Varberg, take Exit 56 and follow the signs.

Not sure whether there are more birds or birdwatchers visiting the **Bird Visitor Center Getteron (25)** on a yearly basis. But nevertheless, it's worth visiting if you want to learn about the flora, fauna and the way the surroundings of Varberg shaped and formed in a cultural and geological way over the years. Open all year, during the winter months only on Friday, Saturday and Sunday.

a. Getterövägen 2A, 432 93 Varberg
t. +46 3408 7510
w. getteron.com

Do as all Varberg's folks do and stroll, walk, jog, bike along Varberg's **promenade (26)**, all the way from the Kallbadhuset near the city centre to Äpelviken beach to the south. It's not a biggie, only 2,5 kms, but it's nice in any weather really, stormy, windy, or warm and sunny. It's not a straight line, it meanders along the water's edge, rounding corners, going ever so slightly uphill and downhill, passing shrubs, green hills, the Varberg Fortress and beaches.

The iconic **Kallbadhuset (27)** sits on its stilts above the sea, and has done since 1903, years into Varberg's fame as a wellness destination. Before the current bathhouse was built, it had already been destroyed by storms twice. Still standing strong and very much active, you can go here, have a swim in the cold sea and warm up in their sauna. Then have a coffee and stare out over the ocean with glowing cheeks and tingling fingers and feet, reminiscing over the fact that people have been doing the very same thing for over a hundred years and felt exactly the same as you do now. Open all year on Wednesday and at weekends.

a. Otto Torells Gata 7, 432 44 Varberg
t. +46 3401 7396
w. kallbadhuset.se

There's a large **skate ramp (28)** next to the car park near the train station, not far from the city centre. Play, play, play, and on Thursday afternoon, make room for the girls: this is when it's girl's only! Yeah baby girl, yeah.

If it's raining, or you want to have more options than just the one ramp, check Varberg's **indoor skatehall (29)**. You'll have 280 square metres with street and mini bowls to do your thing. Open all year.

a. Tingsgatan 12, 432 45 Varberg
fb. Varbergs Skateboardklubb

You'll notice pretty soon that - besides surfing - SUP and yoga are the next big thing in Varberg. Sometimes it's just SUP, or only yoga, and then of course there's doing yoga on a SUP. Here are some mighty fine choices to get lean, long and strong:

Supcoachen (**30**) is located opposite the Kallbadhuset, adding a bit of nostalgic feel to your workout. They offer SUP yoga classes, a 60-minute experience of yoga and meditative paddling. Another experience on a SUP is their 3-hour tour at sea in cooperation with Getterö boats. During this tour a boat takes you out to the Getterön peninsula and you'll paddle along its nature reserve. There's a slight chance of being accompanied by seals. Open (by reservation) from May to September, and daily in July and the first week of August.

- **a.** Otto Torells Gata 7, 432 44 Varberg (at the beach opposite Kallbadhuset)
- **t.** +46 709 665 368
- **w.** supcoachen.se

Himmel och Jord (**31**) (Heaven and Earth) has their yoga studio in the centre of town. Courses, workshops and drop-in classes available, with a choice of Yin yoga, Yoga Flow and the option to book a yoga massage. Open all year.

- **a.** Borgmästaregatan 2, 432 41 Varberg
- **t.** +46 761 366 880
- **w.** himmelochjord.com

And then there's **Juice o Yoga** (**32**)! As the name implies, there are juices and smoothies, freshly prepared, and there's yoga. All to be enjoyed in the open air, surrounded by birch trees, the sound of the ocean and the peaceful vibe that comes with it. This lovely, summer only, pop-up yoga shala and juice bar is the brainchild of Malin Palm. Returning to Sweden after a 4-year stay in Australia, the fear of getting bored made her come up with this plan.

An outdoor yoga studio, a place to get together, a place to enjoy a juice or coffee in the sun or shade, and hang around all day if you like. The idea came from working in a juice bar in Australia for some time where students of the opposite yoga studio came round after class. You'll find Juice o Yoga in Kärleksparken, the little park between the Varberg Fortress and Kåsa beach. Yoga classes are held 4-5 days a week, with either Malin or a guest teacher, mostly at 08:30 hrs in the morning. They provide yoga mats, blocks and blankets. A class is 100 kr (10 €), show up a few minutes before, no need to make reservations beforehand. Every Sunday there's kids yoga class at 11:00 hrs, free or on donation. Sometimes there are events where all money collected from yoga class goes to a street kids charity in Bali called YKPA. The café's open every day. Oh, and did you notice, their name in short spells JoY... Open from June to August (unless it's crazy windy, which in Sweden means there are waves, so they'll all be out surfing!).

- **a.** Kärleksparken, Ringvägen 130, 432 52 Varberg (along the promenade)
- **t.** +46 734 401 518
- **w.** juiceoyoga.se

Somewhat south of Varberg, **Kajplats Balans** (**33**) offers a fusion of yoga sorts, such as Hot Yoga and Hatha yoga, all in one class. From their studio you have a view of the ocean. Rather be even closer to the water? Join their SUP yoga classes. Drop-ins welcome.

- **a.** Strandbackavägen 136, 432 74 Träslövsläge
- **t.** +46 737 057 696
- **w.** kajplatsbalans.se

If you've got some jumpy youngsters in the back of your car, let them have a go at the **Bounce Camp (34)** trampoline park in Träslövsläge, just outside Varberg. The park has 5 trampolines and a large foam pit. Kids may have all the fun, but why not join them, it's said to be a great workout! Open all year.

a. Nätvägen 5, 432 74 Träslövsläge
t. +46 727 400 023
w. bouncecamp.se

EAT/DRINK/HANG OUT
◆

Smack in the middle of the town centre sits the lovely **Kassett Kaffe Etc (35)** in a late 1700s building. The 'Kassett' in the name refers to owner Cecilia Vennsten's singing career and hours upon hours in her youth spent with her cassettes and recorders in front of the radio and television. Her many cassettes on the wall on entering the café are proof of that. Stepping into the first room of the café you'll soon find out what the 'Kaffe Etc' stands for. Oh boy, there's coffee indeed! In bulk, or small packages, blends from all over the world. In the en suite room you can set yourself and your company down for some mighty fine 'fika' - time spent with friends over coffee and sweets. Best you stay the whole afternoon, so you can order multiple times. The choice of baked goods, all sorts of coffee and tea is too good to leave at just one order. And by the time you want to leave, settle the bill, see if you can resist all the other goodies you can shop for, like books, chocolate or home decorations, some clothes even. Our absolute favourite in town. Open all year. ◆€◆ ◆€€◆

a. Torggatan 11, 432 41 Varberg
t. +46 340 692 980
w. kassettvarberg.com

At Varberg's largest beachfront, Apelviken, are a few of the city's nicest (and best) restaurants. Obviously they all have a perfect view over the ocean, so now we got that clear, let's talk some details:

Brittas Strandveranda (36) is a lively place, at almost any hour of the day, but especially around lunchtime. Easy going, good vibes and hearty food, anything else? Big sunny terrace perhaps? Check! Open from April to September. ◆€€◆

a. Tångkörarvägen 2, 432 54 Varberg
t. +46 703 223 611
w. brittasveranda.se

BBQ restaurant **John's Place** (**37**) is somewhat of a household name in Varberg and beyond. Over the 25 years he's owned the place, Dorthe Florin has made locals and visiting guests return to his restaurant over and over, no matter what the trend, or the flavour of the day is. In summer the terrace serves as an extension of the restaurant, a canvas roof providing shade from the summer sun. In winter a large fireplace warms the place. As does the charcoal grill, where your food's prepared with lots of tender loving care and no-nonsense. And the John in John's place is the name of the former owner, Dutchie Jan Bakker. As Dutch do when abroad, they adapt their names to something all people can pronounce, hence John. Open all year. ♦€€♦

a. Tångkörarvägen 4, Apelviken,
432 54 Varberg
t. +46 3401 0903
w. johnsplace.nu

You can hardly miss the big 1967 British double-decker bus housing **Le Bistro Roulant** (**38**), run by the same owners as Brittas. Its location at the large car park next to the beach couldn't be more convenient. Whether going to or coming from the beach, before or after a surf, a swim, a day of sunbathing, playing, building sandcastles or hiking with a gale force wind in the back, sit on deck inside (done up real nicely in a vintage, beachy manner), outside, or order a take-away sandwich, cooling drink, or coffee. No need to dress up, it's the beach remember! Open in summer from June to August. ♦€♦ ♦€€♦

a. Tångkörarvägen, Apelviken parking,
432 54 Varberg
t. +46 727 002 920
fb. Le Bistro Roulant

We were given the word on Majas by many, usually with a reference to their live concerts and good atmosphere. But **Majas vid Havet** (**Majas by the sea**) (**39**) turns out to be a lot more than a music venue. It looks like any old warehouse from the outside, but inside it's like a barn turned into cosy and lively café with lots of tables to enjoy their delicious and mostly organic food. Open from June to August and all year for groups or special occasions. ♦€♦ ♦€€♦

a. Tångkörarvägen 15, Apelviken,
432 54 Varberg
t. +46 3401 4151
w. majas.nu

The **Surf Saloon** (**40**) is a little sparkler, you'll be in a tropical mood even on the rainiest of days due to their colourful tiki bar-like décor. Obviously there's a strong surfy vibe, and on Tuesday and Friday mornings in summer there'll be yoga chicks and geezers enjoying their healthy breakfast after class - you can join in, drop-in classes available! What else is on their menu? Cocktails, some mighty fine burgers, cakes, live music and friendly staff. Open from May to September. ♦€♦ ♦€€♦

a. Tångkörarvägen 17, Apelviken,
432 54 Varberg
t. +46 727 302 200
w. surfsaloon.se

&Olles (**41**) sits at the end of Apelviken bay. This easy going bar and restaurant is popular with locals and tourists alike, sharing tables and therefore stories, and who knows, in the end phone numbers… We like the place to bits and on top of it being a very friendly place, it's pretty good value for money too. Open from June to August. ♦€♦ ♦€€♦

a. Tångkörarvägen 10,
at the end of Apelviken, 432 54 Varberg
t. +46 709 171 528
w. olles.nu

Queue up for some scoops at **Tre Toppar** (**42**) near Varberg's fishing harbour. While waiting your turn you can try choosing from their 60 different flavours of ice cream. Open every weekend in March and daily from April to September. ♦€€♦

a. Storgatan 2, 432 75 Träslövsläge
t. +46 340 671 230
fb. tretoppar.se

On your way down south from Varberg, and in need of a coffee, sweet treat or still looking for that one souvenir, money burning in your pocket? Stop by at farm cafeteria and shop **Barley Dalsgård** (**43**) in Tvååker. Set in an old barn, surrounded by green, horses, grass and flowers, you'll find they may have something of your liking, if you're into vintage stuff, local crafts or need a bit of inspiration for your home décor. Old fashioned in the best sense of the word. Open all year. ♦€♦ ♦€€♦

- **a.** Korndal 1, 432 77 Tvååker (just off the E6)
- **t.** +46 734 388 735
- **fb.** Korndalsgard

SHOP
♦

Market: Every Wednesday and Saturday in the main square of Varberg centre, with stalls selling seasonal goods like fruits, vegetables, and some local handicraft. Open all year.

Obbhultsgård (**44**) is a farm from 1752, converted by couple Lars and Kicki Lennartsson into a shop and café. They kept the old style and look. No better place to sell handpicked antiques and vintage items, but they also sell some brand new interior items and fresh flowers. Their café offers home baked goods, with seasonal flavours. And coffee of course, you won't want to miss Fika time while you're out here. On Saturdays and Sundays they serve breakfast. Open from May to September (but do check their site for updates, they're not always open on weekdays). ♦€♦ ♦€€♦

- **a.** Obbhult 13, 430 16 Rolfstorp (just outside Varberg, on the other side of the E20)
- **t.** +46 702 474 337
- **w.** obbhultsgard.se

Walking from the sea towards Varberg's centre you'll pass the old harbour warehouses, dating back from 1874. The warehouses are restored and have become a 4-storey high creative hub for the city. Several galleries and workshops are open to the public, such as **Galleri Hamnmagasinet** (**45**), which serves as a central meeting place. There are regular art and crafts exhibitions, usually exposing work from regional artists, and sometimes concerts are held.

- **a.** Sjöallén 6, 432 44 Varberg
- **t.** +46 3408 8183
- **w.** konsthallenhamnmagasinet.se

How can we not mention **Kustbageriet** (**46**)? The Seaside bakery! To name just a few treats they have on sale: organic breads, baguettes, cinnamon buns and a choice of marmalades and muesli. Of course, all made and manufactured by themselves. You'll find them near the harbour, and if you come in before 10 in the morning you can have a rich breakfast for 98 krona, serving a grand choice of their good stuff. Open all year.

a. Skeppsgatan 10, 432 44 Varberg
t. +46 340 690 300
w. kustbageriet.se

A shop we just couldn't resist: **Basement Design** (**47**). They've got unique interior items, cosmetics, and stuff you won't want to miss in your kitchen. The best thing, besides all is to die for, most items have either a story, and are ecological, organic, locally handcrafted, or all the above-mentioned. Open all year

a. Kungsgatan 31, 432 44 Varberg
t. +46 3401 6260
w. basementdesign.se

Surfers Paradise (**48**) is the largest surf shop in Sweden, going strong since 1985. You'll find them in a large warehouse just outside the centre of Varberg. They've about all and everything you need, and more, for all water sports. Their staff is friendly, but more importantly, knowledgeable, since they're all surfers and (sea)water people. You can also rent all the equipment you may need, from boards to suits.

a. Södergatan 22, 432 44 Varberg
t. + 46 340 677 055
w. surfers.se

SLEEP
◆

The grand Fortress along Varberg's seaside was built in the late 13th century, with some adjustments made in the 18th and 19th century. Its first job was obviously to protect the city from military attacks. Later in life, until 1931, the fortification was used as a prison, this time protecting the city's citizens from alleged murderers and thieves. Nowadays it houses a museum, 2 restaurants and the **Fästningens Vandrarhem** (**49**), the fortress hostel. The hostel sleeps up to 73 people in single, double and shared bedrooms. The single rooms used to be the prison cells. The basic furniture and their stone walls, now painted white, add to the character of the place. There's a shared kitchen and lounge area. Open all year. ◆€◆ ◆€€◆

a. Varberg Fortress, 432 44 Varberg
t. +46 3408 6828
w. fastningensvandrarhem.se

The rooms of **Okéns Bed & Breakfast** (**50**) are light, bright and almost all white. But the small family-run hotel's a warm and welcoming place to stay, steps away from the shops and restaurants in the centre of Varberg. Their breakfast buffet is an all-organic feast and all 4 rooms have their distinct character. Open all year. ◆ €€ ◆

a. 25 Västra Vallgatan, 432 41 Varberg
t. +46 3408 0815
w. okenshotellvarberg.se

The quaint beach cabins, **Strandhyddan** (**51**), rented out by old windsurfer and shaper Ulf Larsson are perfectly located, right at Apelviken beach. They fit the Swedish 'Lagom' - perfect simple - lifestyle: not too little, not too much, just as much as is needed. We think they also fit Ulf, he's a character: sweet but no-nonsense, full of interesting stories and history, but not bragging about it. The beach huts and the small terrain they're built on are very surfer friendly. Ulf lives right next door in his self-built house. Open from April to November. ◆€◆

a. Apelviksleden 2, 432 53 Varberg
t. +46 708 622 007
e. clssurf@tetia.com

The beach cabins and houses of **Apelvik Strand** (**52**) are a bit larger and more upscale, but also less personal and on a bigger terrain, with an ever so slight 'park life' feel to it. But again, perfectly located at the beach. The cabins sleep up to 4 people, the houses up to 8 people. Open all year. ◆€€◆

a. Surbrunnsvägen 2-8, Apelviken, 432 53 Varberg
t. +46 3408 6828
w. apelvikstrand.se

You won't be having any trouble finding a decent campsite around this area. Come to think of it... not anywhere in Sweden really! Here are just 3 suggestions we picked because of either their location, close to the beach, or because they're nice and calm.

Camping Apelviken (53) is a large campsite, at the north end of Apelviken beach. They've got pitches, cabins, and a restaurant. Open all year. ♦€♦ ♦€€♦

a. Sanatorievägen 4, 432 53 Varberg
t. +46 340 641 300
w. apelviken.se

Agrell´s Camping (54) is a small and quiet family friendly campsite with large pitches, and sea view, located some 150 metres from Apelviken beach. Open from April to September. ♦€♦

a. Ullebovägen 14, 432 53 Varberg
t. +46 3401 2054
w. agrellstugor.se

Hostel and camping **Rödlix (55)** is not exactly at the beach, but close enough. It's located in the countryside, on a farm, amid fields full of animals, approx 10 kms south of Varberg. You can either stay in the hostel, rent a cabin, stall your campervan or pitch your tent. Open from April to September. ♦€♦

a. Galtabäck 17, 432 76 Tvååker
t. +46 706 740 182
w. rodlixvandrarhem.se

At the farm lodge **Strömma (56)** you can stay in one of their 4 rooms, done up tastefully, 'rustically stylish' as they say themselves. It's a tranquil and very peaceful place in the countryside just south of Varberg. Besides the lodge they have a shop and café - serving pancakes, soups, sandwiches and sweets. Open all year. ♦€€♦

a. Strömma, 432 77 Tvååker
t. +46 702 527 425
w. strommafarmlodge.com

SURF

Since the Kattegat is only 40 metres deep, and there's no groundswell, a study of wind, wind direction, and which beach, bay, or rocky headland to surf takes a bit of time. (Forecasts for Kattegat can be checked at dmk.dk). To sum it up: your best surf circumstance is strong onshore wind and a corner to get some protection. Luckily Varberg has some avid and stoked surfers that don't mind sharing their knowledge, and even let you in on a secret or two, just as long as you don't tell, post a photo, and state exact locations. Which means all the information below can be maximised if you befriend an Åsa or Varberg surfer…

Åsa Gårda Brygga (I) is next to a harbour wall and is a right pointbreak over rocks. To get surfable waves it needs a strong S-SW wind. ◆ *All levels/rocks/easy parking/toilets.* ◆

Åsa Sörvik (II) is a beachbreak near the campsite, needs SW winds. ◆ *All levels/sand/easy parking/toilets/surf school.* ◆

Next to Varberg's Fort and protected by a harbour wall is **Castle (III)**, a good spot that doesn't work often. It needs strong S or SW wind to wrap around the harbour wall. It has a rocky bottom but you can access at the beach of the Kallbadhuset. ◆ *Advanced level/rocks/difficult parking in summer/restaurants/toilets.* ◆

SCHOOL RENTAL REPAIR

Kåsa (IV) is a small beach along the seafront promenade. It needs a strong W or NW wind, and has some protection from the headland.

◆ *All levels/sand/easy parking/toilets/campsite.* ◆

The endless bay of **Apelviken (V)** is mostly known as a windsurf and kite spot. It's a very shallow beach, perfect for beginners. Apelviken needs a S, W or NW wind. ◆ *All levels/sand /easy parking/surf school and shop/toilets/restaurants/campsite.* ◆

Träslövsläge - Läjet (VI) is a large but shallow bay, south of Varberg, needing SW wind. There's also a left point breaking over rocks next to the harbour wall that needs a strong S-SW wind to wrap around it. ◆ *All levels at beach, advanced level at point/sand and stones/ easy parking/toilets/restaurants.* ◆

There are several rocky spots that are slightly sheltered and need N winds around **Halmstad**. The long stretch of sand at **Mellbystrand (VII)** needs SW-NW wind. ◆ *All levels/sand/easy parking/surf shop/restaurants.* ◆

Next to Åsa Camping you'll find **Surfskjulet (57)**. The school's recently changed owners, from 102.se to Surfskjulet; at time of printing the info the new school isn't finished yet, but they should have surf and SUP lessons, and boards for rent.

a. Stora Badviksvägen 10, 439 53 Åsa
t. +46 300 569 300
w. surfskjulet.se

The very friendly character, Ulf Larsson of **CLS** (**58**), Custom Line Sailboards, has been around for quite some time. He's been in the shaping and repair business for 40 years, shaping custom windsurf boards first and adding surfboards and kiteboards to his shaping and repair skills later on. If you need any repair done to your board, know it's in good hands. Ulf started his career as a trainee at no other than the family Nalsh. He fixes your board AND has a good story to tell, for sure.

- a. Apelviksleden 2, 432 53 Varberg
- t. +46 708 622 007
- e. clssurf@tetia.com

Surfskolan (**59**) offers kitesurfing, SUP and surf lessons in Varberg, but depending on the wind they also drive towards Österlen in Skåne. Besides lessons and rental you can join a SUP fitness, or SUP yoga class.

Open from April to October.
- a. Tångkörarvägen 2, Apelviken 432 54 Varberg
- t. +46 707 986 522
- w. surfskolan.se

Fahlén (**60**) have a surf shop in Varberg and a surf school at Apelviken beach. They offer lessons and courses in surf, kite, windsurfing, and SUP.

- a. Birger Svenssons Väg 38, 432 40 Varberg (shop)
- a. Tångkörarvägen parking, Apelviken, 432 54 Varberg (school)
- t. +46 3408 3750
- w. fahlensurf.se

You can't miss **Surfers Center** (**61**), smack in the middle of Apelviken, next to the Surf Saloon. Surfers Center is a shop and school providing lessons in SUP, surfing and windsurfing. For the surf courses they pick the right circumstances, you get a message when the conditions are good. They also offer SUP tours. They've been around over 20 years and happily share all their ocean experience. There's a small skate ramp in front of the shop, free to use. Open from May to August.

- a. Tångkörarvägen 17, 432 54 Varberg
- t. +46 725 254 176
- w. surferscenter.se

Photo: Mathieu Turcis

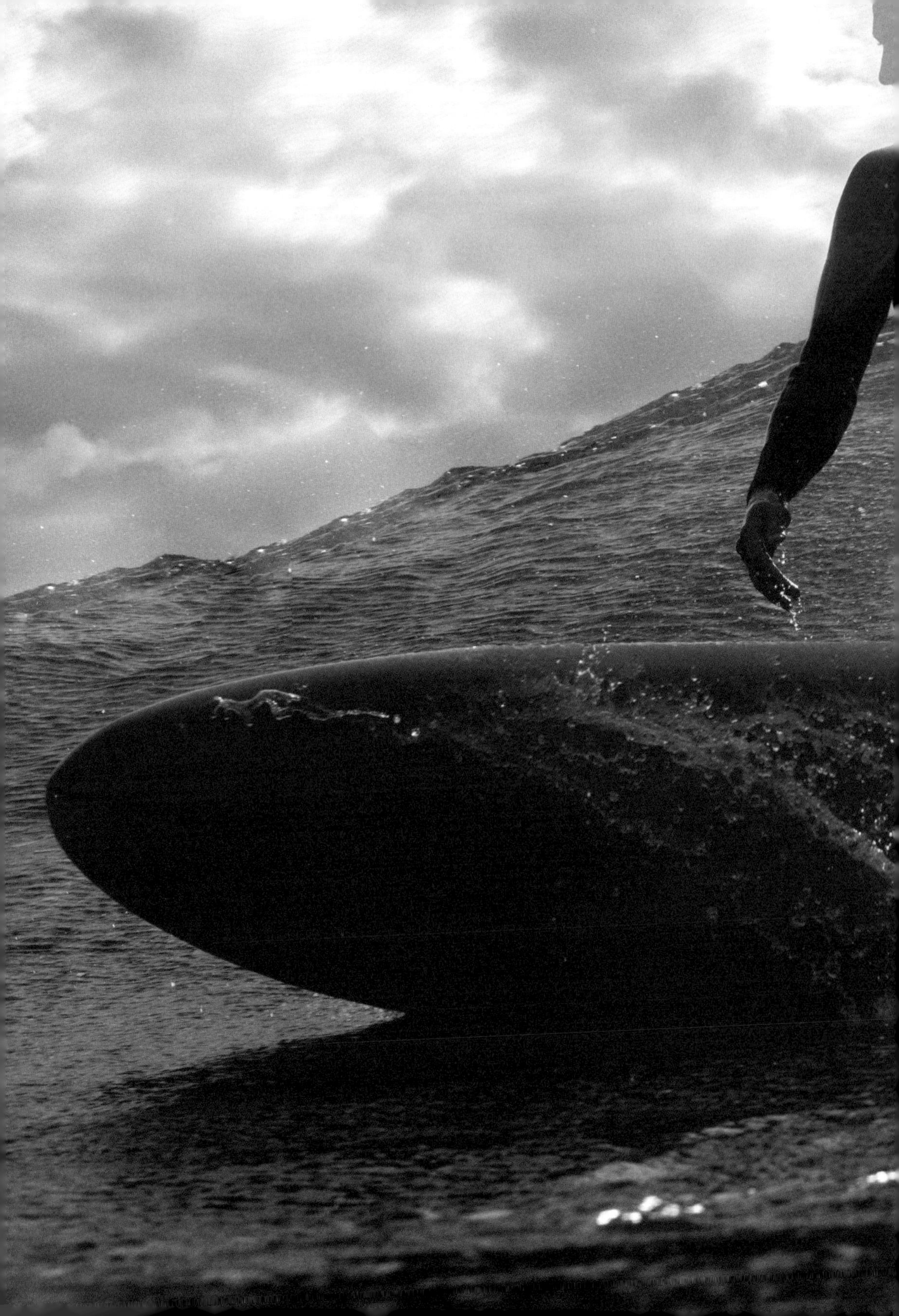

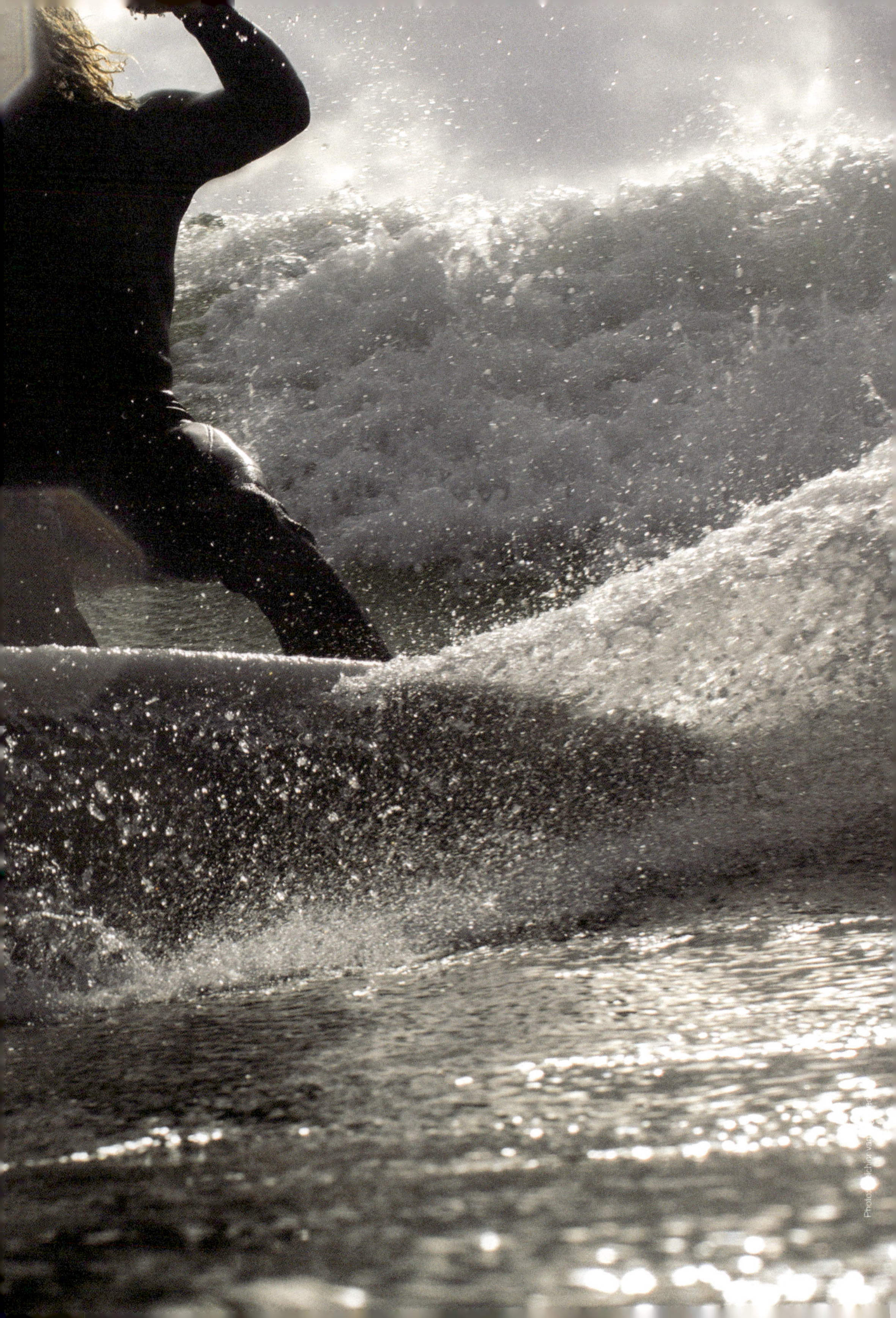

MELLBYSTRAND

SKOTTORP

BÅSTAD

1,2
VÄXTO

Skåne

◆ 15
FÖRSLÖV

MÖLLE
(1)
◆ 3,5-13,20-23,34,35
MÖLLE
◆ 4,18,19
ARILD
◆ 16,24   ◆ 17
SKÄRET

◆ 27,31-33
JONSTORP

ÄNGELHOLM

◆ 14,25,26,29,36
HÖGANÄS

◆ 28
VIKEN

HELSINGBORG

HELSINGØR

Denmark

◆ 30
LUND

SKÅNE

Sweden's southernmost province offers all a seaside lover could wish for: white sandy beaches, small friendly communities, nature parks, forests, cliffs, lighthouses, art, and good food. Organic farms sell their wholesome and healthy stuff along the roadside or at their shops, there are vineyards, and wines to be tasted, galleries and potteries to be visited - just look for the signs saying 'keramik'. And, for some mysterious reason, a whole bunch of awfully good pizza places. They're the in-thing in Skåne it seems! And if you've had just about enough of farms, fields, empty beaches, and fancy a bit of an urban spark, there's the surprisingly groovy city of Malmö. There's even a bit of mystery and craziness to be found. The standing stones at Ales Stenar have a serious Stonehenge feel, and the fascinating driftwood and stone artwork Nimis near Mölle leaves you wondering what one strong-willed human being can achieve. The south and southeast coast are such a different sight. At some beaches you'd swear you can order a green curry for tea, they resemble Thai islands that much!

TRAVEL INFO

Although a car gets you everywhere, the ferry, bus and train networks in Skåne are well organised.

BY AIR

One of Europe's biggest airports, Copenhagen Airport (Københavns Lufthavn Kastrup) is so close to Malmö, and therefore used by many Swedes and tourists as their portal to Sweden. A 30-minute train ride, crossing the famous 16 km long Öresund bridge, takes you to the centre of Malmö.

w. cph.dk

BY PUBLIC TRANSPORT

Perfect train and bus connections make even remote areas in Skåne accessible, and it's allowed to take your bicycle on the train. Timetables and information on local transportation are provided by Skånetrafiken.

w. skanetrafiken.se

BY FERRY

There's a regular 20-minute ferry connection between Helsingborg in Sweden and Helsingør in Denmark.

w. scandlines.com

IN AND AROUND MÖLLE

At the far end of the Kullen peninsula sits Mölle. Oh, if ever we loved a town more in Sweden... Mölle is a sweet little seaside town, its few winding roads lined with stately 19th century houses, wooden houses, small and grand, you can dream of yourself living in, looking out over the harbour and sea. There are a handful of peachy places to eat, drink, enjoy fika, or try to befriend a local who might help you getting your hands on one of those houses. When there are no waves it's pretty hard to imagine there ever will be, but once there are and you hit the water the backdrop is a treat. Forested hills surround the small town, its scenic harbour's a busy hub and centre for tourists, locals, fishermen, sailing, kayaking and surfing water people alike. The very tip of the peninsula rises from the sea, with a scenic lighthouse on top of its cliffs and hiking paths to explore. Nearby Arild and Skåret are old fishing villages, now characterised by lavish gardens, art galleries, and cosy teashops. You may notice the lines of vines growing on the slopes of the peninsula. Some vineyards offer wine tastings, though you can't actually purchase the wine, since in Sweden alcohol can only be purchased in state owned shops.

Tourist office at Centralgatan 20, in Höganäs.

TO DO

The **Vallåsen Bike Park** (**1**) is located on the northern slope of Hallandsås, a horst with elevated areas up to 224 metres, between Halland and Skåne. The slope is used as a skiing area in winter. You can take the chairlift all the way up to the top and choose between 9 tracks to go down, with levels varying from easy-going to dare-devilish. Either take your own bike up, or rent bike and protective gear from the bike park. Open from May to October.

a. Vallåsen Skidanläggning, Yllevad 154, 312 98 Våxtorp
t. +46 5413 2600
w. vallasen.se/bike-park

Flying down the same Hallandsås ridge from a 740-metre long zipline, dropping some 70 metres, at **Kungsbygget Adventure Park** (**2**). Or perhaps catapult yourself 25 metres up in 2 seconds on their bungy rocket, why don't ya! Then there's the opportunity to go for a rodel-ride, the rodel taking you at a dizzying speed, 935 metres down through fields and forest, and have their bungy slingshot for pudding maybe? Open from April to October.

a. Kungsbygget 44, 312 98 Våxtorp
t. +46 4303 0060
w. kungsbygget.com

The **Kullaleden Hiking Route** (**3**) is a 70 km long route, part of the Skåneleden trail SL5, that takes you around the Kullen peninsula from

Helsingborg to Utvälinge. It's easy to follow only parts of it, like the route taking you from Mölle to the lighthouse (5 km) and back. This part is a moderately easy walk with some steep sections, and well sign-posted.

w. kullaleden.se

The small seaside settlement of **Arild** (**4**) nowadays is as much fishing village as it is residence for many artists. Somebody say cute? Set in a coastal nature reserve, the pastel painted houses and their gardens lined with roses are a sight for sore eyes. Same as in Mölle, the harbour seems to be the place to be. Line up for a hot dog, ice- cream or hot bun at the small cabin at the harbour, admire the hollyhocks hugging the houses, or go for a swim from the pier at the far west end of town.

Kullabergs Islandshästar (**5**) offers horse riding tours on the back of their Icelandic horses, a breed known for their gentle character. Enjoying the company of the horses, nature and views, you'll be taken along the surroundings of Mölle, at the Kullen peninsula.

a. Himmelstorpsvägen 48-7, 263 77 Mölle
t. +46 706 277 165
w. kullabergsislandshastar.com

Nimis (**6**), or 'the Royal Republic of Ladonia' is as fascinating as it is eccentric as it is brilliant. In 1980, Swedish artist Lars Vilks began creating driftwood sculpture Nimis, and in the 1990s a second one, Arx, made of concrete. That in itself isn't too extraordinary, but the site he chose to build them is a hard to reach, and therefore desolate rocky beach in the Kullaberg National Park. Somewhat north of Arild you can park your car in the forest and walk up to the 18th century farmstead Himmelstorp. From here a 2,5 km path starts into the forest and soon becomes a steeper descent - and sometimes climb - down towards the artwork. It's easy to miss the yellow 'N' painted on trees, leading you towards the beach. Although the way down is part of the adventure, for sure, climbing and walking in and around the driftwood labyrinth is downright fun and amazing. Amazing in the sense you keep asking yourself why a man would choose this place as a workshop, where did he collect all that driftwood, how many nails must he have brought every time he came down to work on his art. You won't find any answers on a leaflet at the tourist office; the art is created illegally. The county council and Vilks have battled Nimis' right of existence in court more than once. And fires have been set, even as recently as November 2016. The battles continue, even after the small site's been declared as the independent nation Ladonia, as a means to rule out Swedish authorities. You can find out how the Ladonia remoni - the republican monarchy, with a queen AND a president - came about and how to apply for citizenship on their website.

w. ladonia.org

Watch the sun set from the cliffs at **Kullens Fyr (7)**, the Kullen lighthouse. It's apparently one of the oldest lighthouse sites of Scandinavia, since there's been light here, in the form of towers and fire to electricity for over 1000 years. As the 1000-watt beam lights its way endlessly across the ocean, so will your view be: sea and sky, your eyes won't bump into anything else up until Denmark. In summer you can visit the lighthouse for a small fee.

a. Italienska Vägen 323, 263 77 Mölle
t. +46 705 822 372
w. kullensfyr.se

At the same site, the Kullaberg at the tip of the peninsula, you'll find the **Kullaberg Caves (8)**. Since the dozens of caves are situated along the shore they're easily reached by boat, but you can reach them by foot from land. The paths are steep and full of boulders, but do-able. Don't forget to bring a torch!

a. Italienska Vägen 323, 263 77 Mölle
t. +46 4234 7201
w. kullabergsnatur.se

Join **Kullabergsguiderna (9)** on a porpoise spotting trip, the small toothed whale that you could easily mistake for a dolphin. The organisation is eco-certified and with their sea safaris they try to make people aware of the beauty and importance of protecting the mammals. They also offer abseil adventures, hiking and snorkelling tours, SPS cave walks, treasure hunts and more activities in the outdoors, most of them perfectly suited for families. Open from July to August.

a. Italienska Vägen 323, 263 77 Mölle
t. +46 739 881 077
w. kullabergsguiderna.se

Maybe not the first thing that comes to mind when thinking of activities done in Sweden, but **Dykcenter Kullen Dyk Mölle (10)** let you discover the underwater world of Kullaberg with their dive courses and excursions. Open from June to August. Dive excursions are also available at the weekend during May.

a. First Camp Mölle, Kullabergsvägen 286, 263 77 Mölle
t. +46 4234 7714
w. kullendyk.nu

Biking, as is hiking, is a perfect way to discover the beautiful environment of the Kullen peninsula. You can rent bikes at Kullakajak **(12)**, Mölle Kajak & Klättercenter **(13)**, Arilds Hamnfik **(19)**, and First Camp Mölle **(37)**. An option could be to follow the Cykelns

Blå Band, a biking trail following a former train rail.

w. kullendyk.nu

Take a guided kayak, SUP, or fat bike tour with **Kullakajak (11)**. If you're not up for a guided tour, but want to go and explore on your own, they also rent out the SUPs, kayaks and fat bikes.

a. Mölle Harbour, Norra Strandvägen, 263 77 Mölle
t. +46 735 257 431 / 767 656 400
w. kullakajak.se

Mölle Kajak & Klättercenter (12) also rent out kayaks and mountain bikes, and offer courses and tours of climbing and kayaking in the surroundings of Kullaberg.

a. Italienska Vägen 6, 263 77 Mölle
t. +46 705 586 657
w. mollekajakcenter.se

Every first weekend of August the **Casseroles Circus' Food and Music Festival (13)** takes place at Mölle Krukmakeri & Café. Yes! Here's a festival we like, we dig, we can relate to: mainly young guest chefs from all over Europe come and prepare a next-level 4-5 course menu. Pick either one chef's menu, or all; you pay per menu. For drinks there are local and not so local wines and beers and for exercise there's music and dancing till the wee hours. And the next day? Go and repeat!

a. Mölle Hamnallé 9, 263 77 Mölle
fb. Casseroles Circus

In need of some smooth concrete? Check the largest skate park in northwest Skåne, **Höganäs Skatepark Kullask8en** (**14**). Located at the Kullagymnasiets skolgård, along the 111 road. Open all year.

a. Långarödsvägen 30, 263 34 Höganäs

EAT/DRINK/HANG OUT
◆

When asked where you can find **Lillaro Caf'e & Musik** (**15**) the answer is: in the middle of nowhere, or at least pretty close. A treat. A treasure. The food that's served is always heavily dependent on mood and season, and on Friday there's the Slofox - pizza baked in a wood-fire stove. Every now and then there's live music and there's always a good vibe. Enjoy your time here, either in their garden or inside, surrounded by some of their quirky decorations. You'll also find Peleka's shop here, with some unique clothes made from fine fabrics. Peleka is the brand and design from one of Lillaro's owners, Eva. Open from Easter to October, mostly Saturdays and Sundays. In July it's open from Thursday to Sunday. ◆€◆ ◆€€◆

a. Lillahultsvägen 118, 269 71 Förslöv
t. +46 4311 0782
w. lillaro.nu

You'll find **Krapperups Slottscafé** (**16**) at the Krapperup estate, a medieval castle and 16th-century manor. If the weather's fair, you can enjoy your fika or lunch in the garden. Go for a pre or post lunch stroll through the surrounding park, or join a guided walk to learn about the history of the place. Café open from June to mid-August, garden open all year. ◆€€◆

a. 13 Krapperups Kyrkovåg, 263 76 Nyhamnsläge
t. +46 4234 4800
w. krapperup.se

Flickorna Lundgren (**17**) or 'the Lundgren girls' is a bit of a household name in this area. Everybody knows it. The restaurant is family run, for some generations now, founded by 7 sisters Lundgren, back in 1938. From the minute you enter the large garden you feel like a character in a Swedish fairy tale. There's a restaurant in the glasshouse, a bakery and lots of seating places scattered throughout the garden. It's pretty big, but with an intimate feel to it just the same. Open all year. ◆€€◆

a. Skäretvägen 19, 263 72 Skäret, Nyhamnsläge
t. +46 4234 6044
w. flickornalundgren.se

You can hardly miss **Arilds Hamnfik** (**18**) the characteristic shack at Arild's harbour. Get your coffee, ice-cream, herring, cinnamon bun or their bestselling product: hot dog, and find a place along the harbour wall to enjoy. You can also rent bikes from here. Open from April to August. ◆€◆

a. Arilds Hamn, 263 73 Arild
t. +46 709 300 380
w. arildshamnfik.se

Small scale vineyard **Arilds Vingård** (**19**) offers wine tours and wine tasting at their 18th century farm. The vineyard also has a restaurant and some rooms to stay. The restaurant is open and tours are available daily in summer. ♦€€♦

a. Lillavägen 71, 263 73 Arild, Nyhamnsläge
t. +46 423 464 20
w. arildsvingard.se

Ellens Café i Ransvik (**20**) sits in a perfect spot, on a hill overlooking the ocean and remote beach of Ransvik, just outside Mölle. There's a natural swimming pool when you walk down from Ellens Café down to the sea. This beach was the first spot in Sweden where men and women were allowed to bathe together - can you imagine a time when this wasn't allowed! The café serves salads, cakes and sandwiches for lunch. Open every day in July. ♦€♦ ♦€€♦

a. Italienska Vägen, 260 40 Mölle
t. +46 423 476 66 / +722 103 013
w. ransvik.se

We simply love the **Mölle Krukmakeri & Café** (**21**). Not just for their tasteful, fresh pizzas, friendly staff and ace Syrian chefs, but the whole setting completes the joy of eating out. On the colourful terrace in the garden you're protected from the wind on colder days, and shaded from the sun on warmer days. Besides pizzas you can choose salads, home-made soup and baked goods. The restaurant is connected to the pottery shop and gallery from artist and owner, Lisa Wohlfart. While you wait for your pizza, do have a look at her fine collection of cups, plates, bowls and more. Open all year. ♦€♦ ♦€€♦

a. Mölle Hamnallé 9, Mölle
t. +46 4234 7991
w. mollekrukmakeri.se

Knafves Café (**22**) is the small café in the harbour of Mölle, where you'll meet local folks, sailors, surfers and tourists.

a. Harbour/Hamnen, 263 77 Mölle
t. +46 4234 7319
fb. Knafves Café

Never did a fire station get a better second life than **Mölle Brandstation** (**23**). Nowadays it's a restaurant with a small food shop section, selling fresh local food and other carefully selected items. Very nicely done up, with a mighty fine balance between contemporary design and decoration, and paying respect to the original details of the eye-catching building. Open daily in summer, Thursday to Sunday in low season. ♦€€♦

a. Södra Strandvägen 5, 263 77 Mölle
w. mollebrandstation.se

You won't want to take your vegetarian friend to **Holy Smoke BBQ** (**24**) in Bräcke. But if you like meat, smoked and barbecued, this is a go-to place. Good atmosphere, bit hipster-ish but not too much, friendly people. Open in summer in the weekends from 11:00 to 17:00, or sooner if they're sold out. ♦€€♦

a. Krapperups Kyrkoväg 116, 263 76 Bräcke, Nyhamnsläge
t. +46 464 277 303
w. holysmokebbq.se

'Junk Food Royal' is what **Garage** (**25**) in Höganäs puts on the menu. Most of what you can find in this sharply smart bar involves the Big Bs: beer, burgers, blues, boogie, booze and er… battoos? Tattoos: the one thing sticking out, on the arms of the bartender to the musician and clientele - not involving a B though. The bar was the idea of 3 friends with a shared passion for food, music and engines. Their travels, and meeting people from around the world left an imprint on them and Garage is an expression of just that. Expect Americano/Tex Mex food, French fries, hamburgers and even Buffalo wings, but all made with quality ingredients. Plans for the very near future involve live music events, pop-up stores and skate shows. Sounds like a perfect place to return to! Open all year.

a. Bruksgatan 36-Z, 263 39 Höganäs (next to Magasin 36 and the Saluhallen)
t. +46 424 539 456
w. garagebar.se

Next door **Höganäs Saluhall** (**26**) is a wonderful place, inspiring you to try out things, make up new recipes, bake some, smell herbs and ask how to use them. It's a restaurant and market hall in one, using and selling organic products and ingredients that are close-to-locally produced, all seasonal and fresh of course. Open all year.

- **a.** Bruksgatan 36-Z, 263 39 Höganäs
- **t.** +46 423 425 01
- **w.** hoganassaluhall.se

SHOP
◆

Kullabygdens Bakgård (**27**) has a cosy café attached to its bakery, built in a former car workshop. Get your ration of sourbread, knäckebröt, biscuits or chocolate. Open all year. ◆€◆

- **a.** Åhusavägen 38, 263 92 Jonstorp
- **t.** +46 736 647 526
- **fb.** Kullabygdens Bakgård

Tomáto, tomato, the farm shop of **Vikentomater** (**28**) has them in all shapes and sizes and colours. Besides the tomatoes, home-made ketchup and tomato marmalade, they sell some yummy Italian delicacies, and their bakery offers all sorts of breads and pastries, also gluten-free, and fika: coffee and cakes. Open al year, products depending on season.

- **a.** Rågången 41, 263 65 Viken
- **t.** +46 424 000 035
- **w.** vikentomater.se

Magasin 36 (**29**) is the third of shops and restaurants we mention here (Saluhall and Garage being the other two) that are located in an old industrial venue, just outside the centre of Höganäs. All have at least one concept in common; using or selling locally produced goods and ingredients. Here you'll find food, drinks, arts, crafts and events. Magasin sells mostly home decoration, cutlery, some clothing, shoes and linen. A bit clean and wholesome, but some surprisingly stylish items too.

- **a.** Bruksgatan 36, 263 39 Höganäs
- **t.** +46 4233 1585
- **w.** magasin36.one

Boardwalk (**30**) is a pretty and well stocked shop in Lund for all those who like the surf, skate and street lifestyle: from wearing the clothes to actually skating or surfing. So if you're here solely to check out some fancy stuff to flaunt your street swagger, that's fine, but you can also find a wetsuit, wheels, deck, board, wax AND have your board repaired!

- **a.** Stortorget 5, 222 24 Lund
- **t.** +46 703 943 980
- **w.** boardwalk.nu

SLEEP

◆

Campervans (31) can park and stay near the harbour of Svanshall, right beside the sea. From here you can hike the coastal trail up to Kullaberg. It has all the basic camper facilities. Open all year. ◆€◆

a. Hamnbacken 23 (Norra Kustvägen), 263 92 Jonstorp
w. svanshall.net

Basic but pretty and tranquil, **Bläsinge Gård (32)**, is situated on the Kullen peninsula. The old farmstead was converted into a small campsite and a hostel with 15 large rooms, the rooms sleeping from 2 up to 5 people. A commonly used kitchen and garden are well equipped to have BBQs and do your own cooking. In high season breakfast is served. Guests from the campsite can also make use of the kitchen, or the breakfast. Open in summer, or on request. ◆€◆

a. Gamla Södåkravägen 127, 26 392 Jonstorp
t. +46 4212 1413
w. jonstorp.com

Guesthouse Villa Kullaberg (33) is located between Jonstorp and Arild. The villa is a spacious and light wooden cabin, with large windows. The 2 to 4 person guesthouse opens up to Skälderviken bay and has direct access to the hiking paths of nature reserve Skåneleden. Highlight? Their sauna with ocean view, a private outdoor deck and jacuzzi under the stars. Open all year. ◆€€◆

a. Tranekärrsvägen 88, 26 392 Jonstorp
t. +46 733 613 154
w. villakullaberg.com

First Camp Mölle (35) is a family friendly campsite, some 2 km southeast of Mölle. There are pitches, cabins, a swimming pool, sauna and you can rent bicycles. Open all year. ◆€◆

a. Möllehässle, Kullabergsvägen 286, 263 77 Mölle
t. +46 4234 7384
w. firstcamp.se/molle

Falknästet (The Falcon's Nest) **(34)** must be one of the most romantic places you could ever stay. Situated close to the Kullen lighthouse, in the midst of Kullaberg nature reserve, Falknästet sits in the old watchtower of the Swedish armed forces. A round bed hangs from the ceiling, the large panoramic windows offering a view over the ocean. Wanna get married already?! Open all year. ◆€€€◆

a. Naturum Kullaberg, Italienska Vägen 323, 263 77 Mölle
t. +47 739 881 077
w. falknastet.se

Campervans (36) can stay and park near the harbour of Höganäs. There are all the camper facilities you need, a shower and toilet. Open from June to August. ◆€◆

a. Höganäs Hamn, 263 39 Höganäs

NSM

WWW.NORDICSURFERSMAG.SE

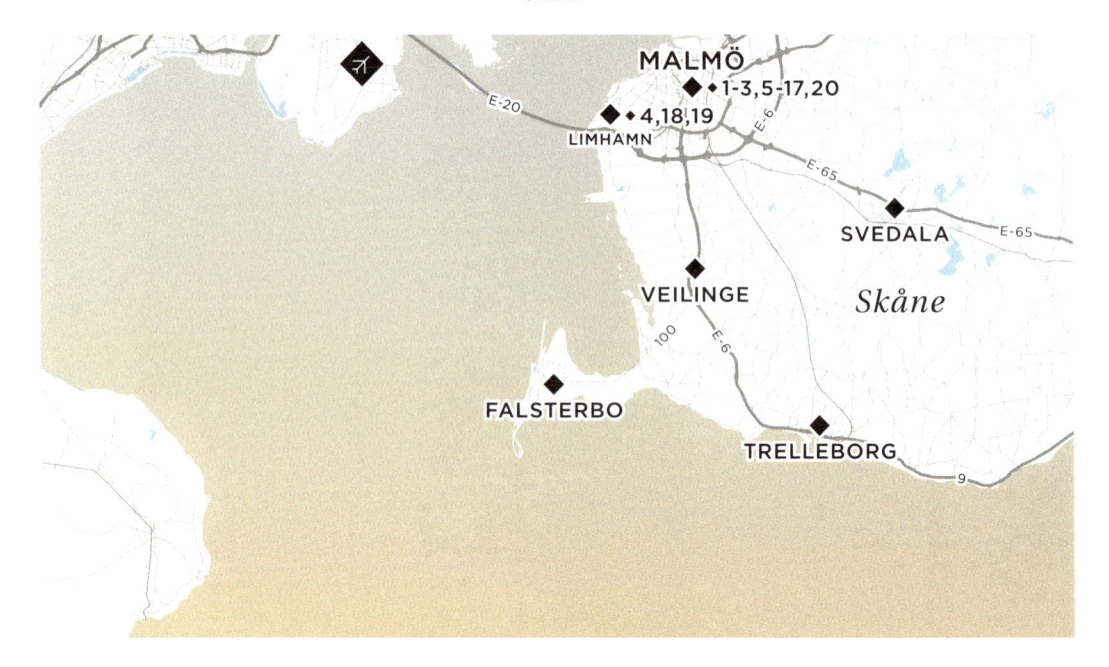

IN AND AROUND MALMÖ

◆

Malmö may not be your most obvious choice of city breaks in Sweden, obviously Stockholm's done a better job at attracting visitors and making a name for itself as a pretty cool city. We tried Malmö. It's on our surf and seaside itinerary after all. And we liked it so much we stayed on a bit and even returned to check out some more of this surprisingly fresh, easy-going and progressive city. Thanks to friendly and knowledgeable locals (tusen tack, Anna B. and Christian M.L.!) we opened our eyes and heart to the city. We learned about the Western Harbour area (Västra Hamnen), once a shipyard, now a spacious and modern area of architectural interest, with apartments, shops and restaurants relying 100% on local renewable energy. And where to find the best falafel and eastern delicacies (try the Möllevången neighbourhood!), skate parks, food halls, saunas, beaches and loads more too that, of course, we'll share with you.

Tourist office at Börshuset, Skeppsbron 2.

TO DO

◆

The city has big, really big **parks** and recreational grounds, green areas, and beaches, so even on warm summer days you can enjoy the city and a bit of sunbathing, swimming, and relaxation. There's Slottsparken, Castle Park, where you find sculptures, woodland, and the castle's mill. In the heart of the city lies Kungsparken, the King's Park. From the 3 km long beach of Ribersborg, backed by the biggest dog park we've ever seen, you have a clear view of the Öresund bridge, connecting Malmö with Copenhagen, and the Kallbadhus sitting on its stilts in the sea. Towards the city you'll see Scandinavia's tallest building, called the 'Turning Torso'. Contrary to what you'd think of a city beach, the water quality isn't poor at all, Ribersborg even displays the Blue Flag.

Travel Shop (**1**) has all sorts of bicycles for rent. They also offer guided bike and food tours. Open all year, find them at these 2 locations:

- **a.** Carlsgatan 4 (behind the old post office, opposite the Glasvasen at Malmö C), 211 20 Malmö
- **a.** Jörgen Kocksgatan 33 (400 m behind the Central Station), 211 20 Malmö
- **t.** +46 4033 0570
- **w.** travelshop.se

Malmö is skate-minded. In fact, it's one of the most skate-friendly cities in the world, it even has its own skate gymnasium (Bryggeriet). There are several **skate parks** (**2**) throughout the city. A small selection:

Indoor skate park **Bryggeriet** is one of the first in Malmö and set a standard for all following, allowing the skate scene to grow and gain respect, nationally, internationally, and from the local authorities. The park has bowls, a vert and street courses. There are special skate hours for beginners, girls-only, and, we like this: the 'Old Bastards' hours for 30+ skaters. It comes with a fully stocked shop and a café. Regularly they organise film, or other skate-related events. Open during indoor season, from September to May.

- **a.** Ystadvägen 44, 214 45 Malmö
- **t.** +46 4092 6585
- **w.** bryggeriet.org

Stapelbäddsparken outdoor skate park sits close to the Turning Torso, in the area of the old shipyard. It offers all the concrete you'll need: several bowls, a pool, a street-inspired area with metal sculptures and granite benches, a café and skate shop. Stapelbäddsparken is one of the largest skate parks in Europe. Open all year.

a. Stapelbäddsgatan 3, 211 19 Malmö
w. stapelbaddsparken.se

The smaller outdoor skate park **Sibbarp** is located in Sommervägen, at the seaside. It has bowls and a street-inspired course with bumps and corners. Open all year.

a. Sommarvägen, 216 11 Limhamn (near the Kallbadhus and the Öresund bridge)

In the same area you'll find **Malmö Wake Park (3)**, close to Västra Hamnen, the Western Harbour. A wakeboarding park with ramps and obstacles, available for all levels and ages from 8 years up. You can also rent SUPs to explore the bay that runs alongside the city. Open from May to September. Close to the Turning Torso in Västra Hamnen

a. Ribersborgsstigen 16, 211 16 Limhamn
t. +46 704 125 431
w. malmowakepark.se

Moana Malmö (4) offers SUP courses for beginners, SUP yoga, tours and workouts, and rents out SUPs as well. They're located near the Sibbarp campsite, at a quiet lagoon looking out on the Öresund bridge. Open from June to August (when weather allows), from Wednesday to Sunday, or on request.

a. Sommarvägen, 216 11 Limhamn
t. +46 706 977 348
w. moanamalmo.se

Ribersborgs Kallbadhus (5) used to be the bathhouse for the workers of the city, back in the days when Malmö was largely dependent on industry and the shipyard. The bathhouse still stands strong on its stilts at the Ribersborg bay. From here you can skinny dip in the sea and warm up in their sauna - there are 2 separate areas for men and women and 1 mixed sauna. The restaurant serves a wholesome brunch, or coffee with cakes. Open all year.

a. Limhamnsvägen, Brygga 1, 217 59 Malmö
t. +46 4026 0366
w. ribersborgskallbadhus.se

Hot Yoga House Triangeln (6) is set out to make you feel healthy and balanced. The friendly and modern studio in the centre of Malmö offers fun yoga classes for all levels, sizes and ages. Drop-in classes available, you can choose hot yoga, vinyasa, yin or hatha lessons.

a. Holmgatan 4, 211 45 Malmö
t. +46 406 188 292
w. hotyogahouse.se

If you're not sure what restaurant to choose, or which dish, snack or drink; try a food tour with **Matkaravan (7)** - meaning as much as 'food caravan'. Matkaravan's offered food walks for over 13 years, so you can bet they're knowledgeable when it comes to culinary specialities, multicultural flavours and, of course, where to find the best places to enjoy them. All guides either are or have worked as a chef, sommelier or food journalist and stylist. The walk takes about 2 to 3 hours, with 4 to 6 stops along the way at shops and restaurants, chosen for their quality and personal approach. You'll be inspired to try new ingredients and recipes at home. If you're more of a sweet tooth, try their Swedish Fika Caravan - sampling chocolate, candy, biscuits and buns with a typical Nordic flavour. And coffee of course. Available all year.

t. +46 707 344 136
w. matkaravan.se

EAT/DRINK/HANG OUT
◆

As you may notice by our list below, we love our share of vegan, vegetarian and organic food. Not always easy to find outside the bigger cities, so now we're here and it's available, we like to highlight them, 'cause we care and we-like-a-lot.

Get into the multicultural vibe of Malmö at the market square **Möllevångstorget** in the district of Möllevången. There's a daily fruit and vegetable market, the surrounding shops and restaurants offer everything from exotic goods from the Middle East to the far west. Get your falafel for less than nothing, but oh so rich in taste.

At food hall **Malmö Saluhall (8)** you'll be getting hungry, greedy, wanting more, even after you're stuffed. There's falafel, ice-cream, fresh coffee beans, Korean street food and much, much more. And bearded chefs with sharp knives, adding to the hipsterality of the place. On warm days you can choose to sit outside on one of the terraces. ◆€€◆

a. Gibraltargatan 6, 211 18 Malmö
t +46 406 267 730
w. malmosaluhall.se

Good fun, and unique to say the least, is **Boulebar Drottningtorget (10)**. It's a restaurant, yes, set in a 19th century riding school. And it's a place to play boule (pétanque), the game we thought only the French played with such passion. The menu is pretty much French bistro orientated, and their Sunday brunches are famous. Enjoyable place with a very friendly staff where you definitely can take the kids along, they won't get bored. ◆€€◆

a. Château de Cheval, Drottningtorget 8, 211 25 Malmö
t. +46 406 222 343
w. boulebar.se

Amongst many other awards, **Kafé Agnez (11)** once won the award for Malmö's Best Café. Even if it was a few years back, they're still going strong. The smell of freshly baked bread and coffee are enough to lure you in, one look at the menu and you decide to stay. Especially on warmer days it's a go-to place, sitting outside in their lovely courtyard. They serve organic and vegan hot and cold meals, have gluten-free options, raw pastries, soups, and an excellent salad buffet. Like! Closed in winter. ◆€◆ ◆€€◆

a. Agnesgatan 11, 21133 Malmö
t. +46 739 916 727
fb. Kafé Agnez

The Surf Shack (12) has, almost as expected with a name like that, burgers on the menu. But they do serve a perfect veggie alternative, made of tofu and black beans. Besides burgers you can order home-made French fries served with garlic and herbs. And don't get their regular burgers wrong either, the meat's from a local farm, free of antibiotics and additives, served with artisanal bread. Open all year. ◆€◆

a. Västergatan 9a, 211 21 Malmö
t. +46 761 764 018
w. surfshacksmashburgers.com

Lively bar and restaurant **Far i Hatten (13)** has good food, live music venues and DJ sets on their menu. On summer nights the buzz from the large terrace will certainly get your attention with the promise of a sparkling night out. Outdoor dining in the best informal atmosphere, some laid-back tunes, chatting or playing a game of, er, ping pong! Go for it, nice place, friendly people, funky settings. Open all year. ◆€€◆

a. Folkets Park, 214 37 Malmö
t. +46 406 153 651
w. farihatten.se

As to be expected, the **A·VO·KA·DO (14)** café has a lot of things avocado on their menu - bowls, smoothies, and desserts. Check this fast-but-healthy-food café if you want a quick shot of energy, a boost for your city-worn limbs, or find out if avocado goes well with a custom brewed coffee. Find the café around the corner from the Hot Yoga House's studio (same owners you see, they like it healthy). Open all year, only in the daytime. ◆€◆ ◆€€◆

a. Holmgatan 4, 211 45 Malmö
t. +46 790 694 630
w. avokadomalmo.se

Raw Food House (15) is yet another little gem of a place with their green hearts at just the right place. Even if you're not a fan of raw food, or have never had a taste of it, you should give it a try at this peaceful place. The creative manner in which the dishes are prepared, all gluten-free, lactose-free and without the use of refined sugar, will change your mind about raw food altogether. The raw food principles imply the food's not heated over 42°c to save the ingredients' nutritional values as much as possible. If you'd like to know more about it and use some recipes yourself, you can buy their cookbook. The place is fresh, friendly and has a large sunny terrace. Find them in the shopping area in the centre of Malmö. Open all year. ♦€€♦

a. Friisgatan 8, 211 46 Malmö
t. +46 401 292 00
w. rawfoodhouse.se

SHOP
♦

When Matthew Baxter started the **Red Snapper Surf Shop (16)** back in 2005, he'd been surfing in Sweden since 1996: "I wanted getting your hands on good suits, gloves and boots made easier". Quite a character, Matthew, and he's been around long enough to know a thing or two about boards, suits and quality clothing. In his shop you'll find all the essential surf gear and smart clothes, caps and accessories.

a. Friisgatan 14, 211 46 Malmö
t. +46 403 036 06
w. redsnapper.se

Skater owned, skater run and with a dedication to skating, **Streetlab Skateboardshop (17)** is one of the very few skateboard shops in Sweden. They've been around since 2001 and it's the go-to place for all your skate essentials, info on the great places to skate throughout Malmö, meeting up and chatting decks with like-minded skater folks.

a. Regementsgatan 12, 211 42 Malmö
t. +46 406 616 102
w. streetlab.nu

SLEEP
♦

Campervans (18) can park and stay overnight at the Limhamn harbour, with views of the Öresund bridge, parks, beach and the city centre within walking distance. It has all the camper facilities you need and there's a shower and toilet. Open all year. ♦€♦

a. Andelshamnen Lagunen, Vaktgatan 9, 216 13 Limhamn
w. lagunen.nu

Camping **First Camp Malmö (19)** is located on the seafront facing the Öresund bridge. There are pitches and cabins for rent, bus services to the town centre (or rent one of their bikes). The large dog park and Sibbarp skate park are within walking distance. Open all year. ♦€♦

a. Strandgatan 101, 216 11 Limhamn
t. +46 4015 5165
w. firstcamp.se/malmo

Another cheap option for a Malmö city break would be the **STF Malmö City Hotel & Hostel (20)**. Clean, friendly and smack in the middle of the centre, next door to Malmö's opera house. They have single, double and dormitory rooms. Open all year. ♦€♦ ♦€€♦

a. Rönngatan 1, 211 47 Malmö
t. +46 406 116 220
w. svenskaturistforeningen.se
/anlaggningar/stf-malmo-city-vandrarhem

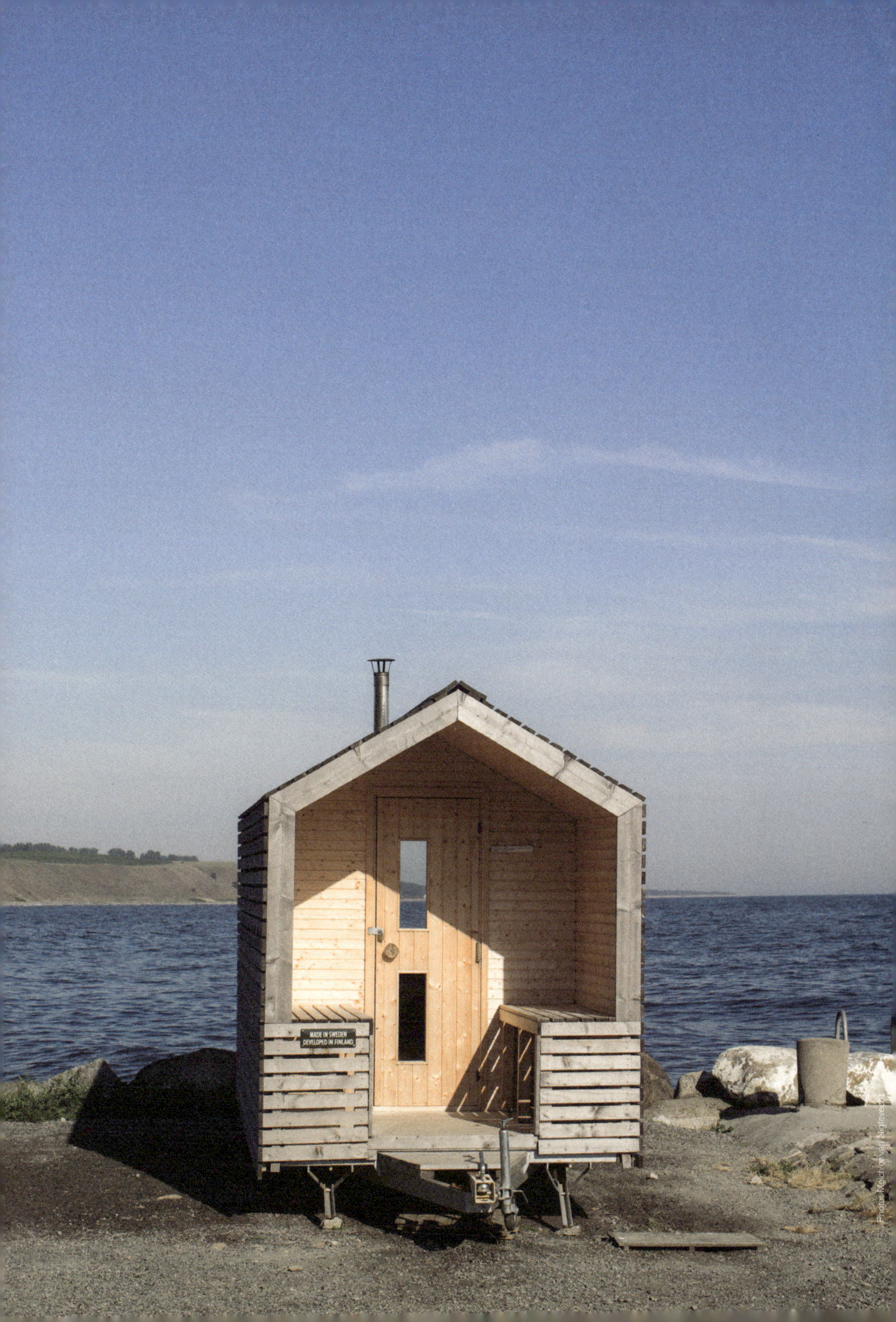

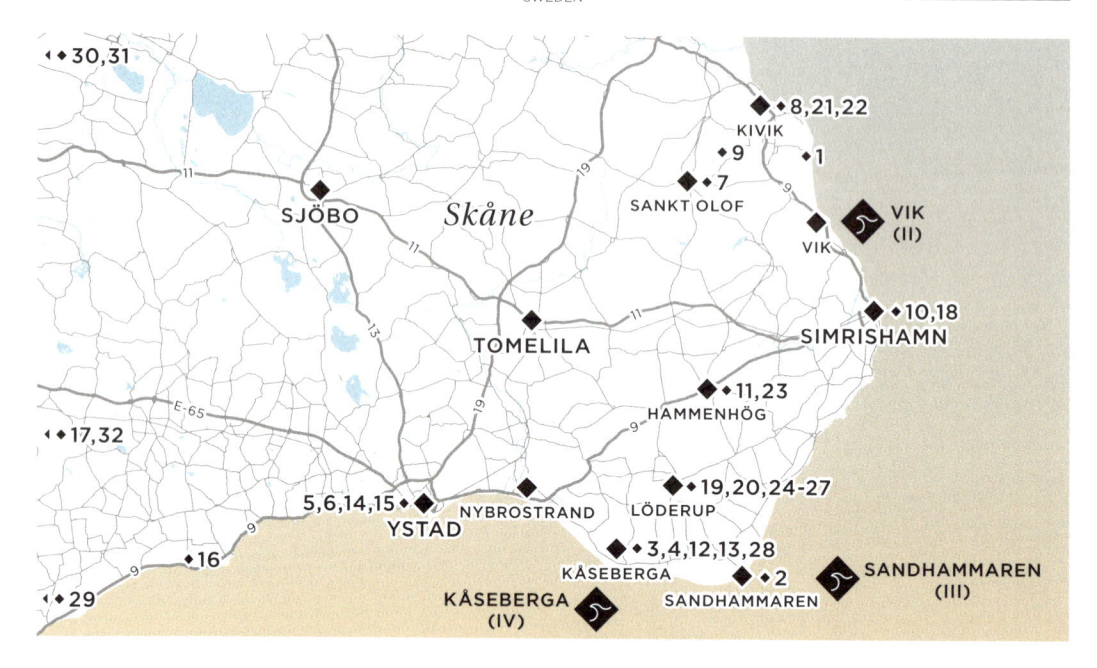

IN AND AROUND YSTAD

◆

South and southeast Skåne are quiet, open, peaceful. It's beautiful and even exotic in some parts: hilly and green, white sand beaches, a clear blue sea. Tranquil, even though the month of July and first half of August everything seems to revolve around tourism. These months the little settlements come to life, a lot of houses serving as summer family homes. The ride along coastal route Västra Kustvägen (road 9) between Ystad and Skivarp, or even further Trelleborg, is one of the most enjoyable rides in the area to get acquainted with the seaside. Ystad and Kåseberga remind us of French villages, with their woodwork houses, town squares and slow living, slow cooking, slow brewing, slow growing of crops, herbs, and grains. The fertile grounds around Vik and Knäbäckshusen make orchards produce juicy fruits. Especially apples - do try to get your hands on the locally produced cider and apple juice.

And then there's this thing. It's a Swedish thing. If you have a farm, you open up a farm shop - makes sense. If you have a pottery, you start brewing coffee and baking cakes to serve to guests that visit your pottery. You have a family house, turn it into a bed & breakfast, open up a shop and, why not, add a little restaurant or ice parlour. And everything's done with all the attention it needs, the love, the tasteful design, the elegant Scandinavian way. Got us all confuselled: should we put this shop under the Sleep section? Because they do rent out rooms in their house and serve breakfast. Put that café under Shop section? Because it does sell all kinds. Anyway, enjoy our picks, wherever they ended up, we love that the Swedes don't care about sections and labels!

Tourist office at Sankt Knuts Torg.

A little note: the island off the coast of Ystad is Bornholm. Since it's officially Danish, you'll find the info on the Bornholm Surf Farm in the Denmark chapter.

TO DO

♦

We love a good folktale, especially one involving trolls, fairies and giants. Too bad we never learned the full story of the giant that apparently lived in a nearby cave at **Stenshuvud National Park** (**1**). But he must've been Sten, since the National Park is named after him - 'Sten's head'. Either way, the almost 100 m high Stenshuvud hill and the luscious forest make the park look like the Garden of Eden; the stretch of fine white sand beneath it resembling an exotic Asian beach. Maybe you're here to check the surf, and if there's none, you might as well check out the park. There's a visitor centre that offers guided tours on Sundays throughout the year, except winter. In summer there's a tour every day. You'll learn of the biodiversity, plant life and what animals live here. But of course hiking without a guide is easy. You'll miss out on what's what, but from the top of the hill you'll have a rewarding view over the southern coastline.

a. Stenshuvud National Park, 277 35 Kivik (between Knäbäckshusen and Kivik)

Sandhammaren beach (**2**), just east of Ystad, seems endless. You think you'll go for a stroll and end up hours later, still walking along the southern cape of Sweden. Backed by dunes and forest, you can switch from shuffling barefoot through fine white sand to strolling along a shaded path between pine trees. Don't forget to size up the remarkable iron skeletal lighthouse, near the parking area at the end of Sandhammarvägen. We think it looks like a piece of art. You can visit the Sandhammaren lighthouse between June 27 and August 20.

Take in a bird's eye view of the southern coastline with **Sky Adventures** (**3**). You'll make a tandem paraglider flight, using the upward winds at the cliffs between Hammarsbackar and Kåseberge. Open all year.

a. Alesväg 5, 271 78 Kåseberga
t. +46 708 600 221
w. skyadventures.se

From the picture-perfect village of Kåseberga with its traditional houses, white fences and abundant gardens, a pretty walk up the cliffs from Kåseberga village takes you to **Ales Stenar** (4). The 59 standing stones resemble similar mystical places such as Stonehenge or Brittany's Carnac stones. As with these two, the mystery of Ales erect standing stones has never been solved. Suggestions that they're a burial ground, an ancient astronomical clock or a place for worshipping are merely that: suggestions. Clock makes sense: they are positioned so that the sun sets at the northwest stone in summer, and rises at the opposite stone in winter. The best time to visit is just before sunset, the magic hour.

Ever seen the brilliant BBC police series Wallander, the Swedish detective played by Kenneth Branagh? Well, then you're aware of the fact that Wallander lives in Ystad, the police station is in Ystad, all the crimes are committed in and around Ystad. Funny thing they all speak English, but who cares! You can visit the **Ystad Studios** (5) and see some of the props and décor used for the series. Or find out in what field the murders and crimes were committed.

a. Elis Nilssons Väg 12, 271 39 Ystad
w. filmiskane.se

Do as the Swedes do, or all Scandinavians for that matter: soak up the warmth of a sauna and cool off (preferably naked) in the cold Baltic sea. If you want a bit of luxury added to that, act out the ritual at **Ystad Saltsjöbad** (6) at the beach of Ystad. They have a heated swimming pool, jacuzzi, sauna, steam room, hot springs and a long wooden path leading straight out to sea.

a. Saltsjöbadsvägen 15, 271 39 Ystad
t. +46 4111 3630
w. ysb.se

EAT/DRINK/HANG OUT

◆

Fancy a copious vegetarian lunch, a chocolate or blueberry cake, home brewed beer or breakfast buffet in a rustic, friendly and hipsteralicious environment? **Byvägen35** (7) is your go-to place. Find them in the tiny village of Sankt Olof, near Stenshuvud National Park. Open all year, from Thursday to Sunday.

a. Byvägen 35, 277 40 Sankt Olof
t. +46 703 398 615
fb. Byvagen35

It seems time stood still since its opening in 1956 at **Kaffestugan Annorlunda** (8) which translates to 'the different coffee shop'. It's located in the midst of the Stenshuvud National Park and has a large garden to enjoy your coffee and cakes and cookies, baked in the same tradition as it's always been done. But then again, inside is where you can reminisce about the older days, when coffee pots were elegant and cups were porcelain. Open from March to October, on public holidays. Open daily from mid-June to end of August. ◆€◆ ◆€€◆

a. Stenshuvud, 277 35 Kivik
t. +46 4147 0475
w. kaffestuganannorlunda.se

Friden Gårdskrog (9) is famous for putting weird things on their pizza. Most of the ingredients used are organic and locally produced, so whatever you find on your pizza, know it's consciously chosen. All pizzas are baked in a wood-oven, and made from sourdough. Creating your pizza takes time, because love is added. While you wait you can choose one of their many beers, or taste their very own juice from apples picked just down the road. Find them 3 km outside Kivik; driving south, turn right towards Vitaby, and right again at the crossing, continue up the hill and turn left just before Mellby Atelier. Open all year. ◆€€◆

a. Friden Gårdskrog 267, 277 35 Mellby
t. +46 4142 1036
w. friden.nu

Mandelmanns Gardens (10) is a fairy tale-like farm with an abundant garden full of flowers, herbs, fruit trees and free-roaming chickens. The organic farmhouse, run by the welcoming couple Gustav and Marie, is sun and wind powered, has a farm shop and garden kitchen. Best to book in advance, they can only take a small number of visitors, which makes it all the more enjoyable. Very child friendly place, kids can run around the farm, play hide and seek, or have a chat with the chickens. Open in summer. ◆€◆

a. Djupadal, Rörum, 272 95 Simrishamn
w. mandelmann.se

In a former Opel garage just off the village square in Hammenhög, the **Garage Project** (**11**) is best described as a social gathering place for lovers of art, theatre, film and music. To keep track of what's going on, check their website or Facebook. Open from April to September.

a. Simrishamnsvägen 1,
   276 50 Hammenhög
t. +46 735 317 589
w. garageprojektet.org

Kåseberga Harbour (**12**) has some mighty fine fresh fish restaurants and smokehouses. Take your pick, you can hardly go wrong, the fish basically just jumped on your plate, right after taking that smokey sauna.

Café and shop Kåsessons (**13**) serves Nordic dishes, sandwiches and fika. The shop sells typical local products and delicacies like mustard and jam. They sometimes organise tastings, and you can order a picnic basket to take with you on your walks. Open all year. ♦€€♦

a. Ales Väg 26, 271 78 Kåseberga
t. +46 705 224 339
w. kasessons.com

Bakery **Söderberg and Sara** (**14**) in Ystad, bakes their sourdough bread in the stone oven, using real butter, leaving out the additives, putting in grain that's taken its time to grow, eggs from free-range local chickens and rapeseed oil from nearby fields. Besides all that, it's a cosy, welcoming place to enjoy a coffee with their goodies. Open all year.

a. Österportstorg 1, 271 41 Ystad
t. +46 4111 2580
w. soderbergsara.se

Open-air beach bar, **Shufflebar** (**15**), just recently opened, and is a perfect hang out for a cocktail or beer on a warm summer's evening, turning ever so slowly into the night. While waiting for your burger or snack, play a game of shuffle with the other guests. How this works? Beats us, but looks mighty fun. They're located next to the Sältsjobad spa. Open from June to August. ♦€♦ ♦€€♦

a. Saltsjöbadsvägen 13, 271 39 Ystad
t. +46 411 237 310
w. shufflebar.se

Luckily we don't have to, but if we had to pick just one café or restaurant in the area, it would be **Hörte Brygga** (**16**), without a doubt. Its location alone, right by the water, a little harbour in front and backed by green fields and trees sets you in the 'let's sit here, chat, eat, watch the sunset and never go home' kind of mood. Either inside, but better yet, outside on the terrace and garden, on barstools or long tables. They serve next level home cooking, take care of the environment by reducing packaging, using the most ('from nose to tail') of the sustainably bred meat, fish and vegetables they prepare. What's left is composted, not thrown away. For drinks there's a choice of natural wines, juices and craft beers. But really, go see this place for yourself and tell us you agree with our choice. Open from May to August. ♦€€♦

a. Hörte Hamn, Dybäck 465, 274 54 Skivarp
t. +46 739 971 342
w. hortebrygga.se

Badhytten (17) at the beach of Skanör is frequented by both locals and tourists, and the vibe's far more laid-back than you'd expect on seeing its smart appcarance. Kick off your shoes, settle into the sand, lounge around or join the free workouts they offer at the beach. Open from April to September. ♦€€♦

a. Skanörs Hamn, 239 30 Skanör
t. +46 406 280 570
w. badhytten.com

SHOP
♦

Locals tipped us about **Sjöfolket (18)** fish shop and restaurant, to get your hands on the best fish, and advice on how to prepare and serve the seafood you just purchased. If you're not about to prepare a dish yourself on your holidays, you can choose from ready-made dishes - or just eat at their restaurant. Open in summer.

a. Svartehallsvägen 11, 272 63 Simrishamn
t. +46 414 401 033
w. sjofolket.se

If you like meat, check out **Södra Kompaniet (19)**; a smokehouse, charcuterie and deli workshop, or a fast-food deli as they say themselves. Simple, but good food, no additives, using the purest and best products with the right seasoning, prepared by 2 dedicated chefs. Open all year from Thursday to Sunday.

a. Hagestadborgsvägen 243, 276 45 Löderup
t. +46 739 223 323
w. sodrakompaniet.se

In spring of 2019 the people behind Södra Kompaniet opened a new beach bar, **Strandkompaniet (20)**, in Löderup Strandbad. On the menu: quality food, the happy-go-lucky vibe you'd expect of a venue at the beach, and a light, bright, colourful interior. But obviously you'll be sitting outside. It's the beach after all! Closed in winter. ♦€€♦

a. Östanvägen 4, 271 77 Löderup
t. +46 73 922 3323
w. strandkompaniet.se

SLEEP
♦

Campervans (21) can park and stay in the small harbour of Kivik for free. No facilities. Open all year.

a. Rusthållsvägen 14, 277 30 Kivik

Hostel and camping **Ängdala (22)** is a small, family friendly campsite and hostel, with pitches, cabins and rooms for rent. Open from April to September. ♦€♦

a. Ravlunda 2115, 277 37 Kivik
t. +46 733 648 420
w. angdalavandrarhem.se

Next to an orchard, amid fields of flax flowers, you'll find Bed & Breakfast **Rävåkra (23)**. Once a farmhouse, the guesthouse now still has the rustic atmosphere of a farm, even after complete renovations, with wooden ceilings and a woodstove, and a lush garden. The rooms are nicely decorated, in a typical Scandinavian way: elegantly minimalistic, light and bright. Open all year. ♦€€♦

a. Vallby 3850, 276 56 Hammenhög
t. +46 708 665 415
w. ravakra.se

Løderups Strandbads (24) is a basic campsite with pitches and cabins that sleep up to 6 people, their unique selling point being its location, right on the beach. Open from April to September. ♦€♦

a. Östanvägen 64, 276 45 Löderup
t. +46 411 526 311
w. loderupsstrandbadscamping.se

Hostel Backåkra Vandrarhem (25) is a perfect option if you don't want to spend too much money on your stay, but do like the place you return to every day, and wake up in, to be clean and cosy. The hostel has shared rooms, double rooms, family rooms, and the communal kitchen, garden and living room are an extension of your holiday house, where you can meet the other guests. Furnished with vintage goods, lots of playground and toys for kids, and even blankets for the more chilled evenings spent outside are provided. Open from May to September. ♦€♦

a. Östra Kustvägen 1231, 271 77 Löderup
t. +46 411 526 080
w. backakra.se

Surrounded by farm fields where seasonal changes are noticeable, boutique hotel **Örum 119 (26)** offers a piece of tranquil country life. Set in a former school, the décor of the 15 rooms is stripped of distracting knick-knacks and brought back to precisely the amount of luxury you could wish for, by using quality materials and just plain good taste. At the back of the hotel you'll find their farm shop, open-air restaurant and artisanal ice parlour. Open from Easter to September. ♦€€♦

a. Örumsvägen 119, 271 76 Löderup
t. +46 411 556 688
w. orum119.se

Bed & breakfast, shop and gallery, **Strandbadsgården (27)**, is located near the beach of Löderup, surrounded by farm fields. They have private rooms in the attic of the bed & breakfast, the communal garden has romantic and secluded corners, a BBQ and there are bikes to be used for free. The gallery and shop open up to the garden, in the shop you'll find clothes, jewellery, linen, bags and shoes from small-scale Scandinavian designer brands and their own brand, Kuddfabriken AB. Lovely and extraordinary place altogether! Open from midsummer until mid-August. ♦€€♦

a. Östra Kustvägen 1085, 271 77 Löderup
t. +46 709 267 100
w. strandbadsgarden.se

Campervans (28) can park and stay overnight on a big grass field, just after entering the village Kåseberga. From here you can walk up to the standing stones (Ales Stenar) on the cliff, or the picturesque harbour. You pay a small fee for staying the night and then are allowed to use the toilets and shower of the neighbouring soccer club. Parking in the daytime is free. Open from March to October. ♦€♦

a. Ales Väg 2, 276 46 Kåseberga
t. +46 708 495 449 (Ronny)

Campervans (29) can park and stay for free at the most southern tip of Sweden, close to the ferry terminal of Trelleborg. There are no facilities, in the harbour you'll find restaurants and toilets. Open all year.

a. Smyge Strandväg 10, 231 78 Smygehamn

SURF

Since magazines and social media have covered the Baltic over some years now, we all know that, yes, there IS surf, the Baltic sea does deliver. But not that often. Fickle? You bet. Windy? Yep. We're staying low in the beautiful south of Sweden, where chances of scoring surf are higher and so are the waves, usually, when they arrive. Expect picture-perfect backdrops, and when you see a wave, jump in, don't hesitate, it can be over before your coffee's finished, or the sauna's heated up.

WEST COAST

Mölle (I) - one of Sweden's finest. A righthander that breaks over boulders, needing a medium to big N-NW-W windswell. You'll see it working from the harbour of Mölle; access from the pier, or the road along the water (climbing over the boulders). • *Intermediate and advanced level/rocks/a few parking spots along the road, or park near the harbour/restaurants/toilets.* •

Secrets remaining secrets… Go and explore the peninsula on both sides for some hidden hotspots.

SOUTH AND SOUTHEAST COAST

The narrow beach of **Vik (II)** is a beauty! Next to the harbour is a right pointbreak that starts working with strong onshore east winds. No surf? No problem, go hiking, take pictures, pretend you're in the Caribbean. • *All levels/sand/easy parking/restaurants/toilets.* •

An endless stretch of fine white sand at **Sandhammaren (III)** offers ample opportunities for medium to big E-SE-S windswell to create surfable waves. On summer days you'll have an audience, since this is a popular holiday beach. • *All levels/sand/easy parking/restaurants/toilets.* •

Next to the harbour walls of **Kåseberga (IV)**, and at the beach itself you'll find waves during a strong E-SE-S wind swell. If not: heat up the portable sauna at the harbour, have some smoked fish, or walk up to Ales Stonar. • *All levels/sand/stones/easy parking/restaurants/toilets.* •

SCHOOL RENTAL REPAIR

ZT Surfboards (30) surf shop, surf school and shaping workshop is owned and run by Zafer Taylor, hence the ZT. Zafer's known for his sharp and critical eye. A lifetime of experience, and being one of the few shapers in Sweden, he understands what a North Sea, Kattegat and Baltic Sea surfer needs. Besides shaping boards, ZT Surfboards offers a range of second-hand boards, a surf school (groups and private lessons), repairs and board/wetsuit rental. In the shop you'll find all your surf essentials.

a. Värmövägen 8, 268 73 Billeberga (between Helsingborg and Malmö)
t. +46 739 044 427
w. ztsurf.com

Johan Denker of **JDshapes (31)** mainly shapes single fins and logs, getting his inspiration from the old classical shapes, with his own modern touch. He started shaping over 4 years ago, out of need actually: "Getting your hands on a proper longboard in Sweden is almost impossible, especially handmade. I'm shaping boards that work for the kind of surf we get here. My garage is rebuilt in to a shape shack, where I do all my shaping and glassing." Shaping's not his core business, but more of a hobby that's getting a bit out of hand. That's because he makes them so beautiful… you can contact Johan - and see his work - through his Instagram.

a. 234 40 Lomma
t. +46 708 680 979
ig. @JDshapes

Ksurf Skanör (32) surf school offers surf and kite lessons, SUP fitness and yoga, surf, SUP and skimboard rental. They're located on the beach, next to Badhytten, at Skanörshamn. Open from mid-April to mid-October.

a. Skanörs Hamn, 239 30 Skanör / Falsterbo
t. +46 760 825 391
w. ksurf.se

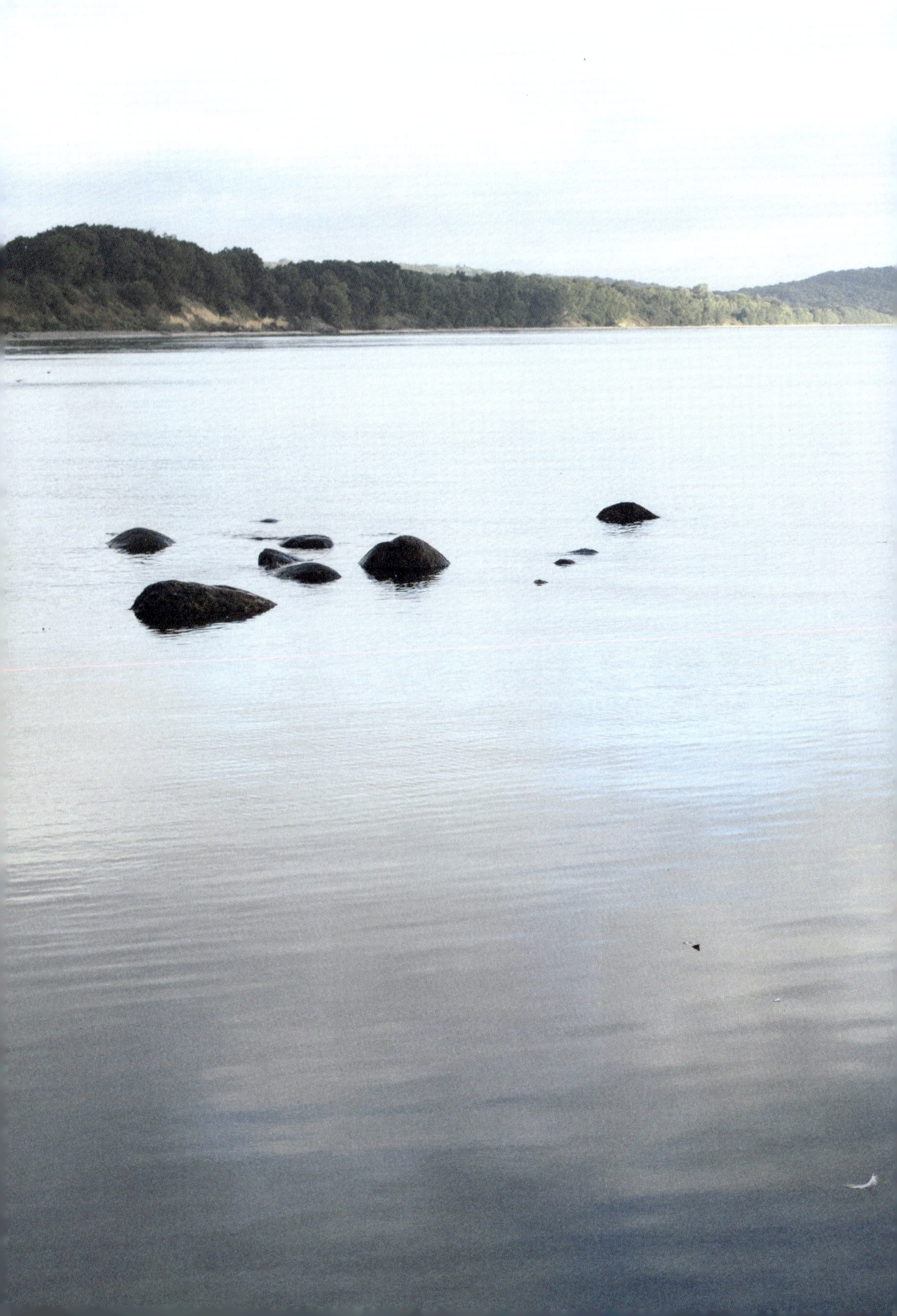

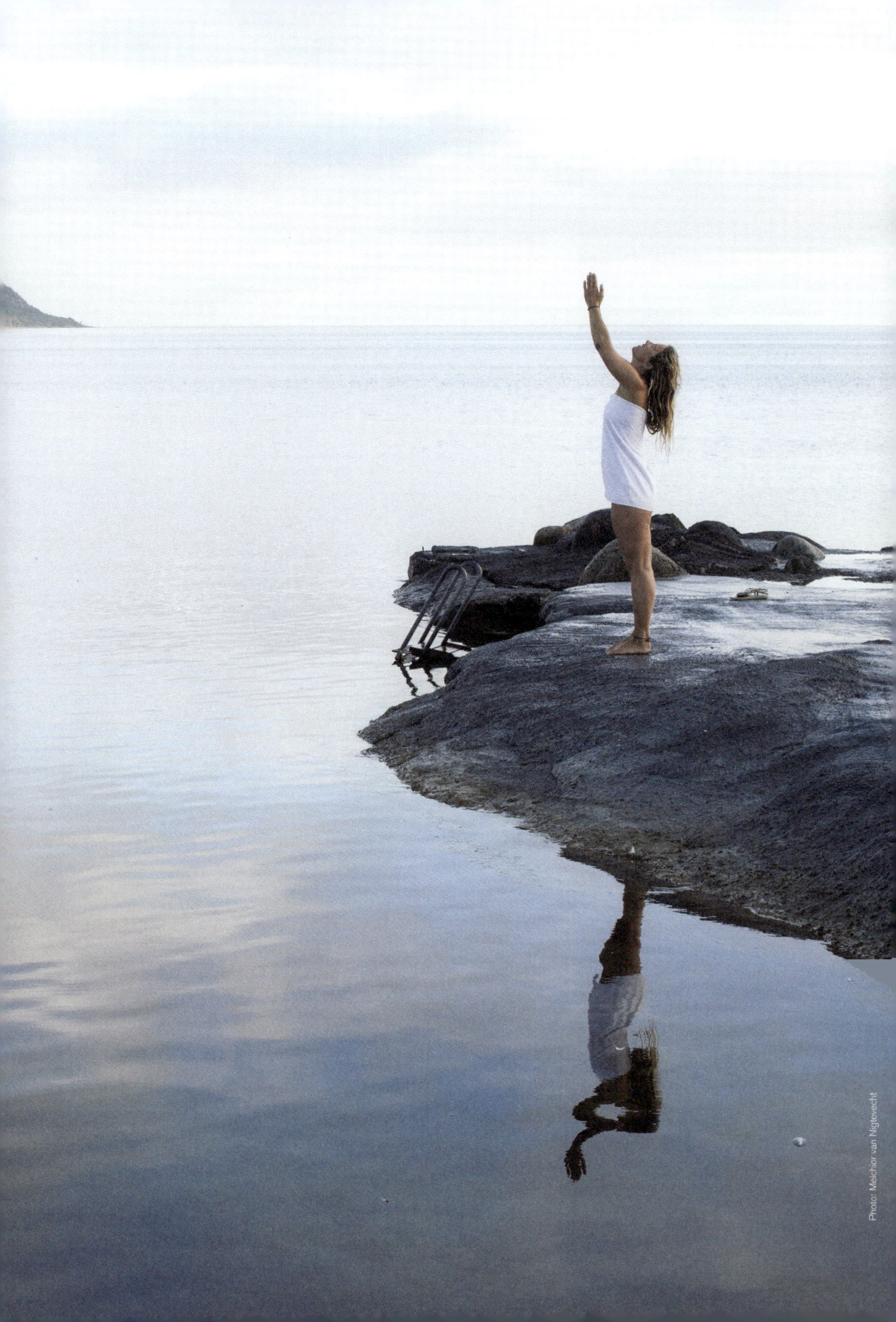

Photo: Melchior van Nigtevecht

Denmark

DENMARK

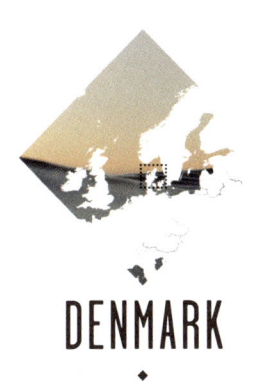

From the urban stylishness of Copenhagen to the Riviera of hip raincoats in north Sjælland, and then on to the honesty boxes, 'selfpluk' fields and endless beaches of Jutland, there's one thing that these three very different Danish destinations have in common, besides being tourist magnets: their freshness. Like young cherubic chubby-cheeked children, rubbed clean in a bathtub.

North Sjælland (Zealand) in the northeast, its seaside toes dipping in the Kattegat, is dotted with small coastal communities whose populations quadruple in summer. Its attraction very clear: white sandy beaches, green cliffs, lively harbours, exclusive eateries, and seawater that can warm up to over 22°C in summer. They may call it the Danish Riviera, the Danes however, will never ever, be blatant about, well, anything really. It's an exception to see anyone flaunting their stuff - clothes, body, house, or car - due to their deep sense of Jantelov. Jantelov, or Jante's Law, the name deriving from a 1920s novel, is a strong group mentality that doesn't allow too much self-appraisal, but promotes and favours group efforts. You won't notice it right away.- it's probably only in hindsight, thinking about your Denmark holidays, appreciating the refined manners of your hosts, that you might detect something out of the ordinary.

Danes like things clean and healthy, and despite their appetite for meat (and especially sausages) you won't have difficulty finding a decent vegetarian or vegan alternative on any menu. Just about every public toilet you use - and there are many - is squeaky shiny clean and miraculously never runs out of paper. Along Jutland's roads you'll find honesty boxes with potatoes, jam and 'honnig' - honey from local beekeepers. At 'selfpluk' fields you're allowed to pick herbs or flowers yourself for a small fee. And litter? Danes don't do litter. Good thing to take home!

SURFER-TRAVELLER TYPE DENMARK

You love a beer, any time, especially from some microbrewery, and open it with whatever's available - your lighter, wax comb, or teeth maybe. Anything really but a regular opener. You like people to form a queue, anywhere, and prefer sitting outside on a terrace, even when it's freezing, but know exactly what they mean by being hygge. You choose dark rye bread as a base for your open-faced sandwich and know where to find the ø, æ and å on your keyboard. You've always dreamed of driving your car right on to the beach and don't mind a bit of studying the wind speed and direction along with the swell direction. And you're not put off by short swell periods.

WORDS AND CONCEPTS THAT MIGHT COME IN HANDY

Skål! - Cheers!

Hej or hejsa - Hi, hello, casual greeting but can be used in shops, meeting strangers or friends.

Tak for kaffe - literally means 'thanks for coffee' but is used all over the place to express surprise or the equivalent of OMG! Put emphasis on tak if you don't mean to thank for the coffee.

Klokken lort - can be used when you go for dawn patrol, meaning something like 'shit o'clock' (literally clock shit), getting up at unreasonable hours, or arriving extremely late.

Hygge - non-translatable word that describes a feeling, a place, or an atmosphere of cosiness, intimacy, warmth. Like being cuddled up on a sofa, have a hot chocolate, chatting with your best friends. Or the way a sweater falls casually of one's shoulder and the light's just perfectly softening the tone of revealed skin. Or having an animated conversation with your kid, a sparkling night out with total strangers, your first coffee after an early morning surf.

FOOD FACTS

SMØRREBRØD

Smørrebrød, literally meaning 'spread bread', is the famous open sandwich, usually with a base of buttered rugbrød, rye bread, and layers of toppings like meat, fish or cheese, vegetables or salad, and cream or sauce. When ordered as a lunch in a restaurant it's usually artfully presented.

FISH

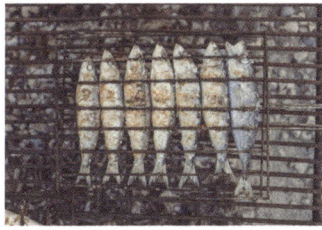

Danes are creative with fish, whether fresh, smoked, cured or pickled, all variations go, and it's pretty easy to find good fishmongers along the coast. If you prefer to do your own fishing, you'll have a good shot at catching trout. There are a few rules and regulations though. You need a fishing licence, which can be easily purchased at tourist offices or fishing shops. You can either buy one for a day, week or year, and it will save you paying a pretty hefty fine if you're caught fishing without a permit. With the fishing licence you'll have the right to fish in both freshwater and saltwater.

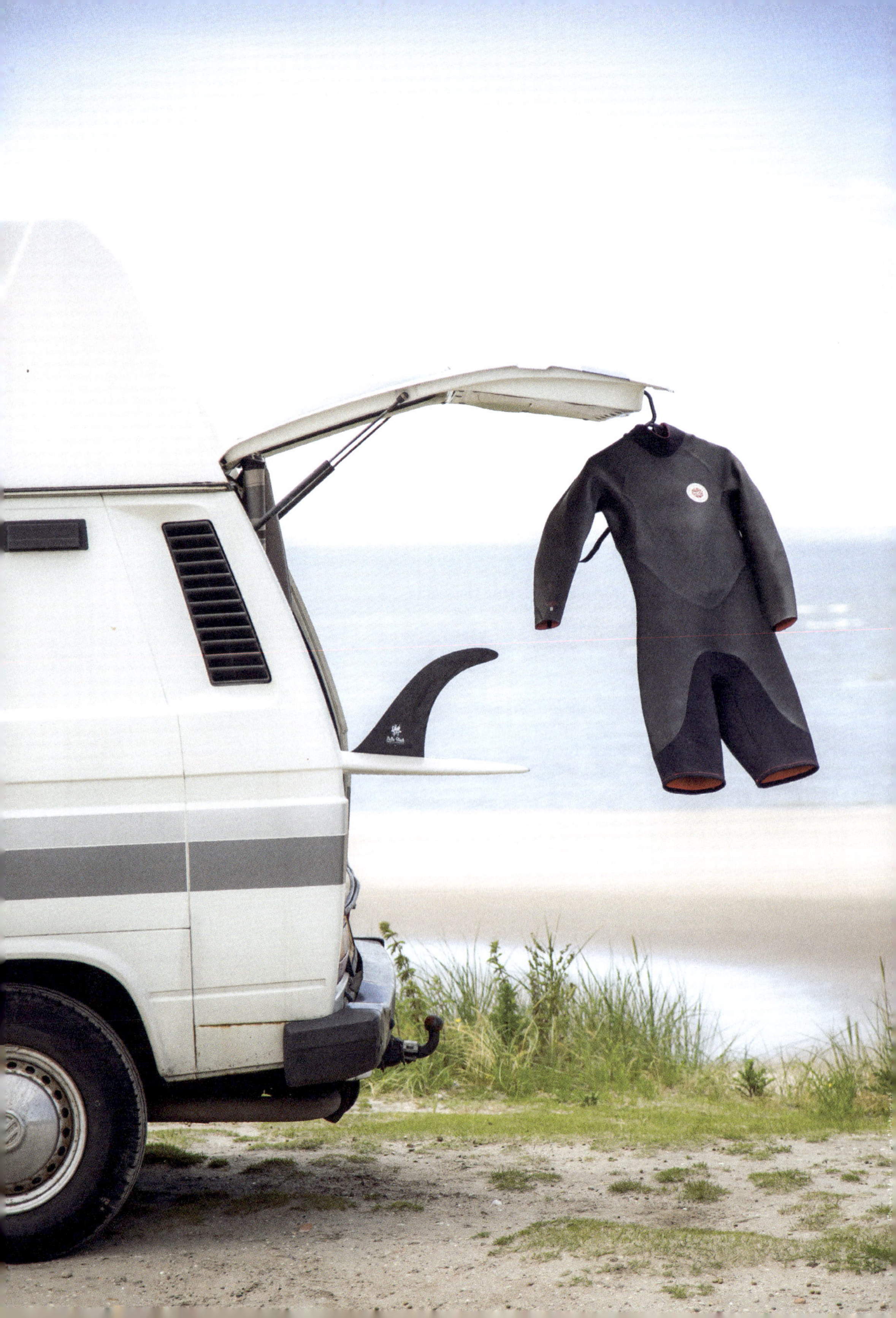

A BIT ON SURF IN DENMARK

Say surf Denmark and every other person will reply "Klitmøller". The town's commonly known as Cold Hawaii, or as Klitten to some... but foremost as a world class windsurf spot, hosting the world cup windsurfing for many years. But the term Cold Hawaii isn't exclusively reserved to this surf-loving seaside village, it's actually the whole west-facing area, from Hanstholm to Agger; blessed with several breaks, piers, jetties, sandbanks, and the beautiful backdrop of Thy National Park.

It's this area where surfing in Denmark started, relatively recently, back in the eighties. Windsurfers making use of their boards on windless days, and travelling surfers coming back home and seeing the potential, sharing the stoke, albeit carefully, since surfers weren't well received by the Danish fishing communities.

Not unlike other northern seaside nations, like Sweden, Germany and Holland, a great number of Danish salt water fans make use of wind AND waves; not just taking up windsurfing or kite or waves, but combining all three, or at least two. It just means more days spent at the beach, in the ocean, using whichever board suits the elements best.

The windsurf scene is still pretty big, but wave surfers are outnumbering them by now. Surfing's becoming more popular in general; boards are available for every level, and wetsuits are getting better, which is a big plus for the northern nations.

So when and where's your best bet for consistent surf in Denmark? Windswell from S to NE winds and, less common, groundswell from SW to NW, produce surfable waves in every season; from the few breaks in the Kattegat up north, and the many North Sea spots on the west coast, to the island of Bornholm in the Baltic Sea, which receives waves from NE-E winds. Most consistent and powerful, however, would be the coast at Thy National Park in Jutland, the aforementioned Cold Hawaii. And it's called that for good reason: you'll have your fair share of waves in summer, for sure, when wearing a 3/2 suit suits just fine. But it's wintertime the North Sea delivers. Spring and fall can be promising too, and not so icy cold. The crowds won't have arrived yet, or have gone, parking spaces ample, shops and restaurants open and accommodation cheaper. Bring your whole winter neoprene collection, though.

Map of Sjælland

Locations marked:

- **HUNDESTED (VI)**
  - HUNDESTED ♦ 28-36, 39, 42-44
  - TORUP ♦ 37, 38, 41
  - FREDERIKSVÆRK ♦ 45
- **SMIDSTRUP (V)**
- **GILLELEJE (IV)**
  - GILLELEJE ♦ 15, 16, 27
- **PLANTAGE (II)**
- **PIER (III)**
- **ÅLSGÅRDE (I)**
  - HORNBÆK ♦ 2-8, 10-14, 17-20, 23-2[?]
- TISVILDE ♦ 21, 40
- GRÆSTED ♦ 9
- HELSINGE ♦ 22
- HELSINGØR ♦ 46
- HUMLEBÆK ♦ 1
- HILLERØD
- *Sjælland*
- ROSKILDE
- COPENHAGEN
- **BORNHOLM (VII)**

SJÆLLAND

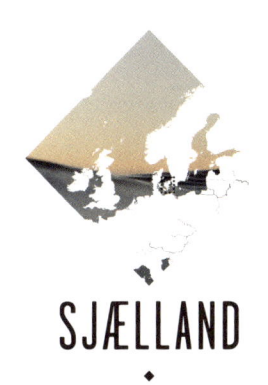

Of all the Danish islands, Sjælland is the largest. Over 7000 km² and connected by bridges from the mainland, you hardly notice that you're on an island. The northern coastal area is sometimes referred to as the Danish Riviera. Since the beginning of the 20th century the area's been a welcoming holiday destination for Copenhagen residents. Makes sense, a home not too far away from home. And the attractions are obvious: white sandy beaches, friendly seaside towns with a, still, thriving fishing culture, all sorts of water sports to do, and there's room to roam. Although Copenhagen isn't officially included in the territory of Sjælland, we do include it in this chapter (we don't mind a bit of border bending). The best part of this area is that you're out and about, wandering through nature, strolling along the beaches one moment, and in less than an hour you can be at a hotspot in the city.

TRAVEL INFO

Using ferries and bridges saves a lot of driving, and time. Coming from or going to Sweden you can cross the impressive 16 km long Øresund bridge, connecting Copenhagen with Malmö in Sweden. The eastern and western parts of Denmark are connected by the 18 km long Storebælt bridge (the Great Belt), across the Storebælt strait.

BY AIR

Both national and international flight companies have direct flights to/from Copenhagen Airport (Københavns Lufthavn Kastrup), one of Europe's biggest airports.

w. cph.dk

BY BOAT

Daily ferries sail between Helsingør on the east coast of Nordsjælland, and Helsingborg in the south of Sweden, and between Rødby, on the island of Lolland, Denmark, and Puttgarden in Germany.

w. scandlines.dk

In the north of Nordsjælland daily ferries sail between Hundested and Rørvig.

w. hundested-roervig.dk

BY TRAIN

Lokalbanen (The Local Railway) and DSB run between almost every town. On the DSB trains you can take your bike.

w. lokaltog.dk / **w.** dsb.dk

IN AND AROUND HORNBÆK AND GILLELEJE

◆

Hornbæk is a popular beach and summer town for Copenhagen city folk. Some have a second home, others just enjoy every free day at the seaside. Where the other, somewhat bigger popular summer town, Gilleleje, has an obvious touristic character, Hornbæk has a distinctive modish, yet breezy, easy-going feel to it. In Gilleleje there's been a little dispute about whether tourism should be handled with more care. Because, the very thing that attracts tourists - the lively, buzzing harbour area and all the goods fishery brings - disables the fishing industry at the same time; unable to do their work properly in high season, they have to close down some of their workspace in summer to make the harbour more attractive to tourists. But all in all, the harbour's still impressively large and colourful, the 'fisk' tastes excellent, and the atmosphere is cheerful, especially on sunny days. We have a slight preference for Hornbæk though. The water temperature during a good summer can reach up to 22 °C, pods of small dolphins and seals are spotted regularly. The harbour's a good place to start exploring town, which can easily be done on foot.

Tourist office Hornbæk at Vestre Stejlebakke 2A, 3100 Hornbæk (in the library).

TO DO
◆

Hornbæk Harbour Festival is a family friendly festival, held each year since 1881 during the last weekend of July. As the name suggests, it celebrates everything maritime or involving the harbour. The festival's a good way to meet the locals of Hornbæk, while you listen to live music, visit the funfair, have a drink or a local bite to eat. There are lots of activities for children.

w. hornbaekhavnefest.dk

Biking is easy-peasy in Nordsjælland, since there's lots of nature, lots of paths, and no hills to speak of. There are several places to rent bikes, or even a delivery and pick up to/from the places along the north coast, from Helsingør to Hundested. Rental at **Hornbæk Cykeludlejning** at Nordre Strandvej 315 (**w.** hornbaekcykeludlejning.dk). Rental, delivery and pick up along the coast at **Nordkystens Cykeludlejning** in Gilleleje.

a. Svend Henriksens Vej 14, 3250 Gilleleje
t. +45 5129 2943
w. nordkystenscykeludlejning.dk

Admire the work from national and international artists at the museum of modern art **Louisiana** (**1**), both modern classics - think Picasso - to contemporary. From their restaurant, a popular spot for Copenhagen's city folk to meet up, you'll have a panoramic view of the east coast. Open all year.

a. Gammel Strandvej 13, 3050 Humlebæk
t. +45 4919 0719
w. louisiana.dk

At **Hornbæk Surf Shop** (**2**) you can rent bicycles to explore the very bike-friendly area. And of course, being a surf shop, you can rent surfboards and SUPs, or book lessons. Open all year.

a. Havnevej 20, 3100 Hornbæk
t. +45 3024 3838
fb. Hornbaek Surf Shop

The **Havreholm Klatrepark** (**3**) is a treetop climbing park, with 4 tracks and a 208 m long zipline. Rather stay on the ground? You can play a 9-hole par-3 game of disc golf - no previous golf experience necessary. Open from mid-August to mid-October, from Thursday to Sunday.

a. Klosterrisvej 4, 3100 Hornbæk
t. +45 3074 0944
w. havreholmklatrebane.dk

Yay, sailing! At **SUPspot** (**4**), home to Hobie SUP boards and Hobie catamarans, you can book sailing classes, or rent SUPs and catamarans. Open from June to August.

a. Løvvænget 13, 3100 Hornbæk
t. +45 2178 2201
w. supspot.dk

It's a thing that fits this area, or rather, the town of Hornbæk; treating yourself to a spa or beauty treatment. Not as an exorbitant luxury, more like maintenance of the body and soul. Like going for a brisk walk, jogging or biking, doing your yoga, eating healthy, and every now and then taking a little spa break. At **Spa og Behag** (**5**), situated at the Hotel Hornbækhus, they offer all sorts of wellness and beauty treatments, including hot stone massages, facial treatments with ecological products, and there's a steam room. Open all year.

a. Hotel Hornbækhus, Skovvej 7, 3100 Hornbæk
t. +45 4970 0169
w. hornbaekhus.com

At the **Kurbadet** (**6**) it actually does look a bit more exorbitant, there's more on offer, but boils down to the same thing: me-time and spoiling yourself with some extra care. They offer hot and cold pools, an open-air pool on the roof terrace, sauna, steam room, and you can book massages or facial treatments. The spa is located in the same building as the restaurant (all in hands of grand dame of Hornbæk, designer Ilse Jacobsen). If you go at dinnertime you'll be distracted by the smells of cooking - not necessarily a bad thing.

a. A.R. Friisvej 16, 3100 Hornbæk
t. +45 7060 6020
w. ilsejacobsen.com/kurbadet

At **Yoga Praxis** (**7**) they offer daily hatha and yin yoga, and pilates classes in a serene studio in Hornbæk. Everything's provided; mats, blankets, pillows, belts, warm cushions and eye pads - all you have to do is show up on the mat. Drop-in classes possible. Check their schedule on the website. Open all year.

a. Engholmvej 19, 3100 Hornbæk
t. +45 2242 9923
w. yogapraxis.dk

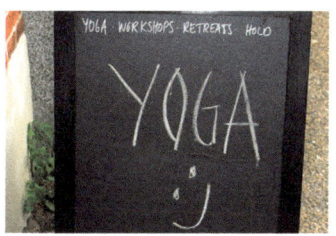

In their small but intimate studio, **Yoga i Hornbæk** (**8**) offer regular classes, and workshops. In the summer months of June, July and August you can join their Drop-In Sommeryoga classes. There are yin yoga, yoga-in-motion and yoga and mindfulness classes available. Check the website for schedules and dates. Open all year, but drop-in classes only in summer.

a. Havnevej 6, Baghuset, 3100 Hornbæk
t. Charlotte +45 2166 5565 / Mia +45 2978 2545
w. yogaihornbaek.dk

Between Dronningmølle and Gilleleje you'll find **Munkeruphus** (**9**). This country house, built in 1916 in colonial style, near the sea, has a 5 acre garden where you can explore the winding paths that open up to the beach, hug old trees, enjoy the views, and admire the architecture of the house itself. The house isn't private any more and now serves as a café, a gallery (inside and outside in the garden) and gift shop. An art-lover's must. Open March to October.

a. Munkerup Strandvej 78, 3120 Dronningmølle
t. +45 4971 7906
w. munkeruphus.dk

EAT/DRINK/HANG OUT

Det Fedtede Hjørne (**10**), which translates to 'The Greasy Corner', was originally set up as a project for the famous Roskilde Festival. Then in the summer of 2016 it ended up in the small town of Hornbæk. The Greasy Corner is a summer mini-festival, event, happening, whatchamacallit, with street food trucks and live music concerts. Open in July and August.

a. Øresundsvej 2, 3100 Hornbæk
fb. det fedtede hjorne

a. Nordre Strandvej 354, 3100 Hornbæk
t. +45 2517 1751
fb. Albi's Kaffebar og Second-Hand

Albi's (**11**) is our favourite place in Sjælland. The coffee bar, restaurant, hang out and second-hand shop's giving the small-scale seaside town of Hornbæk a bit of an urban, fresh and natural spirit. Run by the ever-smiling happy people, Camilla and Michael Mengers, who put their heart, soul, passion and vibrant personalities in the look, the food, and the vibe of the place. Albi's is definitely more a restaurant and café than a shop, but all items you see in their vintage interior are for sale. Their menu offers home-made everything, from the cakes and breads to the granola, jam, juices and shakes. Albi's regulars and irregulars are a fine mix of local folk, passing cyclists, surfers, families, kids and tourists. You can either sit inside their cosy restaurant and admire all the second-hand objects, outside on the terrace, or in the garden. In summer they have regular live music gigs in the garden. Open all year. ♦€♦ ♦€€♦

Close to Albi's, in the main street of the little village, is another favourite; family-run **Det Luc's** (**12**), a juice and sandwich bar. They strive for a 100% organic menu, and you can be sure you get a health and energy boost after choosing from their many shakes and juices. All fresh ingredients; ginger, fruits, herbs and much more. To help you choose, Det Luc's very friendly and exotic family (with Danish, Indian, Cape Verdean and Senegalese blood running through their veins) are at your disposal. We had a hard time choosing between their great coffee and juices. So drank both. And went for a refill, so tasty! Open all year. ♦€♦ ♦€€♦

a. Nordre Strandvej 345, 3100 Hornbæk
t. +45 5120 9345
fb. Det Luc's Hornbæk

CRÊPE Hornbæk (**13**) obviously have crêpes on their menu, but also delicious ice-cream. Good to know in summer, when you've got a craving… Open from March to August. ♦€♦ ♦€€♦

a. Nordre Strandvej 357, 3100 Hornbæk
t. +45 2640 5559
fb. crepe hornbaek

For genuine stone-oven pizzas, Italian-made, check in at **La Vera Pizza** (**14**) in Hornbæk. Besides tasty pizzas they have lots of other yummy Italian dishes on the menu: cold plates with prosciutto, bruschetta, and paninis, and hot meals such as cannelloni, lasagne and of course, the 'dolces', sweet desserts: tiramisù and panna cotta. Open from June to August. ♦€♦

a. A R Friis Vej 8, 3100 Hornbæk (there's another good Italian, run by the same owner, in Øresundsvej)
t. +45 4921 3031
w. laverapizza.dk

Cafe Flora (**15**) is one of the nicest cafés in Gilleleje, for either a coffee, breakfast, lunch, great salad, or a cake. Oh yes, the cakes! And the staff. We have to mention the very friendly staff. Smiles all over the smart place. Although you can sit outside, one almost hopes for colder weather. Inside it's hygge to the max: brick walls, wooden tables, and their lighting makes everybody look beautiful. Bring your book, laptop, friends, and stay on a bit. Open all year. ♦€♦

a. Vesterbrogade 9D, 3250 Gilleleje
t. +45 6012 2643
w. cafeflora.dk

No better place to go for a herring than one of the many fish restaurants and fish shops in the **harbour of Gilleleje** (**16**). Herring on an open sandwich, rye bread, pickled, sweet, sour or spicy, take your pick. There's Adamsens Fisk and the shop Fiskehuset Gilleleje, well, you can hardly go wrong, can you. This is the heart of herring country. If you're lucky enough to be here on August 1st, you can join in the celebration of Gilleleje Rotary Herring Day. On this day, you can eat all the herring sandwiches you can eat for just DKR 50, (choose between over 10 different kind of preparations). All around the harbour there are celebrations and music and sorts. The herring eating takes place in the Auction Hall.

SHOP
♦

The local **Hornbæk Surf Shop** (**17**) is a small and friendly place, a few steps away from Hornbæk's main break. The owner, Rex Degnegaard, welcomes all and everybody to his shop, whether for a new surfboard, some wax, a new Hawaiian shirt, shorts or hat, or just want to chat about waves and weather. You can do just that, enjoying a coffee, cold drink or hot chocolate while you're at it. Or rent a board and book a lesson. By far one of the most open surf shops we've encountered, with a very positive vibe. Open all year.

a. Havnevej 20, 3100 Hornbæk
t. +45 3024 3838
fb. Hornbaek Surf Shop

On weekend mornings people are lining up at **Bakery Bagt** (**18**). They offer all sorts of bread and delicious pastries, traditional Danish and French biscuits and baked goods. Open all year.

a. Nordre Strandvej 339, 3100 Hornbæk
t. +45 4970 0051
w. bagt.nu

Maybe you're not specifically looking for home décor when on holiday, but have a peek at **Rooms Galore** (**19**). Some shop owners just have a flair for perfectly balanced sugar and spice, everything nice. We're pretty sure you'll find something you never thought you needed but now can't live without. Open all year.

a. Nordre Strandvej 341B, 3100 Hornbæk
t. +45 3089 0030
w. roomsgalore.dk

You'll be praying for some rain and wet weather to justify entering designer **Ilse Jacobsen**'s (**20**) store. Lady Jacobsen is born and raised in seaside town Hornbæk, her designs, especially her iconic rainwear - boots and coats - are well known and sold in shops far beyond Denmark. Open all year.

a. A.R. Friisvej 1, 2D and 3, 3100 Hornbæk
t. +45 4970 0390
w. ilsejacobsen.com

Esthers Garage (**21**) is a vintage shop with a quirky mix of new, old, industrial and antique knick-knacks, bric-a-brac, bits and bobs, odds and ends, miscellanea and more. Open all year.

a. Tibirkevej 17, 3220 Tisvildeleje
t. +45 2966 3498
fb. Esthers Garage

Ørby Vingård (**22**) like to spread the love of Danish quality wine. They sell their own white, rosé and red in the farm shop. Bet you didn't know about Danish wine at all, did you? Maybe first have a tour and tasting before buying? This can be arranged. Open all year.

a. Maglebjergvej 16, 3200 Helsinge
t. +45 4077 9367
w. oerbyvingaard.dk

SLEEP
♦

DCU-Camping Hornbæk (**23**) is a family campsite with pitches and cabins, located next to the Hornbæk Plantage (public woodland with walking trail). It's nothing too special, but it's modern, and clean, kids have 2 playgrounds to choose from, and it's less than 1 km away from the beach and dunes. Open all year. ♦€♦

a. Planetvej 4, 3100 Hornbæk
t. +45 4970 0223
w. camping-hornbaek.dk

It might make you wish you lived here, but a couple of days will give you a fine time to pretend you do, at **Pension Ewaldsgaarden** (**24**). The 150-year-old country house, with a big courtyard and shady garden, although located in the middle of Hornbæk, is a haven of tranquility. Every room is individually decorated. Open from June to August. ◆€€◆

a. Johannes Ewalds Vej 5, 3100 Hornbæk
t. +45 4970 0082
w. ewaldsgaarden.dk

Hotel Hornbæk Hus (25) is a pretty special place, a bit unusual, set in a historic building in a leafy street near the town centre. When you enter you'd swear you just stepped back in time, but look closely and see that it's all cutely charming. It may remind you of a boarding school, but sitting at a large table sharing dinner with strangers makes the strangers feel like friends real quick. Maybe your new friends invite you for a walk or bike tour, or maybe you meet them again during yoga class. Rooms don't need much more than they already have, nothing too special really. Staff are friendly, prices are good value, the location is central and easy to walk to and from beach, woods, town, shops and restaurants. The hotel was undergoing construction work soon after our visit in summer 2017, so some things may have changed (to even better?). Open all year. ◆€◆

a. Skovvej 7, 3100 Hornbæk
t. +45 4970 0169
w. hornbaekhus.com

You'll encounter a lot of 'gamle hus' in Sweden, it means 'old house'. **Det Gamle Hus (26)** in Hornbæk is indeed one of the town's oldest houses. It used to be a fisherman's house, hence close to harbour and beach. You'll feel right at home, that's for sure. Of course it's been renovated for holiday lets, but they didn't try to make it hip, instead kept the atmosphere of a fisherman's family house. The whitewashed stone house is perfectly suited for a couple, or a family with max 2 small children, and has a little courtyard. Open all year. ◆€€◆

a. Øresundsvej 22, 3100 Hornbæk
t. +45 2323 8444
w. detgamlehus3100.dk

Campervans (27) can stay at the big farm garden of Pudsagergård, in Gilleleje. It has all basic facilities. Open from May to September. ◆€◆

a. Ålekistevej 24, 3250 Gilleleje
t. +46 4830 3064
w. pudsager.dk

IN AND AROUND HUNDESTED

The name Hundested literally means 'dog town', the dog in this case being a seal (it's a language thing, seal in most Germanic languages translates to 'sea dog'). There used to be a reef just offshore where hundreds of seals found a home. But the reef's long gone, used up building and constructing harbour walls and such. Of course the occasional seal still pops its head up, but not in the numbers they used to do. Beach and harbour are a good place to hang out. At Hundested harbour, the fine line between rough and rumbling fishing industry, handicrafts, arts and tourism is perfectly balanced. They all profit from each other, in a good way. Just behind the row of restaurants there are dozens of small shops and workshops where designers, artists and craftspeople work with glass, ceramics, leather or wood. The old wharf is still used for boat repair, but also for wood handicraft. All in all it's a pretty good example of how today's touristy harbour areas can keep their charm and character, and still keep up with the times.

Tourist office Hundested at Havnegade 20.

TO DO

Himmelstorm Festival is an intimate and family-friendly event, held annually since 2011 at the Dyssekilde eco-village. There's music and dance, acrobats and workshops and entertainment for all ages. Think: yoga, hip-hop dance classes, hula hoop and Zumba, art installations, jugglers, and musicians from all over the world. There's one big outdoor stage, a circus tent and a smaller tent for the workshops. The festival was initiated to promote the possibilities for an alternative and sustainable way of living, the way it's done at the eco-village. Of course all the values of the village vibrate through the festival: a strong sense of community, the importance of music and art, and all products sold are either organic, recycled or locally produced. Himmelstorm is held at the end of July.

a. Hågendrupvej 9, 3390 Hundested
w. himmelstorm.dk

To start the summer in the saltiest way, seaside town Hundested kicks off the season with the **Lyn-X Open Water Sports Festival**. There's SUP, kite surfing, windsurfing, kayaking, snorkelling even, and all sorts of water activities to be tried in Lynæs Harbour. Besides activities, of course, there are drinks, food, events, and a lively atmosphere in the evening. The festival's held every year over the second weekend of June. Lynæs Harbour is just south of Hundested's harbour.

a. Lynæs Havnevej 8, 3390 Hundested
t. +45 2987 7766
w. lyn-x.dk

To explore this part of Sjælland from the water, you can **rent canoes** at the campsite and youth hostel in Frederiskværk, paddle through the canal into the great wide open water of Arresø, the biggest lake in Denmark.

Or discover the beauty of the coast by renting a craft from **Kajak & SUP** (**28**). From June to August you can rent one or the other or both from several places along the coast: in Gilleleje at Tinkerup Strandvej 32, in Tisvildeleje at Hovedgaden 112, in Liseleje at Lisehøjvej 10, and in Hundested at the Frisk Strandbar:

a. Amtsvejen 3, 3390 Hundested
t. +45 9155 0005

If you're curious about the alternative and sustainable way the eco-village **Dyssekilde** (**29**) works (the village that organises the Himmelstorm Festival), you can visit them, and even take a guided tour (only available in summer). Learn how the community built their village using exclusively ecological materials, and produces its own energy. And don't forget to stop by at the shops to take some of their tasty and fresh organic goods home.

a. Solen 15, 3390 Hundested
t. +45 4798 7026
w. dyssekilde.dk

At the organic farm Røjlegården, between Frederiksværk and Hundested, you'll find **Dyssekilde Yogacenter** (**30**). In summer they offer daily morning yoga classes at 8:00. When weather allows it, the yoga will be outdoors, smelling the flowers and counting the sheep in the field. If you want to stay on a bit at the farm (good way to make sure you're in time for the morning classes) you can pitch your tent, sleep in the shed, or rent a room at Røjlegården (w. roejle.dk).

a. Torupvejen 98, 3390 Hundested
w. dyssekildeyoga.dk

Children will like the sand sculptures, or better yet, love the opportunity to build their own at the Hundested **Sand Sculpture Festival** (**31**), held in Hundested harbour's boat hall. Not really a festival, more an exhibition of large sand sculptures, made by international sculptors, with a different theme each year. Half of the site is indoors, the other half in an enclosed open-air area. There's a café and a sandbox where kids can create their own piece of sand art. Open from mid-May to mid-September.

a. Kajgaden 7, 3390 Hundested
t. +45 5047 9830
w. sandfestival.dk

The sea sport centre **Lynæs Surfcenter** (**33**) offers courses, drop-in lessons and events involving kite and wind surfing, kayaking or SUP surfing. Their shop also rents out windsurfing gear, kayaks, SUPs, mountain bikes and fishing rods. Open from April to September.

a. Lynæs Havnevej 8, 3390 Hundested
t. +45 2987 7766
w. surfcenter.dk

The **Maritime Experience Center** (**32**) teaches children and adults about the marine environment and maritime professions at the Experience Platform. Every day fishermen bring examples of their catch in a small basin. Children can learn in an interesting way about the creatures that live in the ocean, and where the fish on their plate comes from. Local biologists explain their importance and role in the maritime system. The Experience Platform is open during school holidays and from July to mid-August.

a. Fiskeriets og Havnens Hus,
   Nordre Bedding 49, 3390 Hundested
t. +45 2928 9899
w. fiskerietsoghavnenshus.dk

EAT/DRINK/HANG OUT

◆

The **Frisk Strandbar** (**34**) in Hundested is located between the busy harbour, the beach and the pier. The part that usually makes up a perfect piece of no-man's land used by maybe a fisherman, a dog walker and a romantic couple. So, expect sea view, harbour view, a bit of a character, perfect coffees, sandwiches, BBQs and a real good vibe. Open all year during the weekends and daily in summer. ◆€◆

a. Amtsvejen 3, 3390 Hundested
t. +45 2986 2281
fb. Frisk Strandbar

In Hundested harbour you'll find the café and brewery **Halsnæs Bryghus** (**35**). A good place to start or end your evening, enjoy a beer, a hearty meal and usually some live music, from local talent to international stars, from jazz to pop and dance music. Open all year. ♦€€♦

a. Nordre Beddingsvej 35, 3390 Hundested
t. +45 2616 7046
w. halsbryg.dk

The former storage warehouse **Proviant** (**36**) is our pick in Hundested. This friendly family-run café and restaurant is not only a sight for sore eyes, but their food is fingerlicking good, original, and served with some fine wines. Coffee and cakes are also a treat. The building itself, which is said to be over 100 years old, is full of stories. It's supposed to have housed an illegal bar, colonial goods were handled, and at one point sailors bought their groceries here. The décor of Proviant is a smart mix between refined taste and historic insight and respect. Open all year during the weekends, and from Easter to October almost every day. ♦€♦ ♦€€♦

a. Havnegade 2A, 3390 Hundested
t. +45 4215 8714
w. provianthundested.dk

SHOP
♦

In the small community of Torup they've adapted the Book Town concept that was once initiated by a chap called Richard Booth from the UK. It comes down to individuals 'running' a bookstore, even if it only means having a shelf with a few books to either sell, rent or swap. Sort of a tiny bookstore movement. The books are donated for free, then sorted for quality and put out for sale. They can operate with the use of honesty boxes - people leave their change in a box or jar. The bookstore owners of **Torup Booktown** (**37**) earn a small income, part of which goes to the Torup Book Town Association, which, in turn, runs the annual Nordic Book Festival with music, films and talks from established authors. Anyway, what it comes down to; you'll find tiny bookstores all over the place in Torup, at the entrance of a farm, on a cart in a field, a stable, the railway station. How very bookish-cool is that!

a. 3390 Torup
w. torupbogby.dk

They like living the good and sustainable life in Torup, that's for sure. Don't miss the twice-monthly organic **Torup Market** (**38**) at the Dyssekilde Station. Torup's finest can be found at the market: food stalls, fresh drinks, fresh veggies, herbs, home-made marmalade, jam and local honey, and much more. Open from June to October, every odd Saturday, from 10:00 to 15:00.

a. Dyssekilde Station, Stationsvej 1, 3390 Torup
fb. Torup Marked

Have a peek at, or visit the many **ateliers, workshops and art shops (39)** in Hundested's harbour. You can choose from a selection of unique art and handicrafts like jewellery, bags, clothes, linen, ceramics, glass art, paintings, and wooden, stone and bronze sculptures.

Most shops are just behind the first row of restaurants on the waterfront, housed in former fishing huts. Not exactly the thing you expect to find at a harbour, and that's exactly what makes the Hundested harbour so unique and worth a visit. Hundested invites and encourages contemporary artists, and inventive start-ups to set up in the harbour, thus generating a creative hub that's attractive for artists and designers, locals and tourists.

Campervans can make use of all facilities at campsites that have the 'QuickStop' availability. This means you can spend your day and park your van wherever, and only use the campsite for a portion of the night, without having to pay the full amount (usually from 18:00 or 20:00 hrs till 10:00 hrs). You pay only for the facilities you use. Ask the campsites if they're part of QuickStop.

Vejby Strand Camping (40) is a family friendly campsite with lots of playground for young and older kids; a pool, tennis court, football pitch, mini golf and table tennis. There are pitches and cabins for rent that sleep up to 6 people. Vejby is also a QuickStop place. Open all year. ♦€♦

a. Rågelejevej 37, 3210 Vejby
t. +45 4041 6788
w. vejbystrandcamping.dk

At the organic and self-sustaining **Røjlegården farm (41)**, proud partners of the Torup Booktown, they rent out private double rooms, and have camping pitches in the garden, or you can stay in a wooden caravan. Your shower's heated by solar, veggies and fruit are from the garden and orchard. A peaceful haven for busy minds that need some time to reflect or calm down, only a 10-minute bike ride from the beach. Open all year. ♦€♦

a. Torupvejen 98, 3390 Torup
t. +45 4798 8016
w. roejle.dk

You can hardly miss the eye-catching **Hundested Harbour Cabins (42)**, looking out over the fishing harbour and Isefjord. The cabins sleep up to 4 people, are basic but spacious, you can bring your own linen or rent it. Open from April to October. ♦€♦

a. Havnegade 2, 3390 Hundested
t. +45 2129 2425
w. havnehytter.dk

Campervans (43) can stay overnight at 2 places in the Hundested harbour and make use of all the facilities in the harbour for a small fee. There are only a few places available. Open all year. ♦€♦

a. Havnegade 8, 3390 Hundested
w. hundestedhavn.dk

Lynæs Camping (44) is a basic campsite, located right by the water's edge of the Isefjord. Open all year. ♦€♦

a. Søndergade 57, 3390 Hundested
t. +45 4793 7907
w. dk-camp.dk/profile/lynaes_camping

Camping and hostel **Frederiksværk (45)** has pitches, cottages, and a circus saloon wagon. The hostel sleeps up to 75 people, most are shared rooms, and also rents out canoes. Open from March to October. ♦€♦

a. Strandgade 30, 3300 Frederiksværk
t. +45 2344 8844
w. fredfyldt.dk

Photo: Geert-Jan Middelkoop

SURF

◆

Not commonly known for surfing, the beaches of the Danish Riviera are prone to wind, and therefore popular with wind and kite surfers. The perk? While you might not have the beach to yourself, because surfing is a growing sport, it's far from crowded. The waves are mostly onshore wind waves, which, as all northern European surfers know, sounds less inviting than it actually is. Meaning it won't get epic, but it can be good. Most Sjælland breaks are perfect for surfers new to the sport, and introducing your children to surfing. And… just like Kelly Slater developed his skills from the sloppy waves of Florida, Sjælland is homeground to Denmark's best surfers, the brothers Christoffer and Oliver Hartkopp.

Ålsgårde (I) is a left pointbreak and beachbreak that needs a strong N-NW-W windswell. There's a jetty you can jump off to get straight into the line-up. A surf and sailing clubhouse sits next to the parking area. From the beach you'll have a view of Helsingør's Kronborg Castle in one direction, and Sweden on the other side.
◆ All levels/sand/small parking/ surf club/no facilities. ◆

One of Hornbæk's better breaks is **Plantage (II)**, a fickle low-tide beachbreak with rocks, that needs a strong NW windswell. Beautiful forested surroundings. ◆ All levels except beginners/sand and rocks/easy parking/no facilities. ◆

Hornbæk's main break is **Pier (III)**, a beachbreak on the east side of the harbour wall, which gives some protection from SW-W wind. Works best with medium to strong N-NW-W windswell.
◆ All levels/sand/easy parking/surf school/use of facilities in harbour. ◆

Beachbreak **Gilleleje (IV)** is on the east side of the harbour wall, which gives protection from SW-W wind. Works best with medium to strong N-NW-W windswell. ◆ All levels/sand bottom/easy parking at the harbour near the fishermen houses/use of facilities in harbour. ◆

Smidstrup (V) is a beachbreak with cobblestones and some concrete jetties. Needs a medium N-NW-W windswell. ◆ All levels/sand and stones/ easy parking/toilets. ◆

SCHOOL RENTAL REPAIR

◆

Hundested (VI) is a beachbreak and has a small pointbreak at the western end of the beach, near the cliffs. Needs a medium NE-N-NW-W windswell, the harbour wall offers some west wind protection. ◆ *All levels/sand/easy parking/bar and restaurant/toilets/showers at beach.* ◆

Bornholm (VII) is a bit of an outsider here. It's an island, it's the Baltic Sea, and according to local Dennie Hilding of Bornholm Surffarm, the island offers surfing for all levels, from heavy slabs, point breaks to soft peeling longboard waves. The north and east coast work best with NE windswell, but, since Bornholm is an island, you'll find some surf at all wave and wind directions. (How to get there, see Sleep section).

One of the oldest shops around is **Dark Blue Board Shop (46)** in Helsingør. Bit of a local hang out, and very well stocked.

a. Klostergade 8, 3000 Helsingør
t. +45 4921 0346
w. darkblue.dk

Hornbæk Surf Shop (47) (in Hornbæk, no less) offers surf lessons, rental of boards and sometimes organises trips with a speedboat to surf the wake. Open all year.

a. Havnevej 20, 3100 Hornbæk
t. +45 3024 3838
fb. Hornbaek Surf Shop

SEASIDE LOCAL: DENNIE HILDING

◆

Dennie Hilding lives on a farm on the Danish island of Bornholm, together with his wife, 6-year-old daughter, a dog, a cat, 3 horses and some chickens. Not just any farm though. This is the Bornholm Surf Farm: a project with a vision: living and promoting an ecological lifestyle and sustainable awareness.

"We cannot force trees and other nature properties to grow faster than they do."

Dennie was born and raised in Malmö, Sweden, where he then worked as a clinical psychologist, lecturer and mental trainer. But surfing was and is his greatest passion. In 2012 Dennie and his wife left their homeland Sweden, took their 6-month old baby, and moved to Bornholm due to its great nature and surf potential. "I had never even owned my own apartment before, and suddenly I was the owner of a farm, a tractor and 4 acres of land." Here, he had the opportunity to develop an idea he'd been dreaming of for a long time, which originated during the time he was travelling the world, backpacking, surfing and bunking at hostels. "My wish was to create the kind of hostel that I myself had been searching for during my travels. One that encourages you to go offline, to be present in the moment and to reconnect with the people and environment around you."

The Bornholm Surf Farm is a place where he and his wife realised all their ideas and dreams. The hostel and campsite offer surfers and outdoor enthusiasts an exciting way to experience the nature and spirit of Bornholm. "The philosophy behind the Surf Farm is based on a simple way of living, a close interaction with nature and the possibility to disconnect from technology distractions and a high tempo city lifestyle. We want guests to experience what it's like living temporarily 'off the grid' and hopefully get inspired to adopt some of our values and concepts back into their everyday lifestyle." He still works as a clinical psychologist today, and the psychologist side of him played a big part in the making of the farm, creating an offline retreat using healthy activities, such as surfing, cliff snorkelling and their horses as therapeutic tools. Setting up the farm wasn't a complete change of lifestyle, but rather an extension of Dennie's core values: "I have always known what kind of a lifestyle I was seeking to have." The Surf Farm will always be in a developing stage. "It is a part of me and it will continue to develop and evolve with me. I like the fact that things take the time they take. We cannot force trees and other nature properties to grow faster than they do. Here we do things the way nature allows." And the essence of what Dennie stands for: "I would like to encourage people to make more time for their passions and dare to take steps into the unknown and discomfort. The reward will be well worth it."

◆

w. bornholmsurffarm.com
Read the full story on **w.** iloveseaside.com/stories

◆

DENMARK

IN AND AROUND COPENHAGEN

There are many guides to Copenhagen, and we're not pretending we can cover the whole city in minutiae. But we like that Copenhagen, København, can literally be an active city break, in the way that you can explore the city by foot or bicycle and by water. We provide you with all sorts of options. And offer just about enough choice in food, drink, and places to stay that you'll enjoy the city as much as we did! If you have only a few days, or even only one day, pick one or two neighbourhoods to discover. Christianshavn, for example, is easily discovered by foot, accessible and close to the city centre. Find quirky shops, restaurants and cafés. On hot days it's best combined with a stroll along the former docks and warehouses on the quay, between the bridges Knippelsbro and Langebro. Vesterbro, just southwest of the centre, used to be a working-class district; today it's a mighty fine mix of entrepreneurs from all walks of life, from sex workers to artists. The main shopping area's found on and around Strøget, a pedestrian street right in the heart of city. Your closest escape to a nice seaside area would definitely be Bellevue Strand, on the northern outskirts. You can't miss the blue-striped lifeguard towers, very Instagram-worthy...

Tourist office at Vesterbrogade 4B.

TO DO

◆

Bicycling: We've been told there are more bikes in the city of Copenhagen than people - indicating the bicycle-friendliness of the city. And isn't it just one of the best ways ever to experience any place, especially a city. There are designated cycling paths, many bike rental stations, and the terrain is flat. Here's our pick of the smartest bike rentals in town:

When you rent your bike at **Baisikeli** (**1**), meaning bicycle in Swahili, you're not only helping yourself to a perfect means to explore the city, you're also helping the poorest of the world in getting access to 2 wheels. The Baisikeli project uses the profits of their Copenhagen bike rental shop to fix and ship used bikes to Tanzania, Sierra Leone and Ghana. Isn't that a sweet idea! We absolutely applaud this concept, and besides, their rental touring bikes are mighty fine, come with 27 gears, optional bike bags, and repair kit. Open all year.

a. Ingerslevsgade 80, 1705 København
t. +45 2670 0229
w. baisikeli.dk

The Nordic countries have a seemingly crazy habit of combining things that you'd never think of, but once combined it seems obvious, perfectly fitting - why didn't you come up with it yourself? **Wecycle Copenhagen** (**2**) is a place where both coffee and bicycle enthusiasts can get their fix. Owners Haukur and his wife select their coffee beans just as carefully as they do the bicycle saddles. Besides renting out vintage, retro-style bikes - that pedal as smooth as summer cherries, no worries - they also sell customised and vintage style bikes and gear, serve a fine beer if you're done with coffee, and Danish sweet treats. Open all year.

a. Islands Brygge 21, 2300 København
t. +45 7518 1855
w. wecycle.shop

Another superb way of traversing the city is travelling the many waterways and canals. You'll see Copenhagen from a surprising perspective, at a tempo that gives you ample opportunity to take it all in. We loved seeing the city from the water with one of the **Kayak Republic** (3) tours. They offer courses and different guided kayak tours; a City tour, Nordic food tour and Architectour. Water enthusiasts can also join a workshop to work on their kayak skills, or, if you're an experienced paddler, rent a kayak and paddle-ho! Your tour doesn't end with you handing over the paddle and kayak though - their location along the quay, with a terrace, Kayak bar, delicious home-made meals and floating beach make for an easy-going hang out to relax after your tour. They've got a changing room and showers too. Making a reservation for one of the tours is recommended. Open daily from April to September.

a. Børskaj 12, 1221 København (under Knippelsbro bridge)
t. +45 2288 4989
w. kayakrepublic.dk

Want a free ride AND satisfy your environmentally responsible self? Join Kayak Republic's **Green Kayak Project**. What's the deal? You and your buddy take a free kayak trip along the waterfront with the task of collecting trash from the water before it degrades into tiny pieces of much-hated microplastic. The project is a non-profit initiative, started and managed by Kayak Republic, funded by CultureHarbour365. If you want to join, act quickly. It's a grand success by both Copenhagen locals and tourists, and clean-up tours are easily booked solid until the end of season!

w. greenkayak.org

Less active but equally tranquil is renting one of the sustainable barges from **GoBoat** (4). The boats carry up to 8 people and the fab thing is; you don't need a licence or even experience to sail away. Even more satisfying is the fact that you drift through the canals in complete silence. The boats have an electric engine, powered by solar. You'll find the eco-friendly principle showing from the solar power to the sustainable wood of GoBoat's pavilion and tables, and the organic drinks they serve. Besides all that the boats are utterly loveable!

a. Islands Brygge 10, 2300 København
t. +45 4026 1025
w. goboat.dk

An equally satisfying way to discover the city, by foot. We selected a few tours by theme:

The name alone! **Hygge & Happiness Tour** (5)! Can you resist? The tour introduces you to a deeper understanding of the oh-so-Danish concept of hygge. What better way to learn than experience the very things that make hygge hygge. In a 3-hour tour you'll be immersed in Danish culture and the importance of hygge, and get useful one-to-one tips to create your own happy hygge. Available all year.

a. Meeting point at the corner of Øster Voldgade and Hjertensfrydsgade, København
t. +45 2082 5287
w. copenhagenurbanadventures.com

The **Alternative Tour Copenhagen** (6) is a 2,5 hour walking tour, guiding you away from the mainstream attractions to get you acquainted with a different side of Copenhagen. Get to know the eclectic, vibrant district of Vesterbro, and learn of the counter-culture of the famous free state of Christiania. As they say themselves: "This tour is an amazing tale of Copenhagen's underground scene, and the people who make it incredible. It's more than just a story of hipsters and down-and-outs; this is a tale of a totally different world questioning their cultural status quo." Available all year.

a. Meeting point: Espresso House Rådhuspladsen, Vesterbrogade 2A, 1620 København
t. +45 4097 3686
w. neweuropetours.eu/Copenhagen/en/sandemans-tours

It feels almost an obligatory to-do, to visit **Christiania** (7), the free state within the city of Copenhagen, set up in 1971. Called a 'social experiment' by one (the government), 'alternative' by others, 'different' by many; could be described as 'easy to find', after all it's in the centre of Christianshavn. Depending on which culture or country you're from, you'll either be impressed, shocked, bored, feel like an outsider, fit right in, feel inspired, or think it's all a bit of a hype. Maybe it's us, coming from Holland, seeing people smoking hasjies in public isn't our idea of an attraction or even that big-a-deal, or the place doesn't really shine through at first sight. It all feels a bit of an act, one that you're not part of, or don't feel too inspired to take part in. But that said, we're not objective... the guide's about what we like, and think you might like too. This one, Christiania, we simply couldn't figure out. But maybe go see for yourself. You might love it! There are guided tours in English led by a 'Christianit', to get an insight into the cultural, political and social life of the self-declared independent state, which will make more sense than just having a look around, like we did. Tours are every Saturday and Sunday at 15:00 hrs. (50 DKK).

w. christiania.org

Fælledparken is one of Copenhagen's most popular parks. It's used as a playground, for sunbathing, jogging, summer concerts and celebrations. Within the park you'll find the **Fælledparken Skatepark (8)**, one of the largest outdoor skate parks in Denmark. All levels are welcome, although advanced skaters are advised to use the late afternoon and evening hours to enjoy undisturbed skate sessions. All wheels are allowed: skateboards, BMX and roller skates. Open all year and free for use.

a. Edel Sauntes Allé, 2100 København

Indoor skating is available at **Copenhagen Skatepark (9)**, a former tram depot. It has a large vert ramp, street sections, ledges and rails, as well as a lounge and balcony to chill or watch. Open all year.

a. Enghavevej 80, 2450 København
t. +45 3321 2828
w. copenhagenskatepark.dk

If you don't want to skip your yoga routine while on a city break, there are options aplenty. The following 2 addresses are in Indre By, the inner city, near the main shopping area of Strøget:

If you like it sweaty and active, you're welcome to join a class at the studio of **Hot Yoga Copenhagen (10)**. Fruit, tea and snacks are waiting for you in the lounge area after class. Open all year.

a. Badstuestræde 11-13, 1209 København
t. +45 5388 1209
w. hotyogacph.dk

At **Hamsa Yoga (11)** you can join in classes of Vinyasa Flow and Hatha. Their studio's a haven of tranquility, designed with that subtle Scandinavian flair. Classes are open to each and everyone, no matter what your level is. Open all year.

a. Klerkegade 19, 1st floor,
1308 København
t. +45 2649 7077
w. hamsayoga.dk

Tivoli Garden is Copenhagen's amusement park, in the heart of the city, near the Copenhagen Central Station and the City Hall. Driving or walking through town, you'll spot a glimpse of it at one point or another, the tops of the wooden Rollercoa13ster sticking out above the trees, or the Vertigo turning people upside down. Every Friday night in summer there's **Fredagsrock (12)**: open-air concerts from national and international rap, rock and pop artists. Fredagsrock is from April to September, concerts always start at 22:00 hrs.

a. Vesterbrogade 3, Tivoli 1630 København
t. +45 3315 1001
w. fredagsrock.dk

EAT/DRINK/HANG OUT
◆

Vesterbrø is becoming more and more popular, but still far from mainstream. At the West Market food stalls you can get a taste of the world kitchen, with different stalls offering all sorts of food, sometimes accompanied by live music (Vesterbrogade 97; w. westmarket.dk). Vesterbrø's Meatpacking District is where Copenhagen's meat industry used to be. The neighbourhood's now a creative hub, known for its nightlife, and choice of small-scale restaurants that serve either unusual, exotic, vegan or experimental dishes and drinks. Same goes for the lively multicultural **Nørrebro (13)** area, otherwise known as 'Little Arabia'. Especially on Jæggersborggade, unknown to many tourists, you'll find some gems; shops, ice parlours, and restaurants. And the friendly **Christianshavn** area, where you'll surely end up at one point, has many, many little shops, eateries and cafés.

You wouldn't carry your Seaside guide if you didn't want to be close to the water most of the time. Luckily Copenhagen is blessed with waterfront eateries and cafés. Our pick is **Kayak Bar (14)**, right on the docks. Whether you've been kayaking or shopping, if you're looking for an unpretentious place to cool down, relax, kick off your sneakers or high heels AND enjoy a delicious meal or tasty snacks and a beer, this is your place. It's a pretty unique place for a city, and we can assure you the food's good and fresh. Open all year. ◆€◆ ◆€€◆

a. Børskaj 12, 1221 København (next to Knippelsbro bridge)
t. +45 3049 0013
w. kayakbar.dk

Smørrebrød, always a good idea. At luncheon restaurant **Ida Davidsen (15)**, one of the oldest restaurants in the city (since 1888, now run by the 5th generation, and still going very strong!) they serve the best open sandwiches. We were tipped off by locals on this one; you'll find it busy with regulars and tourists alike, which is always a good sign. Located in the city centre, Indre By. Open all year. ◆€◆ ◆€€◆

a. Store Kongensgade 70, 1264 København
t. +45 3391 3655
w. idadavidsen.dk

SHOP
◆

All the above-mentioned neighbourhoods, especially Christianshavn and Vesterbrø, have perfect shopping options if you're looking for a Scandinavian and more exclusive or alternative look. Around Strøget, in the inner city, you'll find the bigger chains and a large choice of shops.

Our perfect pick and fab favourite by far, the beautiful shop - and brand - **Oh Dawn (16)**. Maybe you've seen their men's collection of smart shirts, trousers and sweaters, caps and basics around, and in select shops all over Europe, but this is home base for Oh Dawn. Visiting their shop you totally get where they find their inspiration. Surrounded by concrete, but oh-so-close to the Scandinavian seaside and raw landscape. Oh Dawn find their roots in the Shred Sled Society, a surf collective of craftsmen and creatives, with a love for quality and clean lines (which, yes, can probably be interpreted as relating to surfing and design).

a. Pilestræde 47, 1112 København
t. +45 301 45 030
w. ohdawn.com

Surfers, photographers and designers Kasper Harup-Hansen and Jane Stub Kirchhoff, opened up the one shop that was still missing in the centre of Copenhagen. **Surf Studio Naami (17)** is a teeny tiny lifestyle and surf shop, bringing beach life and aloha to the city.

You'll find photographs, books, unique apparel, eco-wax, stylish fins, good vibes, and yep, cold drinks are served as well. Open all year.

a. Puggaardsgade 7, 1573 København
t. +45 2442 0248
w. naamilife.com

SLEEP
◆

Family-friendly **Hundige Strand Familiecamping** (**18**) is Denmark's oldest campsite. Within walking distance of the beach and with a regularly running 15-minute train ride from the centre. Open from April to October. ◆€◆

a. Hundige Strandvej 72, 2670 Greve
t. +45 4390 3185
w. hsfc.dk

Backpacker hostel **Sleep in Heaven** (**19**), love that name, is located in the heart of Nørrebro. Yes, the lesser-known neighbourhood filled with arty shops, cool bars and small eateries. If you're lost for choice where to go and what to do, ask the friendly staff, they'll be happy to inform you and give you insider tips. A lively hub, with light but cosy communal areas, a bar with a daily happy hour, and the best place to meet fellow travellers. They offer walking tours and bike hire. You can choose between dorm-style rooms that sleep from 3 to 16 people. Open all year. ◆€◆

a. Struenseegade 7, 2200 København
t. +45 3535 4648
w. sleepinheaven.com

One of the cosiest hostels of Copenhagen must be the **Bedwood Hostel** (**20**). Situated in a former 18th century warehouse in the Nyhavn district, the 2 owners of the hostel built it up from scratch and created a stylish place. It's within the budget reach of a hostel, but not a party-hard place. There's a downstairs bar, and a quiet courtyard, perfect for the sunny days; it's plenty hygge and sociable. Choose between dorm-style rooms, where each bunk bed has curtains for privacy, or private rooms. Within every detail of the hostel you can tell the owners are avid travellers themselves, they seemed to have figured out all the needs for both city dweller and backpacker. There's no age limit, they have bicycles for rent, there's a small communal kitchen, and every morning a breakfast buffet is served. Open all year.

a. Nyhavn 63, 1051 København
t. +45 6142 6146
w. bedwood.dk

Although it's nowhere near Copenhagen, the island of Bornholm, just off the coast of Ystad, Sweden, is Danish. And easily reachable from Copenhagen, thus the eco-certified **Bornholm Surf Farm** (**21**) finds its place in this section. It's one of the most extraordinary places we offer in this guide. Everything on the farm is designed around and based on the quest for a simpler way of living, slowing down the up-tempo city lifestyle and being aware of fast consumption and processes in our day-to-day lives. And the good thing is, it's so enjoyable! It's not about taking away luxuries, but adding moments of awareness, enjoying moments we tend to overlook or take for granted, like cooking, or taking a shower. And of course there's surfing! And SUP safaris. What, you're on an island, surrounded by the sea! The hostel has dorm-style rooms, and there's a private room available as well, or you can rent a tent or pitch your own. All rooms have ocean view. The farm has a large communal kitchen and room with books and a pool table, you can use the BBQ, oven and fridge. From Copenhagen you can reach the island either by flight (30 minutes) or bus/train/car via Ystad, or boat (3 hours). By bus, Rute 700 takes you straight from Copenhagen to Bornholm (**w.** rute700.dk). Open all year. ♦€♦ ♦€€♦

a. Vassebækvej 5, 3760 Gudhjem, Bornholm
t. +45 6151 9506
w. bornholmsurffarm.com

Photo: Tim Wendrich

North-Jutland

NORTH JUTLAND

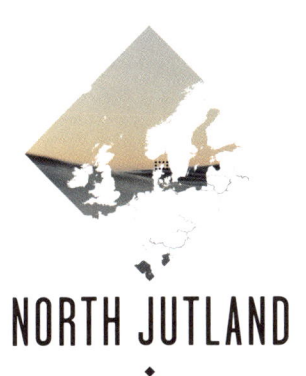

In the north of Jutland's peninsula you'll find sand dunes, forests, farmers' fields and endless beaches - some of them you can drive your car over! Prevailing winds from the west have bent trees forever eastwards. The north of Jutland is separated from the south by the not-actually-a-fjord Limfjord (we'll save the geology lessons for later). The emptiness, the surrounding water and yellow fields of grain produce a special kind of light, that makes even cloudy days seem somewhat sunny. From Skagen at the very tip, along the Limfjord, to surf paradise Klitmøller, water is omnipresent. Small fishing settlements, now turned into summer resorts, are still very much thriving on fish, adding to the genuine character of the little seaside towns. If you're prone to agoraphobia, the fear of large spaces, this is not your ideal destination. If you love vast landscapes of nothing and nobody, get in the van. Or on the bus, train, plane. You've found your heaven on earth.

TRAVEL INFO

◆

Public transport in Denmark is well organised, whether using bus or train, or both, you'll get to your destination - even the smallest community - one way or another.

BY BOAT
◆

Ferries sail to/from Sweden and Norway to/from Hirtshals or Frederikshavn in North Jutland.

w. colorline.dk / fjordline.com

BY CAR
◆

If you want to drive the most scenic routes through Denmark, follow the Marguerite Route: clearly marked by brown signs with a white and yellow marguerite daisy. The route's named after the favourite flower of Margrethe II, Queen of Denmark. The route's easy to follow, leave and pick up again.

Photo: Tim Wendrich

IN AND AROUND LØKKEN

The rows of white beach huts and fishing vessels on the beach, the small town with its yellow-washed houses right behind the dunes, and of course its surfing possibilities, all add to Løkken's charm. In summer it's a popular seaside resort, in winter a desolate fishing village, just like almost all other seaside towns along the north Jutland coast. The area between Løkken, Tranum and Blokhus, to the south, feels like the dreamed up landscape of a poetic forester. There's the endless stretch of beach, first and foremost, with a backdrop of woodland, fields that either look ravaged by strong winds, or picture-perfect, wheat waving in greens and browns, horses and big horned cows in matching colours. Choose any thoroughfare from the main road between Løkken and Blokhus, and you'll end up at the beach eventually, passing lonely houses hidden in the dunes. But, what are we rambling on about! You'll be there already, obviously, since this is one of the very few places in Europe where you're allowed to drive your car on the beach!

Tourist office at Jyllandsgade 15, 9480 Løkken (next to SuperBrugsen supermarket).

TO DO
◆

You know that cliché of the journey being more important than the destination? Maybe you should remind yourself of it, walking from the parking area at Grenen, just north of Skagen, towards the point where the Skagerrak (North Sea) meets the Kattegat (Baltic Sea). There are few places in the world where you can witness such a phenomenal sight, and it's definitely worth going. Don't expect big colliding waves, but there's a certain serene and almost cleansing feel to sticking your toes in the sea at the very tip of the **colliding seas at Grenen** (**1**). Consider the long walk to the point, usually accompanied by other tourists from all over the world, and some nosy seals popping their heads up, as a tiny pilgrimage...

a. Grenen, 9990 Skagen

The migrating sand dune **Råbjerg Mile** (**2**) is Denmark's largest dune, shifting ever so slowly northeast. Stay long enough and you may almost notice it. Nah. Think not. But it does move away from the ocean with the speed of some 15 m each year! There are hiking paths aplenty, but please stay on the trails, we don't want any seaside-lovers disappearing in the quicksand areas.

a. Råbjerg Mile, 9990 Skagen

Ah, best thing ever! **Driving your car or van alongside the North Sea** (**3**), on the beach, between Blokhus and Løkken. No need for a four-wheel drive, any old campervan will do! Another section where you can drive on the compacted sand of the beach is between Kandestederne (south of Skagen) and Skiveren.

In the seaside village of Lønstrup, small white and yellow houses line the Strandvejen, the main road that leads to the beach. In some of them you'll find artist's workshops and galleries. Why'd you end up in the picturesque settlement? It's close to **Rubjerg Knude Fyr** (**4**), probably Denmark's most photographed, or at least most photogenic lighthouse. While it's still here. Fact is: the lighthouse is being swallowed by the sand. First casting its light over the ocean in 1900, from what was the highest point inland, some 200 m from sea, the lighthouse was lit for the last time in 1968 after being slowly consumed by ever-increasing dunes around the building. It's top is still the highest point of this part of the west coast, looking straight out to sea, but not for much longer, as it's been accepted that to struggle against nature is futile in this instance. Another building due to disappear within the next 10 years or so: the remains of the medieval Mårup Kirke - just south of Lønstrup sits this church on the cliff, awaiting its doom. Now only 10 m away from the eroding clifftop, it's bound to crash down to sea at one point or another, the harsh surroundings and weather relentless, and indifferent to its stories and history.

Saga Heste (5) riding centre offers horse riding tours in the surroundings of Skallerup. You'll be riding along the beach, through forests and dunes, on the back of Icelandic horses, one of the gentlest of horse breeds.
a. Nørlev Strandvej 391, 9800 Hjørring
t. +45 2346 2182
w. sagaheste.com

Yoga at the beach, and a sauna afterwards? During the summer months **North Shore Surf (6)** offers yoga lessons on the beach. Toes in the sand, stretching your body towards the sun and afterwards you can slough that last bit of stress in their beach sauna. Perfect! You can register for a session in the surf café, at the entrance to the beach in Løkken.
a. Søndre Strandvej 18, 9480 Løkken
t. +45 2070 8643
w. northshoresurf.dk

Løkken Bryghus (7) brews in the tradition of the old craft breweries. You can visit and learn about the art of brewing beer, and of course taste examples, during a guided tour. Open all year.
a. Vrenstedvej 12, 9480 Løkken
t. +45 5010 8330
w. loekkenbryghus.dk

Rent a (fat)bike at **Hune-Blokhus Cykeludlejning (8)** and pedal along the North Sea shore, from Blokhus up north, or down south, wherever you like, you're on a fat bike! To the north, however, you'll be biking on the beach over compacted sand where cars are also allowed. Fat bikes can be rented straight from the beach in summer months. Open all year.
a. Pirupvejen 7, Hune, 9492 Blokhus
t. +45 2578 8620
w. lejencykel.dk

The Blokhus Dune Plantation is a mostly forested area of some 640 hectares, serving as a recreational area, with hiking trails, picnic areas and a playground. A well signposted 10-km long **MTB trail (9)** runs through the plantation. Beginning and end are east of Blokhus Gateway at the Plesnersvej, just off road 559 (Aalborgvej).

EAT/DRINK/HANG OUT
◆

You'll easily spot the **Keramikcafé Møllehuset (10)**, right next to a typical Dutch windmill (how did that end up there!), just off the Lønstrup coast. Great place to sit outdoors on a sunny day, munching on their delicious homemade cakes, eating a sourdough sandwich for lunch or having a refreshing juice. All served on or in their own ceramic plates and cups. And if you like them, go inside the shop, and get your hands on some beautiful pottery stuff. Lots of cobalt blue, since that's the favourite colour of the lady who creates them, Kerstin Feldkamp. Open all year from Tuesday to Sunday, in December from Thursday to Sunday. ◆€◆ ◆€€◆
a. Skallerupvej 810, 9800 Hjørring (close to Lønstrup)
t. +45 9898 1616
w. mollehuset.com

The most perfect hang out at the beach of Løkken is the friendly and nicely decorated **North Shore Surf Café (11)**. At the entrance to the beach, nestled in the dunes, you can either sit outside on the terrace that extends to the beach, order inside or at the Food Truck, have a pre-beach coffee or an after-surf sauna and don't worry about closing times, since they vary with the weather and activities. So even for a late night beer you could well end up here. Open every day from June to September. ◆€◆ ◆€€◆
a. Søndre Strandvej 18, 9480 Løkken
t. +45 2070 8643
w. northshoresurf.dk

SHOP
◆

While you're at their beach café, why not take a short jaunt into town and check out the shop-restaurant-bar-boutique hotel of North Shore Surf: **Havs (12)**. Smartly decorated and exhaling everything surf related. You'll find all necessary surf gear, boards, fishing rods, clothes, books and more. Open all year. Hotel info in Sleep Section.

a. Søndre Strandvej 16, 9480 Løkken
t. +45 2760 5098
w. husethavs.dk

SLEEP
◆

Campervans can make use of all facilities at campsites that are part of the 'QuickStop' scheme. It means you can spend your day driving around wherever and then use the campsite only for the night, without having to pay the full amount (usually from 18:00 or 20:00 till 10:00 hrs the next day). Ask at the campsites to find out whether you can make a QuickStop.

Campervans (13) can also park and stay at Løkken Mobile Home Park. It's just a field without facilities to empty toilet/waste water, but there's electricity and you can shower in the owner's house. Open all year. ◆€◆

a. Løkkensvej 875, 9480 Løkken
t. +45 2299 4134

Campervans (14) can stay overnight in the lovely garden of Galleri Munken in Løkken, a private terrain. Simple but clean facilities, and a quiet place to sleep. There are limited pitches, so reservation is recommended. Open from May to October. ◆€◆

a. Munkensvej 11, Ingstrup, 9480 Løkken
t. +45 7026 9050
w. gallerimunken.dk

Løkken Familie Camping (15) has large pitches and rents out cabins and cottages on a large plot surrounded by nature. They're also part of the QuickStop scheme. Open from April to September. ◆€◆

a. Løkkensvej 910, 9480 Løkken
t. +45 9899 1238
w. lokkennord.d

The former boutique hotel Løkken Strand teamed up with North Shore Surf and combined the shop, bar and restaurant with the hotel to create **Havs (16)**. Even closer to the beach, surfer friendly, still run with heart and soul, and decorated with love and a personal touch. Open all year. ◆€€◆

a. Søndre Strandvej 16, 9480 Løkken
t. +45 2760 5098
w. husethavs.dk

Svinkløv Camping (17) holds deep respect for nature, and their pitches are decidedly shaped by nature's own way – picking your pitch is an experience in itself they say! For sure you'll find privacy, peace and quiet and perfect views of the North Sea. The campsite's close to the quiet stretch of beach of Slettestrand. We love this one! Open from March to October. ◆€◆

a. Svinkløvvej 541, 9690 Fjerritslev (close to Tranum)
t. +45 9821 7180
w. svinkloevcamping.dk

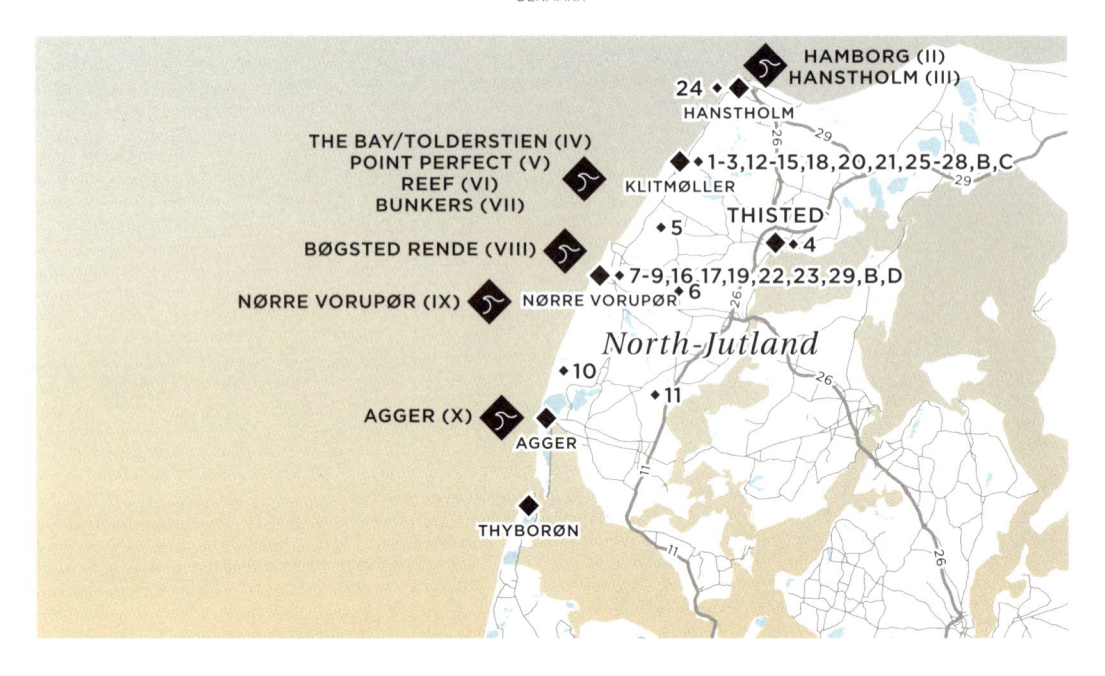

IN AND AROUND KLITMØLLER AND NØRRE VORUPØR

Cold Hawaii and Vegas, these two names pop up regularly when talking about either Klitmøller (Cold Hawaii) or Nørre Vorupør. The latter's not known for its gambling and showgirls whatsoever. It's just easier to pronounce for, well, everyone that's not Danish. The Cold Hawaii for Klitmøller is more obvious. It's known for consistent surf, whether you prefer using a sail, kite, board or SUP. However much we love the sound of Cold Hawaii, we figure 'Hossegor of the North' fits better. Especially when referring to its vibe and the way everybody (young enough to get away with it) dresses like dudes and dudettes. And every other bar and shop has something to do with surfing.

Both villages were heavily dependent on fishery, and trade with Norway - mainly grain and meat shipped from Klitmøller. Nørre Vorupør still has a thriving coastal fishery community. Boats are pulled back onto the beach with a hydraulic winch and you'll see fishermen piling up boxes loaded with lobster. Surrounded by squalling seagulls, waiting for leftovers, often the undesirable parts of crab. Where Nørre Vorupør has a more genuine fishing village feel to it, Klitmøller has perfectly integrated modern architecture into its surf-mindedness. The promenade, Foreningsvejen, links beach and town in smooth style; with the local surf club, instead of being a shed on the beach as standard, integrated into it. The surrounding Thy National Park covers an area of 244 square km, including the rugged, windswept coastline (with some WWII German bunkers as silent reminders of less pleasant times past), dunes, forests, lakes and moors. The ideal playground for hikes, bike rides, a bit of bird watching, or whatever you feel like doing in nature, as long as you don't harm it.

Tourist office at Store Torv 6, 7700 Thisted.

TO DO

◆

Surfjoint is an annual surf festival, organised by Cold Hawaii and the Klitmøller surf club NASA (North Atlantic Surf Association). It's big, with over 1000 people attending from all over Europe. What to expect? Surfing of course, with international comps in wind, wave and kite surfing, live music, films, BBQs and free surf lessons. The festival's usually held at end of July.

fb. surfjoint

The **Klitmöller Skatepark (1)** is a small 'street plaza'. It includes banks, ledges, stairs, curbs and a mini vert. The park's located near the harbour and all levels are welcome. Open all year.

a. Ørhagevej 150, Klitmøller, 7700 Thisted
w. skateparks.dk/nordjylland

Vahine, short for Vahineura, the Tahitian born surfer and yoga teacher of **Ocean Yoga Dance Studio (2)**, teaches her own style of Vinyasa yoga. Drop-in classes available, and if you like her style, why not join one of her long-weekend retreats? Send a text message for her next class.

a. Ocean Yoga Dance Studio, Ørhagevej 89, Klitmøller, 7700 Thisted
t. +45 2814 7799
w. vahine.dk

Admire the innovative architecture of the beach promenade (Foreningsvejen) and the **North Atlantic Surf Association Surf Club (3)** at the far end of the village, opening up to the ocean. The building's called the Hummerhus, the Lobster House, since it's built on the former fishermen's landing site. You can check the waves from its roof, or hide from the rain under its roof. The clubhouse is only open to members, but if you ask politely, a friendly member might let you have a peek.

a. Ørhagevej 189, Klitmøller, 7700 Thisted
w. nasa.coldhawaii.eu

The **Thy Cablepark (4)** is a child friendly active water park where you're pulled by a cable instead of a boat, making it easier to try your hand at wakeboarding or water skiing. Find them east of Klitmøller, at the Thisted Bredning, part of the Limfjord. Open from April to September.

a. Vibedalsvej 2, 7700 Thisted
t. +45 3131 0902
w. thycablepark.dk

At the Tvorup Dune Plantation, in Thy National Park, there are 2 signposted **MTB trails (5)**. The white route is easy, 6 km long, and goes along gravel roads. The green route is 10 km long, a challenging route with steep vertical climbs. Start and end at the sign 'Tvorup MTB rute' on the Tvorupvej, in Torup, just southeast of Klitmøller.

Thy Whisky (6) offers guided tours and whisky tasting. Danish Single Malt Whisky, no less! The whisky's made with organic ingredients grown in and around the Thy National Park and from the family farm of one the producers, Nicolaj Nicolajsen. Together with his good friend and distiller, Anders Bilgram, he started Thy Whisky in 2009. You'll love the characteristic scent of old bourbon and sherry casks in their cellars. The casks, which they collected from an American and Spanish distillery, add to the flavour of their whisky. Open all year, on reservation.

a. Gyrupvej 14, 7752 Snedsted
t. +45 2275 4819
w. thy-whisky.dk

There's a small **skate ramp (7)** at the site of surf shop Westwind in Nørre Vorupør.

Pretty special, and safer for children, is the **Havbad (8)**, the Sea Bath, on the south side of the pier in Nørre Vorupør. A concrete pool's been created so you can take a saltwater dip while protected from the North Sea, whatever the wave and wind circumstances are.

Try a very early morning stroll along the beach and **Stenbjerg Landingsplads (9)**, before anyone else (except perhaps some fishermen and dog walkers) is around. Built in the early 20th century, the old Landingsplads still look exactly the same. A row of white fishermen's huts line the street towards the sea, which were used for storage of fishing equipment like nets and ropes until the beginning of the 1970s. When no longer needed, the local community couldn't stand the sad sight of the huts wasting away and so initiated the restoration works of 2000 and 2012. Some huts are now used for recreational fishing. At the old lifeboat station you can see an exhibition of the history of the place. Every year in July there's a music and food celebration, the Stenbjergdagen, on Stenbjerg day, although it's pretty much a people-party for the locals, you're sure to be welcome. Stenbjerg Landingsplads is off road 181, between Klitmøller and Agger.

w. stenbjerglandingsplads.dk

The 35 m tall granite tower of the 19th century **Lodbjerg Lighthouse (10)** offers a splendid view over Thy National Park. Saves you time exploring the park, you just have to climb the few steps up. If you do want to hike, now that you've seen the beauty of it, the lighthouse is the starting point for hikes through the park, one of which leads up to the high dune of Penbjerg. The lighthouse is open daily, between 7:00 and 21:00 hrs.

a. Lodbjergvej 33, 7770 Vestervig

Have it all done: nails, face, body. Or just enjoy the Finnish sauna and a dip in cold water afterwards. **Sydthy Kurbad (11)** is a luxury spa offering all sorts of massages, baths, scrubs and treatments. Bit of me-time, why not!

a. Idrætsvej 5, 7760 Hurup Thy
t. +45 9917 3160
w. sydthy-kurbad.dk

EAT/DRINK/HANG OUT

◆

Klitmøller Street Food (12) is a small cluster of food trucks, near the beach. Using mostly local produce, the different trucks offer dishes such as veggie burgers, sandwiches, coffee and cakes. You can either sit on their terraces or order take-away. Open in July and August. ◆€◆

a. Ørhagevej 169-171, Klitmøller, 7700 Thisted
t. +45 5186 1125
fb. Klitmøller Street Food

Experience the joys of a slow coffee, prepared with the AeroPress, or go for a quick fix from the espresso machine. Either way, café **Haandpluk (13)** serves a mighty tasty coffee, made with love and special care, no matter which you choose. While waiting for your coffee, have a look around at the products for sale: hand-picked choices of tea, cheese, chocolate, beer and well errr… coffee. Sit inside or in the large garden. Recently, the owner of Haandpluk started brewing his own 100% organic beer, 3 Crates Brewing. So, coffee or beer, what's it going to be? Both maybe? Get them here, in a garage, steps away from Klitmøller's centre - follow the signs from the main street. Open all

year from Thursday to Sunday. ♦€€♦

a. Vestermøllevej 18, Klitmøller, 7700 Thisted
t. +45 3122 8088
w. haandpluk.dk

The Garden Poké Bar (14) in Klitmöller is the brainchild of surfer/yogini Vahine. On the menu you'll find vegetarian or vegan variations of poke bowls. And drinks, ice-cream and smoothie bowls too. Friendly hangout, take-away available. Closed in winter. ♦€♦

a. Ørhagevej 147, Klitmøller, 7700 Thisted
t. +45 9797 5430
w. gardencafe.dk

The pancake café **Kesses Hus (15)**, on the last corner of Klitmøller's main street towards the beach, serves the most delicious crêpes and galettes, with heaps and heaps of different fillings. You'd swear owner Mai Knudsen's French, if you'd only taste her pancakes. Good news for the gluten intolerant; galettes are gluten-free. Inside it's hygge enough, but on warm days we'd recommend sitting in their lovely garden. Open every weekend from Easter to October, and daily in July and August. ♦€♦ ♦€€♦

a. Bavnbak 4, Klitmøller, 7700 Thisted
t. +45 6169 3816
w. kesseshus.dk

Something about pancakes and Danes. **Pandekagehjørnet (16)**, Pancake Corner, in Nørre Vorupør, also serves extremely tasty and large pancakes. Besides, their mighty fine hot chocolate with whipped cream isn't bad at all, au contraire. You'll feel satisfyingly stuffed for the day after one of each. Open from Easter to October. ♦€♦ ♦€€♦

a. Vesterhavsgade 129A, Nørre Vorupør, 7700 Thisted
t. +45 6082 3373
w. pandekagehjoernet.dk

Not in the most obvious location, but well hidden places are usually the best. The ice parlour **ISmejeriet THY (17)** is a little gem, where friendly and enthusiastic staff help you pick from many, many tastes of their own-made ice-cream. Vegan choices available, we like! They're situated at the end of the harbour. Open from Easter to October. ♦€♦

a. Vesterhavsgade 147, 7 Nørre Vorupør, 7700 Thisted
t. +45 2015 1234
fb. ISmejeriet THY

SHOP

♦

The beautiful store **Klitmøller Collective** (**18**) stands out from any shop, whether surf or fashion related. But it does have a definite connection to both. A connection to the ocean for sure: "We're not a surf brand", says owner Robert, "we're an ocean brand." There's no polyester or acrylic used in their knitting, it's either wool or cotton, and produced in Portugal. The look and feel of the clothes they design, the sustainable approach towards creating them, and the creators themselves, all strongly bond with living close to the sea. Their attire has a distinctive no-fuss, clean cut, quality feel to it, like the shop itself: stylish, but sturdy. No big logos needed, it's good taste all over the place. Open all year.

a. Ørhagevej 80, Klitmøller, 7700 Thisted
t. +45 5350 4062
w. klitmollercollective.dk

Slow Works (**19**) is the little shop and studio right next to the co-working space and Guest House Klitmøller. Locals Benthe and Troels, who run the shop, sell their own Slow Work label products and attire. And just like the Klitmøller Collective, they're strongly connected to the seaside, the ocean and have typical clean Scandinavian design. Nice to know that all their indigo-coloured clothes are a reference to the ocean, and besides, naturally dyed with indigo. Open all year.

a. Ørhagevej 84, Klitmøller, 7700 Thisted
t. +45 2324 0434
w. slowworks.dk

In **Cold Hawaii Board Shop** (**20**) you'll find all your surf necessities, like wetsuits, wax, leashes and their own brand of boards, Columbus. The Columbus surfboards are designed by owner and avid surfer Mor Meluka. Originally from Israel, Mor's made quite a name for himself due to his surfing style and skills, and enthusiasm for surfing and the area in general. The shop also serves as a café and relaxed hang out for local and visiting surfers. Their bar serves coffee, home-made cakes, and craft beers. Open from Easter to November.

a. Ørhagevej 151, Klitmøller, 7700 Thisted
t. +45 2910 8873
w. coldhawaiisurfcamp.com

One of the many surf shops of **West Wind** (**21**) sits right next to the beach and has a large choice and stock of all surf necessities. Their perk? The surfers' sauna! To warm up after your cold water session. Open from Easter to November.

a. Ørhagevej 150, Klitmøller, 7700 Thisted
t. +45 9797 5656
w. klitmoller.westwind.dk

Besides Patagonia wetsuits, the smart little **VØ Surf Shop** (**22**) exclusively sells their own brand of clothing, Nørre Vegas, and other apparel from Danish designers and brands, most of it also produced in Denmark. Owned and run by a very friendly couple who also offer surf lessons, and SUP tours on the lakes if there's no surf. They work closely with a local shaping bay who can help you shape your own board. Perfect place to go shopping for some unique t-shirts or unexpected presents, even if you're not interested in surfing at all, but like stylish stuff. Closed in winter.

a. Hawblink 2, Nørre Vorupør, 7700 Thisted
t. +45 3131 5087
w. surfkollektiv.dk

You'll find another **West Wind** (**23**) surf shop in Nørre Vorupør, offering a large selection of clothes, and new and second-hand boards. They recently put up a skate ramp in front of the shop. Find them at the parking, just behind the beach. Open from Easter to October.

a. Hawblink 4, Nørre Vorupør, 7700 Thisted
t. +45 6185 5060
fb. westwindVorupor

SLEEP

♦

Campervans (24) can use the service station with all facilities, for free, at the Circle K Hanstholm.

a. Bødkervej 25, 7730 Hanstholm

The idea behind small-scale **Guest House Klitmøller (25)** is to be a place where you and your family, or partner, can truly relax, feel at home after a long day in the water or at the beach, and have all the luxuries you need, without the feel of an anonymous hotel. It's easy to meet other guests in the communal areas, like the dining room or kitchen. The guesthouse has double rooms with private bathrooms and some with shared bathrooms, one single room, an outdoor sauna and bathtub. Open all year. ♦€€♦

a. Ørhagevej 84, Klitmøller, 7700 Thisted
t. +45 4166 0477
w. guesthouse-klitmoller.dk

Cold Hawaii Surf Camp (26) has a large house, divided into 8 private rooms, a shared kitchen and living room, and garden. The house is less than 1 km from the beach, close to the centre and the local supermarket. Open from Easter to November. ♦€♦

a. Ørhagevej 69, Klitmøller, 7700 Thisted
t. 45 2910 8873
w. coldhawaiisurfcamp.com

Klitmøller Hus (27) is a beautiful family house, sleeping up to 10 people, in the middle of the dunes that surround Klitmøller. It has 2 bathrooms, a sauna, wood-burner, well, just about everything you could wish for to make your holidays more comfortable than your own flat.

w. klitmollerhus.com

The **Nystrup Camping Klitmøller (28)** has pitches and cabins for rent that sleep up to 6 people. The campsite is completely surrounded by trees, sheltering you from wind and shading from the sun. Located right next to the beach and smack in the middle of National Park Thy. The campsite rents out bicycles as well. Open from March to October. ♦€♦

a. Trøjborgvej 22, Klitmøller, 7700 Thisted
t. +45 9797 5249
w. nystrupcampingklitmoller.dk

The **Strandgaardens Camping (29)** in Nørre Vorupør is also directly by the sea, and close enough to town to walk to shops and restaurants. Open March to October. ♦€♦

a. Vesterhavsgade 85, Nørre Vorupør, 7700 Thisted
t. +45 9793 8022
w. strandgaardenscamping.dk

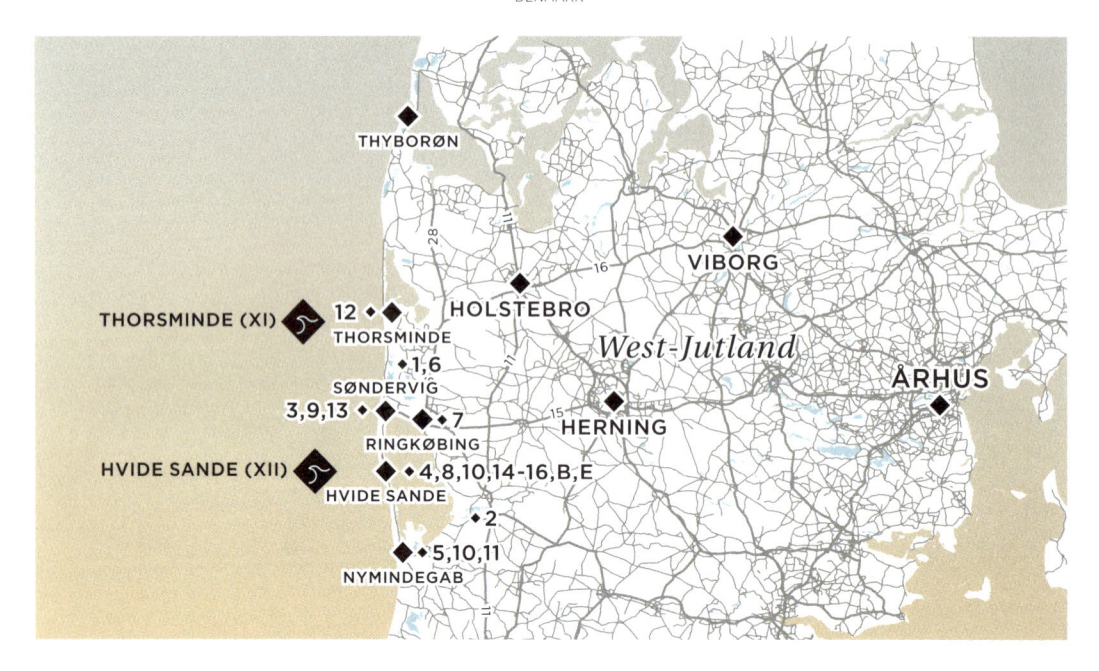

IN AND AROUND HVIDE SANDE

It's all quiet and peaceful at the Hvide Sande front. Even in the midst of summer, the season that West Jutland and the Ringkøbing fjord area come to life, you can find yourself all by your lonesome, all day long. It's exactly what attracts tourists, most deriving from the northern European countries. The chance to wander great lengths without encountering many people. To look and see beyond horizons, without your eyes bumping into houses, towns, or any urban signs for that matter. The land's flat as a pancake, so the horizon reaches far. From Klitmøller to Agger you'll be driving along and through the Thy national park, with many options to hop off the highway, go hike, picnic, bike, check beaches. From Thyborøn, nestled by the Limfjord, to the Ringkøbing fjord, it's dunes, beaches, small settlements centred around a white-washed church, golden fields of grain, some windmills and a horse or two. Hvide Sande itself, meaning 'white sand', sits on the small stroke of land between the fjord and the North Sea. Being surrounded by water, obviously fishery is thriving. Driving through the village of Thorsminde, just north of Hvide Sande, gives an indication of what to expect from its bigger brother. It's a mini version of Hvide Sande, with its harbour, fish auction and smokehouses. Less touristy, more genuine.

Tourist office at Nørregade 2b, 6960 Hvide Sande (in same building as Fiskeriets Hus).

JUTLAND

TO DO

♦

The Nordic people really do love the kindly Icelandic horse. **Vedersø Ridecenter (1)** takes you through forested areas and along the beach on the back of these very gentle breed, tours varying in length and level. Open all year.

a. Vesterhavsvej 5, Vedersø, 6990 Ulfborg
t. +45 6110 7409
w. vedersoeridecenter.dk

Perfect family day out: the **WOW-Park (2)**, offers some challenging tree-top adventures, experiencing a forest from up above. Open from Easter to September.

a. Løvstrupvej 1, 6900 Skjern
t. +45 2329 1130
w. wowpark.dk

Every year some 40 artists build sand sculptures at the **Søndervig Sand Sculpture Festival (3)**, based on a different theme each time. Kids can put their hands into sculpting their own creative fantasies in a special sand basin. Open daily from May to October.

a. Lodbergsvej 44, Søndervig, 6950 Ringkøbing
t. +45 2889 7844
w. sandskulptur.dk

At **Wakepark (4)** near Hvide Sande, on the lakeside, you can try your wakeboard and water skiing skills, whether you're a first-timer or experienced. You'll be pulled by a cable, not a boat, the cable being able to draw up to 10 people at once. There's a little eatery serving burgers and coffee.

Open from May to October.

a. Gytjevej 15B, 6960 Hvide Sande
t. +45 2872 8000
w. kabelpark.dk

A beautiful way of spending a windless and waveless day is to SUP your way through the Ringkøbing fjord and waterways. **Windsport (5)** organises SUP tours, rents out SUPs, and gives SUP lessons in sea and lake. Open from Easter to October.

a. Vesterhavsvej 326, 6830 Nymindegab
t. + 45 2142 8797
w. windsport.dk

233

EAT/DRINK/HANG OUT

◆

Scandinavians love their coffee, and are good at doing what they love. At the **Fjand Gårdbutik (6)** you can enjoy a good cuppa, home-made cakes and light lunches. In the shop you can choose between different sorts of coffee, tea, pottery and... Norwegian knitwear. Ehm. You never know when you might need it! Fjand Gårdbutik has more on offer: regular exhibitions, in summer a weekly buffet accompanied by live music, with folky, singer/songwriter and jazz musicians. And if you'd like to stay a bit longer, they have a B&B as well. The very friendly staff love to help you out, show you around, or just have a chat about the surroundings. Closed in January and February. ◆€◆ ◆€€◆

a. Klitvej 49, 6990 Ulfborg (near Fjand Strand)
t. +45 9749 6460
w. fjand-gaardbutik.dk

Café and shop **Kræs (7)** in Ringkøbing makes for a nice stop off as you're driving by. It has a view of the red wooden fishing huts, sometimes cod hanging to dry, and the reflecting water of the fjord. On sunny days you can sit outside, half shaded under the trees, and feel almost as if you're part of it all. The shop's got a selection of wine, local specialities, coffee, tea and books. Open all year. ◆€◆ ◆€€◆

a. Ved Fjorden 2B, 6950 Ringkøbing
t. +45 9732 4288 / +9732 0456
w. cafekraes.dk

Find the teeny tiny hang out and café, **Westwind Surf Café (8)**, tucked away in the dunes, next to the entrance for Hvide Sande beach.

a. Tungevej 8, 6960 Hvide Sande (at the camper parking)
t. +45 4061 7559
fb. Westwind Surf Café

SHOP

◆

We do have a soft spot for all things made at home, local and in the countryside, but especially at a coastal area. The **Vestkystens Gårdbutik (9)**, or West Coast's Farm Shop, has all these things: home-made products from their farm, meat and dairy products from their free-range cows, and goodies from the salted earth, like cranberries. The farm's been in the family for hundreds of years, and uses old insights such as making the best use of the soil, taking good care of the animals, and living with the seasons. Definitely worth a visit. Open all year.

a. Houvig Klitvej 77, Houvig, 6950 Ringkøbing
t. +45 9733 1599
w. vestkystensgaardbutik.dk

You might have seen a couple of these already in other sections of the guide.

It's not us, it's them, being everywhere, the **West Wind Shops (10)**. Some shops are pretty basic in decoration, most are well stocked, and some a tad nicer, with all sorts of activities on offer. At Hvide Sande there's Nord and Syd, at Hemmet there's Bork. Syd's a very nice shop, with a good choice of surf and street-style clothing. It's a big water sport centre, located on the lakeside, where you can take up SUP, kayak, catamaran, windsurf, kite surf lessons, or rent the gear. The shops on the North Sea side of Hvide Sande have surf lessons and rent out boards. Open from March to November.

a. Sønder Klitvej 1, 6960 Hvide Sande (Syd)
t. +45 9731 2899
w. syd.westwind.dk

Small and cosy **Windsport (11)** at Nymindegab has been around since 1992, offering all kind of surf-related essentials. They have their own brand of surfboards, especially created for North Sea conditions. They also offer SUP tours and surf lessons. And coffee! Open from Easter to October.

a. Vesterhavsvej 326, 6830 Nymindegab
t. + 45 2142 8797
w. windsport.dk

SLEEP

◆

The dunes surrounding Hvide Sande are dotted with want-have houses - houses you'd love to own as your summer house. Good news is; you can have 'em! At least for a little while, because most of them are for rent. The houses are almost all privately owned houses, and rental's usually arranged by the local tourist office, or through sites like these…

w. danwest.dk / esmark.dk / feriepartner.dk

Campervans (12) can park and stay at the end of Thorsminde Harbour, close to the beach. Showers and toilets. Open all year. ♦€♦

a. Vesterhavsgade 1a, Thorsminde, 6990 Ulfborg

Søndervig Camping (13) is a friendly campsite with pitches, cabins and apartments for rent. If you want your own private bathroom next to your tent or campervan, you can choose a pitch with a little bathroom attached. The campsite is also a QuickStop, so you can stay at night, use the facilities and pay less. Open from April to September. ♦€♦

a. Solvej 2, Søndervig, 6950 Ringkøbing
t. +45 9733 9034
w. soendervigcamping.dk

Nearby and at the harbour of Hvide Sande there are 3 options to park and stay with your van or camper. At the **Hvide Sande Autocamperplads (14)** though, right behind the beach, you'll be right at the surf spot. There are squeaky clean showers and toilets. Open all year. ♦€♦

w. hvidesandecamping.dk

The **Bjerregaard Camping (15)** is a true water sport focused campsite. They've got their own tiny beach at Ringkøbing fjord and perfect views over the bird sanctuary Tipperne. You can rent canoes or a SUP to explore the lake, or bikes to go to town or the beach. They have pitches, cabins and mobile homes that sleep up to 5 people. Open from Easter to September. ♦€♦

a. Sønder Klitvej 185, 6960 Hvide Sande
t. +45 9731 5044
w. bjerregaardcamping.dk

Oh, you'll be sleeping like a prince or princess on the **Mamrelund houseboat (16)**, floating in Ringkøbing fjord. Although anchored at the small harbour of Hvide Sande, you'll have wide views from the first floor over the fjord. The boat's got 3 bedrooms on the ground floor, sleeping up to 5 people, and a light and spacious living room on the first floor. Depending on the hour of the day, and whether you want sun or shade, you can sit on the east or west terrace. The boat's moored within walking distance from shops, restaurants and, more importantly, the beach. Open all year. ♦€€€♦

a. Mamrelund 39, 6960 Hvide Sande
t. +45 9731 5040
w. esmark.dk/sommerhus-f4265

SURF

The northwest of Jutland is less blessed with waves than the southwest, since Norway gets in the way, but it still gets its fair share. It's mostly windswell, and your best bet is the stretch of beach at Løkken, due to its west facing position. From Hanstholm all the way down to Hvide Sande there are spots along the endless stretch of beach, with Klitmøller and Nørre Vorupør the most consistent, the best known and therefore the most crowded surf beaches of Denmark. Especially from Klitmøller down to Agger you'll hardly ever surf alone. Since it's so close to home for German surfers, you'll see lots of them driving up north if the forecast's good, in holidays, at the weekend, or even for an evening and morning session.

A 200 m long jetty gives shelter at the north side of **Løkken (I)**. Works best with W-S-E windswell, at low to mid tide. A perfect spot for beginners because of the shallow waters. Friendly atmosphere in the water and hardly ever too crowded. • *All levels/sand/easy parking/toilets/beach bar/surf school/surf shop.* •

Hamborg (II) is an exposed NW facing beach that works best with a small to medium W-NW-N windswell, at all tides. A 100 m long jetty gives some protection from the wind. The spot is popular with wind and kite surfers. • *Intermediate level/sand and stones/easy parking in the dunes overlooking the break/no facilities.* •

Hanstholm (III) is also referred to as Fishfactory because of the nearby fish factory action (smell). There's a harbour wall and a small jetty, which the line-up is just west of. Works from small - and holds big - SW-W-NW windswell, at all tides. The harbour wall offers some protection from the wind. Hanstholm is also a popular wind and kite surf spot. • *All levels/sand and stones/easy parking/no facilities.* •

Klitmøller has several spots - and we don't mention all here, so exploring respectfully could be worth your while:

The Bay/Tolderstien (IV) starts working with a small S to N windswell, or medium to big SW swell. Works best on a medium SW swell with a SE wind, but holds up to head high. Depending on sandbanks, low to mid tide would be preferable, beware of strong currents. With stronger wind there'll be lots of wind and kite surfers. ◆ *All levels/sand/ ok parking, but busy in summer/toilets/ restaurants/surf shops/surf schools/ wind and kite surfers.* ◆

At **Point Perfect (V)**, despite its name, you usually see lots of beginners and surf schools. It can get perfect, but most likely it won't happen while you're there on your holiday... (but you can always mindsurf a perfect left point-break). Works only with a small W to NE swell. ◆ *All levels/sand and stones/ ok parking, but busy in summer/toilet/ restaurants/surf shops/surf schools.* ◆

The **Reef (VI)** is pretty popular and easy to check from the boardwalk, it's right in front of the surf club. The outer (mussel) reef creates easy long left and right waves, so be prepared to share it with lots of SUPs. When it gets bigger, and the inside starts working, you'll have a much faster, hollow wave. At any swell, there'll be lots of surfers of all abilities. Works best on a medium to big W-NW swell, at all tides. ◆ *All levels/reef with mussels/ok parking, busy in summer/toilets/restaurants/ campsite/surf shops/surf schools.* ◆

Klitmøller's **Bunkers (VII)** is known as one of the best waves of Denmark, not suitable for beginners. It's an A-frame reef creating right and lefthanders, working best from medium to big W-NW swell, from mid to high tide. ◆ *Advanced level/rocks/easy parking/ no facilities.* ◆

North of Nørre Vorupør you'll find **Bøgsted Rende (VIII)** along the stretch of beach, an exposed break that can produce powerful hollow waves. Works best with a medium W-NW-N swell, tide depending on the sandbanks. Easily blown out, and strong currents. ◆ *Intermediate to advanced level/sand/easy parking/toilets.* ◆

The stretch of white sand beach a bit further north of the pier at **Nørre Vorupør (IX)** offers peaks aplenty.

SCHOOL RENTAL REPAIR

Left, in front, and to the right of the half sunken bunker on the beach, you can take your pick. Depending on sandbanks they work best with a medium W-NW swell and upcoming tide. The Pier is a fun lefthander, popular with longboarders and SUPs. ◆ *All levels/sand/easy parking/restaurants/toilets/surf shops/surf schools.* ◆

Agger (**X**) has 2 long piers protecting north and south side from strong winds. Agger works best with a medium SW-W-NW swell, depending on sandbanks, at all tides. Further south you'll find more spots that work in stormy W-NW swells. Beware of strong currents. ◆ *All levels/sand/easy parking/restaurants/toilet/campsites.* ◆

Next to the jetties at **Thorsminde** (**XI**) you'll find some fun hollow peaks, usually the breaks north of the harbour work best. Starts working from small W-NW to bigger SW and N swells, at all tides. ◆ *All levels/sand/easy parking/restaurants/toilets.* ◆

Hvide Sande (**XII**) has several spots: North is protected from south winds, next to the long harbour wall. Betweens and Hvide Sande South can be good spots for beginners when there's not too much wind and a small W-NW swell. When it gets bigger it can produce fun waves for all levels. ◆ *All levels/sand/easy parking/beach bar/toilets/showers.* ◆

During its rather short season, **North Shore Surf School** (**A**) offers about all and everything you could wish for as a seaside lover: surf and SUP lessons, beach yoga, BBQ nights, an outdoor sauna and hot tub. And then there's their café at the beach, a shop and a restaurant in town, all done up in a smart seaside style and full of feelgood vibes. Open in July and August.

a. Sønder Strandvej 18, 9480 Løkken
t. +45 2070 8643
w. northshoresurf.dk

The **Westwind** (**B**) shops and schools offer all kind of lessons, courses and rental, from surf and SUP to wind and kite. Their surf camps include optional accommodation, and for the colder days they have a surfers' sauna (Klitmøller and Hvide Sande) and a skate ramp for waveless days (Nørre Vorupør). Open from March to October.

w. westwind.dk
w. klitmoller.en.westwind.dk

Cold Hawaii (C) surf school and surf camp offer packages, either with or without accommodation, surf and SUP lessons, and rentals. You can also opt for a private lesson with owner, and coach of the Danish National surf team, Mor Meluka, to work on your skills. If you're interested in the shaping process, you can visit their Columbus Surfboards shaping bay. Open from Easter to November.

a. Ørhagevej 151, Klitmøller, 7700 Thisted
t. +45 2910 8873
w. coldhawaiisurfcamp.com

Vegas Surf School (D) in Nørre Vorupør offers both surfing and SUP for all levels. The VØ crew share as much of their stoke for novices as they do for experienced surfers. Ask at their shop if you need any board repair, or are interested in the shaping process of boards. Closed in winter.

a. Hawblink 2, Nørre Vorupør, 7700 Thisted
t. +45 3131 5087
w. surfkollektiv.dk

Drive Thru Surfcamp Hvide Sande (E) offers accommodation in a 200-year-old farmhouse, and surf, SUP, kayak, yoga and longboarding lessons and rentals. When you choose to stay here you'll be in good hands, the friendly staff make sure you'll be taken care of and all food and drinks are locally produced where possible. For example, your apple juice will be from a nearby orchard. Guests can use all equipment at reduced costs. Open all year. ♦€♦ ♦€€♦

a. Holmsland Klitvej 10, 6960 Hvide Sande
t. +45 2143 0944
w. drivethru.de

VAN LIFE

♦

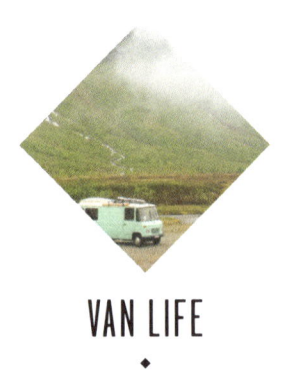

Travelling with a campervan is a dream for many, a holiday escape for others, and a way of life for some. Since its popularity's growing and the first signs of annoyance amongst local people has become apparent, we teamed up with some seaside locals to consider how best we can all avoid giving van life a bad reputation. Belgian couple Gijs Vanhee and Marijke van Biervliet, live permanently and travel in their converted trustworthy 1978 Mercedes 508, so they know all the ins and outs, dos and don'ts. Together we came up with some tips to share; simple reminders and unwritten rules of van life, to ensure we can all continue to enjoy the freedom of travelling this way in the future. (Ah. So. As of now the unwritten rules are written!)

♦

The first and simplest: Treat everything with respect; nature, locals and the sites where you're camping. Obviously leave no trash behind and try to keep everything inside, or attached to your vehicle, especially at night, so it doesn't feel like you're claiming the spot.

♦

Second: Be humble towards locals and all passersby. Smile! After all, you may be intruding on people's daily routines, their places, and home grounds. Also, chances are you might need their help one day, if you have an unexpected problem.

♦

Then there's the issue of toileting. If you have a toilet on board, easy; use it and empty its contents only, really, only in designated places. Luckily there are a growing number of service stations. Apps such as Camper Contact tell you exactly where the nearest service station is, and where you can park or stay for the night. (w. campercontact.com)

♦

If you don't have a toilet in your van, why not go to one of the many quirky cafés we recommend in the guide. You support a local business, and treat yourself to an undisturbed place where you can, you know, do your business. If you're in the middle of nowhere, with not a loo in view, find a quiet place, dig a little hole, do your thing, cover the hole, and please take your paper with you to get rid of in a bin. Nothing can disturb nature, dogs, locals, hikers, and yourself more than having a load of shit (and dirty paper) around.

Be considerate. Don't block the view from someone's house, restaurant or terrace.

Do enjoy your own view, soak it up, forget about posting a perfect #vanlife pic and enjoy time in the real world, talk to strangers, watch the sunset, get up before dawn, love the journey, equally love the destination.

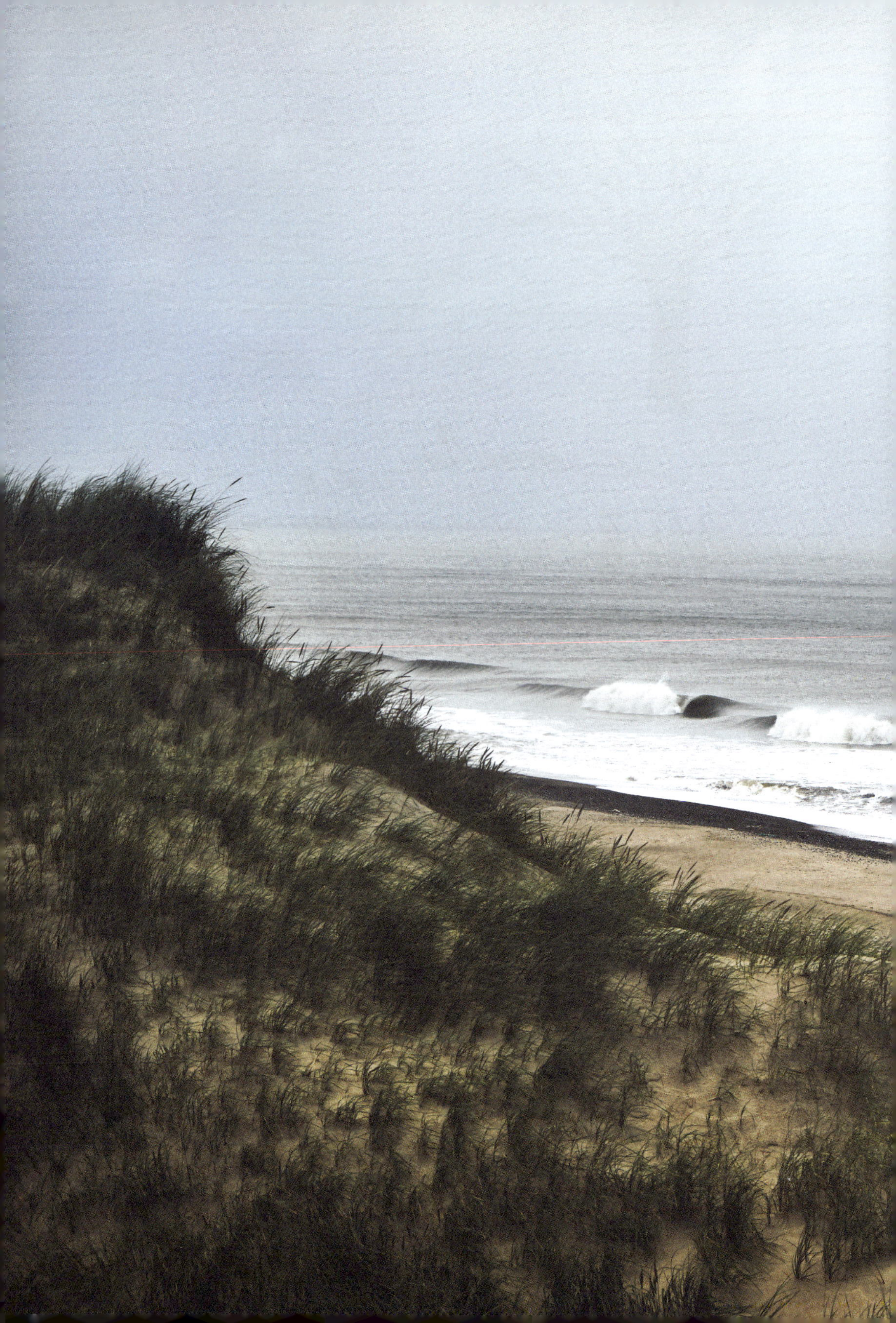

Photo: Tim Wendrich

Germany

GERMANY

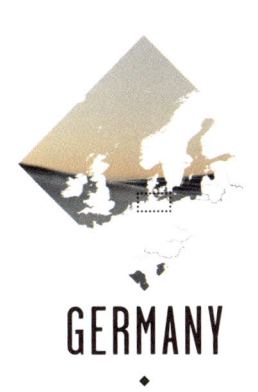

Although a large number of our Seaside readers are German (Hallo!) and it's a big country, it's only a small section in this guide. Because surfing is on our itinerary, we stick to the coast, and we even narrowed it down to just two East Frisian islands. Nevertheless, these are two little jewels, with which we're sure you'll be pleasantly surprised; beauty and surfing wise. On all our travels along the European coast we meet so many Germans, and it becomes more obvious that their adventurous spirit is rooted in their own curiosity and open-mindedness. And it's refreshing to see that it's not because they dislike their own country, they're proud of it alright. They like to explore the rest of the world just as much as they like to explore, and share, their own riches.

SURFER-TRAVELLER TYPE GERMANY

◆

You love Dinkelbrot, or like to find out what it is and what it tastes like, and you're not afraid of big, big bottles of beer. You like things well organised, and on time. You like getting straight to the point, and don't feel offended if there's not much small talk going on. You like to meet a German surfer on their homeground for a change, and feel obliged to learn some German words, since your English is not always easily understood. You don't believe that all Germans eat sauerkraut and listen to Rammstein. They don't.

WORDS AND CONCEPTS THAT MIGHT COME IN HANDY

◆

Ja! - Yes!

Nein! - No!

Moin Moin - North Germany's informal way to say hi, hey, bye, hello.

Guten tag and *Hallo* - Hello, formal and informal.

Tschuß - Bye, although 'ciao' will do fine as well.

Bitte - Please. As in " *Zwei bier, bitte.*"

Schnapsidee - an idea you got while drunk which seemed brilliant at the time but turns out to be, well, a *schnapsidee*.

Alles hat ein ende, nür die würst hat zwei - This profound expression literally translates to 'Everything has an end, only a sausage has two.' Meaning as much as everything must come to an end. Try it at the end of a party, after a perfect dinner, a perfect wave or perfect day.

GERMANY

FOOD FACTS

KARTOFFELN

Potatoes; anything potatoes. Baked, boiled, crispy, mashed, oiled, peppered and herbed. Germans are extremely creative when it comes to potatoes. One of the tastiest variations we had was the Kartoffelpuffer, which are small shallow-fried pancakes. Usually they're made out of a mixture of potato, flour, and egg, seasoned with onion, salt and pepper. But there's a sweet version as well, with sugar and cinnamon.

BREZEL

The pretzel! Known, sold and eaten all over the world but German bakeries beat them all when it comes to taste and texture. Pretzels are made from flour, water and yeast, simple as that, but apparently the trick is how much or little of what, and when, you add. Of course the finishing touch is the sprinkled sea salt. Try as many pretzels as you like at any bakery, preferably while they're still warm. They all taste slightly different, yet never disappointing.

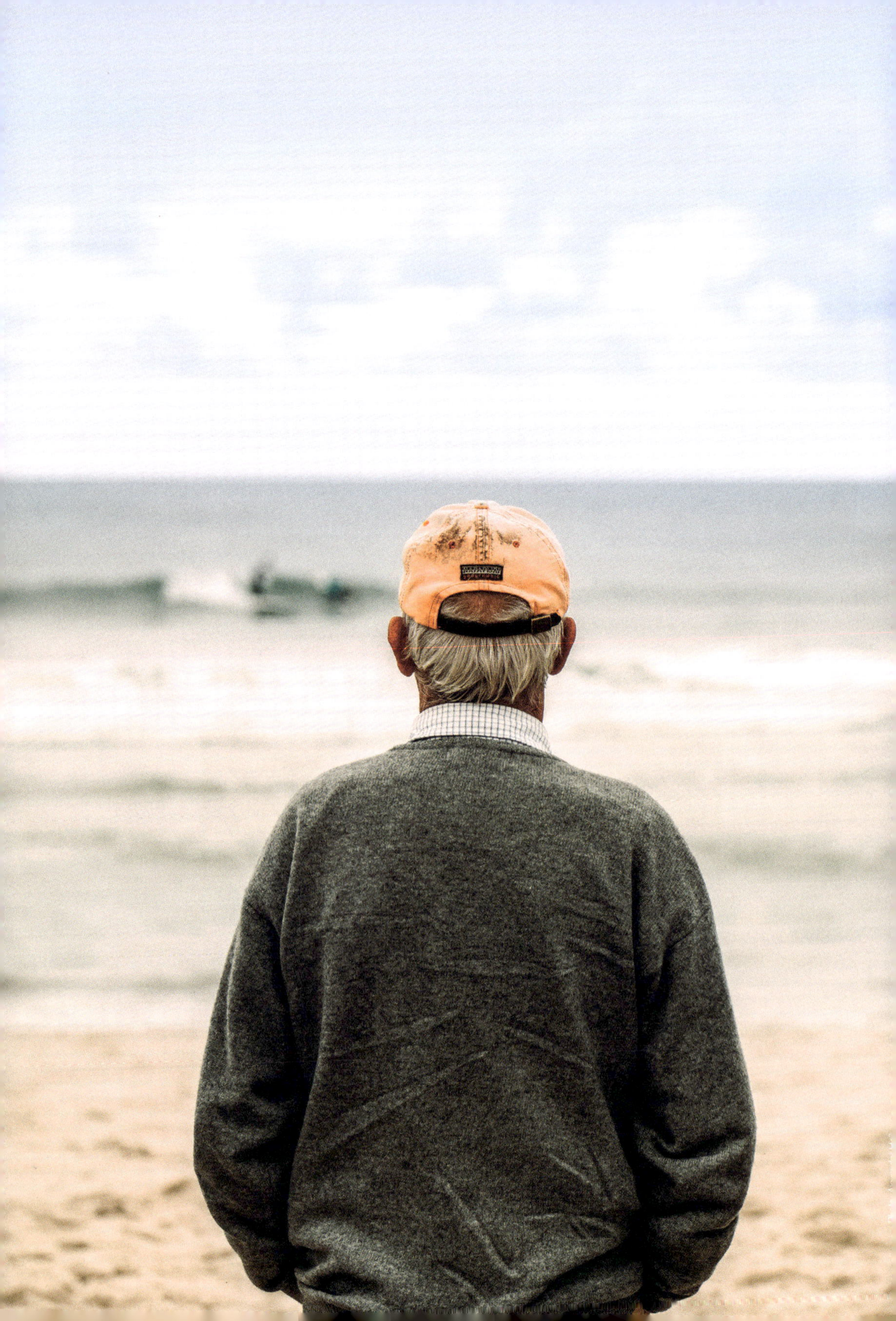

A BIT ON SURF IN GERMANY

•

The German coastline's relatively small for such a big country, and there are 83 million Germans. Suppose one percent of those 83 million want to go surfing or spend time at the seaside and you can imagine why you meet so many of them travelling the shores of... pretty much everywhere. We came up with this little theory, there's no scientific proof whatsoever to this, except that we keep bumping into German surfers and travellers, everywhere we roam along the ocean. They are an adventurous lot, they are.

Despite their short coastline and only the North Sea and Baltic Sea to choose from, Germany's surfing history goes as far back as the 1950s. Lifeguards on the island of Sylt, watermen by nature, started using their paddleboards to stand up. After a bit of travelling to the south of France 'real' surfboards were brought back to the island. Not surprisingly, the first German surf club started in Sylt, founded in the early 1960s.

So when and where is your best bet for consistent surf in Germany? If it wasn't for the UK and Scandinavia being in the way, the west-facing coast of Germany would be a North Sea wave garden, receiving every available ripple. But in reality the swell's got to pass the small gap between Scotland and Norway. So when it does, during a rare N-NW groundswell, German surfers, and especially the ones on the East Frisian Islands (Ostfriesische Inseln), have all the fun. The rest of the time it's windswell, mostly produced by strong W-SW winds, with the most northerly North Sea island, Sylt, getting the best of it. All you have to do is find a corner, jetty or harbour wall to seek shelter from the wind, or wait for the wind to die off, to surf what's left of the swell's energy, preferably with a bigger board. Most North Sea surfers are capable of surfing different volumes of boards; like any sea species, adapting to their habitat. From late summer until October you can surf in a 3/2 without hoodie, boots or gloves. You might want to start wearing your 4/3 from late September. From November on to April, have all your neoprene at hand.

If you want to learn more about German or Nordic surf culture, pick up a copy or check the websites of the beautiful, German and English language, magazine Blue (**w.** bluemag.eu), the longstanding and well-informed Surfers Mag (**w.** surfersmag.de), or stylish Waves & Woods (**w.** wavesandwoods.de). Don't worry if you don't get the words, the pictures speak for themselves. Nord / NordWest Surf Film Fest is a yearly 3-day festival, held in July in Hamburg, dedicated to anything related to contemporary Nordic surf and skate culture.
w. nordnordwestsurffilmfest.de

Rømø

• 1
LIST

KAMPEN (I)
• 2, 11, 20
KAMPEN

WENNINGSTEDT (II)
• 3, 16, 21, 23
WENNINGSTEDT-BRADERUP

BRANDENBURGER (III)
• 4-6, 12, 17, 18, 24, 25, 28
WESTERLAND

OSTERIA (IV)
• 26
TINNUM

Sylt

• 19
RANTUM

HÖRNUM K4 (V)
• 27

HÖRNUM CAMPINGPLATZ (VI)
• 7-10, 13-15, 22
HÖRNUM

Föhr

SYLT

Although geographically closer to Denmark, Sylt is the northernmost of Germany's East Frisian islands. With 40 km of exposed white sandy beaches, chances are that you'll be catching some waves, even in summer. Sylt's quite a hotspot for well-to-do Germans who like things laid-back and prefer traditional over glamorous. Mix this with old-fashioned promenades, beaches dotted with the classic German 'strandkorb' - the iconic roofed wicker beach chairs - infinite dunes and heaths, red cliffs, reed-thatched houses, and Germany's oldest surf culture, and you have the short version of Sylt. To get the full version, you'll have to go and visit yourself, eh! For sure there's enough to do and see, even on wave-less days. Getting there is a pretty cool trip all in itself.

TRAVEL INFO

Hindenburgdamm is the 11 km long causeway that connects the island to the mainland, but the only way to cross the causeway is by train.

BY BOAT

To properly get into the island feel you could choose to enter from the water. There's a daily ferry between Rømø in the south of Denmark and List in Sylt. Before you hop on the ferry, we recommend you watch Roman Polański's 2010 political thriller, 'The Ghost Writer'. Sylt, and especially the ferry, featured as an alternative to the Martha's Vineyard ferry; Polański being unable to travel legally to the US and film the real thing (as the subject of an Interpol Red Notice for sexual offence charges from the 70s).

w. syltfaehre.de

BY TRAIN

Ever so easy: drive your car, campervan or bike on to the shuttle at Niebüll, sit back (in your car or van, probably not on your bike), relax and enjoy the 45 minute journey, views of farmland, wetland and the Wadden Sea crossing. If you don't have a comfy seat of your own you can travel on the Sylt Shuttle Plus. Both trains use the Hindenburgdamm causeway to Westerland, Sylt. RV travel may be restricted due to size and roof type - check info on website.

w. syltshuttle.de

IN AND AROUND WESTERLAND
◆

Let's start by saying Westerland is the least attractive town of the island. But it's centrally located and usually the starting point, if you arrive by shuttle. It's also the largest town on the island, with one of the best surf spots. The centre of town has some nice shops, and the weekly market on Wednesday mornings is worth checking out, but there's more concrete than you'd wish for on an island holiday. To the north you'll pass family and surf friendly Weningstedt, before entering Kampen. Kampen's perfectly manicured reed-thatched cottages and costly cars along the road foretell that you'll end up with some Louis Vuitton or Hèrmes items if you go shopping there. But if you want to spot some German celebs, get your Joop! perfume out and your Chanel socks on, wine and dine, and pay (what's that all about?!) to get to the beach... On to the south it's a different story: Rantum, in the narrowest part of the island, is a small village amidst relaxed, never too busy stretches of - dog and child friendly - beaches. If you like your fish fresh or smoked, try one of the smokehouses at the small marina, like Der Hafenkiosk 24. To the far south you'll find the laid-back seaside village of Hörnum. You can walk the southernmost headland, from North Sea to Wadden Sea, with beaches east and west of the village.

Tourist office at Friedrichstrasse 44, Westerland, 25980 Sylt.

TO DO

Hike and bike: first and foremost, a warning to tread carefully. Sylt's got numerous hike and cycle paths, but their coastline is rapidly eroding, losing land to the sea. All sorts of measures are taken, but the best protection right now - the beautiful fragile dunes. They're all nature reserves with marked paths. If you stray off the paths and trample the plants and grasses, the roots loosen and the sand is at higher risk of erosion from wind and water. That's nature's way, so please respect the signs and use the paths. There are plenty of them!

Naturgewalten Sylt (1) - Forces of Nature Sylt - is a great place to learn about the ocean, waves, and the island and its changes over time. With the help of headphones you'll be guided through the exhibition (English language available). There's a water tank for an interactive lesson on how waves are formed, how they hit the beach, and you can even take control over the wind (in the tank - that's obvious though, right?) to see how it affects the waves. Or see the underwater world of seals and dolphins from a crab's perspective in the Wadden Sea tunnel. Lots of interactive hands-on stuff makes it a perfect place to take youngsters. Open all year.

a. Hafenstraße 37, 25992 List
t. +49 4651 836 190
w. naturgewalten-sylt.de

A pretty unique longboard festival takes place every year on the second weekend of September. **Buhne 16 Longboard Festival (2)** initiator, and owner of the Buhne 16 beach bar, Sven Behrens, (the son of Uwe Behrens who set up the first surf club in 1966) believes the festival is born under lucky stars. It's never suffered a lack of waves on its chosen weekend! Sven started the festival in 1999 after he switched from being a lifeguard to bar owner, having been afraid he'd lose the time to hang out and surf with his friends. Thus the festival is held in September, after the busy summer season, when the water's at its warmest, the weather just fine and waves can be expected. Buhne 16 quickly became a popular event, bringing hundreds of people to the beach to enjoy surfing, contests, live music, films, food and drinks and a generally good vibration.

a. Listlandstr 133b, Buhne 16, 25980 Kampen
t. +49 4651 4996
w. buhne16.de/the-festival

Learn all about edible (and poisonous!) plants, how to build a fire and an outdoor shelter, understand how birds spot other animals and humans, read footprints, find water and your way around without the use of a compass or your mobile phone, and lots more, in the **Wilderness Courses** (3) of Matthias Poppek. You can join for one or more days of excursions. It's the best way to make use of all your senses, connect with nature and just have a really exciting time outdoors. Suitable for all ages!

a. Buchholz Stich 4, Biolandhof Dethlefs, 25996 Braderup
t. +49 1724 046 967
w. workshop-sylt.de

Yoga mit Maren (4) offers yoga classes at different locations in Wenningstedt, Westerland and Hörnum. If weather allows, classes are on the beach from June to September. The classes are easy to follow Hatha yoga. Open all year.

a. Am Bastianplatz 4, 25980 Westerland
t. +49 1785 831 538 / 4651 878 9005
w. yogamare.de

Release all the tension from your muscles and at the same time get body and mind energised with a traditional **Thai massage** (5). Perfect before, after, or if suffering from lack of surf. Open all year.

a. Andreas Nielsen Straße 3, 25980 Westerland
t. +49 1578 241 2132
w. sylt-thai.de

Do things you don't do at home, try new experiences - isn't that the purpose of travelling? Well, at least your holiday… So, why not pick up archery, get to know bow and arrow, feed the inner warrior. **Youksakka** (6) is a 'Bow & Fun company' offering traditional bow making and introductory archery courses. And once you get to know your bow and arrow, you're allowed to shoot free at their court. We think it's a pretty cool thing. They think everybody can learn to make and shoot a traditional bow. Well, everybody between 6 and 99 years old. Open from March to October.

a. Keitumer Landstraße, 25980 Westerland
t. +49 1778 027 309
w. youksakka.de

Claudia Niehues of **SUP Surf Sylt** (7) takes SUP tours in different areas of the island, depending on wind and wave conditions. You can also join her SUP fitness or yoga classes. Open from May to October.

a. Oststrand, 25997 Hörnum
t. +49 1702 484 843
w. sup-surf-sylt.de

On the southernmost tip of the island you'll find **Strandsauna Hörnum** (8). After a sweaty session in the Finnish cabin on the dunes, you can walk some steps down to the nudy beach and take a refreshing dip in the North Sea. Open all year.

a. Süderende 25, 25997 Hörnum
t. +49 4651 880 300
w. strandsauna-sylt.com

Yowa. What's that! Yoga on a SUP, that's what. Book your spot at **Suedkap Surfing** (9) in Hörnum. Or if you just want to paddle a bit, they rent out SUPs as well. Open from Easter to October.

a. Strandpromenade 1, 25997 Hörnum
t. +49 4651 9954 410
w. suedkap-surfing.de

Climb to the top of **Hörnum's lighthouse** (10). You'll have to take a guided tour, but groups are small, and reservation is recommended. Tours are held every Monday, Wednesday and Thursday, and a magnificent view is guaranteed. Get your ticket at the Hörnum Tourist Office. Open all year.

a. Rantumer Straße 20, 25997 Hörnum
t. +49 465 196 260
w. hoernum.de

EAT/DRINK/HANG OUT

◆

Beach bar **Buhne 16** (**11**) is the living breathing soul of Germany's surfing history. In 1981 brothers Uwe, Conrad and Dieter Behrens, avid surfers and lifeguards at the time, started Buhne 16. These days it's cousins Tim and Sven Behrens who run the bar, maintaining the same laid-back vibe instigated by their predecessors. Besides Buhne 16's shrewdly surfing-style décor, they serve good food, cold beers, and have regular live music events, a big campfire at Easter, and the yearly Longboard Festival, attracting surfers of all ages, their friends, families, and future friends. Although Kampen and its beach are known for a jet-set-ish atmosphere, everybody's welcome, flip-flops and t-shirts being more the dress code than designer jeans. Leave your ride at the car park and wander the calming walk through the dunes, over the hilltop, to the first ever beach bar on Sylt. Open from Easter to October. ◆€€◆

a. Listlandstraße 133b, 25999 Kampen
t. +49 4651 4996
w. buhne16.de

The small wooden kiosk **Beach Box** (**12**) sits right behind the dunes at Westerland's south promenade. It's the place to go when you crave a large portion of food, and especially crave a tasty burger. You won't be disappointed on either point. And there's a vegan option as well. Open all year. ◆€€◆

a. Käpt'n-Christiansen-Straße 40, 25980 Westerland
t. +49 4651 9428 891
w. beachbox.juisyfood.com

Bakery, pastry shop, ice-cream parlour and restaurant **Lund** (**13**), in the centre of Hörnum, is one of those fine, fine, fine spots you'd like to go every day, to taste something new - and get another of what you chose yesterday too, it was so good! Lund is a family run place that's been around since 1940. Their passion and heart for creating tasteful, wholesome and honest products permeates directly through with your first bite of their cake, bread, ice-cream or whatever you choose to pamper your taste buds with. Good to know that whenever you choose something with fruit and vegetables, it'll be prepared with seasonal products, from the island, mostly coming from the organic farm 'Strawberry Paradise'. The restaurant serves, fish, meat and vegetarian dishes. Closed in winter. ◆€◆ ◆€€◆

a. Rantumer Straße 1-3, 25997 Hörnum
t. +49 4651 881 034
w. lund-sylt.de

"Save the fish, eat more crêpes" is the philosophy that the small crêperie **Hafen Liebe** (**14**) holds dear. We dig that philosophy, and their crêpes! They sell drinks and ice-cream too, from their wooden shack on Hörnum's promenade. Open every day from spring to autumn, only closed during storms. ◆€◆

a. Hafenstraße 4, 25997 Hörnum
t. +49 1713 358 488

At the western beach of Hörnum sits restaurant and café **Kap-Horn** (15). Completely snuggled down into the dunes, you'll pass it on your way to/from the beach. It's an unpretentious easy-going beach bar with a large selection of wines - here's a good spot to taste some German wein while you listen to the waves. Open from March to November. ◆€€◆

a. Süderende 24 (Weststrand), 25997 Hörnum
t. +49 4651 881 548
w. kap-horn-sylt.de

SHOP

Get your ecological veggies and fruits from **Erdbeer Paradies** (16) in Braderup. Eckehard, Bettina, their son Jens (an avid Sylt surfer) and daughter Rike have created a true paradise; not only growing and selling juicy strawberries, but edible flowers, extremely tasty tomatoes, potatoes and other vegetables, and some home-made goodies like marmalade and honey, in their farm shop. Visit their paradise on Tuesdays and Fridays from 10:00 to 17:00, or find them in the market in Westerland on Saturday and Wednesday mornings.

a. Terpwai 17, 25996 Braderup
t. +49 4651 443 69
w. erdbeerparadies-sylt.de

Inselkind (17) in Westerland is one of Sylt's nicest shops. They've created their own line of clothing, with a stylish relax-a-lotta beachy look. As well as their t-shirts, hoodies, caps, hats, bags and pants, they also sell the locally designed Norden surfboards, prints, art, books and jewellery. Open all year.

a. Stephanstraße 8, 25980 Westerland
t. +49 4651 446 7977
w. inselkind.com

Every Wednesday there's a fresh **market** (18) in Westerland. Open all year, from April to October, also on Saturday morning.

a. Alte Markthalle, Rathausplatz, 25980 Westerland

Café and coffee roasters, **Kaffeerösterei Sylt** (19), has some tip-top tasting coffee, freshly roasted and prepared with the utmost care. Christian Appel's café lures you in with the scent of coffee and cakes. Vegan cakes no less. Find his good looking and great smelling place in Rantum, just south of Westerland. From the shop you can spot birds, conveniently they have a pair of binoculars at hand. Open all year. ◆€◆

a. Hafenstraße 9, 25980 Rantum
t. +49 4651 2995 757
w. kaffeeroesterei-sylt.com

SLEEP

There are rental holiday houses galore on the island. Look for signs saying 'Ferienwohnung' or ask at the local tourist office.

Campervans and caravans can park and stay at **Campingplatz Kampen** (20), tucked away in the dunes surrounded by green. Open from March to October. ◆€◆

a. Möwenweg 4, 25999 Kampen
t. +49 1713 012 042 / +49 465 142 086
w. campen-in-kampen.de

Campingplatz Wenningstedt (21) is a family campsite right behind the dunes, steps away from the (surf) beach and close to the town of Wenningstedt. Open from March to October. ◆€◆

a. Osetal 3, 25996 Wenningstedt
t. +49 4651 944 004
w. campingplatz.wenningstedt.de

Campers (22) can stay in a specially arranged field, in the middle of the dunes, near the (surf) beach of Hörnum. It has all the basic facilities, and a restaurant (Meermann) within walking distance. Open all year. ◆€◆

a. Rantumer Straße 31, 25997 Hörnum
t. +49 4651 8358 431
w. hoernum.de

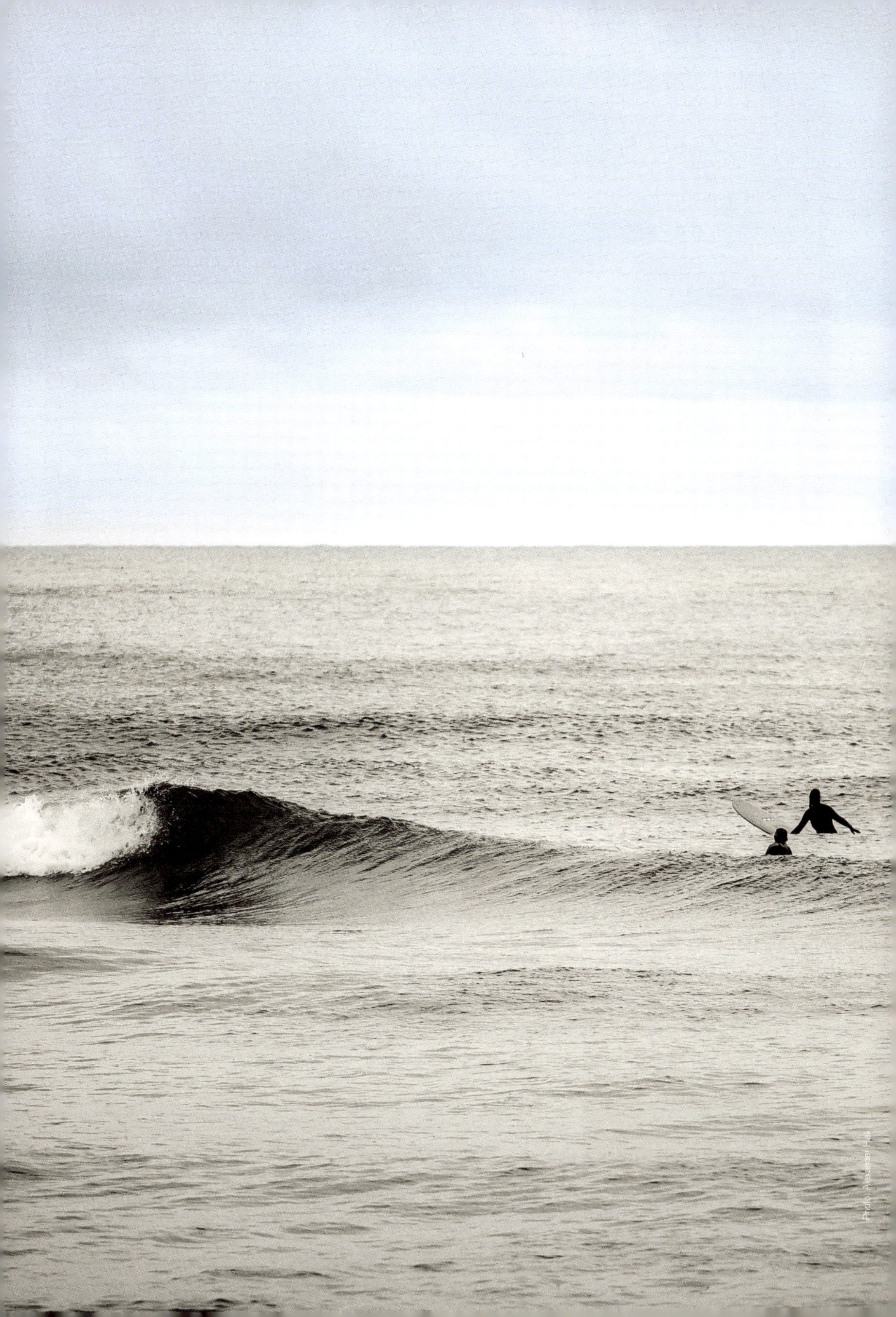

SURF

About every break in Sylt is exposed to both swell and wind, and most are west-northwest facing. After summer you'll have a good shot at getting some groundswell, but mostly you'll be surfing windswell. Nothing wrong with that, especially when the wind turns offshore, or drops off altogether. If that happens, usually you have a few hours after the wind dies to surf clean waves. Depending on sandbanks you can make use of all boards, but boards with a bit of volume are going to give you more fun.

After a bit of a walk through the dunes you'll reach **Kampen (I)**, in front of beach bar Buhne 16. This beach works best at higher tide with a small to medium SW-W-NW or N swell. ◆ *All levels/sand/paid parking/paid beach access/restaurant.* ◆

In the seaside village of **Wenningstedt (II)** some jetties help shape the waves for the better. Works on all tides, from small to medium and even holds big swells from the SW-W-NW and N. It's also popular with wind and kite surfers. ◆ *All levels/sand/paid parking/paid beach access/toilet/restaurants/surf school/camping.* ◆

The beach at **Westerland - Brandenburger (III)**, is a famous windsurf world cup stage where jetties help the waves shape up. Works best at lower tide with a medium to big SW-W-NW or N swell. Not surprisingly you'll find wind and kite surfers here, depending on the wind. ◆ *Advanced levels/sand/paid parking/toilet/shower/restaurants/surf school.* ◆

The exposed **Westerland - Osteria (IV)** beach works with a small to medium swell from SW-W to NW, all tides ◆ *All levels/sand/paid parking/all facilities/restaurant/camping.* ◆

The large stretch of beach at **Hörnum K4 (V)** offers several peaks. Have a good look from the top of the dunes to decide where to go in before you head down to the beach. Works best on the push to high tide, with a small to medium SW-W-NW swell. ◆ *All levels/sand/free parking and free beach access/no facilities/surf school.* ◆

SCHOOL RENTAL REPAIR

Hörnum Campingplatz (VI) sits, as the name suggests, right in front of the campsite. Works best at mid-tide with a small to medium SW-W-NW swell.
* All levels/sand/free parking and free beach access/restaurant/camping. *

Südkap Surfschule (23) works with small groups for their lessons, they also rent out surfboards and SUPs. Südkap offers weekend and weekly surf camps: 'From bed to board' is their saying. The accommodation, Hostel Nordseeheim, is right at the surf spot.
a. Dünenstraße 333b, 25996 Wenningstedt
t. +49 4651 9570 373
w. suedkap-surfing.de

Surf Shop Sylt (24) was founded in 1977 (as Surf Line Sylt) and is not only one of the oldest surf shops on Sylt, but in the whole of Germany. They have all the essentials you need for surfing, kite surfing, windsurfing, SUP and body boarding. Open all year.
a. Wilhelmstraße 5 (near the station), 25980 Westerland
t. +49 4651 7734
w. surfshop-sylt.de

Sunset Beach (25) surf school and restaurant is run by Hans Heinicke, since 1987. (Bit of insider's info, for those familiar with the old windsurf scene: Sunset school used to be owned by Jürgen Hönscheid, one of the best German windsurfers, who emigrated to Fuerteventura in 1987 and has since been shaping surfboards.) Meanwhile, Sunset offers lessons in surfing, kiting, and catamaran sailing. Closed in winter.

- **a.** Brandenburger Straße 15, 25980 Westerland
- **t.** +49 4651 271 72
- **w.** sunsetbeach.de

Surf and skate shop **BLP Sylt (26)** has all your surf and skate essentials, and clothing. Open all year.

- **a.** Zur Kratzmühle 2, 25980 Tinnum
- **t.** +49 4651 332 00
- **w.** blp-sylt.com

Angelo Schmidt's surfing school, **Inselkind (27)**, offers surf courses for small groups, rental of surfboards and SUPs, and organises the Inselkind Ocean Camps. Their school's based in an old elementary school on top of the dunes, overlooking the harbour and neighbouring islands. It's a bit of a meeting place for watermen and women between 8 and 18 years. From Monday to Thursday mornings in summer, children can take part in a water sport every day at the camp. Depending on the wind, waves and tides, they can practise either surfing, kiting, SUP, sailing or windsurfing. The surf school has a wooden shack at Hörnum beach as well. Closed in winter.

- **a.** K4 beach access, 4 kms outside Hörnum
- **t.** +49 173 2001 120
- **w.** inselkind.com/surfschule

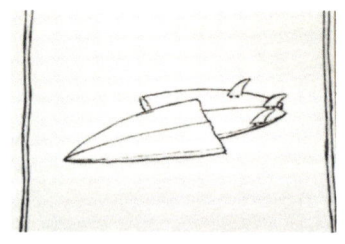

If you have a board to repair, contact **Dirk Effler (28)**.

- **a.** Kiarwai 28, 25980 Westerland
- **t.** +49 173 3966 669
- **w.** ilovekitesurf-sylt.com

PROTEST

WWW.PROTEST.EU

SEASIDE LOCAL: ANGELO SCHMITT

Meet Angelo Schmitt, a Sylt local, surfer and family man, and a curious, creative human being with a tremendous amount of energy. Angelo was born and raised on the German island, 'south of heaven', Sylt. He lives here with his wife, son Tay, and daughter Joy. His upbringing awakened his love for the unusual, and being aware of himself not quite fitting in. His parents took him and his sister abroad a lot, and not just holidaying in France - they took a proper break of 2 years, travelling in a campervan to India. 15 years later, Angelo went on another extended trip around the world, enjoying different cultures and their views on life. The trip may have ended after 20 months, the lessons he got from it are still alive today.

"It's all in the love. See what's there and not bitch about what's missing. Life's full of opportunities - use them!"

He's thankful for living on the island: "Raising kids and living here is a wonderful thing, I'm thankful for it. It's safe, nature's stunning. Being a local boy and getting in touch with your surroundings, giving back through volunteering work with the surf school, beach clean-ups, raising a voice when things tend to go wrong, tourist-wise, it's always been important to me."

Trying to pin down Angelo to one thing is selling him short. He's an agile person when it comes to initiatives or work. He says: "I always have new ideas, trying to escape the norm, do something fun and creative." He runs a surf school, produces his own brand of surfboards, Norden, and is one of the founding members of Blue, a stylish yearly magazine on surfing and travelling. "Besides this, I help out our local surfing youth, and organise beach clean-ups too. With my #shadesoftrash I feed a passion to do good and contribute to mother Nature. Surfers can be a bunch of selfish dudes! Not all of them of course, but it's about time to give back. The plastic madness has reached crazy dimensions. Spreading the word about it to the uneducated, partaking in beach clean-ups are some examples to act." The other project he's proud to be involved in is Meer Leben, started on Sylt some 10 years ago: "We take kids who are suffering from cancer and are struggling with life to surf, SUP and skate. This, and taking kids out in the water in general... I could fill books on the topic. Their youth and their stoke - even in the most crappy waves the vibe in the water is fantastic!" How does such a whirlwind channel all his energy, and stay positive and constructive? "It's all in the love. See what's there and not bitch about what's missing. Life's full of opportunities - use them!"

Find Angelo at his surf school in summer, the rest of the time if you want to chat island, try the shop he runs with his wife, Inselkind, in Westerland. **w.** inselkind.com

GERMANY

JANUSKOPF
(III)

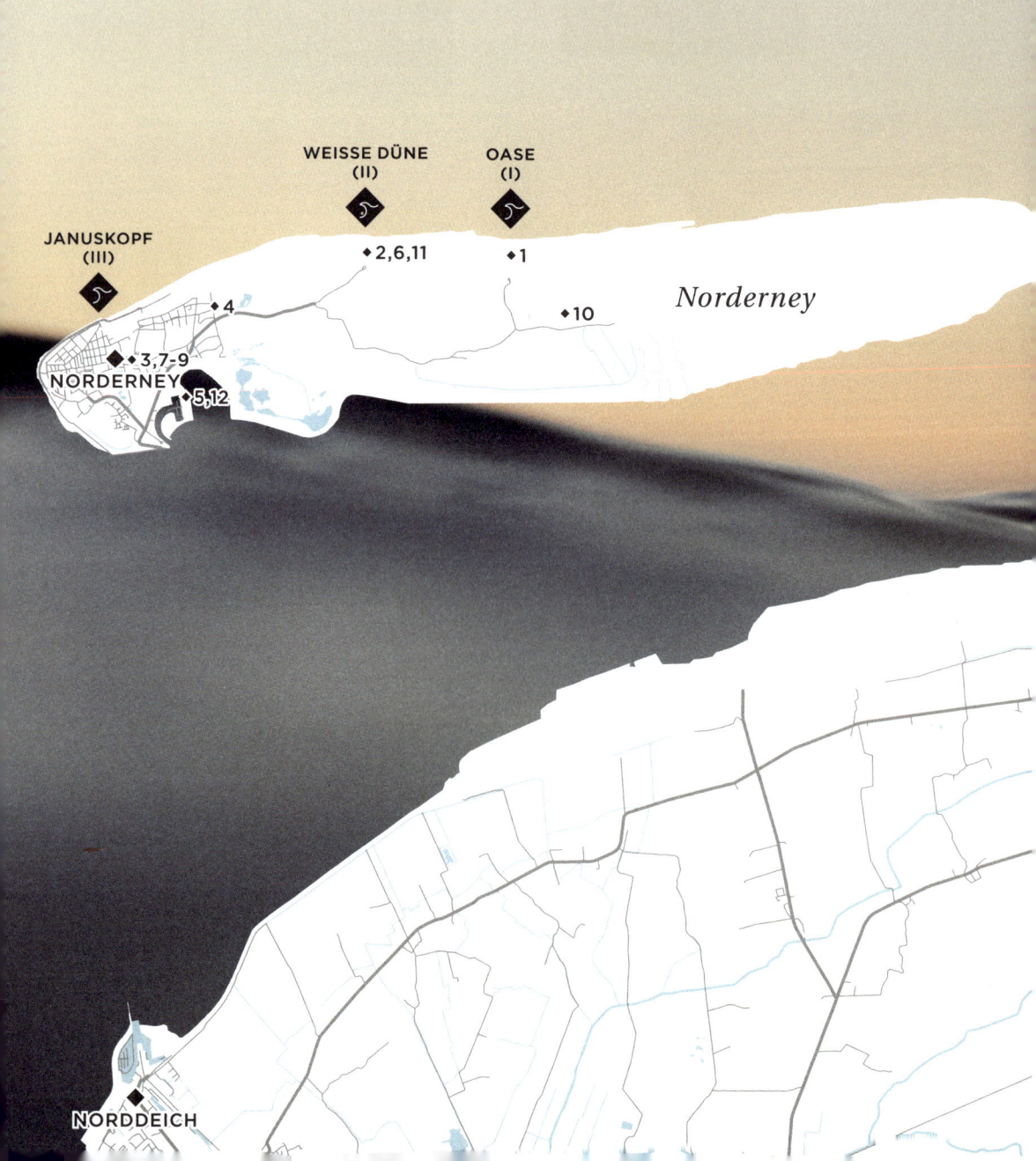

WEISSE DÜNE
(II)

OASE
(I)

◆ 2,6,11   ◆ 1

◆ 4   ◆ 10   *Norderney*

◆ 3,7-9
NORDERNEY◆
    ◆ 5,12

◆
NORDDEICH

NORDERNEY

♦

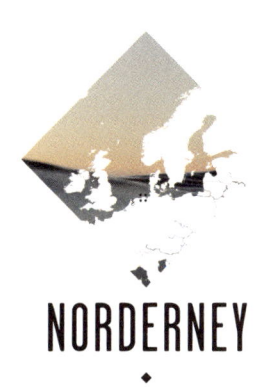

The third in the chain of Germany's East Frisian islands, just off the coast of the mainland, Norderney's been long-time famous as a spa resort but not known for its surf. We appreciate it's been kept a bit under the radar, like some other islands, and so apologise to all Norderney locals to have picked up on it. It's just that you have such a loveable little island. We love the fact that you can officially park a horse at the beach. It's like a spot where you put your bike: a designated place to leave your horse, while you go for a dip in the sea, or a coffee at the beach. We love that you can sleep in one of those iconic wicker beach chairs. We love the size of the island. There's actually no need to take your car, since you can either walk or bike to pretty much every spot. There are coastal wetlands, 14 kms of fine white sand beach, salt marshes, rolling dunes, and 85% of the island is in the Wadden Sea National Park.

TRAVEL INFO

♦

The island is only 14 km long and 2 km wide. It's possible to take your car on the ferry but there's really no need to drive. Best to leave your vehicle at the port in Norddeich, on the mainland, and either take your own bike or rent one.

BY BOAT

♦

The only way to get to the island is by ferry (sailing up to 13 times a day) from Norddeich on the mainland. In summer it's advisable to book in advance.

w. reederei-frisia.de

IN AND AROUND NORDERNEY

◆

The main town of the island bears the same name as the island itself. It's a pretty town, with whitewashed and red brick houses lining the streets and the sea wall. The island being a hotspot for thalassic treatments, you'll find enough spas and wellness places to fill your days. But spending your days, and maybe nights, at and around the beach, in or near the sea, you'll have all the thalassotherapy you could wish for. Since everything is within walking or biking distance of town, there are a lot places that offer bicycle rental, so don't worry if you didn't bring your own.

Tourist office at Am Kurplatz 1, 26548 Norderney.

TO DO

♦

The **Summertime Festival** is a 5-day event full of concerts, DJs, parties, and sports at Januskopf at Norderney's Nordstrand. The yearly festival takes place during the last week of July.

w. summertime-norderney.de

Who ever came up with the idea of putting a sauna on the beach deserves a medal, we think. Luckily the island of Norderney's got them too! Find the **Strandsauna** (1) at the nudist beach (FKK) Oase, in the northern part of the island. There are actually 2 of them, with a sun terrace to relax in between sessions. And, of course, the North Sea to cool down in, just steps away. Both saunas have panoramic views of the ocean. Open from April to October.

t. + 49 4932 474
w. norderney.de/strand-meer

At Weiße Düne beach you can get an open-air **massage** (2). Very Bali or Thailand style: no need to book in advance, just whenever you feel like it, go up to the little wooden booth at the beach. Only available in the warm summer months of July and August (obviously).

a. Weiße Düne, 26548 Norderney
w. norderney.de/strand-meer

Badehaus Norderney (3) values the German spa tradition and offers thalassic style saltwater baths, saunas and steam baths, a floating bath and massages. Open all year.

a. Am Kurplatz 2, 26548 Norderney
t. +49 4932 891 400
w. norderney.de/badehaus-norderney

Reitschule Junkmann (4) takes you horse riding along the beach. There are different tours depending on your level, and the timing of the tours depend on the tide - 2 hours before to 2 hours after low tide. Open all year.

a. Lippestraße 23, 26548 Norderney
t. +49 4932 924 10
w. reitschule-junkmann.de

Paddle across the Wadden Sea on a SUP or kayak with **Surfschule Norderney** (5). You can either join their 2-3 hour tours, or rent the equipment and go explore on your own. Of course you have to consider the tidal differences! The school also offer courses and rentals for windsurf, surf, sup, kayak and kitesurf. Open from mid-March to mid-October.

a. Am Hafen 17, 26548 Norderney
t. +49 4932 648
w. surfschule-norderney.de

EAT/DRINK/HANG OUT

Warm up by the large fireplace after a walk or dip in the ocean - or, let's think positive thoughts, work on your tan while lounging in beach chairs on the terrace - at the stylish beach restaurant **Weisse Düne** (**6**). Ideally located between the dunes and the sea. Open all year. ♦€€♦

a. Weiße Düne 1, 26548 Norderney
t. +49 4932 935 717
w. weisseduene.com

Along the western headland, Januskopf, you'll find the **Surf Café** (**7**). A perfect spot to meet up with visiting and local surfers alike, or beach goers, dog walkers, well, basically everyone who loves the beach. If you want to spice up your own house when you get back from holiday, and need a little inspiration to make it into a bright beach-style house, you can surely find it here. They serve breakfast, lunch, brunch, dinner, drinks, and everything in between. Open all year. ♦€♦ ♦€€♦

a. Am Januskopf 9, 26548 Norderney
t. +49 4932 935 750
w. surfcafe.info

The sturdy looking **West Strand Bar** (**8**) serves their own brewed beers, snacks and, of course, other drinks as well. The bar's from the same owners as the Norderneyer Brauhaus and Brauhalle. So, we recommend highly that you order a beer, you won't be disappointed. Find them along the boulevard on Norderney's western headland. Open from early Easter to October. ♦€♦

a. Am Weststrand, 26548 Norderney
t. +49 171 5500 466 / 932 935 087
w. norderneyer-bier.de

SHOP

Coffee roaster and chocolate shop **Bittersüss Norderney** (**9**) serves, and sells, damn good coffee, tea and hot chocolate. And all the additional stuff that makes a person happy, like homemade chocolates. Need more? Another stash of chocolates, truffles, or nougat perhaps? Bittersüss, bittersweet, is a happy place altogether. Closed in November and December.

a. Strandstraße 7, 26548 Norderney
t. +49 4932 4980 426
w. bittersuess-norderney.de

SLEEP

Like all other East Frisian islands, there are plenty of holiday houses for rent, usually private owned, but taken care of by a coordinating organisation or the local tourist office.

Reiterhof Harms (**10**) sits on the outskirts of Norderney in a tranquil location. There's a guesthouse and campsite to choose from, and a farm where you can book horse riding tours. Open from March to October. ♦€♦

a. Am Leuchtturm 11, 26548 Norderney
t. +49 4932 2108
w. reiterhof-harms.de

We were only fantasising about sleeping in one of those iconic beach chairs, then it turns out you actually can! At Weisse Düne - the White Dune - you can rent the **Schlafstrandkorb** (**11**). Your bed in the dunes is wide and long enough for 2 people to sleep comfortably, and comes with bed linen. It has a wind and water resistant tarpaulin with windows, and can be closed completely. But you don't want it closed, do you! You can either rent the schlafstrandkorb at the beach chair rental place, or make a reservation online. Available from April to September. ♦€€♦

a. Weiße Düne 1, 26548 Norderney
t. +49 4932 891 300
w. norderney.de/norderney-shop/schlafstrandkorb

SURF SCHOOL RENTAL REPAIR

The surf spots at Norderney are all along the 14 km long strip of white sand beach on the North Sea side of the island. Since all spots are facing north, it's pretty obvious all spots are offshore with south winds. The south side of the island is Wadden Sea, no waves to be found there, except maybe the bow waves from the ferry. Most of the swell that reaches Norderney is windswell, and the occasional groundswell.

Located at the FKK nudist beach you'll find the peaks of **Oase (I)**. Oase works best on an upcoming tide with a small to medium NW-N swell. ♦ *All levels/ sand/easy parking/toilets/restaurant/ camping.* ♦

Weiße Düne (II) is a little west of Oase and needs pretty much the same conditions: small to medium NW-N swell, working best on upcoming tide. ♦ *All levels/sand/parking/toilets/restaurant/sleeping beach chair.* ♦

The main surf spot is **Januskopf (III)** on the northwest end of the island. It's where you find the surf café and the surf school. The beach has some jetties and works best on incoming tide with small to bigger W-NW-N swells. It'll be offshore with southeast wind.
♦ *All levels/sand/parking/toilets/restaurants/surf school.* ♦

Having the looks of a North Sea stilt house, the 2 wooden huts of **Surfschule Norderney (12)** are a pretty sight. It's a nice place to hang out, before or after your session, popular place for windsurfers and surfers alike. They offer lessons and rental of equipment. Open from mid-March to mid-October.

a. Am Hafen 17, 26548 Norderney
t. +49 4932 648
w. surfschule-norderney.de

#creaturescountry

this is creatures country

CREATURES OF LEISURE

SUPPORTED BY SURFEARS

SURFER'S EAR

♦

On surfer's ear, Tom Carroll, earplugs, and why we should use them!

At least one of our team, and several of our friends, suffer from surfer's ear. Whether you're a coldwater surfer, or travelling and surfing a lot in waters that aren't all blue flag beaches, infection of the ears is a painful by-product of spending so much time in the water. Excessive exposure to cold water and air, or polluted waters – of which we're often unaware – can lead to ear problems and eventually to surfers ear. Pursuing your passion can, in the case of frequently chasing waves, lead to bone growth inside the ear, narrowing the ear canal. It's a freakish thing our bones do, to try and protect us from the cold water, and it's called exostosis ('new bone' in Greek).

Once your ear canal's narrowed, it's harder to drain (sea)water, or dry out after a surf session. And since seawater isn't as clean as we'd all like it to be, and bacteria really appreciate the warm damp environment of your ear canal, the ear can get infected very easily. To protect your ears, and prevent developing exostosis, it's definitely wise to wear earplugs.

SurfEars were developed by Swedish surfers (who happen to be product designers as well) looking for the perfect device to protect the ears from water, cold air and contaminants, but also let the sound in: a very important aspect of surfing, to stay balanced and connected to the surroundings. The development team of SurfEars worked closely with 2-time surf champ and waterman, Tom Carroll, to make improvements to their product. The result being earplugs that are truly experience-based and constantly tested, practical products, which work! They've a modified ear sizing for young guns (Junior Surfears), and besides eco-packaging, a wider size range in the improved SurfEars 3.0 for a perfect fit.

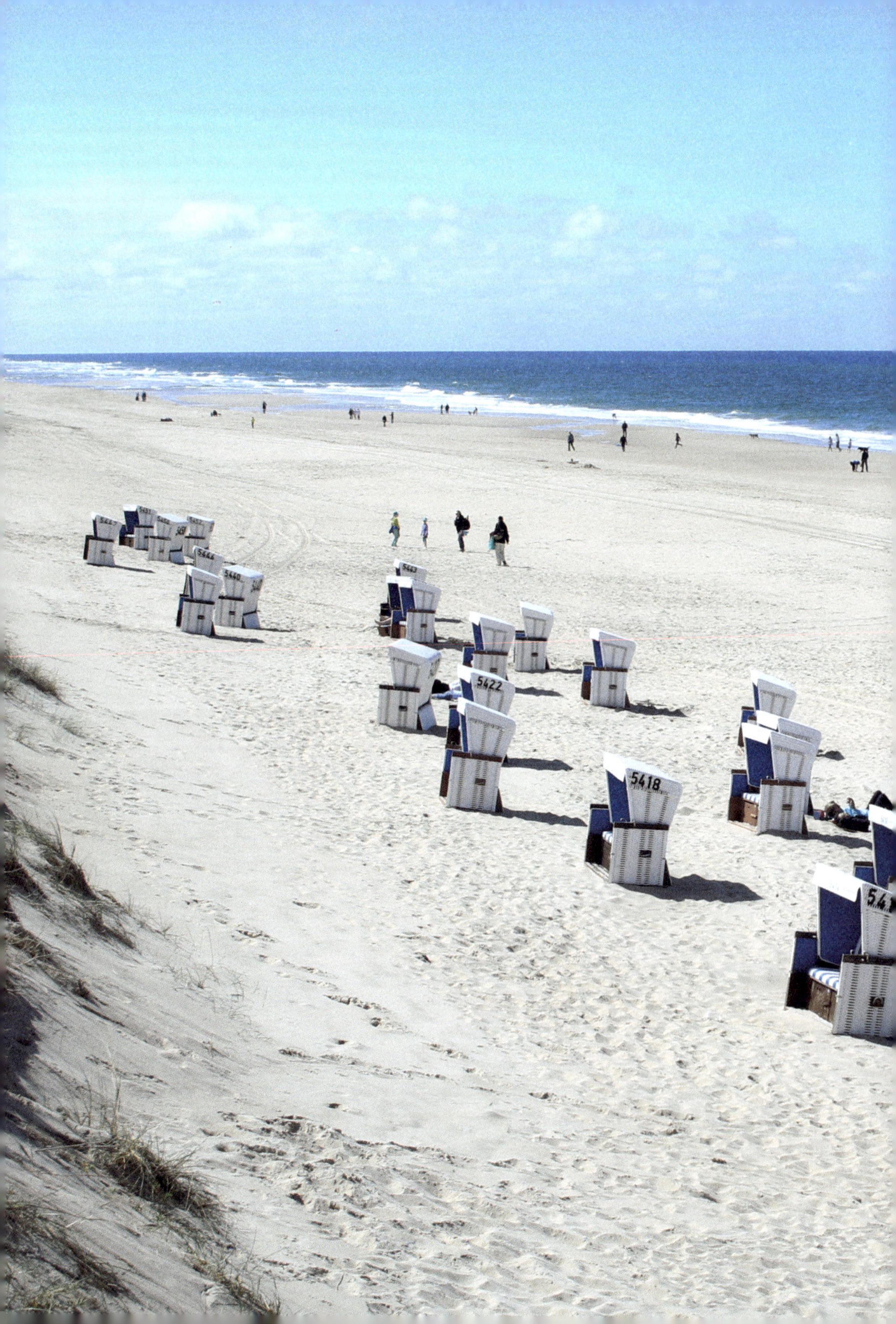
5422
5418

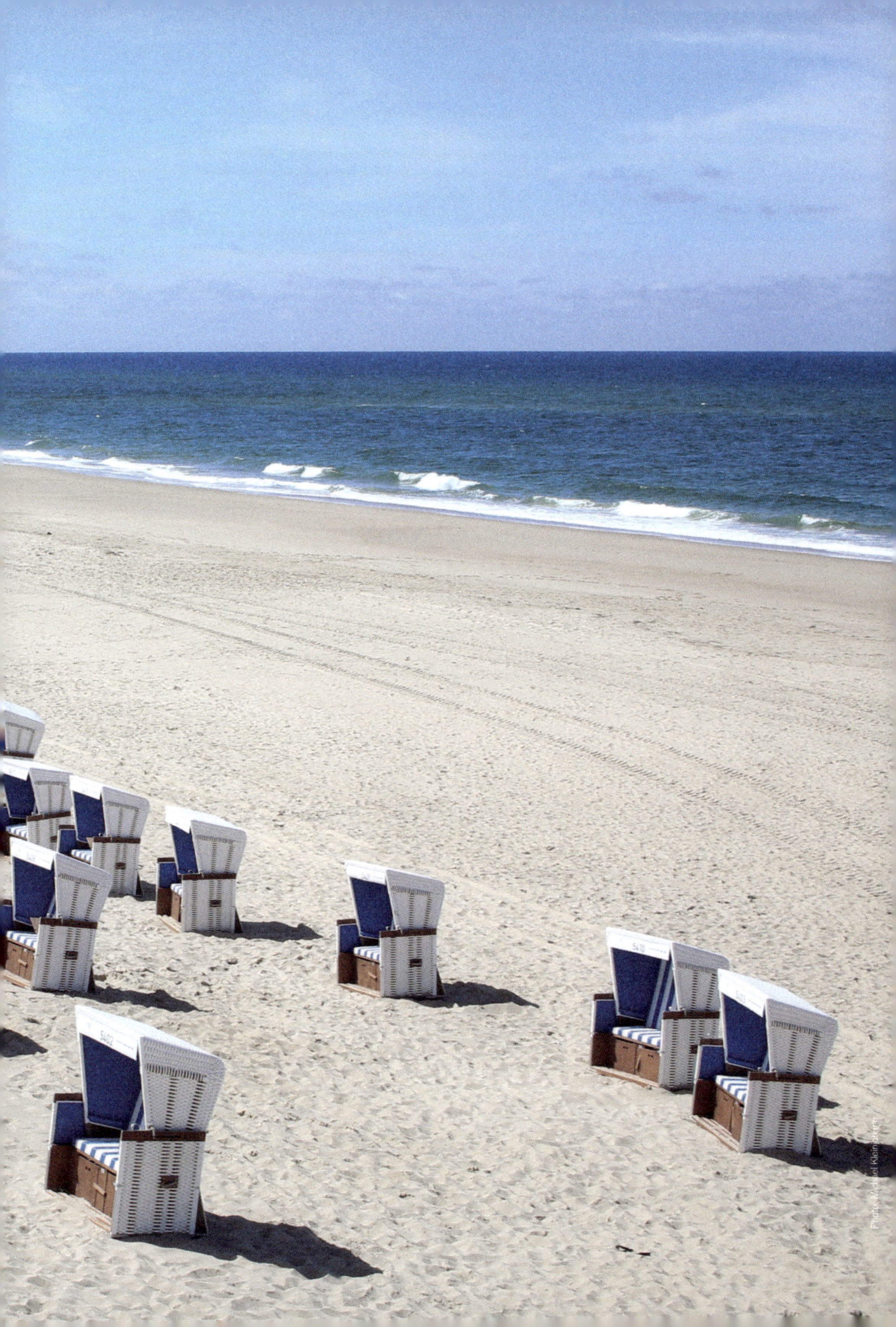

Holland

HOLLAND

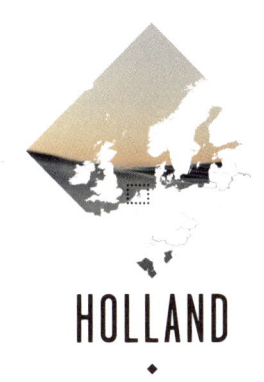

Holland, or The Netherlands, has over 500 kms of coastline; you won't find many Dutch that haven't been to the seaside at least once in their life. On a sunny day, especially the first sunny days after a long greyish and cold winter, all roads leading to the seaside will be full, if not blocked for hours. And it will be busy at the beach, think towels, or what? people! rubbing shoulders, the smell of sunscreen and French fries stronger than the salty ocean. But! But... that's just in some parts, usually around a cluster of beach clubs, or along a boulevard. Only go 2 km away from the scene that's reminiscent of ants crawling round a sugar lump, the beaches will be all yours, and a lonesome dog walker's perhaps.

Dutch love their coast, beaches and seaside life, the sea being the largest natural site in the country. The beach clubs right on the sand - usually open between April and October - are a unique sight. The modest size of Holland makes it easy to combine sea and city in just one day. From Amsterdam you can be at the nearest seaside resort or surf spot in under an hour.

And what about the free-spiritedness? It's what they're known for. We don't know if the Dutch are any more free-spirited than the next people, but the saying 'Wie goed doet, goed ontmoet', translates to 'If you do good, good will be done to you'. And we like to think that travelling ocean-loving people per definition have the tendency to be open-minded, no matter where they're from, and welcome all walks of life. So, that includes you, right?

SURFER-TRAVELLER TYPE HOLLAND

You like to see where you're going; having no hills to speak of to obstruct your sight. You kinda dig that faint whiff of marijuana every now and then, the colour of the sea to be greenish-grey or chocolate-brown, and seeing people use their bicycle to move furniture, take dogs out, transport themselves, surfboards and their entire family. And you don't feel offended hearing ggg, ggg, ggg in every other word they're saying. The fact you're below sea level doesn't scare the shit out of you and you fully trust the Dutch to fight off any floodwaters.

WORDS AND CONCEPTS THAT MIGHT COME IN HANDY

Hoi! - Hi! Just as informal as you would use Hi in English.

Lekker! - Meaning good, fine, yummy, and can be used to describe your food, a hot-looking lady or lad, or something you enjoy, such as sunshine on skin, catching a nice wave, or a song you like.

Gezellig - Ah, so typical Dutch, it's hard to translate. It comes down to cosy, feeling good in particular company, the way a place is decorated, a setting, enjoying a chat with a close friend, having dinner with your loved ones. You can even combine the two. Try '*Lekker gezellig!*' when you're waiting for your next wave in the busy line-up at Scheveningen.

Bakkie doen? - An invitation to go for coffee, even if you end up drinking tea.

Koekebakker! - Kook! Dutchies' very own surf lingo. Literally: the one that bakes the cookies.

HOLLAND

FOOD FACTS

HERRING

A must while at Holland's seaside: 'Haring happen!' That's right, Dutch don't eat their herring like any other food, they bite chunks off, raw nonetheless! Here's how you do as the locals do: order your fresh herring with raw onions, don't have it cut into easy bite-size pieces, and DON'T use a fork.

Hold the paper with the onions in one hand, take the herring by its tail, dip it in the onions then lift it up so you can bite off bits from the other side. Don't worry, its head's already been cut off, and its intestines removed right after you ordered. Eet smakelijk. Don't eat the tail though!

STROOPWAFELS

These waffles are the best gift you can bring home from Holland. Consisting of two thin layers of crisp grilled dough, and a filling of syrup. Best eaten at markets, or from street vendors, selling the waffles fresh and hot with syrup dripping off. If not fresh from the griddle you can warm them up by placing your waffle on top of a steaming cup of tea or coffee (preferably your own) for a few minutes.

277

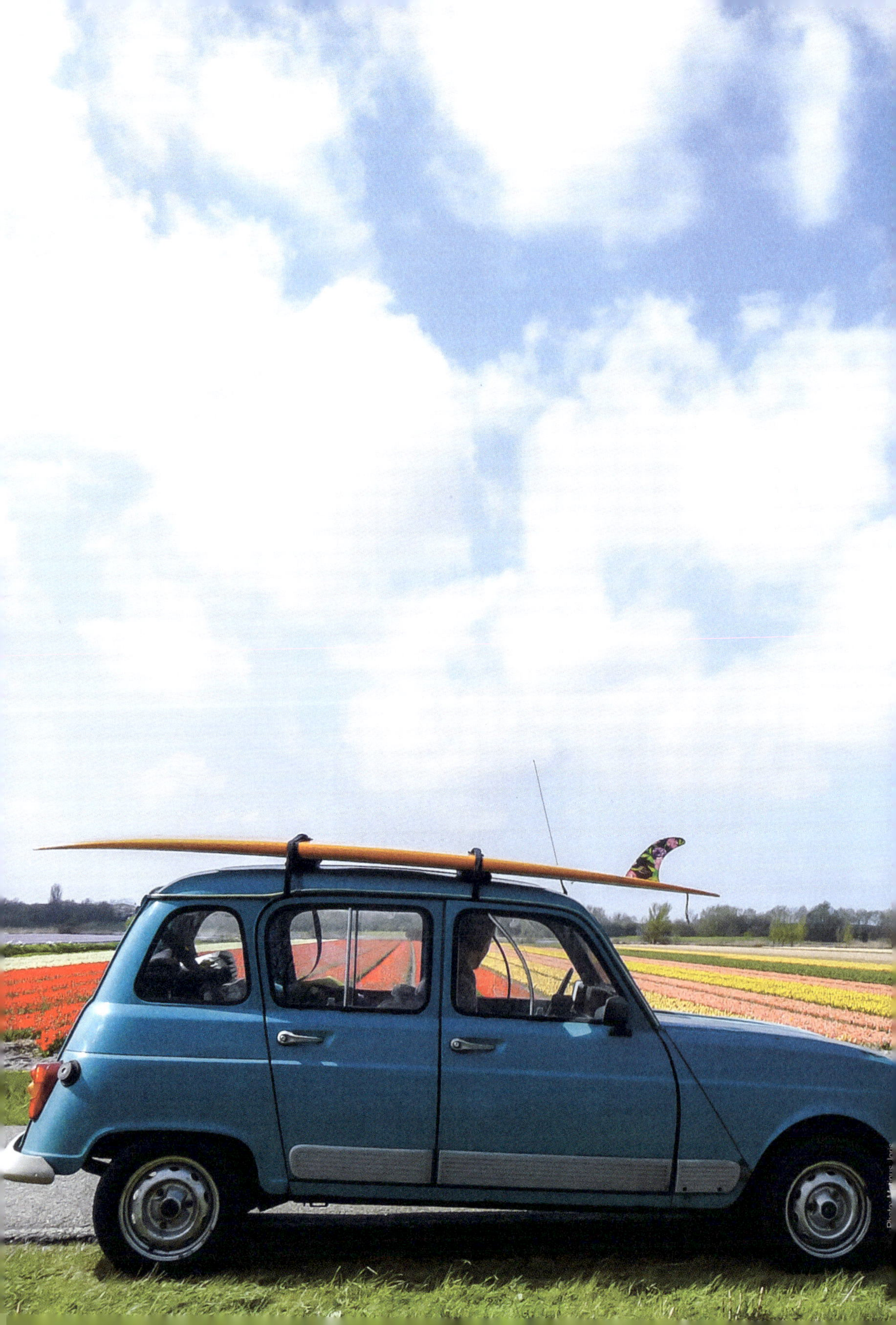

A BIT ON SURF IN HOLLAND

Holland's seaside may not be exactly a swell magnet, but it has plenty good surf days - more than you'd expect. Than anyone expects really. Its location and the N-NW facing coastline means good groundswell from storms off Norway, and SW windswell. The high level of surfing is surprising for a North Sea nation, as is the stoke. Dutch surfers will surf anything, from onshore, southwester storms to clean knee-high ripples, usually having a quiver that suits all circumstances, or taking up kite, SUP or windsurfing to extend playtime in the ocean.

Although a surfer's been sighted as far back as the 1930s, surfing in Holland started in the late sixties, in Scheveningen. A forgotten surfboard at a sailing club was used by the members on windless days and ignited a spark of stoke. The first surfers in Holland didn't bring boards from Australia or even France, but the UK. Surf trips were adventurous from the start, from roadtripping in a used-up car to Morocco, to flying to South Africa and bringing back better boards. Back in the days the line-up in Scheveningen was like the bar in that TV series Cheers, 'Where everybody knows your name'. Nowadays it's more like a rave party, with a few tight-knit members of the surf tribe still knowing each others' names.

So when and where's your best bet for consistent surf in Holland? Although Scheveningen pops up in everybody's head when talking of surfing in Holland, Domburg in Zeeland, Wijk aan Zee in Noord Holland and the Wadden Islands also have aces tucked up their sleeves. Reading the forecast charts will puzzle any surfer from the south of Europe, what with a north swell, 6-second period and 0.9 m wave height being near perfect. And although most surf guides (off and online) will tell you summer is flat, no such thing is definite. Perfect clean peelers can roll in on a hot August day, with the advantage of wearing a 3/2 wetsuit or even a shorty. October and November you can surf in a 4/3, maybe start wearing booties from then on. December you'll need full gear, 5/4/3, hood, gloves and boots, up until April-May.

If you want to learn about or see more of surf in Holland, pick up a copy of surf magazine 6 (**w.** 6.soulonline.nl) or Mui (**w.** muimagazine.nl). Stories will be in Dutch, but there are lots of pictures showing memorable North Sea glory.

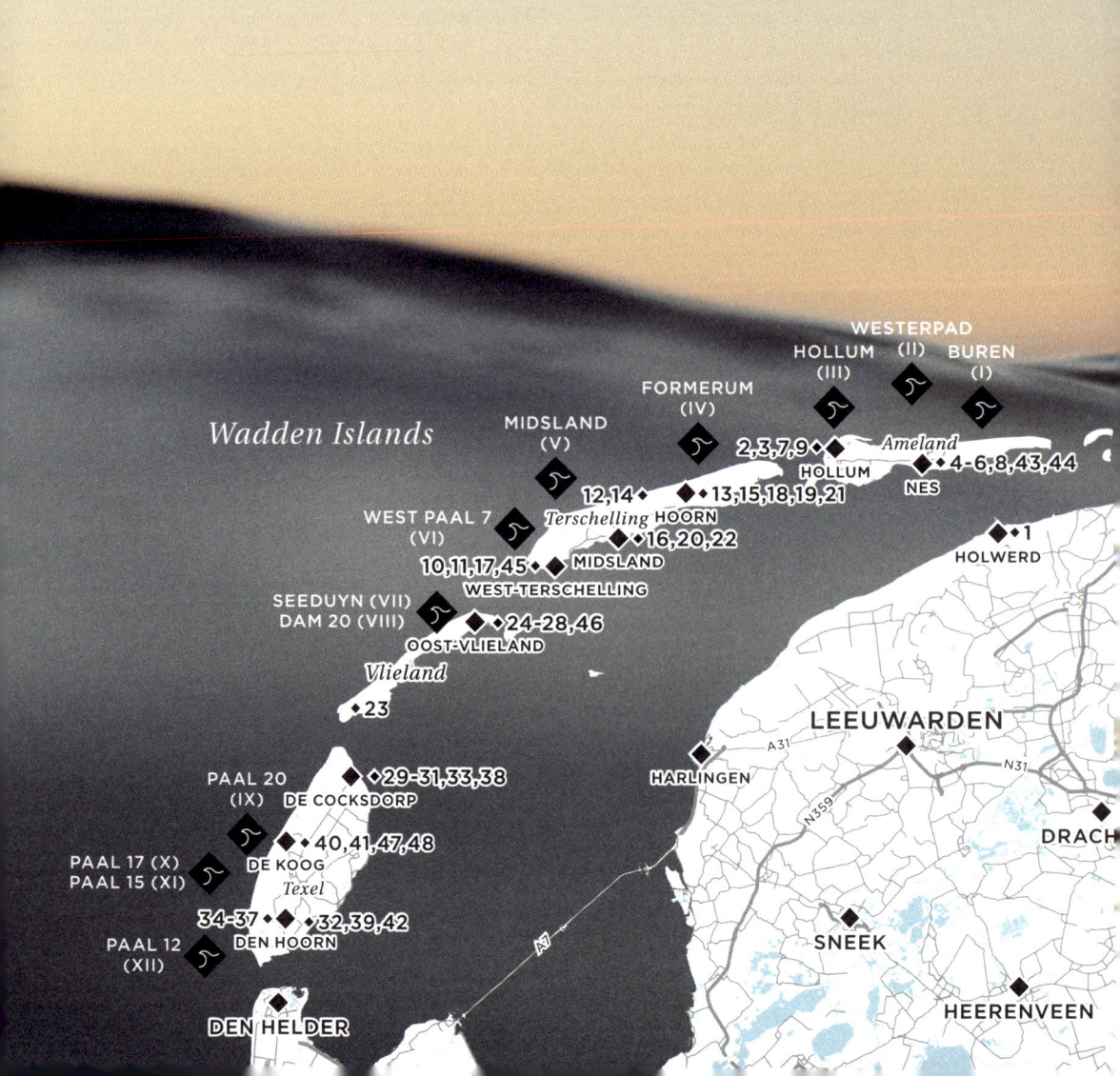

Wadden Islands

WESTERPAD (II)
HOLLUM (III)
BUREN (I)
FORMERUM (IV)
2,3,7,9
Ameland
HOLLUM
4-6,8,43,44
NES
MIDSLAND (V)
12,14
13,15,18,19,21
HOORN
WEST PAAL 7 (VI)
Terschelling
16,20,22
1
HOLWERD
10,11,17,45
MIDSLAND
WEST-TERSCHELLING
SEEDUYN (VII)
DAM 20 (VIII)
24-28,46
OOST-VLIELAND
Vlieland
23
LEEUWARDEN
PAAL 20 (IX)
29-31,33,38
DE COCKSDORP
HARLINGEN
DRACH
40,41,47,48
PAAL 17 (X)
DE KOOG
PAAL 15 (XI)
Texel
34-37
32,39,42
DEN HOORN
PAAL 12 (XII)
SNEEK
DEN HELDER
HEERENVEEN

WADDEN ISLANDS

The Dutch West Frisian islands, pearls in the same chain of islands as the German East Frisian islands, are commonly known in Holland as the Wadden Islands. Named due to their location, they shield the Wadden Sea - tidal mudflats that lie between the islands and the Frisian coast - from the North Sea. Hence, the north and northwest coasts of the islands are wide open to a lot of surfing potential.

Dutch kids have to learn the names and order of islands by heart, using the memory aid term 'TV tas', a silly name meaning 'TV bag'. From west to east it stands for Texel, Vlieland, Terschelling, Ameland and Schiermonnikoog. Almost all Dutch have been to at least one of the islands, at one point in their lives, and usually have fond memories of it. Especially folks from the densely populated west of Holland enjoy the Wadden's sheer emptiness, small settlements and rambling stretches of beach, dunes and forests. We hop from island to island, highlighting what we love about them. Although we skip Schiermonnikoog, this should not stop you exploring the tiniest community of Holland. The entire island is declared National Park, no cars are allowed and over 250 bird species love the place for its ever-shifting dunes, salt marshes and mudflats.

TRAVEL INFO

The islands can only be reached by boat (unless you dare walk the mudflats at low tide, gear and surfboard under arm…). Travel info for each island is in the island's individual section. Note: Cars are unwelcome on some of the islands. To use a car in Vlieland a special permit is needed: available to residents only.

BY BUS

Day passes are available for local buses, and the regular OV-chip cards, used for all public transport in Holland, can be used on all islands except Schiermonnikoog.

BY TRAIN

Direct trains go to/from Amsterdam and Den Helder (to Texel), and Harlingen (to Terschelling and Vlieland). Info on all public transport to plan your routes at:

w. 9292.nl

IN AND AROUND AMELAND

Electric buses and cars, thousand of solar panels and other innovative technologies; Ameland uses all the elements in an effort to be self-sustainable for water and energy by the year 2020. Despite it being an island, there are over a hundred roe deer roaming around. It started with one male who went exploring from the mainland, walking across the mudflats and swimming the channels. The people of Ameland thought he'd be pleased to have a lady friend for company and so brought a female roe deer to the island. Et voila! A healthy number of their offspring can be seen nowadays. Clearly he heard how beautiful the island is, and we're sure he appreciates it as much as we do! Visit late summer to find out what we love best about it; checking the surf from dune tops with whiffs of sea-lavender pleasing the senses, one eye on the waves and the other looking out for roe deer.

Tourist office at Bureweg 2, 9163 KE Nes.

Getting there:
A quick 45 m trip on the Wagenborg ferry takes you from Holwerd (Friesland) to Ameland. **w.** wpd.nl

TO DO

Learn to capture Wadden at its finest during a photography workshop with lens man **Harmen Piekema**. We love his work, you know why? Every now and then we, Dutchies, in a very rare moment of patriotism, are proud of our typical landscapes. We see glimpses of them, driving home at sunset, commuting on an early train, cycling to our next appointment in the freezing cold. Harmen's able to stop time and still those moments, so we have a forever reference to Holland's finest moments. You want to know how to do the same? Join a workshop to learn about composition, timing, location, lighting techniques, and tides (!) - an important factor when shooting at the Wadden. You'll be out and about all day, immersing yourself in nature, which is precisely what Harmen aims for in his workshops. Harmen also has more workshop destinations on offer, like Lofoten, Norway! Check the website for details and dates.

w. foto-shoot.com

The **MadNes Festival** at Nes beach is a weekend celebration of music, culture and outdoor activities. 45 plus bands and DJs perform, both national and international. There's graffiti workshops, salsa lessons, massages, surf, skate, slacklining, archery, kayak, beach rugby and, whooph! many, many more clinics and new things. MadNes aspires to be a sustainable festival, as much as possible: they make use of electric festival buses, their merchandise t-shirts are made from ecological cotton, there's a grand scale beach clean-up, you can rent a sustainable tipi, and there are additions to the list every year. The festival's held on the first weekend of July.

w. madnesfestival.nl

Family-friendly **Rôggefestival** is a street festival held every year on the first Friday of August, in the village centre of Nes. Expect live music, theatre, fireworks, a parade and lots of people being jolly, frolicking about, dressed up, singing, dancing. Feel free to participate.

w. roggefestival.nl

Wadlopen (**1**), mudflat walking, must be the most unique way to experience the Wadden. What you do is: start your hike from the mainland, walk some hours on grounds varying from slippery, sandbanks, wade through knee-deep (or deeper) water for 3 maybe 4 hours until you reach the island. What's so special? You'll be walking on the bottom of the sea! The wadloop tours are at low tide only, and under guidance (guides know exactly the region, changing tides and the speed of the sea). The guides share info about the plants, birds and sealife, and it's very likely you'll have a close encounter with a seal or two. You do need to be fit for this one.

a. Departs from restaurant Land en Zeezicht, Grandijk 2, 9151 AE Holwerd
t. +31 595 528 345
w. wadloop.nl

Paracenter Ameland (**2**) takes you skydiving. You'll be safely harnessed and attached to the instructor. You're allowed to scream in their ears. They're quite used to over-excited peeps.

a. Strandweg 21, 9162 EV Ballum
t. +31 519 554 880
w. paracentrumameland.nl

Take the 236 steps up to the top of the **lighthouse Bornrif** (**3**). You'll be awarded with views from 55 metres high, over the island and sea. Open all year. Check website for exact opening times.

a. Oranjeweg 57, 9161 CB Hollum
t. +31 519 542 737
w. amelandermusea.eu

EAT/DRINK/HANG OUT

Sjoerd (**4**) (a sturdy Dutch boy's name) is a mighty fine looking beach bar at Nes beach. Sjoerd's been voted the most sustainable beach restaurant in Holland, that's how we heard about it. It's not just because the drinks and food (delicious traditional Mediterranean and street food) are where possible organic, and locally produced or brewed. Their takeaway cups and other packaging are of biodegradable material, they use solar energy to heat their water, LED lighting, and efficient energy usage in general. Although it's quite big, light and bright, it's a warm and welcoming place at a stunning beach. Open all year. ◆€€◆

a. Strandweg 70, 9163 GN Nes
t. +31 519 542 524
w. sjoerd-ameland.nl

Ask any Dutchie about their traditional meals and you get a sour look, or a long silence before answering, "nothing special really." Luckily it's changing, albeit slowly, and the Dutch are getting more self-conscious about food traditions. Regular supermarkets stocking 'forgotten vegetables' and people cooking at home making increasing use of grandmother's recipes. Restaurant **Boerenbont** (**5**) doesn't shy away from good old-fashioned Dutch traditional and very tasty recipes, but offers them the limelight on the menu. The word Boerenbont refers to the typical Dutch crockery, white porcelain with flowers painted on. The restaurant describes their menu and décor as the 'no-nonsense of Oma' - Oma being Grandma. Although most of the meals are meat or fish dishes, the chef offers a creative vegetarian option. Closed in winter. ◆€€◆

a. Strandweg 50, 9163 GN Nes
t. +31 519 542 293
w. restaurantboerenbont.nl

SHOP
◆

Going to shop for shoes, end up with a surfboard, or the other way round? At **vanDonia** (**6**) you'll find a collection of shoes, accessories, and bags. Not the usual surf suspects though, no Billabongs, nor Vans, but you can find their own brand VanAmeland t-shirts and sweaters. And surfboards and wax. Open all year.

a. Rixt van Doniastraat 10, 9163 GR Nes
t. +31 519 346 971
w. vandonia.nl

SLEEP
◆

Eco-farm and camping **Tussen Wad en Strand** (**7**), meaning 'between mudflats and beach', offers pitches for tents and campervans on their small-scale but spacious campsite, surrounded by green. Or you can rent from a selection of Mongolian yurts, wooden cabins with curved roofs, or circus wagon. Or add a bit of glam by choosing the fully equipped safari tent. The campsite is self-sustainable, using solar power and other green techniques. Closed in winter. ◆€◆

a. Smitteweg 8, 9162 EC Ballum
t. +31 519 542 941
w. tussenwadenstrand.com

Camping Duinoord (**8**) has pitches in the dunes and fields, and rents out chalets, canvas tents, or comfortable wooden tents that sleep up to 6 people in 2 separate bedrooms. Open from April to September. ◆€◆

a. Jan van Eijckweg 2, 9163 PB Nes
t. +31 519 542 070
w. campingduinoordameland.nl

Sier aan Zee (**9**) and **Huisje Duin** are both run by the same couple. Sier aan Zee is their family-friendly hostel with lots of playground space for kids. The separately located and gorgeously secluded Huisje Duin is everybody's little getaway dream house. It's set in the middle of the dunes and forest area, directly under the lighthouse. This white-washed wooden house is only accessible via an unpaved path through the dunes. Don't need to fill you in on the tranquility and the view, do we? Open all year. ◆€◆ ◆€€◆

a. Oranjeweg 59, 9161 CB, Hollum, Ameland
t. +31 519 555 353
w. sieraanzee.nl

IN AND AROUND TERSCHELLING

Bring your bike! Or rent one, it's easy enough, coming off the boat you practically bump into the first two of many rental companies on the island. Terschelling, one of the larger Wadden Islands, has bicycle paths galore. It also has lively villages, the 400-year-old iconic Brandaris lighthouse, 30 kms of beaches and 80% of the island is all-natural beauty. You can both party all night long, and go exploring outdoors without meeting a soul all day. The north coast picks up any available swell, add that to all other options and you're well on your way to falling in love with this sturdy member of the Wadden family.

Tourist office at Willem Barentszkade 19A, 8881 BC West-Terschelling.

Getting there:
From Harlingen (Friesland) you can take the regular ferry (2 hrs) or the fast ferry (45 min). An inter-island ferry sails regularly between Terschelling and Vlieland (30 min). **w.** rederij-doeksen.nl

TO DO

During the **Oerol Festival** the whole island becomes a natural stage celebrating art, theatre, music, dance, science, nature, society and everything in between for a unique 10-day festival that sells an average 130 thousand tickets each year! Oerol, in Frisian, means 'all over the place'. Anything can serve as a festival location, from beach to bar, campsite to dune, forest to lighthouse, barn to street. It's fun, it's 'gezellig', and above all it's magical. At times you don't know whether you're an onlooker, part of a play, a piece of art, or a concept. The annual festival is held in mid-June, special festival buses leave from Utrecht and Amsterdam to the ferry port at Harlingen.

a. Westerkeyn Zuid Midslandweg 4, 8891 GH Midsland
t. +31 562 448 448
w. oerol.nl

Try different levels of walking, climbing, hopping, gliding obstacles in the forest playground at **Klimbos Klimdaris** (**10**). Not to worry, you'll get extensive instructions before you're off! Open from April/May to August. Reservations recommended, by phone or online.

a. Sportlaan, near Dobe swimming pool, 8881 EP West-Terschelling
t. +31 637 244 762
w. klimdaris.nl

During the summer months yogini Ezra Goudzwaard offers **yoga for surfers** (**11**) at Ieders Plak in West-Terschelling. In highly accessible hatha yoga classes she'll give you tools to increase flexibility and strength and stay in shape. The classes aren't just for surfers, they're for anyone who could use a little extra self-care, whether beginner or advanced, surfer or non-surfer. Every Friday at 20:00 hrs from July to mid-September. Ieders Plak is open all year and offers all sorts of yoga, meditation, and sports lessons, and massages.

a. Sportlaan 9, 8881 EP West-Terschelling
t. +31 562 450 942
w. iedersplak.nl

EAT/DRINK/HANG OUT

Elvis is still alive. And some of his long lost rock 'n' roll pals, like Chuck Berry, Buddy Holly and Johnny Cash. Find them all at the beach bar and restaurant **Heartbreak Hotel** (**12**). At least their soul, spirit and sound are being kept very much alive in Heartbreak Hotel's music, décor, and menu. A choice of dishes like the vegetarian Stray Cats and Patsy Cline, the June Carter sea bass, or the Burning Love burger, and add the fact that this is a one-of-a-kind beach bar. Open all year. ♦€♦ ♦€€♦

a. Badweg Oosterend 71,
   8897 HD Oosterend
t. +31 562 448 634
w. heartbreak-hotel.nl

Since beach restaurant **Kaap Hoorn** (13) can only be reached by bike, on foot or horse, we like it no matter what. And the fact that it's smaller and more intimate than most beach bars and restaurants. What else? Their surroundings; a small valley between forest, dunes and beach. The menu, the fresh juices, and the tranquil vibe tick all other boxes. Open from April to October. ♦€♦ ♦€€♦

a. Badweg Hoorn 16, 8896 KC Hoorn
t. +31 562 448 367
w. kaaphoornterschelling.nl

Okay, just one more beach hangout, then we'll be off, exploring the interior of the island. **ZandZeeBar** (14) adds a little oriental feel to the island. Bit of Bali, bit of Indian, bites from the East, and colours of Africa. But only the Dutch can come up with 'Patatje Rendang': French fries and beef (from Terschelling's local herds), prepared with Indonesian style and flavour. It's on their menu, check it out. Open from April to October. ♦€♦ ♦€€♦

a. Badweg 6, 8896 KW Formerum
t. +31 562 445 172
w. zandzeebar.nu

Colourful place this is, restaurant **De Reis** (15). Bit big, but then again, it's in the heart of the village Hoorn, we guess you have to be able to host lots of hungry guests. In its former life the restaurant was a farm. Although not much of it reminds you of the daily milking of cows, the owners kept its robust character, added quirky paintings and small Hispanic details, like miniature cactus plants and vivid, bright colours. On the menu? Tapas. You guessed that right. Open all year. ♦€♦ ♦€€♦

a. Dorpsstraat 58, 8896 JG Hoorn
t. +31 562 448 424
w. tapasopterschelling.nl

Lots of love, hard work and family spirit went into the making of **Pura Vida** (16). Mother and son run this welcoming place in Midsland, where you can enjoy a good choice of organic, vegan and vegetarian goodies, but also snacks, coffee, healthy burgers and breakfast bowls. Done up in smart, tasteful style, they're a great addition to the island's choice of bars and restaurants. Ask them about the surf and yoga lessons they organise in summer. Open all year. ♦€♦ ♦€€♦

a. Oosterburen 36, 8891 GC Midsland
t. +31 611 855 457
w. puravidaterschelling.nl

Although it's not at the beach, restaurant **DE ZEE** (17) in West-Terschelling has all the beachy feel you could wish for. Photos of waves, drawings of sea birds, the ever so slight use of colours blue and green, driftwood details, and surf and sailing memorabilia. The kitchen's equipped with an original Italian wood-oven in which some delicious dishes are prepared, using as many locally and responsibly produced ingredients as possible. Expect a Mediterranean menu with a bit of island flair. Open all year. ♦€♦ ♦€€♦

a. Boomstraat 33,
   8881 BS West-Terschelling
t. +31 562 442 539
w. restaurantdezee.nl

SHOP
♦

The free roaming sheep of organic farm **De Zeekraal** (18) graze on a rich diet of herbs. Twice a day they come back to their barn to be milked. And from this milk all sorts of tasty cheese and ice-cream is prepared, such as cranberry and elderberry. You can also get your hands on, and rub them with it while you're at it, ever so soft hand cream made with the sheeps' milk. If you wish to linger, you can sleep in one of their tents. Open all year.

a. Oosterend 17A, 8897 HW Oosterend
t. +31 562 449 278
w. dezeekraal.nl

Zelfpluktuin Groenhof (19) is an idyllic place absolutely bursting with fields of wild flowers, strawberries, and various other berries and small fruits. As soon as the first fruits start to ripen, you're welcome to pick your own fruit and flowers. And it's all sustainably grown! Open from June to whenever all fruit and flowers have been picked, usually September.

a. Hoornerkooiweg 1, 8897 HW Oosterend
t. +31 643 831 731 / 614 325 959
w. zelfpluktuingroenhof.nl

De Ouwe Smidte (20) in Midsland specialises in coffee, tea and chocolate. Yay! Just entering the shop will lighten up your mood, whiffs of all three heavenly substances filling the air. The coffee beans are freshly roasted, the chocolate's from fair trade and the tea's hot enough. You can either buy some for home or enjoy a cup of what you fancy on their small terrace. Open daily in summer.

a. Oosterburen 37, 8891 GA Midsland
t. + 31 562 448 069
w. deouwesmidte.nl

SLEEP

The apartment **Graceland (21)** takes you right back to the fifties and sixties of last century, with a really rather retro interior including a jukebox and record player. Choose your tunes to wake up to; bet it's Elvis, or a bit of Be-Bop-A-Lula. Open all year. ♦€€♦

a. Dorpsstraat 5, 8896 JA Hoorn
t. +31 646 261 808
w. heartbreak-hotel.nl/graceland-terschelling

Almost all campsites on the island of Terschelling are nicely located, pretty much small-scale and near nature and beaches. Although relatively big, camping **De Kooi (22)** is for tents only. Located between Midsland and West-Terschelling, it's pretty much in the middle of everything: forest, dune and beach are just a bicycle ride away. And you can take a dip in the lake bordering the campsite. Open mid-April to mid-September. ♦€♦

a. Heester Kooiweg 20, 8882 HE Hee
t. +31 562 442 743
w. campingdekooi.nl

IN AND AROUND VLIELAND

Ah, no cars. Well, hardly any cars. Imagine that. It's just one of the many charms of the island. Vlieland's only got one village, Oost-Vlieland, which makes it all the more compact and clear, and so, so attractive in these busy times. It's a bit of a getaway for Dutch artists, actors and TV personalities, but you won't notice a thing. Everybody's got their reason to choose Vlieland over other destinations, but it usually comes down to its tranquility, laid-back vibe and sheer beauty.

Tourist office at Dorpsstraat 150, 8899 AN Oost-Vlieland.

Getting there:
Vlieland only allows cars on the island with a special permit. And tourists/travellers get no permits. You can leave your vehicle at the designated parking area in Harlingen. To Vlieland from Harlingen (Friesland) by regular ferry (1,5 hrs) or fast ferry (45 min). Also an inter-island from Vlieland to Terschelling (30 min). **w.** rederij-doeksen.nl

TO DO

Yes, that's correct. **Into The Great Wide Open** is a Tom Petty song. It's also Vlieland's 3-day long fab festival; celebrating music, culture and film. And most importantly, nature - well, what else would you celebrate on an almost car free island, with a name referring not only to Tom, but the great wide open that Vlieland represents. The festival's very child friendly, with lots of fun stuff for kids to do, see and experience, while you enjoy a little dance or two. What to expect? Some indie, African, pop, rock, jazz, reggae, folk, blues and soul, and some more, the stuff that can't be labelled. We love the fact that the sea borders the festival terrain, rather than some fence. The island itself serves as the stage - beaches, dunes, maybe a church or a ship. Great and wide as it may be, the festival's one of the most intimate, peaceful, one-of-a-kind events you'll ever attend. Every year on the first weekend in September.
w. intothegreatwideopen.nl

Earlier in the season, a prelude to Into The Great Wide Open is held; a celebration of what's to come (big clue about that in the name of this one) at the small-scale **Here Comes the Summer** festival. Join in the fun during the first week of May, at and around the campsite of Stortemelk.
a. Kampweg 1, 8899 AM Oost-Vlieland
w. intothegreatwideopen.nl

The Vliehors Expres (23) takes you to a place called the Vliehors, also known as 'the Sahara of the North'. You'll board their big yellow truck and drive along the 20 km long stretch of sand on the west side of the island, all the way to the tip of the island. It's not uncommon to see seals, and all kinds of birds. Part of the trip is a visit to what was formerly a refuge for stranded sailors, fishermen and others saved from the sea. It's now being used as a quirky wedding location, and a museum filled with stuff that's been washed up on the beach. Trips are made all year round, but regularly from mid-July through August.

a. Middenweg 41, 8899 BA Oost-Vlieland
t. +31 621 820 842
w. vliehorsexpres.nl

EAT/DRINK/HANG OUT
◆

Enjoy home-made cakes, fair trade and specially selected coffee and tea, organic drinks, smoothies, spelt flour open sandwiches with layers of local ingredients and much more at **Leut** (**24**). The drinks, snacks and dishes are as fresh as their interior. (If you like the place, they also rent out 3 stylishly decorated rooms, from February to November). Open all year. ◆€◆ ◆€€◆

a. Dorpsstraat 118, 8899 AM Oost-Vlieland
t. +31 562 853 791
w. leutvlieland.nl

SHOP
◆

't Snoepwinkeltje (**25**) is a treat if you have a sweet tooth. It's filled to the brim with typical Dutch candy: lollipops, sour mats, tiny syrup soldiers, and of course 'drop', liquorice, in all sorts, tastes, sizes and shapes. How about a metre of it, rolled up into a tight little bundle? Open all year.

a. Dorpsstraat 58, 8899 AA Oost-Vlieland
t. +31 562 451 328
fb. Het Snoepwinkeltje

The **Eb en Vloed Holiday Store** (**26**) offers all sorts of items, with one thing in common, as they say themselves: "We only sell good feelings." You can easily walk into the store with the whole family in tow, there's some for everyone, you see. Home decoration, bodycare products, books, wine (oh, like the combo!), selected food items and clothes. Not buying any? Sit back and relax on their garden terrace, tasting some of that fine wine, or tea, coffee, whatever you fancy. Eb en Vloed has a heart for durability, sustainability and quality, which is reflected in their choice of items.

a. Dorpsstraat 5, 8899 AA Oost-Vlieland
t. +31 562 451 782
w. eb-vloed.nl

SLEEP
◆

Stortemelk (**27**) is one of few campsites on the island. Besides pitches just behind the dunes, a stone's throw from the beach, they also rent out some wonderfully located cottages. The wooden, oval-shaped houses are in the middle of a forested area and are sustainably built. They sleep up to 4 people, have a spacious terrace - even beyond spacious, since the forest is your extended garden, isn't it! If you want to stay at the campsite but didn't bring your camping gear, you can rent a fully furnished and equipped tent, sleeping up to 6 people. Open all year. ◆€◆ ◆€€◆

a. Kampweg 1, 8899 BX Oost-Vlieland
t. +31 562 451 225
w. stortemelk.nl

De Lange Paal (**28**) is a quiet, basic, nature campsite located between the dunes and woods. You'll wake up to the birds chirping, the wind rattling leaves in trees and the waves - oh that blissful wonderful endless sound of surf. There are pitches and you can rent one of their tents, with all camp necessities included. Open from April to September. ◆€◆

a. Postweg 1A, 8899 BZ Oost-Vlieland
t. +31 306 977 749
w. logerenbijdeboswachter.nl

IN AND AROUND TEXEL

The largest island of the Wadden archipelago, and the most attractive to tourists. Doesn't mean you can't escape the crowds! Plenty of dunes, forests and beaches; each marked by a post with a number, for example: Paal 11. And De Slufter - Paal 27 - part of the Dunes of Texel National Park, even when the green route's closed for the bird breeding season, still offers plenty more paths. Think long strolls, looking for shell fossils, meeting birds, rabbits, hares, frogs, butterflies and bees, the latter attracted by the sea-lavender. That's one to look out for: try to get your hands on sea-lavender honey - lamsoor honing - it's said to do a world of good for your health. Texel's also known for its many sheep, and products made from sheep's milk or wool. There's even a spa where you can indulge in a bath of soft sheep's wool! Other activities include skydiving, mountain biking, sailing, wind, kite and of course, just plain old good old surfing.

Tourist office at Emmalaan 66, 1791 AV Den Burg.

Getting there:
A quick crossing (20 mins) on ferries sailing regularly between Texel and Den Helder (Noord-Holland).
w. teso.nl

TO DO

Sample, or just get a sniff of, all the local delicacies at the Beach Food Festival. You'll find oysters, smoked fish, herring, seaweed and lots more on the menu. Different food trucks offer a wide array of fresh, cold and hot drinks, snacks, tasty slow food, and healthy fast food. From beer to brownie: all locally grown, produced, prepared or brewed. And there's music too! A perfect family outing, sitting on hay bales used for benches, dancing and listening to live music, eating honest food. The festival takes place on the third weekend of July each year.

a. Waddenstrand, Oudeschild
w. beachfoodfestival.nl

At sailing school and Nacra test centre **De Eilander** (**29**) you can learn to sail a catamaran, either in the flat water of the Wadden Sea, or the waves of the North Sea. Lessons are given at the northernmost point of the island, at Paal 33. Open from April to September.

a. Volharding 6, 1795 LH De Cocksdorp
t. +31 620 634 413 / 620 634 413
w. deeilander.nl

We'd almost say it's a must-do, indulging in a sheep's wool bath at **Spa Woolness** (**30**). The spa uses all sorts of natural products from the island. You can choose a sheep milk massage, several beauty treatments, use the sauna or steam bath, self-massage your feet on the designated barefoot path, or choose the unparalleled wool bath. Open all year.

a. Postweg 134, 1795 JS De Cocksdorp
t. +31 222 311 237
w. hoteltexel.com

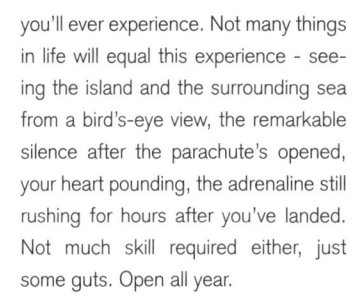

Do the thing birds do best and try a little freefall with **Paracentrum Texel** (**31**). Whether you like to learn how to operate a parachute yourself, or take a tandem jump with one of their instructors, skydiving is one of the best feelings, and closest to the feeling of flying, you'll ever experience. Not many things in life will equal this experience - seeing the island and the surrounding sea from a bird's-eye view, the remarkable silence after the parachute's opened, your heart pounding, the adrenaline still rushing for hours after you've landed. Not much skill required either, just some guts. Open all year.

a. Postweg 128, 1795 JS De Cocksdorp
t. +31 222 311 464
w. paracentrumtexel.nl

Sukha Texel (**32**) offers yoga lessons and weekend meditation retreats, treatments based on Ayurveda, and classes or workshops on vegetarian cooking. You can join a retreat, take a class, book a treatment, or stay for a bit longer and sleep in a yurt or an ayurvedic-based homestay. Check website for schedules and dates. Open all year.

a. Schilderweg 208A, 1792 CK Oudeschild
t. +41 222 315 782
w. sukhatexel.nl

EAT/DRINK/HANG OUT
♦

There are beach bars galore. Every beach is marked by a post 'Paal' with a number, and lots of the bars have simply adapted the corresponding post and number. We selected a few of our favoured places, most are open from April to October unless stated otherwise.

At the northernmost point of the island you'll find **Strandpaviljoen Kaap Noord** (**33**), at Paal 33. No fancy pants, but rather flip flops or bare feet, and bring your dog along, it's one of the few beaches where dogs are allowed all year. Open all year. ♦€♦ ♦€€♦

a. Volharding 4, 1795 LH De Cocksdorp
t. +31 222 316 340
w. strandpaviljoenkaapnoord.nl

Strandpaviljoen Vijftien (34) is a laid-back, unassuming and welcoming place, at, you guessed it, Paal 15. In summer you can book a massage, join yoga lessons on the beach, or vigorous beach boost classes if you want to sweat and tone those muscles. They rent out little whitewashed beach huts - very difficult to get your hands on, they're popular so book ahead. Easy to portray and take Insta-beach-worthy photos with though. ♦€♦ ♦€€♦

a. Westerslag 4, 1791 PP Den Burg
t. + 31 222 314 847
w. strandpaviljoenvijftien.nl

Strandpaviljoen Twaalf (35) is a lively place, perfect for those who long for never-ending summer nights. They host a funky reggae festival every year on the last weekend of July. Every Friday in July and August they organise Barefood Beats; evenings filled with music, DJ sets, outdoor cooking sessions and cocktail drinking. ♦€♦ ♦€€♦

a. Jan Ayeslag 2, 1797 RM Den Hoorn
t. + 31 222 319 737
w. strandpaviljoen-twaalf.nl

With a well balanced mixture of locals and tourists, the quirky eatery, **Inn de Knip (36)** in the village of Den Hoorn, is a cosy place to grab a bite, enjoy a good coffee, chat, read, swap your book, fix your bike tyres - Inn de Knip welcomes cyclists! Colourful setting and décor, friendly staff and vibe, and a menu based around local products. Do you need more reasons to visit? Open all year. ♦€♦ ♦€€♦

a. De Naal 2, 1797 AC Den Hoorn
t. +31 222 319 946
w. inndeknip.nl

SHOP
♦

Novalishoeve (37) is a care farm, using dynamic biological methods to process their dairy, fruits and grains, resulting in incredibly tasty products. You can not only buy their products, like droolicious ice-cream, cheese, tea, you can stop for a drink, and also witness how organic farming works. All is done with love and attention; the farm works with young people that need extra care, educating and teaching them so much more than just organic farming methods. Open all year.

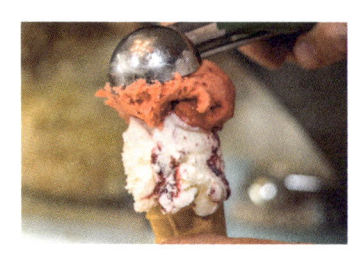

a. Hoornderweg 46, 1797 RA Den Hoorn
t. +31 222 319 482
w. novalishoeve.nl

SLEEP
♦

Hotel Texel (38) is a boutique-style stay, offering luxurious rooms and suites, authentic and traditional island dishes, and their absolutely unique Spa Woolness (see To Do section). The hotel's located near De Slufter nature reserve and close to both villages De Cocksdorp and De Koog. Open all year. ♦€€€♦

a. Postweg 134, 1795 JS De Cocksdorp
t. +31 222 311 237
w. hoteltexel.com

Eight classic silver Airstream caravans are lined up at **Camp Silver (39)**, the Island Hideaway. A large dome tent serves as a pavilion for breakfast, lunch and dinner. Think camping? Well, yeah, but in the best possible, and most comfortable, way. One of the Airstreams even has a private sauna! All Airstreams have their own patio, breakfast buffet is included, and each sleeps 2 people. Camp Silver is in a secluded spot, surrounded by nature, and has one strict rule: no kids allowed... Perfect romantic getaway anyone? Open from April to November. ♦€€♦ ♦€€€♦

a. Eendenkooiweg 2, 1794 GA Oosterend
t. +31 222 318 571
w. campsilver.nl

Ruige Hoogte (**40**) is a small-scale campsite and bed & breakfast. Their pitches are all separated by hedges, giving you ample privacy. You also have the option to rent a completely furnished and fully equipped safari tent. The bed & breakfast has 2 rooms available. Open from March to October. ♦€♦ ♦€€♦

a. Maaikeduinweg 1, 1796 MN De Koog
t. +31 222 317 626
w. ruigehoogte.nl

Smack in the middle of the dunes, just steps from the beach, **Camping Kogerstrand** (**41**) offers some 900 pitches. Yes, that's a lot, so no, it's not your small and personal campsite. But then again, it's smack in the middle of the dunes! And because you're surrounded by nature, you'll have the feeling you have it all to yourself. Open from March to October. ♦€♦ ♦€€♦

a. Badweg 33, 1796 AA De Koog
t. +31 222 390 112
w. krim.nl/overnachten/camping-kogerstrand

Either stay in a yurt or enjoy an Ayurvedic homestay at **Sukha** (**42**). Get inspired by the philosophy of Ayurveda - living in harmony with nature and the elements. You'll feel well balanced just by entering the warmly decorated yurt and homestay. Their breakfast is, obviously, based on the Ayurvedic idea, organic as much as possible and vegetarian. If you're interested you can join meditation classes or book an Ayurvedic treatment. From March to October. ♦€€♦

a. Schilderweg 208a, 1792 CK Oudeschild
t. +31 222 315 782
w. sukhatexel.nl

SURF

The Wadden Islands are the pièce de résistance of surf on Holland's seaside menu. Not too crowded, consistent, and the backdrop is simply stunning. Sometimes you have to do a bit of rambling, biking, climb a dune top or two, to get to your dish of the day, but then it's all yours, apart from the occasional seal you might be happy to share with. Venture away from obvious areas with care and respect, and you'll probably find way more spots than mentioned below. Some are obviously lacking lifeguards, so be aware of currents. Holland's coastline can appear deceptively calm, but especially some spots around the Wadden have strong undercurrents. Almost all beaches are exposed, so strong onshore winds can be spoilsports, but all available north and northwest swell is at your disposal. Windswell mainly - groundswell rare but oh so good. A strong south wind gives offshore pretty much everywhere, and every slight bend in the coastline can make a difference to conditions. Make time to explore…

AMELAND

Buren (I), on the stretch of beach to the east of Nes. Works with a small to medium W-NW-N-NE swell, best from mid to high tide. Beware of strong currents. ◆ *All levels/sand/easy parking/toilets/restaurant.* ◆

Westerpad (II), best from mid to high, with a small to medium W-NW-N-NE swell. Strong currents here too. ◆ *All levels/sand/only reachable on foot or bike/restaurant/surf school.* ◆

Hollum (III), (between Paal 3 and 4), tucked in a bit to the west and offering slight protection from W-NW wind. Works best from mid to high tide with a small to big NW-N-NE swell. You'll usually find fast, hollow waves, and there are strong currents to be reckoned with. ◆ *Intermediate to advanced level/sand/only reachable on foot or bike/no facilities.* ◆

With a W-NW-N or NE-E swell it pays to check the breaks between Paal 8 and 22, best from mid to high tide.

TERSCHELLING

♦

The exposed beach of **Formerum (IV)** works at all tides with a small to medium W-NW-N-NE swell. Beware of strong currents. ♦ *All levels/sand/easy parking/restaurant.* ♦

The main surf break, **Midsland (V)**, an exposed NNW facing beach that works on all tides with a small, medium to big W-NW-N-NE swell. ♦ *All levels/sand/difficult parking in summer/restaurant.* ♦

Same for **West Paal 7 (VI)** but doesn't handle a big swell as nicely as Midsland. All tides, small to medium W-NW-N-NE swell makes for the most fun. ♦ *All levels/sand/easy parking/restaurant/campsite/surf school.* ♦

VLIELAND

♦

NW facing **Seeduyn (VII)** has some jetties, works at all tides with a small to medium W-NW-N-NE swell. ♦ *All levels/sand/toilets/restaurant/surf school.* ♦

Dam 20 (VIII) also has some jetties and works on all tides with a small to medium W-NW-N-NE swell. It's an isolated beach, beware of strong currents. ♦ *All levels/sand/only reachable on bike with a bit of a hike on top/no facilities.* ♦

TEXEL

♦

Kogerstrand Paal 20 (IX) is a NW facing beach that works best on up-coming or higher tides with a small to medium W-NW-N-NE swell. ♦ *All levels/sand/easy parking/toilets/restaurants/campsite.* ♦

Ecomare Paal 17 (X) and **Westerslag Paal 15 (XI)** work best on outgoing to low tide with a small to big SW-W-NW-N-NE swell, and also have jetties. Both beaches are popular with wind and kite surfers. ♦ *All levels/sand/easy parking/toilets/restaurants/surf schools.* ♦

West facing **Jan Aye Slag Paal 12 (XII)** works best on low to mid tides with a small to medium SW-W-NW swell. There are some jetties, and it'll be offshore with east winds. Strong currents, also popular with wind and kite surfers. ♦ *All levels/sand/easy parking/restaurant.* ♦

SCHOOL RENTAL REPAIR

AMELAND

Beach Ameland (**44**) offers kite, surf, SUP, bodyboard, kayak, rafting, yoga and blokarting (sailing in a little kart on the beach) lessons, and rental of gear.

a. Westerpad 1A, 9163 HP Nes
t. +31 627 226 906
w. beach-ameland.nl

Ameland Adventure (**45**) has surf school and rentals, and offers all the other beach and water adventure and fun you'd expect; blokarting, kite buggying, SUP and kayak. Open in summer.

a. Westerpad 1C, 9163 HP Nes
t. +31 612 930 357
w. amelandadventure.nl

TERSCHELLING

Surf Village (**46**) have a surf and SUP school, close to beach bar West aan Zee. They also have a little shop selling all your surf essentials, accessories, gifts and clothes. Ask them for any info you need, have a chat or book a wonderful SUP tour in the south side of the island's calm Wadden Sea. Open all year (winter: Thursday, Friday and Saturday only).

a. Boomstraat 25,
8881 BE West-Terschelling
t. +31 629 541 190
w. surfvillage.nl

VLIELAND

Vlieland Outdoor Center (**47**) organises surf lessons, kayaking, power-kiting, kite surfing, and some genuinely endearing outdoor activities such as outdoor cooking workshops. They also host the free Surffilm Festival, every year on the second Wednesday in August. Expect films and documentaries on anything surf (kite, wave, wind), good food and music. Open at the beach daily in summer, other seasons by reservation only.

a. 400 m west of beach pavilion 't Badhuys
t. +31 651 460 152
w. vlielandoutdoorcenter.nl

TEXEL

◆

At De Koog, Texel, you'll find **Surfschool Foamball (48)**, offering surf lessons and courses, rentals of all gear, summer camps and events. Find them south of Paal 19. Open from April to October.

a. Ruijslaan 44, 1796 AD De Koog
t. +31 624 632 238
w. surfschoolfoamball.com

Surfschool Texel (49), located at Paal 17 in De Koog, offer surf courses and lessons, rental of all gear, boards and SUPs. Ask the friendly staff for more info on surfing in Texel, or hang out in their hammocks. You can also store your own board at their school.

a. Ruijslaan 96, 1796 AZ De Koog
t. +31 610 956 959 / 610 956 959
w. surfschool-texel.nl

DEN HELDER

JULIANADORP

JULIANADORP & CALLANTSOOG (I)

CALLANTSOOG

PETTEN (II)
◆ 13, 35, 36, 43
PETTEN

CAMPERDUIN & HARGEN (III)
◆ 1, 14, 44
HARGEN

◆ 2, 15   ◆ 3, 15, 16
BERGEN AAN ZEE   **BERGEN**

ALKMAAR

BERGEN & EGMOND (IV)
◆ 4, 17-19, 28, 29, 37, 45, 46
EGMOND

Noord-Holland

CASTRICUM (V)
◆ 5, 20, 38, 39, 44, 47
CASTRICUM

WIJK AAN ZEE (VI)
◆ 6-8, 21, 22, 48
WIJK AAN ZEE
◆ 55

IJMUIDEN (VII)
◆ 23, 40, 49
IJMUIDEN

◆ 24, 25, 41, 50, 51
BLOEMENDAAL
◆ 9, 30, 56
HAARLEM

BLOEMENDAAL & ZANDVOORT (VIII)
◆ 10, 11, 26, 27, 42, 52-54
ZANDVOORT

AMSTERDAM
◆ 12, 31-34

NOORD-HOLLAND

The province of Noord-Holland, North Holland, holds one of the most extensive areas of dunes, forests and expansive beaches in Holland that's still largely free to roam. The vegetation-rich territory around Bergen, Schoorl, and Groet are popular mountain biking and hiking terrain. Some coastal communities are divided into 'at sea' and 'inside' parts, like Egmond and Bergen, with a distinctive difference in vibe, look and of course, locals. Especially the 'at sea' species of native will emphasise they're from Egmond/Bergen/Wherever aan Zee. Why, what? Cos they can skip-hop to the beach in a heartbeat, instead of joining the nagging traffic jams in summer to get to the sea, right?

Small as some villages may be, they're all close to the bigger towns like Den Helder, Alkmaar and of course, Amsterdam. Therefore the more popular beaches will always be crowded from the moment the first rays of sunlight hit the sand. Especially Zandvoort and Bloemendaal, with their hip-and-happening beach clubs. But finding a stretch of white sand just for you and your favourite travel companion is easy. Move away from the beach entrances and beach bars and you'll have the place to yourself. Promise.

TRAVEL INFO

In Holland, everything's near. Even from the far north to the far south is only 3 hours by car. The country's small, people are many, and cars plenty. Roads will always be busy, and trains well filled, but except for rush hour, everything runs pretty smoothly.

BY AIR

International flights from both established and budget airlines fly to/from Amsterdam Schiphol Airport.

w. schiphol.nl

BY TRAIN

An extensive and reliable train network, run by the Nederlandse Spoorwegen (Dutch Railways), takes you from the far north to the far south, west and east of the country, and back.

w. ns.nl

BY BUS/WATER TAXI

Several bus, tram and metro companies make sure you can get to even the remotest areas in the country. During the summer months there's a water taxi running 4 times a day between IJmuiden (Pontplein) and Wijk aan Zee (Noordpier).

w. pont-noordzeekanaal.nl
Plan all your public transport routes at:
w. 9292.nl

IN AND AROUND WIJK AAN ZEE

Beauty is in the eye of the beholder. Wijk aan Zee, and neighbouring IJmuiden, are therefore loved and loathed. Where one sees a unique sight that brings a smile to the eyes, another drily notes a set of the Tata steel plant blast furnaces, known as the 'Hoogovens'. Let's stick with the unique sight. Surfers would want to enter the beach of Wijk aan Zee on the north side, close to the northern end of the long harbour wall (technically in Velsen-Noord, but everyone agrees it's ok to call Wijk aan Zee). A long road through the dunes, pipes sticking out at the south end, takes you to a seemingly never-gonna-end beach, backed by a dune reserve that stretches to the north. Zandvoort, just south of Wijk aan Zee and IJmuiden, is also a popular beach resort. Having a Formula One race circuit right by the beach helps attract even more daytrippers. Like most Dutch seaside towns, the old city centres of Wijk aan Zee and Zandvoort are cute, the boulevards a mixture of fast-food and chip shops, 19th century houses, modern restaurants and hotels built by virtue of developers and financers who, in hindsight, maybe didn't have such good taste after all.

Tourist office at Voorstraat 12, 1949 BH Wijk aan Zee.

TO DO

Much loved beach festival **Surfana** celebrates the good life, in every sense. Imagine a perfect day out and about with friends, one that spontaneously slides into a vibrant night; with campfires being lit, music and dancing going on, and new friends being made. That, multiplied many times, is the good feeling of the Surfana festival. And it's not just a day, it's a long weekend. The festival takes place in National Park Zuid-Kennemerland, with the beach and dunes as playground, stage and hangout. Surfana is surf-focused, kinda obvious, eh! But it's more about people enjoying all that's on offer. Daytime you can participate in workshops, clinics and classes, evenings are filled with music and dance, and there's good food throughout. Usually held on the second weekend of June.

w. surfanafestival.com

Bakkum Vertelt is a fun cultural festival, held at the open-air theatre stage of Camping Bakkum on the second weekend in July. Everybody's welcome, you don't need to be a camping guest. Expect lots of live music, performances, theatre, food trucks, and kids and grandparents, dads and mums, all dancing.

a. Zeeweg 31, 1901 NZ Castricum
t. +31 251 661 091
w. campingbakkum.nl

Beach bar and surf school The Spot, in Zandvoort, recently started the first drag races on the beaches of Holland. Festival **Bikes and Boards** must be on your tick-list if you're anything into custom built engines, or classic and old skool surfboards and logs. Every year in the first week of September there'll be bikes, boards, competitions, a classic board expo, and brands ready to make a special offer. There's a barber, and beer and a hot smoking BBQ. The festival's for everyone to enjoy, whether you're just a curious onlooker, are competing, or own a log, bike, beard...

a. The Spot, Strandafgang Barnaart 23A, 2041 KB Zandvoort
w. bikesandboards.eu

De Jongens uit Schoorl (**1**), 'The Boys from Schoorl', take you and a SUP out to sea, or to the calm lagoon of Camperduin. When there are waves, they take you out surfing. If it's windy - kite/wind surfing, or to learn power kiting on the beach. Loads of energy between them. And for the record: the Boys aren't all boys, some of the Boys are actually powerful and enthusiastic ladies. Open all year, on reservation.

a. parking Camperduin, Heereweg 334, 1871 GM Schoorl
t. + 31 725 092 773
w. djus.nl

Jetty Stammes of **Yoga Bergen** (**2**) takes her classes outside in summer. Her Hatha yoga classes are easy and relaxing, nothing strenuous. Classes from May to beginning of September, in Bergen aan Zee: Saturday mornings at Blooming Beach, Sundays at Strandpaviljoen Noorderlicht. Drop-ins welcome.

t. +31 655 113 494
w. yogabergen.nl

Before you know it, you're **Uked** (**3**)! Well, it's what happens to every other person that attends one of the ukulele workshops of the Uked girls, Liselotte and Barbara. They appreciate the simple things in life, downsizing, and simplifying. Doesn't being able to play a few songs on a ukulele tick the boxes above? Liselotte, Barbara and their small team of ukulele lovers guarantee that by end of the workshop you'll be able to play at least one, but probably a few simple tunes. Even if you've never played an instrument before! Besides their monthly workshops you can get inspired in their shop in Bergen. They've got some high-end ukuleles that, even if you never lay fingers on strings, will look absolutely gorgeous on your wall, in your campervan, or lying next to you in a park or at the beach. Workshops are held throughout the year, the shop opens by reservation.

a. Oude Bergerweg 1, 1862 KH Bergen
t. +31 645 544 701
w. uked.nl

Take a fat bike tour with the **Beach Bastards** (**4**). You'll cycle the beach, following the shoreline on a chubby tyred bicycle. They also have mountain bike courses on offer. If you want to explore on your own, rent one of their ATB's or 'normal' bicycles. Open from April to October.

a. Pompplein 5, 1931 AD Egmond aan Zee
t. +31 727 112 804
w. beachbastards.nl

Strandvondsten Museum Castricum (**5**) is dedicated to treasures that have washed up on the shores and is located in one of the most beautiful spots of Castricum, at the entrance to the North Holland Dune Reserve. Besides all sorts of flotsam and jetsam on display, there are videos, guided tours, and lots of stories about the beach, beach combing and curious discoveries. Some of the findings date as far back as 1910, most of them were found by the late legendary local strandjutter (beachcomber), Thijs Bakker. Open all year.

a. Geversweg 2A, 1901 NW Castricum (behind the NS station)
t. +31 622 923 226
w. strandvondstenmuseum.nl

Enjoy a Hatha and mindfulness yoga class with sea view at Wijk aan Zee beach. Yogini Kalinke, of **Aloha Yoga** (**6**), teaches her classes every Saturday and Sunday morning at beach pavilion Aloha Beach. Open all year.

a. Reyndersweg 2, 1951 LA Wijk aan Zee/Velsen-Noord
t. +31 251 374 130
w. alohabeach.nl

Outstanding Events (**7**) (couldn't think of a better name!) offers speedy sailing at the beach in blokarts. The 3-wheeled karts have a mast and sail to send you whizzing along the wide beach of Noordpier. It's one of the few beaches in Holland where you're allowed to sail in these fast karts. Open all year, by reservation only.

a. Reyndersweg 2, 1951 LA Wijk aan Zee/Velsen-Noord
t. +31 251 750 500
w. outstandingevents.nl

Bruutbikes (**8**) offers clinics and tours on fatbikes, or you can just rent one. The tyres are as thick as 10 cm, enabling you to pedal on soft sand, no problem. Open all year, tours by reservation only.

a. De Zwaanstraat 14B, 1949 BC Wijk aan Zee
t. +31 645 648 386
w. bruutbikes.nl

Safe Waterman (**9**) will take you on a stunning SUP tour through the channels of the city of Haarlem, and river Het Spaarne. Tours take 1,5 hours and are guided by an experienced instructor. Available in summer, by reservation only.

t. +31 655 861 312
w. safewaterman.nl

You'd never guess that diving in the grey-greenish looking North Sea is possible, eh! **Scuba Republic** (**10**) will change your mind about that, and show the beauty and possibilities of it, especially wreck diving. From VOC ships to war boats, cargo ships and yachts; the North Sea bottom is littered with a smorgasbord of shipwrecks. And the marine life attracted by such wrecks in, on and all around them! Open all year.

a. Boulevard Barnaart 12, 2041 JA Zandvoort
t. +31 237 433 000
w. scubarepublic.nl

At Zandvoort you can breathe it all in, and love it all out during a class of **Yoga with Deva** (**11**) on the beach. If the sun's out and it's warm enough lessons are on the shoreline, if it's too cold or windy, the mats are rolled out at Mango's Beach Bar. Every Sunday morning from May to August.

a. Mango's Beach Bar, Boulevard Barnaart 15, 2041 JA Zandvoort
t. + 31 621 454 479
w. yogametdeva.nl

Since everything's close by in Holland, you might as well visit Amsterdam. It's only 45 minutes by car from Wijk aan Zee, or better yet, a 1 hour train ride. Amsterdam itself is best explored on foot or rented bike (lots of rental stations about), or on a SUP! Check the City SUP tours of Morene Dekker's **M&M SUP Amsterdam** (**12**). Morene takes you out paddling along the many canals of the city, discovering it from another perspective. One of the very first in Holland to offer SUP tours and lessons, Morene knows a thing or two about boards, paddles and the worthiest routes! If you'd rather just have a SUP lesson, or want to join a yoga class on the SUP, you're very welcome at Blijburg beach - the mighty fine city beach of Amsterdam - or at the floating SUP studio. Open all year. SUP lessons available from April to September. City SUP tours only by reservation.

a. Pampuslaan 501, 1087 HP Amsterdam
t. + 31 621 202 222
w. mm-sup.com

EAT/DRINK/HANG OUT

♦

Restaurant Buiten (**13**), in Petten, serves pancakes, snacks made with locally produced ingredients, and craft beer at their cosy restaurant. Surfers will feel right at home in the wooden hut with wood-stove and outdoor terrace, chilled out décor and laid-back vibe. Kids can entertain themselves on the trampolines or play a round of mini-golf. Open from Easter to October. Oh, and waffles! ♦€♦

a. Spreeuwendijk 4, 1755 LD Petten
t. +31 226 381 644
w. buitenpetten.nl

In the middle of the forest area of Schoorl, restaurant **De Berenkuil** (**14**) is the ideal spot to take a break between bike rides and long hikes. In summer you can find a shaded or sunny place on their terrace, on cold days a crackling fireplace makes sure you'll never want to leave. Open all year. ♦€♦

a. Schoorlsezeeweg 2, 1871 PA Schoorl
t. +31 725 091 892
w. deberenkuilschoorl.nl

Strandpaviljoen and **Stadspaviljoen Noord** (**15**), in Bergen aan Zee and Bergen Binnen, respectively, have the same owners and stylish signature all over. The newly designed beach bar is smartly decorated, modern but with all the right beachy details - as can be expected when Dutch designer Piet Hein Eek has a hand in it! Their shop in the quaint little village of Bergen (inland from Bergen aan Zee, at Plein 63) offers all sorts of kitchenware and home deco, clothes and accessories from small designer labels. Open all year. ♦€€♦

a. C.F. Zeiler Boulevard 3, 1865 BB Bergen aan Zee
t. +31 725 814 940
w. strandpaviljoennoord.nl

Coffee roastery and tea company **González Café & Té** (**16**) in Bergen sells specially selected coffee beans and tea. Most (about 80%) of their products are organic and they buy their beans directly, thus the growers get a fair price. Of course you can taste, and treasure, their delicacies extensively at their café. Open all year. ♦€♦ ♦€€♦

a. Jan Oldenburglaan 14, 1861 JT Bergen
w. casagonzalez.nl

Don't let the exterior and surroundings of restaurant **EAZEE** (**17**) fool you, the interior is a warm bath of fancy, smart and tasteful design. You may even feel a bit inspired. We especially like their colour scheme of green, grey, blue and use of metal and wood. Open all year. ♦€€♦

a. Boulevard 7, 1931 CJ Egmond aan Zee
t. +31 727 502 015
w. eazee.nl

If you prefer a place where your kids will have as much of a good time as yourself, restaurant **Natuurlijk** (**18**) is an amiable option. Nice big terrace at the front, regional and mostly organic dishes on the menu, and at the back a mini-golf course where children can be happily busy. Open all year. ♦€♦ ♦€€♦

a. Doctor Wiardi Beckmanlaan 8, 1931 BW Egmond aan Zee
t. +31 725 062 749
w. natuurlijk-egmond.nl

Toast Egmond (**19**) is a sweet little café in the centre of Egmond aan Zee. Lots of typical Dutch sweet treats on the menu; freshly baked cookies, waffles with strawberry and cream, and 'poffertjes', mini pancakes - you order them in portions. Very friendly staff, you can sit either inside or on their terrace facing the shopping street. Open all year. ♦€♦

a. Voorstraat 122, 1931 AP Egmond aan Zee
t. +31 623 150 000
fb. toast egmond

Find **Club Zand** (**20**) at the beach of Castricum. Cuddle up in their sun loungers, or huddle up at their fireplace. It's a cosy enough place for it! They've got regular live music events (every Friday night), and you're going to love their menu: home-made pizzas, lots of vegetarian options and varied salads, gluten-free is never a problem and all dishes are made with organic ingredients as much as possible. Open all year. ♦€♦ ♦€€♦

a. Zeeweg 70, 1901 NZ Castricum
t. +31 251 658 161
w. clubzand.nl

Bar, hangout and restaurant **Aloha** (**21**) sits at the beach of Wijk aan Zee. Every surfer in Holland has been at least once, probably more often, to Aloha. After an unfortunate fire in 2014 which left the regulars and many of the surfing community in shock, Aloha reinvented itself and is going strong as ever. It's still the place where they don't mind you coming in for a warm drink, still wearing your dripping wetsuit and leaving the floor a sandy mess. More often than not they've got something going on, live music, a party, or a surf event (check their Facebook for updates). Aloha's kitchen works with organic ingredients, all fish served are according to the fairest rules of sustainability, cakes and pies are made fresh every day. Open all year. ♦€♦ ♦€€♦

a. Reyndersweg 2, 1951 LA Wijk aan Zee
t. +31 251 374 130
w. alohabeach.nl

Timboektoe (**22**) is the other laid-back hangout near the main surf spot, Wijk aan Zee. Like the neighbours at Aloha, they serve some mighty fine dishes, snacks, salads and shakes. All, including their meat and fish, sustainably and/or organically sourced. Events, live music and parties are also on the menu, as are lazy days that turn into wickedly spontaneous nights. Check them out, you'll like! Open all year.
♦€♦ ♦€€♦

a. Reyndersweg 1, 1951 LA Wijk aan Zee
t. +31 251 373 050
w. timboektoe.org

At **Hightide Surf & Food** (**23**) it's agreed that being in and around the ocean all day, playing, surfing, building sandcastles, has to be rewarded with healthy but delicious food. Ordering from the menu of this low-key, relaxed beach club, you'll be sure to get some good food on your plate. Regional products if possible, animal and human friendly, prepared with love. Hightide's also a surf school, giving lessons and renting out gear and arranging storage for your board(s). On Sunday mornings in summer you can join a yoga class. Open from April to September.
♦€♦ ♦€€♦

a. Kennemerstrand 802,
   1976 GA IJmuiden - IJmuiderslag
t. +31 255 763 996 / 615 097 289
w. hightidesurfandfood.nl

Along the beaches of **Bloemendaal** and **Zandvoort** are a large number of beach bars and restaurants; we've only selected a few. These are the places that have been around for so long they've become household names.

Woodstock '69 (**24**) is the place to be if you want to party all night long, chill out all day, and, well, do a bit of the other in between. Woodstock's as easygoing as their namesake once must have been. Fav hangout for the beach loving, colourful city folks of Amsterdam. Open from March to September. ♦€€♦

a. Zeeweg 94 - Tent 7,
   2051 EB Bloemendaal aan Zee
w. woodstock69.nl

Brightly decorated **Rapa Nui** (**25**) is also popular with the Amsterdam party squad. They even took the vinyl dance event 'Zwarte Liefde' (Black Love) to the beach. p.s. The Black Love's got nothing to do with skin colour, it's the black gold, vinyl, you know, putting the record player on. Check their Facebook or site for regular updates on events and parties. Open from March to October. ♦€€♦

a. Boulevard Barnaart 27,
   2041 JA Zandvoort
t. +31 235 737 060
w. rapanui.nl

The Spot (26) is where the local watermen and waterwomen hang out. A perfect mix of water sports centre and beach bar, organising and hosting regular events, such as a SUP festival, the Dutch kiting championship and the Bikes and Boards festival (see To Do section). Their menu is varied, healthy, and offers lots of organic and vegetarian choices. Open from March to September. ♦€♦ ♦€€♦

a. Boulevard Barnaart 23A,
   2041 JA Zandvoort
t. +31 235 717 600
w. gotothespot.com

Restaurant and beach bar **Tijn Akersloot (27)** has been around since 1965, when a guy named just that decided to start a little beach hangout, and named it after… himself. Fast forward some 50 years and Tijn Akersloot's hangout's still around! Bit bigger though (that's quite an understatement, it's gone large!), almost always busy, known for quality cuisine and friendly staff. Open all year. ♦€€♦

a. Boulevard Paulus Loot 1,
   2042 AD Zandvoort
t. +31 235 712 547
w. tijnakersloot.nl

SHOP
♦

Get your nautical artefacts at **Strand 142 (28)**, a quirky looking shop in Egmond aan Zee's centre. Boat clocks and ship lights, measuring instruments, and a plethora of ocean-related bric-a-brac on sale. Open all year.

a. Voorstraat 142,
   1931 AP Egmond aan Zee
fb. strand 142

Bicycle and board shop **Beach Bastards (29)** found their niche in cycling and surfing. In cooperation with local Backyard surf shop they offer a range of bicycles and all sorts of surf stuff. Besides the gear for sale in the shop, they also rent out bicycles, and offer guided bike tours. Open all year.

a. Pompplein 5, 1931AD Egmond aan Zee
t. +31 727 112 804
w. beachbastards.nl

For the fashion-savvy sea people out there, don't miss **Drifter store (30)** in the city of Haarlem (the namesake of NY's Harlem, which was named after this 'original' Haarlem), near seaside villages Zandvoort and Bloemendaal. Drifter's one of those heart-run stores that we simply adore, the bright interior a perfect display for the lovingly selected items they sell. Small brands, Scandinavian, Japanese and Dutch design, sustainable items, sneakers, sunglasses, inspiring books, amongst many other very likeable bits n bobs. Open all year.

a. Gierstraat 2, 2011 GA Haarlem
t. +31 235 836 040
fb. drifterstore

Visiting Amsterdam? You don't need us to guide you around, Amsterdam will guide you all by itself, no worries. Although we just can't help ourselves by adding a few of our favourite shops:

Right after leaving Central Station, don't follow the hordes, but turn right, towards the Haarlemmerbuurt. At the Haarlemmerdijk and Haarlemmerstraat distinctive and remarkable shops rub shoulders with small but exquisite restaurants. We're pretty sure you're going to love **Sukha (31)**. The shop's bigger than you initially think, offering a constantly changing array of handcrafted, timeless items to either decorate your home or yourself, or give to a friend. It's a spacious haven of peace and calm, and in remarkably good taste. A big perk; everything's produced ethically and sustainably, with the use of natural materials. Yay to style and consciousness! Open all year.

a. Haarlemmerstraat 110,
   1013 EW Amsterdam
t. +31 203 304 001
w. sukha.nl

The 2 shops of **The Old Man** (**32**) in Amsterdam have a bit of, well, everything on offer if you're anything into board sports - snow, street or ocean. Well equipped, and adding a little Amsterdam feel to it with their choice of smoke supplies. At their shop in the Rijnstraat in the south of Amsterdam you can also enjoy a coffee or grab a bite. Open all year.

a. Damstraat 14, 1012 JM Amsterdam
t. +31 206 270 043
a. Rijnstraat 205, 1079 HE Amsterdam
t. +31 207 237 400
w. theoldman.com

The capital holds the most stylish surf shops, at **Behind the Pines** (**33**) you'll be inspired by the choice of streetwear and all things outdoor, snow and surf. You'll find quality brands, and their cooperation with **Sea Sick Shop** (**33**), selling their finger-licking beautiful custom-made logs, fish and fins in the Behind the Pines store, is a big asset. Open all year.

a. Ceintuurbaan 248, 1072 GG Amsterdam
t. +31 203 376 718
w. behindthepines.eu

On a city break, exploring Amsterdam, suddenly feeling lost with so many choices what and where to eat in the sea of plenty? With so very many cafés, bars and eateries, why not stick with the very best the ocean's got to offer:

At **The Dutch Weed Burger Joint** (**34**) you won't end up space-faced and silly-hopping the city for the rest of your day. Because we're talking weed as in a 100% plant-powered and plant-based menu, enriched with seaweed and algae from a Dutch seaweed farm. What to expect? Besides next-level vegan food, the bigger picture is a paradigm shift, but they start with a warm welcome to anyone who loves good food. On the menu: The Dutch Weed Burger takes a wedge alongside classics such as Seawharma, the Dutch Weed Dog, and the weed bites of the Wish 'n Chips dish. Desserts (Sweeds) include chocolate fudge brownies, cheesecake, or the oh, so very Dutch tompouces. All created with the explosive flavour and nutrient-rich ocean greens, sustainably cultivated in the Nationaal Park Oosterschelde. Open all year for your guilt-free pleasure. Eat weed live long! ♦€♦ ♦€€♦

a. Nicolaas Beetsstraat 47,
   1053 RJ Amsterdam
t. +31 203 312 930
w. dutchweedburger.com

SLEEP

•

Camperverhuur Petten (35) rents out 7 fully equipped campervans, sizes from ample to large. Available all year. ♦€€♦

a. Westerdelle 3, 1755 RD Petten
t. +31 226 383 252
w. camperverhuurpetten.nl

At camping **Corfwater (36)** you can either use your own tent or campervan, rent a characteristic safari tent - sleeping up to 7 people - or a small cabin, perfect for a couple. The campsite's only 100 m from the beach, no need for any other entertainment! Open from March to October. ♦€♦ ♦€€♦

a. Strandweg 3, 1755 LA Petten aan Zee
t. +31 226 381 981
w. corfwater.nl

Instead of the obligatory bottle of wine or picnic basket, there's something much more adventurous awaiting you at **Kust (37)** - the nicely decorated and spacious summerhouses of Bastiaan and Nanda, in Egmond aan Zee. Since Bastiaan is a passionate paraglider, he'll take guests on a tandem flight for free (if conditions allow it). How's that for a welcome gift! There are 3 houses to choose from, sleeping from 2 to 5 people. Open all year. ♦€€♦

a. Dokter Wiardibeckmanlaan 99, 1931 BX Egmond aan Zee
t. +31 621 832 733
w. zomerhuiskust.nl

Camping Bakkum (38) is known for its free-spirited atmosphere and events - you'll meet a lot of new friends from Amsterdam, camping Bakkum being their favoured nearby place for a quick getaway. All kinds of quirky tents, tent-houses, lodges and bungalows are for rent. We especially like the Panorama tent: you literally have panoramic views through the many windows, and the best thing is the panorama roof, offering a magical view of the night sky. The tent comes with a custom-made double bed and a bunk bed. Open from March to October. ♦€♦ ♦€€♦

a. Zeeweg 31, 1901 NZ Castricum
t. +31 251 661 091
w. campingbakkum.nl

Farm camping **Ormsby Field (39)** lets you get acquainted with farm life. Their 70 cows are curious and friendly, especially towards children, and kids can help with feeding the calves. The campsite's 30 pitches are in the typical Dutch polder landscape, bordering the dunes, and the beach is only a 20 minute bike ride away. Open from April to October. ♦€♦

a. Hollaan 2, 1902 RW Castricum
t. +31 251 652 950
w. ormsbyfield.nl

NOORD-HOLLAND

Family-run camping **Schoonenberg (40)** sits smack in the middle of forest and dunes; a truly tranquil place to pitch your tent or campervan. Campfires are built regularly, children can explore the woods, and the site's surrounded by biking and hiking paths. Open from April to October. ♦€♦

a. Driehuizerkerkweg 15D,
   1981 EH Velsen-Zuid/Driehuis
t. +31 255 523 998 / 654 728 699
w. campingschoonenberg.nl

Stay in an old skool US school bus, a fully equipped canvas tent with veranda, or an Airstream trailer at camping **De Lakens (41)**, situated just 200 m from Bloemendaal beach. Bus and tent, called the Beach Lodge, are equipped with hammock and slackline, and there's plenty privacy. The Airstream trailer comes with the added privacy of your own sauna. Budget options are to sleep in your own tent or campervan, or stay in the backpack shack - a converted shipping container. The campsite's got more up its sleeve: there's the so-called 'Wellness bus', offering massages and beauty treatments, and yoga classes held in the Zen Zone. Some say camping is going back to basics. We say: if a beauty treatment, sauna and daily yoga classes are your basic necessities, you're damn right camping is like going back to basics! Open from March to October. ♦€♦ ♦€€♦

a. Zeeweg 60,
   2051 EC Bloemendaal aan Zee
t. +31 235 411 570
w. campingdelakens.nl

While most hotels, campsites and guesthouses may be within walking distance from the beach, the **Beachhouse Hotel (42)** is actually at, on, over, right by the beach. You'll literally wake up to the sound of the ocean, seagulls screeching, and be able to immediately open your windows to smell the salty air and complete your surf check. Well, if you even closed them. Double rooms, luxury suites and family rooms are on offer. Open all year.
♦€€♦ ♦€€€♦

a. Boulevard Barnaart 59E,
   2041 JA Zandvoort
t. +31 203 337 247
w. beachhouse.nl

SURF

From Den Helder, in the north, to Zandvoort down south, the long stretch of white sandy beaches offers surf breaks aplenty. But, with windswell being predominant, all comes down to the shape of sandbanks and, ideally, harbour walls or jetties. The ever so slightly curving, west-facing coastline is exposed and easily blown out. All spots with jetties, and harbour walls even more so, are much sought after on windy days. Beware of strong currents all along the coast. Most of the surf spots are also popular with kite and windsurfers.

The stretch of beach near **Julianadorp & Callantsoog (I)** have jetties and work on all tides, best with a small to medium W-NW-N wind or groundswell, or big S-SW windswell. ◆ *All levels/sand/easy parking/toilets/restaurant/camping/surf school.* ◆

At the beach of **Petten (II)**, new sand's been added, the jetties have disappeared, and the beach made wider; luckily it still has its marvellous backdrop of dune tops. You can surf through the tides, but lower tides tend to work better. It needs a small to medium W-NW-N ground or windswell, or big S-SW windswell. Petten is one of the more consistent spots in the north of Holland. ◆ *All levels/sand/easy parking/restaurants/camping/surf school.* ◆

Camperduin & Hargen (III), and **Bergen aan Zee & Egmond aan Zee (IV)** work best with the same conditions as Petten, on all tides, but are less consistent. ◆ *All levels/sand/easy parking/restaurants/camping/surf school.* ◆

Castricum & Zee (V) works on all tides. Best with a small to medium W-NW-N wind or groundswell, or big S-SW windswell. ◆ *All levels/sand/easy parking - paid in summer/restaurants/camping/surf school.* ◆

NOORD-HOLLAND

Photo: Ruben Snieksar, surfphotography.nl

Wijk aan Zee (VI) is your best option in strong south and southwest winds, the long harbour wall offering protection. You won't be by your lonesome though. It's one of the most popular spots, with locals and surfers from Amsterdam and surrounding areas. Works best at mid-tide with a small to medium W-NW-N wind or ground swell, or big S-SW windswell. ◆ *All levels/sand/easy parking/toilets and showers/restaurants/surf schools.* ◆

At **IJmuiden (VII)** the coastline slightly bends, and the beach faces southwest, so it'll be offshore in northeast winds. The long harbour wall offers protection from strong north and northwest winds. Works best at mid-tide with a small to medium W-NW-N wind or ground swell, or big S-SW windswell. ◆ *All levels/sand/easy parking/toilets/restaurants/surf school.* ◆

Bloemendaal & Zandvoort (VIII) are easily blown out and messy, and work at all tides with a small to medium W-NW-N wind or ground swell, or big S-SW windswell. ◆ *All levels/sand/difficult parking - paid in summer/toilets and showers/restaurants/camping/surf school.* ◆

311

HOLLAND

SCHOOL RENTAL REPAIR

♦

Surf School Petten (**43**) offers surf, SUP and bodyboard lessons, and rentals. Groups are always kept small, max 8 persons per instructor. They're very keen on safety and educating pupils about how the ocean and currents work. Since the surf school's a partner of Surf Rider Foundation, regular beach clean-ups are organised. Open from May to October.

- **a.** Strandweg 2, 1755 LA Petten aan Zee
- **t.** +31 655 861 312
- **w.** surfschoolpetten.nl

Get your smart-looking surf and street-style clothes, bikinis and beach accessories at **Boardridersclub Egmond** (**45**). The well-stocked shop for all your surf necessities, boards and rental of boards and wetsuits, comes with a very friendly staff. Open all year.

- **a.** Voorstraat 158,
    1931 AP Egmond aan Zee
- **t.** +31 725 064 076
- **w.** quiksilver-egmond.nl

At **Surf School Castricum aan Zee** (**47**) they like it personal and have an approachable way of teaching, both to beginners and intermediates. They offer surf, SUP, bodyboard and yoga lessons and have summer camps for children. Open from May to October.

- **a.** At the beach, close to restaurant 'De Deining', Zeeweg 45,
    1901 NZ Castricum aan Zee
- **t.** +31 681 298 820
- **w.** surfschoolcastricum.nl

The **Quiksilver Surf School** (**44**) operate from 2 different locations: Hookipa beach in Camperduin, and Sports at Sea in Castricum. They offer surf, windsurf, kite, SUP lessons and summer camps, and rental of gear. Open from June to October.

- **a.** Heereweg 403, 1871 GL Camperduin
- **t.** +31 72 509 2773
- **w.** quiksilversurfschool.nl

Backyard Surfshop (**46**) in Egmond aan Zee sells classic logs and single fin boards, new, custom-made and second-hand. They also have a range of selected clothing brands and fine pieces of surf art. If you haven't found a place to stay yet, ask them about the Californian-style house they rent out, the Barefoot Beachhouse, only 200 m from the sea. Open all year.

- **a.** Voorstraat 102,
    1931 AN Egmond aan Zee
- **t.** +31 622 229 992
- **w.** backyardsurfshop.nl

Either join a surf or SUP lesson, rent your gear, visit their shop, or watch the surf from the terrace at **Ozlines Surf School** (**48**). There are showers (warmed by solar panels), and lockers and good vibrations all around. Very likeable place. Maybe the owner being an Aussie's got something to do with it? Open all year.

- **a.** Reyndersweg 3E, 1951 LA Velsen Noord
- **t.** +31 251 292 410 / +31 613 107 519
- **w.** ozlines.com

Hightide Surf & Food (49) has 2 locations - one's a surf school, at the Kennemer beach, the other a shop. Surf & Food offers surf lessons and rental of surf and SUP boards, the possibility to store all your water sport gear. If there's no surf you can choose to participate in one of their longboarding (skate) courses. On Sunday mornings you can join a yoga class. The Hightide surf shop has all your surf, windsurf and SUP necessities. Open all year.

- a. Kennemerstrand 802, 1976 GA IJmuiden - IJmuiderslag (Surf & Food)
- t. +31 255 763 996 / 615 097 289
- a. Trompstraat 21, 1971 AA IJmuiden (Shop)
- t. +31 255 512 494 / 614 477 105
- w. hightidesurfandfood.nl / hightidesurfshop.nl

If you become a member at **Surfana Zandvoort** surf club **(50)** you can join their weekly scheduled sports and surf lessons. If not, not to worry, they have surf lessons and rental of surfboards and SUPs on offer for everybody. Open daily in July and August, from March to September at weekends, and all other days if there are waves.

- a. Boulevard Barnaart 27, 2041 JA Bloemendaal aan Zee / Zandvoort, next to beachclub Rapa Nui
- t. +31 620 249 031
- w. surfzandvoort.nl

Mifune Watersports (51) in Bloemendaal aan Zee offers surf, kite, SUP and catamaran lessons, rental and storage of gear. They have a bar for pre and post drinks and snacks.

- a. Parnassiaweg 7, 2051 EC Bloemendaal aan Zee
- t. +31 235 391 277
- w. mifune.nl

The Spot (52) in Zandvoort is the place to be if you want anything water sports related. They offer surf, kite, SUP and catamaran lessons, you can rent all sorts of gear and boards and make use of storage. You can also join their ocean-fit classes or longboard (skating) clinics. And you'll find it's a relaxed place to hang out before, between and after sessions. Open from March to September.

- a. Boulevard Barnaart 23-A, 2041 JA Zandvoort
- t. +31 235 717 600
- w. gotothespot.com

First Wave Surf School (53) offers surf, SUP, skate and slackline lessons, and rental of surf gear. They organise a very special surfing event each year called 'surfen op gevoel'. They take blind and visually impaired people out surfing, letting them really feel the waves and participate in something they'd otherwise never experience. Big thumbs up.

- a. Boulevard de Favauge, beach exit 13, 2042 TV Zandvoort
- t. +31 683 023 230
- w. firstwavesurfschool.nl

Van den Berg Surf (54) is a well stocked shop for all water sports, and water sport related lifestyle clothes and accessories. Open all year.

- a. Passage 36, 2042 KV Zandvoort
- t. +31 235 718 600
- w. vandenbergsurf.nl

If you need a repair, drop your board off to Otto from **Ding Repair Beverwijk (55)**. If you're around in winter, he offers shaping clinics as well! Open all year on appointment.

- a. Parallelweg 7, 1948 NK Beverwijk
- t. +31 623 607 827
- w. dingrepairbeverwijk.nl

Redrose (56) in Haarlem also does repairs and shapes boards, and organises shaping clinics in winter.

- a. Dijkstraat 10, 2011 AM Haarlem
- t. +31 651 291 111
- w. redroseboardsenrepairs.nl

SEASIDE LOCAL: NIENKE DUINMEIJER

From unpredictable and mushy North Sea waves to competing in the European WSL longboarding tour, preferably without a leash, Dutch longboarder Nienke Duinmeijer's come a long way.

"I just love having ten toes wrapped around the nose of the board, approaching surfing in a personal, classic way."

She's tall, blonde, slender, and wears a big smile above a zipped-up wetsuit. She's a stylish lady glider who stays far away from striking bikini girl poses. It's all about surfing. And she's beyond obsessed with playing in the ocean, as much as she can, in particular riding her longboard: "I just love having ten toes wrapped around the nose of the board, approaching surfing in a personal, classic way." Nienke's from the small coastal town of Camperduin, in the north of Holland. Being an active child who loved the beach more than anything, she joined the local lifeguarding community and learned to surf with them, and then paddled further afield; the lack of quality waves were good reason to travel abroad from an early age. After improving her surfing skills, longboarding especially, she started entering national and international competitions, competing at a high level and in 2017 she won the famous longboard contest in Salinas. When she started surfing though, Nienke says she wasn't a natural: "I was just determined to get better at it. So far it only brought me good things in life."

A few years ago, Carlos and Rúben from Spanish surfboard brand CeCe crossed her path, asked her to join their team, and have helped her develop her classic style. "Since I joined their team, my level of surfing has gone up a lot. Just by surfing together, watching them and get some tips in the water. They have been my mentors in surfing for the past time." Rúben and Carlos are also part of the coaching team of Nienke's 'Single Fin Surf Travel', which organises trips to places with the best conditions for longboarding, so surfers can work on their skills for a week of consistent playtime. Getting in the water every day makes such a difference to progressing. If you can get in 2 or 3 times a day… even better!

Nienke prefers longboarding to shortboarding (which she's pretty good at too) because she can add her own twist to it. "I think it's more cooperating with the wave. You have to draw lines while longboarding. It's more stylish, and at the same time more technical." Competing is a bit of a love-hate affair for her though: "I actually think longboarding and competitions aren't a very good combination. But I'm a competitive person and competitions are forcing me to show my best surfing. From 2018 I like to participate in the whole European WSL longboarding tour. But I'll do it my way; if conditions are suitable I'll use my Single Fin and leave the leash at home. As a good friend of mine says, 'Leashes are made for disobedient dogs, not for surfboards…'!"

HOLLAND

Photo: Robin Bakker

Photo: Jelle Mul

315

NOORDWIJK
(I)
◆ 1,15,16,44,45,52,5
NOORDWIJK
◆ 35,36

KATWIJK
(II)
◆ 17,37,38,46,54,55
KATWIJK

◆ 47
WASSENAAR

LEIDEN

SCHEVENINGEN NOORD (III)
SCHEVENINGEN ZUID (IV)
◆ 2-14,18-32,39-42,48,49,56-62
SCHEVENINGEN

DEN HAAG

Zuid-Holland

TER HEIJDE
(V)
◆ 43,50,63
TER HEIJDE
◆ 51,65
'S-GRAVENZANDE
HOEK VAN HOLLAND
(VI)
◆ 33,34,64
HOEK VAN HOLLAND

DELFT

MAASVLAKTE
MV2
(VII)

ROTTERDAM

HELLEVOETSLUIS

ZUID-HOLLAND

◆

Most of the seaside settlements and villages of South Holland have roots in, or a strong connection with, fishery and tourism alike. Their identity's similar, but not so alike. What they do have in common are tight-knit communities. Even in these days of fast changes, and people seemingly having more cyberspace connections than real-life friends, the seaside folks of Noordwijk, Katwijk, and Scheveningen, especially those born, raised and rooted for generations, meet in the streets, the harbours, the boulevard and local pubs. They don't need appointments, check-ins or a new plant-based-only lunch hotspot (although we kinda like those…). In every one of these seaside resorts you'll find the elders - usually old seafaring or fishermen - gathering at a set time, at a set bench, at or near the harbour, talking weather, ships, fish, and days-long-gone. There'll still be some ladies wearing the traditional gear, and speaking their dialect amongst themselves. From their last names you can figure out which village they're from; try counting the many Vrolijks, Rogs, or Spaans you encounter in Scheveningen.

TRAVEL INFO

◆

Nothing's too far away to reach within a drive of 3 hours or so in this busy little country, but many people makes for good transport infrastructure; so trains and roads are reliable/smooth cruising. The time we advise you avoid is rush hour - it's easy to linger longer at your coffee or beer, keep your toes in the sand and watch the sea until the busy period switches back to a steady flow, then head at leisure to wherever you choose to go.

BY AIR
◆

International flights have regular schedules in and out of Rotterdam Den Haag Airport or Amsterdam Schiphol Airport, established and budget airlines.

w. schiphol.nl / rotterdamthehagueairport.nl

BY TRAIN
◆

Nederlandse Spoorwegen (Dutch railways) runs a reliable and extensive train network from the far north to the far south, west and east of the country, and back.

w. ns.nl

BY BUS
◆

Several bus and tram companies make sure you can get to even the remotest areas of the country. Public transport routes, timetables and info at:

w. 9292.nl

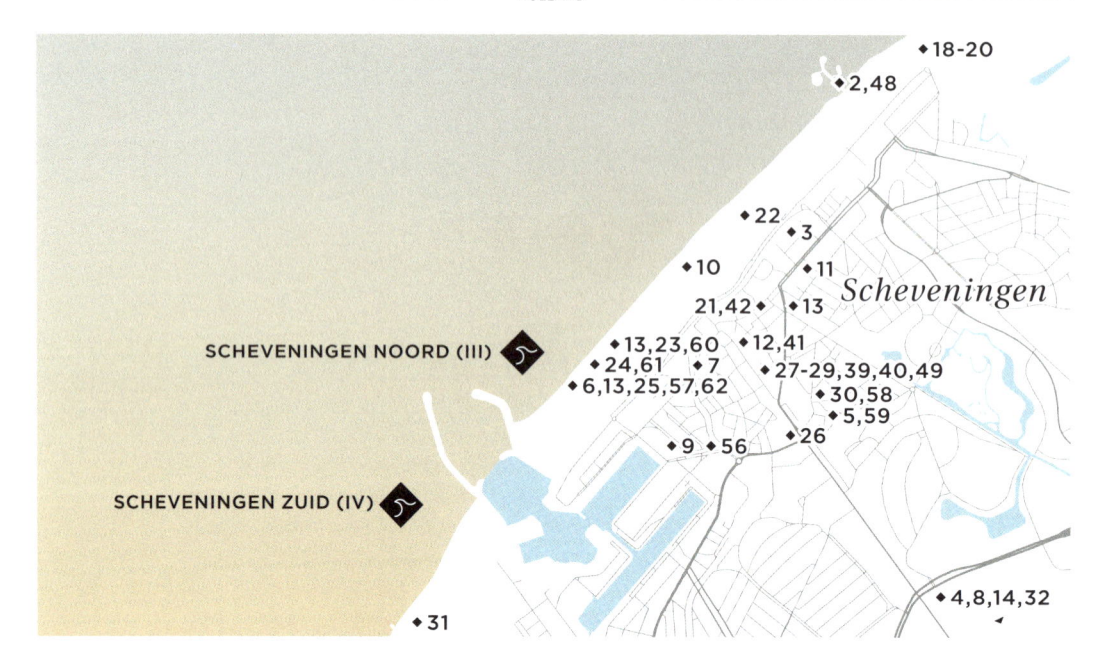

IN AND AROUND SCHEVENINGEN

◆

If the old town and beaches of Scheveningen were on the market, they would be South Holland's bestselling product in the summer sales. Popular with both the masses and a smaller community of like-minded souls with a dainty appetite, seeking one-of-a-kind hangouts, a choice of surf breaks, seaside activities, and an escape route, away from the busy boulevard. I Love the Seaside catering for the latter's got nothing to do with us being highbrow fancy-pants, it's just… Scheveningen is our home town. And we love it to bits! We also love seeing more and more small-scale initiatives that are run with heart and soul popping up. As much as we love traditional Scheveningen's old centre with its fishermen's houses, extensive coastline and backdrop of dunes and forest, the mix of modern additions (managed with care) tend to fit in rather well. The city centre of Den Haag (The Hague), and all other small villages along the coast are only a bicycle ride away. Through the dunes of course.

Tourist information at bookshop AKO, Gevers Deynootweg 990-58, 2586 BZ Scheveningen.

TO DO
◆

Events, festivals, celebrations; Scheveningen has many. There's a **Kite Festival** on the beach with hundreds of kites of all shapes, sizes and colours flying, held at the end of September. **The International Fireworks Festival** draws people from all over to the coast, usually held over the second and third weekends of August. Celebrating all the good that comes from the North Sea, and the many ways to prepare North Sea delicacies, is the culinary fish festival **VISSCH**, held in the summer each year, w. vissch.nl. On **New Year's Eve** some of the world's largest bonfires, made from wooden pallets, are set alight; one at the beach south of the harbour and one at the northern end. Yearly the 'Noord' and the 'Zuid' compete to see who's able to build the highest. Here are some more of our favourites:

On **Vlaggetjesdag**, Flag Day, the first herring catch of the year is celebrated. Herring's a biggie in Scheveningen, as you'll see by not just the dark blue flag with 3 white herrings, each wearing a golden crown, but you'll see the 3 herrings symbol everywhere. Vlaggetjesdag's about more than the start of herring season - it's one of the few days you'll witness some true Dutch folklore and traditions; old crafts, fishermen choirs, board fishing vessels, children playing old Dutch games, ladies dressed up in traditional attire, there's music and, of course, the new herring. Note: it's eaten raw and in one piece, holding the fish up by its tail! Flag Day is held yearly in June and takes place mainly in and along the harbour and the Keizerstraat.

During **Aircooled Scheveningen** the boulevard turns into an open-air exhibition of literally cool vehicles. Hundreds of air-cooled VW buses and Beetles gather and can be admired – the name referring to old motors that are air-cooled. Photogenic material, this festival. You'll spot sixties and seventies models, T-2 campervans, cabriolets, old fire engines and ambulances, and custom built vans. Usually held at the end of May.
w. aircooledscheveningen.nl

At the very beginning of the season the free 2-day **Bonfire Beach Fest** sets off the summer vibes in the best possible way. It's a magical sight, right after sunset; hundreds of lights flickering, in squares, forming letters, turning slowly in circles. A large area in front of museum Beelden aan Zee, between beach clubs Sol Beach and The Fat Mermaid is freely open to the public, to either sit at campfires, listen to intimate live concerts at small stages made from shipping containers, or dance to DJs playing at the beach bars. Bonfire's a friendly and enchanting festival, and a welcome addition to the already fairly extensive list of summer events in Scheveningen. Held every year at the end of April, most beach bars at the north side of the harbour wall participate.
w. bonfirebeachfest.com

Op de Neus, On The Nose, is a small, extremely amicable longboarders' gathering and competition; the gathering more valued than the competition. Style is judged though, just as the seconds on the nose are counted. It's strictly a single fin hang-five hang-ten event, save the hardcore cutbacks for another day. The call to arms (or toes) is usually mid-May, with a waiting period of a month, with skippers meeting and briefing (and drinks and snacks) at surf school The Shore.
a. Strandweg 2A, 2586 ZZ Scheveningen
t. +31 649 392 095
w. hsa.nl/op-de-neus

Park Pop is Holland's biggest free pop festival with an international line-up. There are 3 stages, a market and lots of food and drink stalls. Park pop's held each year at the end of June in the Zuiderpark in the Hague.
w. parkpop.nl

By **hike or bike**, ramble the many paths directly behind the beaches of South Holland. From Scheveningen you can head north towards Noordwijk, or south to Hoek van Holland, using well-marked paths through the dunes. Bike rental stations are easy to find in almost every town - you're in Holland, remember! If you prefer a one-way ride only, rent your bike at Du Nord Rijwielen in Scheveningen, and use their pick-up service. Open all year.

a. Keizerstraat 27, 2584 BA Scheveningen
t. +31 703 554 060
w. fietsverhuurzuidholland.nl

Roos of **Rozananda Yoga** (**1**) is a surfer and yogini teaching all kinds of yoga; vinyasa, yin, and hatha, at several places in Noordwijk. In summer you can join her beach yoga classes at beach club Zon en Zeebad. Drop-ins are very welcome. Check her website for locations, dates and times. Open all year.

a. Zon en Zeebad, Koningin Astrid Boulevard 107, 2202 BD Noordwijk
t. +31 616 531 146
w. rozanandayoga.nl

For over 65 years **De Pier** (**2**) has been the landmark of Scheveningen. Some say that its concrete ugliness is actually attractive, in an artful way. But pretty? It's pretty unique, that's for sure. There are more seaside resorts with a pier, however De Pier in Scheveningen recently reinvented itself. Food's served from hipster-worthy food trucks, there's a choice of small shops, 2 bigger restaurants, a bungee jump on top, hotel suites with panoramic seaside view, a modern Ferris wheel, regular markets and events, and a zipline flying you along 350 m, from the top of the bungee tower to the boulevard, at a speed of 70 km/h. (w. zipholland.nl). Open all year.

a. Zeekant Scheveningen
t. +31 610 386 859 / 702 211 521 / 702 211 138
w. pier.nl

Beelden Aan Zee (**3**) museum exhibits contemporary sculptures of national and international artists. Quite worth a visit, even if art's not your main interest. Only a stone's throw from the busy boulevard, half visible as it hides in the dunes, it's a haven of tranquility. From the boulevard it's hard not to notice the funny fairy-tale bronze figures created by American sculptor Tom Otterness. The eye-catching herring-eating figure is some 12 m high! The sculptures are a public installation as an extension of the museum, which is open all year.

a. Harteveltstraat 1, 2586 EL Scheveningen
t. +31 703 585 847
w. beeldenaanzee.nl

You'll find **Gemeentemuseum**, **GEM** and the **Foto Museum** (**4**) conveniently at one site, so you can easily hop from one to the next. At the Foto Museum you'll find human-focused exhibitions from national and internationally renowned photographers. GEM has contemporary art and installations on display, and Gemeentemuseum's got room after daylit room of fashion, modern, contemporary, and decorative art. It houses some 300 works by Dutch painter Mondriaan. The art-deco building of the Gemeentemuseum was designed by the late H.P. Berlage; a Dutch architect famed for his influence on modern Dutch architecture. Open all year.

a. Stadhouderslaan 43, 2517 HV Den Haag
t. +31 703 381 111
w. gem-online.nl

How about building your own wooden surfboard! Surfer and craftsman, Olaf de Vries of **Ollywood** (**5**), shares his love and knowledge of boards, wood and building-your-own. At his workshop he helps out, and passes his knowledge on to surfers who'd like to build their own wooden board - and surf it eventually. If you'd rather leave it to the master's hands, you can have Olaf make you a custom board, or choose from his existing quiver of classic single fin or twin set-up retro fish, and longboards. Besides boards, you'll find wooden hand planes and surf-related pieces of art - wooden, obviously. Open all year.

a. Vijzelstraat 85, 2584 GK Scheveningen
t. +31 614 361 368
w. ollywoodsurfboards.com

She's energetic, playful, inspiring; Kim Padding, the CIO or Chief (n)Ice Officer of **N-ice World** (**6**). Offering experiences that contribute to your health and happiness, as she likes to put it, Kim guides you towards this state of bliss by practising yoga, and using 'Ice man' Wim Hof's breathing and focus exercises. If you dare, or want to take your experience a step further, you can dunk yourself into an ice bath. Sessions are held at the Pier, overlooking the North Sea. Open all year, on reservation.

a. De Pier, Zeekant Scheveningen
t. +31 643 008 009
w. n-ice.world

Surrender to the relaxing hands of surfer girl Tamar of **Massages en Zee** (**7**) and get your sore surf muscles massaged into their natural state of ease. Find Tamar at her bright studio near the lighthouse, or - on sunny days - at the beach. Massages by appointment only. Open all year (unless she's on a surf trip to the tropics).

a. Hoekerstraat 33, 2583 XJ Scheveningen
t. +31 685 318 505
w. massagesenzee.nl

Visiting **Planet Jump** (**8**), located in an old church, is the best thing you can do for toddlers and children (up to 16 years). A sea of trampolines, an obstacle course and rotating climbing wall will make them never want to leave. Luckily you can have a coffee in the lounge area, sit back and relax, or read - keeping one eye on your kids, one on your book. Open all year.

a. Stadhoudersplantsoen 28, 2517 JL Den Haag
t. +31 707 796 180
w. planetjump.nl

Visit and taste local craft beer at **Brouwerij Scheveningen** (**9**). Learn all there is to know about the brewing process, the ingredients, the time and love put into it, and of course taste their brews, like the Zuidwester, or Scheveninger bockbier. Proost! Open all year, on appointment.

a. Treilerweg 74B, 2583 DD Scheveningen
t. +31 707 785 860
w. proeverijscheveningen.nl

Ralph Groenheijde is Scheveningen's very own hero. The 40-something avid skateboarder's got the energy of a 16-year-old, the wisdom of a 60-year-old, and owns the power of persuasion like the next businessman. His business? Keeping our beaches and ocean clean! Not money business of course. For Ralph, who started **TrashUre Hunt** (**10**) some years ago, it's a necessity; a must to teach especially the young about the trash that ends up in the ocean, killing sea life and threatening our own health at the same time. Everyone can join Ralph's trashure hunts, the bin being the treasure chest, or rather, trashure chest, the trashure hunters pirates, chasing cigarette butts, cans, plastic. After a large piece of beach is cleaned, the pirates will make a piece of art from all trash collected, before everything's put away safely in the bin. TrashUre Hunt also organises clean-ups/hunts in combination with skating (the reward being a skate lesson), music workshops or - brilliant - turning your clean-up into a bootcamp! Check the website for dates, hunts and meeting point, or contact Ralph.

a. Beach and boulevard Scheveningen
t. +31 642 626 391 / 611 470 472
w. trashurehunt.org

Yoga Seads (**11**) is in a beautifully restored former milk factory. You can join one of their many yoga classes, 7 days a week. There's vinyasa, yin, hatha, iyengar and kids yoga on the menu, as well as regular workshops and courses like mindfulness and SUP Yoga. Check their schedule on the website and see what else is on offer. Open all year.

a. Maaswijkstraat 24D,
   2586 CD Scheveningen
t. +31 645 710 503 / 618 393 529
w. yogaseads.nl

At the cosy little **Yoga Studio Zowat aan Zee** (**12**), in the heart of old Scheveningen, you'll find a tranquil spot to roll out your yoga mat, just a skip-hop away from the busy boulevard and beach. All levels, ages, newbies, drop-ins, or regulars are welcome to the small-scale studio, to reconnect, breathe, stretch and make some new friends. Besides regular classes they offer workshops, intensives and private lessons. Check the website for schedules and their Facebook to see what's on.

a. Keizerstraat 40b,
   2583 BK Scheveningen
t. +31 655 150 428
w. zowataanzee.nl
fb. yogastudio Zowat Aan Zee

Scheveningen's got lots of places to **skate** (**13**), with the longest, smoothest and best on offer being the recently renewed boulevard itself.

Find a **skatepool**, **kids zipline** and small **animal farm** along the Haringkade. A large concrete **ramp** sits next to surf school Hart Beach, on the boulevard, and a **mini ramp** can be found at surf school The Shore.

Want to see a bit more of Scheveningen and The Hague, but rather stay close to the water? Join the young and enthusiastic captain Corjan of **Boot Varen** (**14**) for a ride in an open boat along the many waterways of the city. You'll get the best perspective and insight of the Hague's neighbourhoods; even locals are surprised the city's got that many green, historical buildings, and so many canals! You can combine your boat ride with a theme, such as tapas, beer, lunch or a picnic.

t. +31 644 442 968
w. bootvarendenhaag.nl

EAT/DRINK/HANG OUT

◆

There are oh, so many **beach clubs**, **bars** and **restaurants**, literally on the beach, along the coast of Holland. It's actually pretty unique and we've never seen it anywhere else in Europe, at least not in these numbers. A few have permission to stay open permanently, most beach clubs however are temporary: built in spring and just before the November storms start, carefully taken apart and stored in a safe place. We selected our faves, and please excuse us for all other perfect places missed! (Maybe we need to write a book on Scheveningen all by itself?)

Sun's shining at beach club **De Koele Costa** (**15**), even when the sky is overcast. The interior seems to absorb every ray of light, making it look bright, brighter, brightest. And when the sun's out, heating things up? You can cool off in their oh, so, adorable little striped beach tents. De Koele Costa's located at the north side of Noordwijk aan Zee. Closed in winter. ◆€€◆

a. Zeereep 21,
   2202 NW Noordwijk aan Zee
t. +31 643 747 935
w. dekoelecosta.nl

With everyone redesigning restaurants, bars and cafés, **Het Koffiehuis** (**16**) is one of those places the Dutch like to call 'bruine kroeg'. Not many of them around anymore. Literally a 'brown pub'; referring to the brown colour of the bar and slightly dim light, but also the atmosphere. A bar where you can enter alone, but won't feel lonely. Where the music's just right, the staff always friendly. Why, what, the staff's probably your mates! Anyway, Het Koffiehuis is a place like that. It's a bit of a local surfers' hangout too, with bands playing regularly and an extensive list of drinks. They also organise a yearly surf event called Groovy Classic, a fun competition, usually held in June (w.groovyclassic.nl). Open all year.
◆€◆ ◆€€◆

a. De Grent 32,
   2202 EL Noordwijk aan Zee
t. +31 713 616 961
w. hetkoffiehuis.nl

Paal 14 (**17**) is a well-established name, the beach club's a bar, hangout and restaurant for many Katwijk locals and tourists alike. A big fire destroyed the old bar recently, but the owners rebuilt the beach bar, which is just as friendly and open to everyone as ever. Open all year. ◆€€◆

a. Boulevard ZeeZijde 7,
   2225 AB Katwijk aan Zee
t. +31 714 014 464
w. paal14.nl

Het Puntje (**18**) is our most favoured beach bar of all beach bars. Only to be reached by either a walk along the beach, or a bicycle ride through the dunes. No sun-loungers out front - use the sand, use your beach towel - and impossible to make reservations, just decide on the spot if you want to stay for dinner. Owners Marcel and Aad don't care about full terraces; they love the beach, and hope you do too. Inside's like visiting a good friend at home, outside's a small terrace, and then there's the big, white sandy beach to enjoy. Since summer 2018 they've added a separate wooden building with doors and windows opening up to the beach and ocean. It serves as a studio for regular yoga classes and all sorts of workshops, like learning the Wim Hof method of breathing exercises, focus and cold exposure. Check the website for dates and events. Open from March to October. ◆€€◆

w. Noorderstrand Scheveningen
t. +31 641 364 778
w. strandtenthetpuntje.nl

Beach club **Buiten** (**19**), like Het Puntje, is one of the very few places in Scheveningen where the Beach is definitely more important than the Club. Music's good, not loud. Food's delicious, healthy, organic, and offers a lot of vegetarian and vegan options. Staff love the beach and ocean just as much as you do. Owners Danielle and Jim for sure know how to throw a party, and seem to have worldwide connections, getting live bands and singer/songwriters from New Zealand, UK, Australia, playing reggae, rock, and fine tunes at their beloved Buiten. Open from March to October. ◆€€◆

a. Zwarte Pad 67, 2586 JL Scheveningen
t. +31 703 586 467
w. ganaarbuiten.nl

At the very end of the boulevard - or the beginning, depending from where you start - you'll find **Patagonia Beach** (**20**). Their smartly decorated terrace and interior will lure you inside, you'll order a drink, maybe two, decide to stay for dinner, and before you know it, day turned into night and you're still here! Something to do with a very friendly staff, lighting, comfy chairs, a menu offering plenty? Open from March to October. ♦€€♦

a. Zwarte Pad 57a,
   2586 HP Scheveningen
t. +31 622 847 873
w. patagoniabeach.nl

At **Byron Bay Lunch Café** (**21**) you can enjoy breakfast, coffee, tea, home-made cakes, lunch (obviously), drinks, frequently accompanied by acoustic concerts or singer-songwriters. Too bad they're only open at weekends; on weekdays the place serves as after-school care – a very cool one, we must add. It's done up in such a refreshing style, parents stick around when they collect their kids. What a great idea to use the place every day! Open all year, weekends only. ♦€€♦

a. Wassenaarsestraat 86,
   2586 AR Den Haag
t. +31 620 261 544
fb. Byron Bay Lunch Café

Done for the day, ready for drinks, good fun and maybe a little dance? Check in at **The Fat Mermaid** (**22**), order your perfect - really, perfect! - gin tonics, and, well, you know, do what you do to unwind, watch the sun set, chat up the DJ to get him to play your favourite funky soul tunes. Open from March to October. ♦€€♦

a. Strandweg 19, 2586 JK Scheveningen
t. +31 703 541 729
w. thefatmermaid.nl

Hart Beach (**23**) has been a surfers' hangout for almost as long as surf's been on the map in Holland. From a tiny shack, back in the days, to the large restaurant, surf school and shop it is nowadays. The late Etsko Schuitema founded Hart Beach in 1984, a lot has changed since, but his 2 sons, Paul and Romke, still manage to maintain the look and feel their dad established in the early days. You like adding a bit of California to your stay in Scheveningen? This is your place. Open all year. ♦€♦ ♦€€♦

a. Strandweg 3B, 2586 JK Scheveningen
t. +31 703 502 591
w. hartbeach.nl

Although their terrace is mighty fine - extended to the beach, sitting either sheltered from the wind or with your feet in the sand - you're going to love **Aloha's Kitchen** (**24**) even when it rains. Sitting inside at the fireplace, or at the sturdy wooden tables and benches, studying the surfboards on the ceiling, or the 20-some different beers to choose from. You can enjoy food and drinks that are either biological, fair-trade, home-made, 100% free range, or all the above - and lots of vegetarian options as well! On a tight budget? Check out their Thursday evening menu for a surprisingly good deal. They've regular acoustic music sessions and other fun events. Open all year. ♦€♦ ♦€€♦

a. Strandweg 2B, 2586 ZZ Scheveningen
t. +31 70 322 7171
w. alohasurf.nl

The Shore (**25**), at the southern end of the boulevard, is one of the more recent additions to the concept beach bar/surf school/restaurant. The guys in charge, however, are veterans in surfing and hospitality, known to the local surf community as highly likable and either surf teacher, lifeguard, or bar manager. The Shore is a perfectly compact and homely place, almost 100% self-sustainable because of the use of solar panels and boilers. A consciously chosen menu of organic and local products offers, amongst other yummy food and cakes, the most delicious pancakes you've ever eaten. And think about it (well, The Shore peeps thought about it actually): pancakes are quick and easy to make, thus energy efficient. And if you top them off with berries, peanut butter, banana, nuts, ice-cream, coconut, or whatnot… Do we need to explain? Go for it! Open from March to October. ♦€€♦

a. Strandweg 2A, 2586 ZZ Scheveningen
t. +31 649 392 095
w. theshore.nl

Check in at **Zo, Zoet & Zout** (**26**) at any time of the day. All smiles at the counter, a sunny terrace, a brightly coloured interior and a meeting place for locals, tourists, daytrippers, blue collar and office workers alike. Their menu is just as varied. From the classic triple-layered club-sandwich and wraps, to their fresh smoothies, shakes and raw vegan cakes. Open all year. ♦€♦ ♦€€♦

a. Duinstraat 1, 2584 AV Scheveningen
t. +31 703 558 040
w. zozoetenzout.nl

Meneer Chocola (**27**) and next door's **Café de Bayonne** (**28**) transport you straight to the French Basque coast. Meneer Chocola offering freshly baked croissants, pains au chocolat, baguettes, croque monsieurs, salads, soups and an extremely tasty coffee. Café de Bayonne starts where Meneer Chocola stops, at the end of the day, with a choice of wines, large portions of pintxos and a changing menu of Basque delicacies. Their own yearly version of Fête de Bayonne is as festive an event as the real deal in Bayonne. Except maybe people not ending up at lampposts at four in the morning. Or maybe they do… Open all year. ♦€♦ ♦€€♦

a. Keizerstraat 124,
2584 BM Scheveningen
t. +31 702 209 451
w. meneerchocola.nl / **w.** cafedebayonne.nl

In the same street you'll find **De Snoeshaen** (**29**). A snug bar, bistro and self-appointed 'gintoneria'. With some 15-odd different sorts of gin to choose from, expect a long night out. But never mind that, it's 'zo gezellig!' and besides, the owner will gladly help you out if you feel lost in the sea of beer, gin and cocktail options. They've got a dish of the day and a small menu on offer, and regular live music events and DJs playing. Open all year. ♦€♦ ♦€€♦

a. Keizerstraat 97, 2584 BC Scheveningen
t. +31 707 622 876
w. desnoeshaen.nl

After years of practice and learning from mentors and masters, helping out others fine tuning their barista skills, young coffee passionisto Vinni recently opened his very own espresso bar, **Tigershark Coffee** (**30**). It's like he opened the doors to his house, where you feel welcome to sit back, chat, read a book, invite more friends and, of course, savour that freshly brewed cuppa. Open all year. ♦€♦ ♦€€♦

a. Badhuistraat 114,
2584 HL Scheveningen
t. +31 624 445 900
w. tigersharkcoffee.nl

South of Scheveningen's harbour, a stretch of beach called 'zuiderstrand' starts: backed by dunes, room to roam, and far less busy than the north end. You'll also find far less beach clubs. Our favourite is **Strandpaviljoen Zuid** (**31**). Food, atmosphere, and their many events, parties and music nights all add up to Zuid being your best bet to hang out at the southern side of the beach all day. Open from March to October. ♦€€♦

a. Zuiderstrand 3,
2583 VB Scheveningen / Duindorp
t. +31 616 926 783
w. strandpaviljoen-zuid.nl

From the same owners as Zuid, cocktail bar **Vavoom Tiki Room** (**32**) in the centre of The Hague, will surely help you have the best of times on a night out in town. Shaking those cocktails is an art, and while waiting till the grand shakedown's finished and poured into your tumbler, admire the inked arms of the ladies and gents bartenders. Vavoom's a genuine Tiki style bar, so expect bamboo, tiger prints, fifties and sixties style hairdo's, surf sounds and rock'n'roll. Time flies when you're having rum! (Ah. That's their line, not ours). Open all year. ♦€€♦

a. Grote Markt 29, 2511 BG Den Haag
t. +31 703 467 506
w. gmdh.nl/vavoom

De Pit (33) in 's-Gravenzande, somewhat south of The Hague, is a downright non-pretentious beach club where you can get your coffee before a morning beach walk, order a pizza after a surf session, or take a dip in their hot tub. Open from April to October. ♦€♦ ♦€€♦

a. Slag Vlugtenburg,
   2691 KW 's-Gravenzande
t. + 31 174 418 309
w. strandtentdepit.com

We love that more and more restaurants at the beach are ditching fast production and pre-cooked food, putting dishes with locally produced ingredients on their menu instead. **PLSTK Café (34)** is taking things a(n important) step further by aiming to run their restaurant completely (single use) plastic free. Not just ditching plastic cups, straws, teabags, etcetera, but also trying to source goods that aren't wrapped in plastic from their suppliers. Moreover, it's a chilled out spot in the dunes, overlooking the sea. Open from March to October. ♦€♦ ♦€€♦

a. Helmweg 7, 3151 HE Hoek van Holland
t. +31 174 785 016
w. plstkcafe.nl

SHOP
♦

Entering **Keunn (35)**, in the heart of Noordwijk, you think you've walked into a quirky little shop with bits and bobs of vintage and design. Next you discover another room full of inspiring delight; from delicate to industrial-looking home accessories and furniture, street fashion, books, and longboards. At the back there's yet another space where they sell selected second-hand clothes on one side, and a hair and make-up salon takes up the other half. We bet you won't leave the shop empty-handed. Open all year.

a. Keuvel 12, 2201 MB, Noordwijk Binnen
t. +31 629 733 757
w. keunn.nl

Near Keunn you'll find French bakery **Pain de Sucre (36)**, a bona fide boulangerie selling all sorts of French delicacies and those vraiment buttery croissants.

a. Kerkstraat 4,
   2201 KN Noordwijk Binnen
t. +31 623 304 429

At concept store **ROEST (37)** in Katwijk you'll find a select group of designers, creative entrepreneurs and craftsmen offering their products. Caps, hats, clothing, home decoration, jewellery, plants, books, candles and soap, lots of the stuff that makes you a favoured guest at parties, because you bring the best presents. There are regular creative workshops on offer. Open all year.

a. Noordzeepassage 103,
   2225 CD Katwijk aan Zee
w. roestconceptstore.nl

At café and shop **Hé Jij! (38)** everything's for sale. Everything but the staff. If you like the chair you're sitting on, buy it! You like that vase with flowers at the table? Leave the flowers, purchase the vase. Hé Jij! is more of a café than a shop, but what shop can you sit down, order some delicious healthy food or a coffee and cake, while looking around for something that would fit your home. Open all year.

a. Zuidstraat 1, 2225 GS Katwijk aan Zee
t. +31 614 790 660
w. hejij.com

Calling your shop 'sturdy' and adding 'nicest shop at sea' to the name, you have to deliver. Luckily **Stoer Wonen, 'T leukste winkeltje aan zee (39)** does sell all sorts of goodies for your home and garden that are definitely nice and sturdy at the same time. Think driftwood, ceramics, linen, used for tables, vases, lamps, and pillowcases. Find them in the old centre of Scheveningen. Open all year.

a. Keizerstraat 48, 2584 BK Scheveningen
t. +31 639 462 166
fb. Stoer Wonen 'T leukste winkeltje aan zee

When you catch a whiff of incense, walking the old centre of Scheveningen, you're close to **La Caldera** (**40**). Offering a choice of jewellery, precious stones, essential oils, and, obviously, incense. While beguiled with the sweet scents, maybe linger and book one of their massages or beauty treatments, or join a workshop to learn all about the use of precious stones as a therapy. Open all year.

a. Keizerstraat 112,
   2584 BL Scheveningen
t. +31 703 063 674
w. lacaldera.nl

For your (international) surf magazines, travel guides and typical Scheveningen paraphernalia such as cards, fish-shaped chocolates and stickers of the 3 herring flag, check out the **Boekenhandel Scheveningen** (**41**). Open all year.

a. Keizerstraat 50, 2584 BK Scheveningen
t. +31 703 229 558
w. boekhandelscheveningen.nl

Ocean Republic (**42**), the workshop and atelier of gold and silversmith Sophie Ruygrok, is where she works her magic. Her jewellery - some of which you might have seen in our crowdfunder - is delicate, artful, and always inspired by the ocean and her (surf) travels. She might have been to Bali and took some inspiration from a piece of seaweed or coral, as an example to recreate the organically shaped ocean beauties in sterling silver, recycled brass or gold. If you want to be inspired, or shop for some of her work, are looking for a uniquely hand-made necklace, ring or bracelet, she has an open atelier and you can always call or send her a message to stop by her workshop. Open all year by appointment.

a. Wassenaarsestraat 93,
   2586 AM Scheveningen
t. +31 645 956 933
w. theoceanrepublic.com

Dreams (**43**), in the small settlement of Ter Heijde, is one of the few, if not the only shop in town! And such a likeable one it is. Find all your surf and skate essentials (and lessons), street-style clothing, shoes and accessories, or check in at their attached coffee and artisanal ice-cream parlour. Meet up with the local crew, maybe chat up surf photographers Michal Pelka and/or Roy Mosterd, and score some pictures of yourself in the - uncrowded - line-up. Open all year.

a. Karel Doormanweg 23,
   2684 XG Ter Heijde
t. +31 174 730 032
w. dreamsshop.nl

SLEEP
◆

What else could you possibly need once you've booked your **beach cottage** (**44**) right at the beach of Noordwijk? They're comfortably furnished, each has their own small veranda, and then there's the boundless stretch of beach in front. Available from March to October. ◆€€◆

a. Zeereep 21, 2202 NW
   Noordwijk aan Zee
t. +31 683 996 004
w. strandhuisjesnoordwijk.nl

Meet an international blend of fellow travellers and staff at backpacker beach hostel **The Flying Pig** (**45**). "At ease", we'd say; the hostel's known for its tremendously laid-back character and evenings of partying in their café. They've got dorms and private rooms on offer. Open all year. ◆€◆

a. Parallel Boulevard 208,
   2202 HT Noordwijk aan Zee
t. +31 713 622 533
w. beachhostel.nl

At camping **De Zuidduinen** (**46**) you can choose to pitch your tent, van or rent one of the cabins, mobile homes, or 'Coco Sweets'. The Coco Sweet's a sort of upscaled version of a hiker's hut. Open from March to September. ◆€◆

a. Zuidduinseweg 1,
   2225 JS Katwijk aan Zee
t. +31 714 014 750
w. zuidduinen.com

Family-friendly camping **Duinhorst** (**47**) is not particularly small-scale or special, but it's a calm place, located near beaches, towns and nature reserve Meyendel. They offer pitches and wooden chalets, sleeping up to 5 persons. Open from March to September. ◆€◆

a. Buurtweg 135, 2244 BH Wassenaar
t. +31 703 242 270
w. duinhorst.nl

Spending your night at the **Pier Suites** (**48**), you'll have a spacious room with a view. And what a view! You'll be sleeping right above the North Sea. Jacuzzi, rain shower, large terrace, and mini-bar included, and the option to roam around naked without being seen… Definitely one of our favourites. Book in advance, there are only a few rooms available and they're in demand! Open all year. ◆€€◆ ◆€€€◆

a. Zeekant Scheveningen (at the Pier)
t. +31 610 720 438
w. pier.nl

Jorplace Beach Hostel (**49**), located steps away from the beach, bars, shops and restaurants, is your best budget option for a short or extended stay in Scheveningen. Their bar and garden with fireplace is a bit of a local hangout as well, so meeting up with old friends or making new couldn't be easier. Jorplace's staff is friendly, well informed and surf-minded, giving you all the inside information that's needed. You can rent longboards (skates) and beach cruiser bicycles, they've dorm-style rooms, a private, and triple room. On offer, optional daily breakfast, hangover and BBQ buffets (also vegetarian options). Open all year. ◆€◆

a. Keizerstraat 296,
2584 BN Scheveningen
t. +31 703 383 270
w. jorplace.nl

In a renovated 1950s house, twin sisters Saar and Aad, run bed and breakfast **Zussen aan Zee** (**50**), Sisters at Sea. They've kept some nostalgic details and mixed it up with modern touches so guests won't lack any comfort. The sisters themed each room: the portrait room, the rose room and the blue room, with typical Dutch Delfts Blauw details. Or choose to stay in the bright family room in the former attic. Open all year. ◆€€◆

a. Karel Doormanweg 26,
2684 XH Ter Heijde
t. +31 653 368 577
w. benbzussenaanzee.nl

Camping **Jagtveld** (**51**), located in the dunes and near the ocean between 's-Gravenzande and Hoek van Holland, is a quiet family campsite. It's got pitches for tents, vans and caravans. Open from March to September. ◆€◆

a. Nieuwlandsedijk 41, 2691
KV 's-Gravenzande
t. +31 174 413 479
w. jagtveld.nl

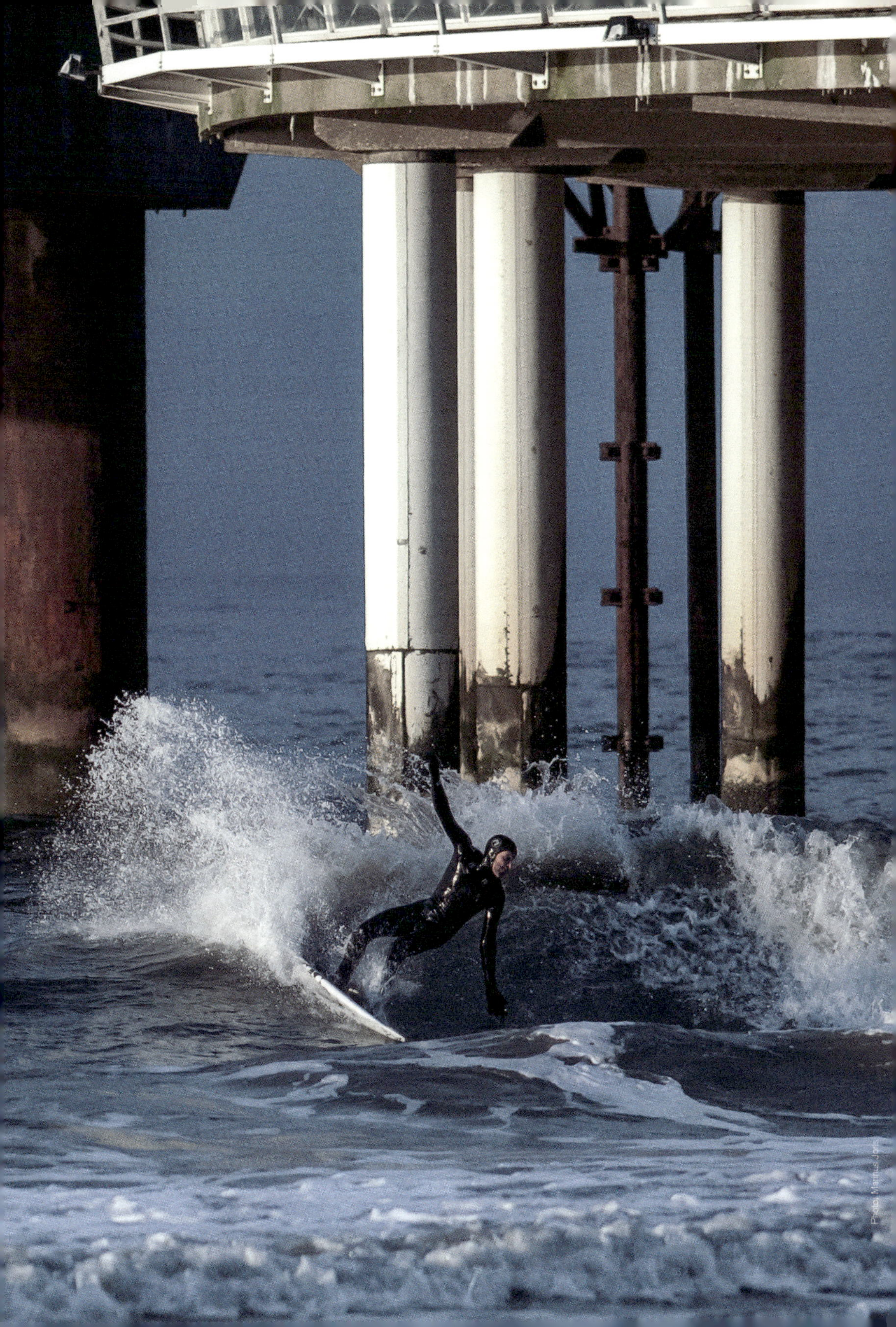

SURF

With all beaches facing west or northwest, apart from those with a harbour wall to offer protection, most are easily blown out. But that said, the south of Holland does have its classic days, more often than you'd expect from a North Sea shore. Especially Scheveningen, with the breakwaters sheltering the beach on both north and south sides of its harbour. The downside: expect crowds beyond belief. Or opt for a little less quality but all the more waves to yourself, by trying the breaks in either direction of Scheveningen's main peaks - Hoek van Holland and De Maasvlakte hold the best cards. All breaks receive both wind and ground swells, the latter being less common. And although in some parts there are designated areas for wave, kite and windsurfers, at most beaches you'll have to share your waves with all types of surf craft.

No wave in sight? Try your luck at **24/7 wave pool** (w. 247waves.com).

West facing **Noordwijk (I)** and **Katwijk (II)** work best at low tide, with a small to large SW-W-NW-N swell. Beware of currents. • *All levels/sand/paid parking/toilets/restaurants/camping/surf schools.* •

WNW facing **Scheveningen Noord (III)** works at all tides; at high tide the shorebreak tends to throw up fast hollow waves, at low tide the outer banks work nicely for bigger boards. Best with a small to big SW-W-NW-N swell. The long harbour wall gives protection from S-SW-W winds. Beginners especially, beware of the currents, and watch out for the rip along the harbour wall. Expect crowds, always. • *All levels/sand/paid parking/toilets and showers/restaurants/surf schools.* •

Scheveningen Zuid (IV) also works at all tides, best with a small to big SW-W-NW-N swell. Expect a little less, but still crowded break, especially with NE-N winds, since the harbour wall on the south side gives protection for this direction. Beware of currents. • *All levels/sand/paid parking/restaurant.* •

Ter Heijde (V) works best at lower tides with a small to large SW-W-NW-N swell. There are some jetties, and very strong currents. Friendly vibe in the water, beautiful backdrop of dunes, and no crowds here! ◆ *All levels/sand/free parking/restaurants/surf school.* ◆

Northwest facing **Hoek van Holland (VI)** works at all tides with a small to big SW-W-NW-N swell. A long harbour wall gives protection from SW-W winds. ◆ *All levels/sand/paid parking/toilets and showers/restaurants/surf school.* ◆

The WSW facing, industrialised **Maasvlakte MV2 (VII)** is not the most beautiful spot, environmentally-wise. But it's loved by the more advanced surfers for its fast and hollow waves when conditions are right. So, be respectful - and wise - before paddling out. Works at all tides with a medium to big SW-W-NW-N swell. Beware of the strong currents. ◆ *Advanced levels/sand/easy parking/no facilities/industrial zone.* ◆

SCHOOL RENTAL REPAIR

Water sports hotspot **Beach Break** (**52**) is a surf, SUP and kite club, school, shop and beach bar. Lessons and rentals available. If you've plans to go kite surfing, best become a member of the club first. It's regulated by the municipality; you're only allowed to kite if you're a member of a club. Open from March to October.

a. Zeereep 106, Noordwijk aan Zee
t. +31 612 098 110
w. beachbreak.nl

Small-scale **Lex Surfschool** (**53**) is located in Noordwijk, but owner and avid longboarder Alexander' uses his surf car to drive to different places, offering surfing wherever the best conditions are. Personal attention, safety (Alex is a certified lifeguard) and fun guaranteed. Closed in winter.

a. Beach Noordwijk
t. +31 611 888 630
w. lexsurfschool.nl

Surf school **Katwijk** (**54**) offers surf, bodyboard and SUP, kite and windsurfing lessons and rental of all gear. If you want to go for something else active; they also have mountain bike, powerkiting and rafting options. In summer their Brunotti beach camps for juniors share the stoke with kids between 12 and 16 yrs. Open from April to October.

a. Boulevard Zeezijde 3, 2225 BB Katwijk
t. +31 642 022 016
w. surfschool-katwijk.nl

Board shop **GEARfreak** (**55**) has been around since 1984, back in the windsurfing heydays. Nowadays, besides windsurf gear, they've got surf, SUP and winter sports apparel, boards and essentials. Open all year.

a. Secretaris Varkevisserstraat 345, 2225 LD Katwijk aan Zee
t. +31 714 013 316
w. gearfreak.nl

Shaper Julian Yoshi's been known for some time as South Holland's Ding Doctor, fixing and repairing any dinged and damaged surfboards. But there's far more to Julian than fixing boards. He runs his shop **Surfhuis** (**56**), and is one of the very few board shapers who's trying to shape boards with as little environmental impact as possible. He's constantly searching for ways to replace the essential elements with non-toxic alternatives and searching for longer lasting and less polluting methods and substances. His shapes are pretty special too, not the average shortboards. Go check them out at his shop and see if you fall in love with them.

a. Zeesluisweg 13,
2583 DN Scheveningen
t. +31 641 469 741
fb. Surfhuis & JY Surf

the two of them they know a lot about boards, shapes, gear, suits and spots. There's an in-house shaper fixing boards, they've got skateboards, books, wetsuits, brand new surfboards and second-hand boards. And fins! They've got an amazing choice: Futures, Featherfins, but also beautiful fins for logs and other boards that require single fins, like the George Greenough and Dewey Weber fins.

a. Badhuisstraat 72,
2584 HK Scheveningen
t. +31 702 015 153
w. noordzeeboardstore.nl

style clothing, accessories, shoes, books and of course surfboards, wetsuits and all other essential surf gear. At the beach you'll also find their surf school offering lessons, rentals, warm showers, a slackline, and in summer special surf camps for kids. Open all year.

a. Vissershavenweg 55b,
2583 DL Scheveningen (shop)
t. +31 703 545 583
a. Strandweg 3b, 2586 JK Scheveningen
(shop, school and restaurant)
t. +31 703 502 591
w. hartbeach.nl

Jana from **Ninety9** (**57**) is a creative and skilled craftsperson. She does wetsuit repairs, and stitches up printed canvas and recycled coffee bags, turning them into smart looking surf socks and board bags. She'll also help you out with curtains and seat covers for your campervan. Open all year, just give her a call or send her a message. You can see samples of her work at surf school The Shore.

t. +31 629 592 151
w. ninety9.nl

Noordzee Boardstore (**58**) is a surf shop owned and run by long-time friends Wouter and Thomas. Between

Shaper Olaf de Vries of **Ollywood** (**59**) shapes - or helps you shape your own - wooden boards and hand planes, or paipos. He also sells some unique t-shirts, printed with typical Scheveningen or surf-related designs. Check his regular posts on Insta, or better yet, give him a call and see what's on offer!

a. Vijzelstraat 85, 2584 GK, Scheveningen
t. +31 614 361 368
w. ollywoodsurfboards.com

One of the oldest surf schools in Holland is **Hart Beach** (**60**). They've got 2 shops, one located at the beach and the other at the harbour. The shops have a large choice of surf and street

Daphne Oedekerk's surf school, restaurant and shop **Aloha** (**61**) offers lessons, rentals, warm showers, kids summer camps, and themed events like a special girls' surf day. Their shop holds a select choice of lifestyle and fashion brands such as Amuse, Volcom, Picture and Rainbow footwear, and surfboards, SUPs, wetsuits, essential gear, books, and accessories. Big perk - the knowledgeable staff, who'll help you out with whatever question you have concerning surfing, surf gear, conditions and such.

a. Strandweg 2B, 2586 ZZ Scheveningen
t. +31 703 227 171
w. alohasurf.nl

Surfles (**62**), from waterman and avid surfer Hans van den Broek, is a very dedicated surf school offering surf lessons, coaching, watermen workouts, and progression sessions - a 1,5 hr session where you learn to increase your wave count, and work on your technique and posture. Learning how to surf is also learning about the ocean and the importance of keeping it clean, so Surfles instructors set an example by following the Pick up 3 principle; every walk from shore to school they'll pick up at least 3 pieces of trash. After your session you can enjoy organic pancakes, and a warm shower, heated by solar boilers, at their beach bar The Shore. Open from March to October.

a. Strandweg 1, 2586 ZZ Scheveningen
t. +31 649 392 095
w. surfles.nl

Dreams (**63**) surf shop and school at the uncrowded break of Ter Heijde offers surf, skate, and skimboard lessons. At their shop you can purchase all your surf and skate essentials, clothing and accessories. Open all year.

a. Karel Doormanweg 23,
2684 XG Ter Heijde
t. +31 174 730 032
w. dreamsshop.nl

Surfschool Hoek van Holland (**64**) offers surf, SUP and bodyboard lessons in small groups, and summer camps for kids in summer. Safe and fun, for beginner and intermediate to advanced. Open from April to October.

a. Rechtestraat 40,
3151 HN Hoek van Holland
t. +31 648 715 056 / 654 236 545
w. surfschoolhoekvanholland.com

The **Dutch Surf Academy** (**65**) is run by two-time Dutch surf champion Kaspar Hamminga. With his long-time friend and surf buddy Erik Ringelberg, they offer surf lessons and coaching for all levels, and ages. Small groups only and safety comes first. Find them next to beach club De Pit at the uncrowded beach of 's-Gravenzande.

Open from May to November.

a. Slag Vlugtenburg,
2691 KW 's-Gravenzande
t. +31 624 165 402 / 636 575 985
w. dutchsurfacademy.nl

Photo: Marcus Jones

SEASIDE LOCAL: YANNICK DE YAGER

♦

Free surfer, Protest team rider and filmmaker Yannick de Jager, lives in Scheveningen, Holland's seriously surf-focused seaside town. But at least half the year he's abroad, travelling, shooting and obviously, surfing.

> *"Scoring quality waves at a place that doesn't receive swell so often is a different experience. It's borderline bizarre."*

Over the years, he's grown from a promising grom, multiple Dutch champ, surfing the QS for a while; to being a free surfer with a philosophical view on life and choosing paths. How'd he do that? "I've been blessed with my upbringing. My parents being unconditional in a way that they gave me all the freedom to do whatever I want. A great gift, but you still need to shape and create the life you want to live. It's a lot safer and more comfortable to just follow traditional paths that society or our environment lays out for us. You have to be willing to go through some struggles, have a sense of discipline and motivation. I think it boils down to following your guts, passion, and taking steps in uncertainty, confronting your fears." Although he does make it sound simple, it's one of the hardest things to do in life, he says. "Although the energy and time that goes into it won't feel as an effort, because you are just going towards the thing you want to do." What Yannick loves most; the ocean, being creative, learning and experimenting with the magical medium of film. "I've always been very visual. I also enjoy reading a lot - and watching films and taking analog photos with my mum. Learning about photography and motion film since I started working with photographers and filmmakers as a young, dedicated, surfing teenager also helped. The ability to capture journeys, surf sessions, moments and stories has always been something that I loved doing naturally... just like surfing." Although he surfs world-class breaks all over while travelling, he loves coming back to the North Sea. "Don't get me wrong, scoring waves in places blessed with decent, consistent surf never gets boring. It's what surfing is about. Whether that's an epic French sandbank, barrelling Portuguese reef, Irish slab, American A-frame skate park, Australian point or some perfect tropical coral. Yet I think scoring quality waves at a place that doesn't receive swell so often is a different experience. You don't take it for granted; you really appreciate it... but really! Like in a different dimension than when you're in a country with consistent quality waves. It's borderline bizarre." But in the end, what keeps his stoke alive: people mostly. "Spending time with family, friends, go surfing together, or people that I work with creating and filming. Just appreciating the little things in life, moments, coffees, being surprised by things... situations that just come together. The smell of the North Sea, the smell of the dunes - and I'm a sucker for sunrises and sunsets."

♦

Check out both Yannick's magical work and his surfing style on his blog **w.** jagershots.tv
Read the full interview on **w.** ilovetheseaside.com/stories

♦

HOLLAND

OUDDORP
(I)

2,8,19,23,24,33,34 ◆

OUDDC

◆ 1,9,18
◆ 10,25

RENESSE ◆

BURG-HAAMSTEDE
(II)

BURGH-HAAMSTEDE ◆

◆ 3

ZIERIKZ ◆

DOMBURG
(III)

◆ 11-14,20,21,27-29,35
DOMBURG
◆ 15

◆ 26
VEERE ◆

Zeeland

WESTKAPELLE ◆

ZOUTELANDE ◆

◆ 4,22
MIDDELBURG

GOES ◆

DISHOEK
(IV)

◆ 5
VLISSINGEN

CADZAND
(V)

◆ 6,32
GROEDE
BRESKENS ◆

◆ 6,7,16,17,30,31,36
CADZAND

ZEELAND

If there's one thing that springs to mind immediately, thinking of Zeeland, it's the incredible light. On the darkest of days, skies seem to let light through thick layers of clouds. It's down to the flat landscape, with mudlands and wetlands and farm fields, and water - everywhere water - reflecting brightly, colouring the sky from the bluest of blue, to pink, purple and red. It attracted painters through the times, it still attracts photographers, and people who like their seaside quiet, peaceful, and spacious.

Zeeland's made up from a number of islands and peninsulas - connected by tunnels and bridges, with a fair few dams giving a helping hand - and a strip of land that borders Belgium. Most of the province being below sea level, it's been flooded and emerged again more than once; hence the flag having a lion rising from the waters. The last major flood was in the fifties, so no need to worry. Besides, you've a wetsuit and a flotation device at hand…

TRAVEL INFO

Although Holland's infrastructure runs smoothly and nothing's too far away to drive to; getting around, and reaching every nook and cranny, in Zeeland takes time. There will be a train, or a bus, eventually, to take you there, you just might need to be patient. Even by car, most roads have 80 km/h as the speed limit, and you'll get stuck behind a tractor at some time or other.

BY AIR

International flights to/from Rotterdam Den Haag Airport or Amsterdam Schiphol Airport, regular schedules for both with established and budget airlines.

w. schiphol.nl / rotterdamthehagueairport.nl

BY TRAIN

Nederlandse Spoorwegen (Dutch Railways) runs a reliable and extensive train network up, down and across the country.

w. ns.nl

BY BUS

There are plenty of bus and tram companies covering travel to even the most remote areas. For info, routes and timetables:

w. 9292.nl

IN AND AROUND DOMBURG

Domburg's special light, nature and teeniest bit of a mundane feel has been attracting artists and painters, and later tourists, since the end of the 19th century. While Zeeland's other seaside resorts are all friendly and unassuming, Domburg has a slight air of arty style. Ouddorp, to the north, technically belongs to Zuid Holland, but most of its star attractions are at or around Brouwersdam. The 6 km long Brouwersdam connects Zuid Holland and Zeeland, with the North Sea on one side, and the large lake of Grevelingen on the other. To the south, the small village of Cadzand's main attraction is its surrounding nature: forested areas, dunes, and - the best bit - Het Zwin nature reserve, where you can find shell fossils and sharks' teeth!

Tourist offices at: Bosweg 2, 3253 XA Ouddorp / Schuitvlotstraat 32, 4357 EB Domburg / Boulevard de Wielingen 44D, 4506 JK Cadzand.

TO DO

Kite-buggying and blokarting are among the most rewarding activities if it's a flat day and your body's yearning for action and adrenaline. At **Natural High (1)** you can learn how to control kite and buggy, or sail in a little kart along the beach. Not too keen on windy activity? Watch the colourful kites from Natural High's stylishly decorated beach restaurant. Open all year.

a. Brouwersdam 22, 3253 MM Ouddorp (Access 16, across from Port Zelande)
t. +31 187 723 900
w. natural-high.nl

Stretch, tone, breathe it in, love it all out - whatever needs to be loosened up or got rid of, you can handle it at either the studio or beach with surfer and yogini Bellatrix van Wingerden. At her **Yoga Studio Ouddorp (2)** she teaches flow yoga, meditation, yoga for surfers, Qigong and Pilates. From July to August classes are outside, at several nearby beaches, such as every Thursday and Sunday morning at Natural High (Brouwersdam). Bellatrix also offers SUP yoga classes. Check website for more info. Open all year.

a. Broekweg 13, 3253 XB Ouddorp
t. +31 642 349 972
w. yogastudioouddorp.nl

From all over the world, tourists, engineers and technically-curious, old and young, come to wonder at and admire the **Deltapark Neeltje Jans (3)**. Here's where you can learn all about Delta Works - the large storm surge barrier which is Zeeland's famously innovative system to protect against flooding. Bit of a thing that is, the Dutch fighting floods from the sea; since half of Holland, and almost all of Zeeland's below sea level and the latter, during a stormy January night in 1953 was pretty much wiped out by floods. Deltapark, located at the foot of the Delta Works, tells all about this natural catastrophe - the reason Holland got so inventive with water defence systems - and how the immense structure works to prevent another disaster. Open all year.

a. Eiland Neeltje Jans, Faelweg 5, 4 354 RB Vrouwenpolder
t. +31 111 655 655
w. neeltjejans.nl

ZEELAND

Middelburg (4) and Vlissingen (5) are definitely worth a visit; however clichéd that may sound. Middelburg might be Zeeland's capital, but like all cities in the province, nothing about it shouts concrete jungle or gives off big-city vibes. Both Middelburg and Vlissingen are like little villages, but with more people, more things to do, shops, bars, galleries, music venues and restaurants. Like Domburg, they both have an ittybit of an artsy feel. While Middelburg's known for its many monumental buildings - including some classic windmills in town, in case you haven't seen any yet - the harbour town of Vlissingen's main attraction is the endless boulevard along the waterway Westerschelde. Check out the wind organ producing some pretty unworldly tunes where the boulevard starts (at the beach end). There's also a 4 km (on foot) or 10 km (by bike) art route through the city, guiding you to public art installations, statues and sculptures. Every September the international film festival, Film by the Sea, is held in Vlissingen.

Go where you normally can't go, on a SUP! Explore the mesmerising nature reserve, 't Zwin, that connects Zeeland and Belgium, with **Cadzand Sports** (6). Even better, go at sunset! They also organise SUP yoga at beach campsite Groede (Zeeweg 1, 4503 PA Groede). Available from May to October.

a. Cadzand, Groede or Terneuzen.
t. +31 621 577 001
w. cadzandsports.nl

You like a bit of a challenge, mud-splattered legs and back, and tiring yourself out to way beyond tired? Try the 35 km long **MTB route Grensstreek** (7), half of which is off-road. The route's well signposted, and you'll be pedalling through both Holland and Belgium, mostly amidst nature, sometimes passing villages, like Cadzand. Starting point:

a. Boerenhoeve Nieuwvliet, Sint Jansdijk 1, 4504 PB Nieuwvliet

EAT/DRINK/HANG OUT

◆

At family-run bistro and wine bar **ZUS** (8), they take into account people like us, who are inclined to try not one, but at least two or more dishes on the menu. So the portions are prepared in

341

such a way you can easily manage to eat an order of at least three, to get a little taste of all sorts of dishes in one dinner. Kind of like tapas, but not. Warm welcomes are offered all day, for coffee, lunch, dinner, or an evening drink. Open all year. •€€•

a. Molenblok 7, 3253 AL Ouddorp
t. +31 187 844 285
w. bistrowijnbarzus.com

If you heard that Zeeland has fertile soil, producing all sorts of vegetables and fruits, you'll expect Zeeland's restaurants to serve fresh and local, and have a stupendous choice. At **Strandpaviljoen Brouw (9)** that's exactly what you get. Fish from the North Sea, veggies from the fields of the islands Goeree-Overflakkee and Schouwen-Duiveland. The beach restaurant likes giving a second life to old things, lamps made of jars, pallets used for loungers. Inside, a large wood-burning stove is the centrepiece for colder days, the terrace perfect for when the sun's out. Open all year. •€• •€€•

a. Brouwersdam 20, Access 15, 3253 MM Ouddorp
t. +31 187 202 010
w. brouw.nl

Restaurant EAT & SEE (10) is an attraction in itself, it's so big, bright and refreshingly designed. There are tree trunk tables and chesterfields, terraces protected from the wind and easy chairs in the sun. The large wooden building with its many windows, located by lake Grevelingen, offers a view of the water, which is usually freckled with all sorts of sailing boats. At the same site they have a smart looking and well equipped surf shop selling all sorts of surf and street-style apparel and surf essentials. Open all year. •€€•

a. Ossenhoek 1 (Kabbelaarsbank), 3253 MH Ouddorp
t. +31 111 671 480
w. brouwersdam.com

Ice-cream parlour **IJsvogel Domburg (11)** serves, well, ice-cream. And coffee, tea, home-made cakes and pie, waffles. But first and foremost: Ice-cream. Artesanal. Mouth-wateringly good. Open all year. •€•

a. Ooststraat 7, 4357 BE Domburg
t. +31 118 583 959
fb. ijsvogel domburg

Just when you think no hipster ever reached Zeeland you bump into **Burger Restaurant De Domburger (12)**. Nah... it's not just another beards, beers and burger joint. Although they do have burgers - one vegetarian option, no vegan - beards have been spotted, and there's a choice of craft beers. And a brick wall. Still, who cares? Burger joint's a burger joint, and we happen to like brick walls and beer. Open all year. •€•

a. Weststraat 22, 4357 BM Domburg
t. +31 118 584 345
w. dedomburger.nl

Get your chai latte, local beers and organic food at **De Domburgsche Bier-en Melksalon (13)**, The Domburg Beer and Milk Salon. A freshly decorated daytime café and restaurant, in a side street off the busy main street, popular amongst local and visiting surfers. Open all year. •€•

a. Weststraat 11, 4357 BL Domburg
t. +31 118 853 810
w. bierenmelksalon.nl

Oh so typical Dutch: pancakes and apple syrup - or any variation of sauce and fillings for that matter. This and other sweet and hearty typical Dutch after-beach-comfort-food is served at pancake restaurant **Vierwegen (14)**. The hearty dish Dutch kids will choose here, over and over, is Appelmoes - a plate of French fries, croquettes and minced apples. Open all year. •€•

a. 't Groentje 10, 4357 BC Domburg
t. +31 118 583 393
w. vierwegen.eu

Tea, tea and more tea (there are 60 blends to choose from) to be enjoyed at **Theetuin De Koektrommel (15)**, Tea Garden The Cookie Jar. Conveniently located on bicycle route 46, just outside the settlement of Aagtekerke. And the cookie jar? Yes, there are home-made cookies and cakes to go with your tea. Open all year. •€•

a. Oude Grintweg 3a, 4363RD Aagtekerke
t. +31 118 436 055
w. theetuindekoektrommel.nl

Beach club **Strand Ruig (16)**, at the stretch of beach at Cadzand, stands out for its architectural feats. It's light and bright, and stone, wood and steel are used for both interior and exterior. If you happen to get stuck with your bike, Strand Ruig's got all the kit to fix your tyres! Open all year. •€€• •€€€•

a. Zwartepolderweg 1A, (Dunepath M12), 4506 HT Cadzand
t. +31 117 396 609
w. strandruig.nl

Restaurant **AIRrepublic** and café **AIRcafé** (**17**), both at the harbour, are the highly accessible offspring of top chef Sergio Herman. Less exclusive than Pure C, the third (Michelin star awarded) restaurant he owns in Cadzand. The restaurant's run by a young chef who's been working with Sergio Herman for over 5 years. If you love seafood, and especially fresh local catch, you'll love their menu, for sure. At the adjoining café you can enjoy your coffee or bite to eat with a view of sea and harbour, in company of locals, boat people and tourists alike. AIRrepublic open all year. AIRcafé open from April to October. ◆€€◆ ◆€€€◆

a. Maritiem Plaza 1, 4506 KZ Cadzand-Bad
t. +31 858 331 919
w. air-republic.com

SHOP
◆

We did mention Natural High in the To Do section and might as well have mentioned **Natural High** (**18**) in the section above too, because their restaurant's as nicely done up as their surf shops. Both shops are well stocked, have knowledgeable staff, are test centre and shop all-in-one, and besides boards and surf essentials they've a choice of lifestyle and streetstyle clothing and accessories. Open all year.

a. Brouwersdam Buitenzijde 22 / Strandopgang 16, 3253 MM Ouddorp
a. Landel Strand Resort, Westerweg 26, 3253 LX Ouddorp
t. +31 187 723 924.
w. natural-high.nl

Dingenliefde (**19**) means love for things. All things nice, in this case. They can be used, old, industrial, new, vintage, organic and fairly produced, collected from all corners of the world. All the nice things are made by and purchased from small businesses. The collection is ever-changing, and you can take a mini tour around the world just by entering the shop. Open all year.

a. Hofdijksweg 14, 3253 KB Ouddorp
t. +31 612 780 874
w. dingenliefde.nl

Sportshop Domburg (**20**) is a household name within the Dutch, German and Belgium surf scene. Still going strong, with everything you need and some more for surfing, beaching, and bumming around in a relaxed fashion. They've a large selection of boards and their staff are a source of information on the area, surf, spots, tides and forecasts. Open all year.

a. Weststraat 2A, 4357 BM Domburg
t. +31 118 586 012
w. sportshopdomburg.nl

Galerie Pop (21) is a café, shop and gallery, all in one. Shop for fair trade items such as pottery, bags, jewellery, notebooks, bet you can't resist the sweet smell of a freshly brewed espresso while you're at it. Almost all food served is home-made, organically grown and produced. They serve breakfast, lunch, drinks and snacks and have regular art exhibitions. Open from March to October.

a. Weststraat 6, 4357 BM Domburg
t. +31 118 584 334
w. galeriepop.nl

You might have guessed we love print, books, and all things ink. At bookshop **De Drvkkery (22)** they spread the love with a fine selection of novels, special editions, children's books, to-do books, art and travel books, special stationery, and regular events, performances, live interviews and music. And a café to sit back and enjoy that newly purchased treasure of words, drawings or photos. Open all year.

a. Markt 51, 4331 LK Middelburg
t. +31 118 886 886
w. de-drvkkery.nl

SLEEP

◆

Small-scale **Camping Zonnewende (23)** is a skip-hop from the beach at Ouddorp, surrounded by the green fields of their farm. Pitches available for tents, campervans and caravans. Open all year. ◆€◆

a. Groenedijk 22, 3253 LB Ouddorp
t. +31 187 681 851 / 610 076 795
w. campingzonnewende.nl

Stay at either the apartment or studio of **New Harvest Inn (24)**. The spacious apartment, set in a former baker's house, sleeps 4-5 people. The smaller studio (The Bakery, 2 persons) was the old bakery itself. Both places have lots of authentic details kept or added, giving them a nostalgic twist. Open all year. ◆€€◆

a. Raadhuisstraat 19 and 21,
   3253 AN Ouddorp
t. +31 612 436 315 / 630 118 922
w. newharvestinn.nl

Oh, don't you wish you could stay forever. Or at least make one of these your own home. The 16 **beach lodges (25)** from sail and surf centre Brouwersdam are built in such a way that you experience the surroundings to the fullest, at the water's edge of Grevelingen's lake. Done up in beachy style, with the use of robust materials, but all the comforts you need. Hammocks and BBQ out at sunset, anyone? Open all year. ◆€€◆

a. Ossenhoek 1 (Kabbelaarsbank),
   3253 MH Ouddorp
t. +31 111 671 480
w. brouwersdam.com

At **Hoeve Banenburg (26)** you'll stay in comfy tents (4 to 6 persons) amidst the farm animals and fields. Kids can play on the haystack, or take up horse riding lessons and help look after the horses. The farm's a 15 minute bike ride from the beach, and close to the village of Veere. Open from March to October. ◆€€◆

a. Weelweg 1, 4352 SM Gapinge / Veere
t. +31 528 229 440
w. boerenbed.nl/locatie/hoeve-banenburg

Pretty unbeatable and far from common, not only in Holland but in the rest of the world as well: sleeping as close to the ocean as possible (if not on a boat, obviously). At **Slaapzand (27)** you stay in a modern, smartly designed beach house on poles, at the beach near Domburg. Available from March to November. ◆€€◆ ◆€€€◆

a. Schelpweg 17A, 4357 BP Domburg
t. +31 654 777 852
w. slaapzand.nl

Olof Sinke is a singer songwriter, musician and surfer, and your host at **De Dromenkamer (28)**. The snug apartment (2 persons) at the back of his house is located within walking distance from both the beach and the town centre. Open all year. ◆€◆

a. Brouwerijweg 11, 4357CD Domburg
t. +31 614 128 128
w. dedromenkamer.nl

ZEELAND

Close to the beach you'll find camping **Noordduin** (**29**), offering pitches and a 4-person chalet for rent. Bike rental available. Open from March to October. ◆€◆

a. Schelpweg 17A, 4357 RG Domburg
t. +31 118 582 666
w. campingnoordduin.nl

Oh so many options to camp at farms in Zeeland. **Mini Camping 10-100** (**30**) only has 25 pitches, each with lots of space and privacy, and endless views of endless green fields. Unless you're looking at the end towards the beach, which is only 500 m away. Open from April to October. ◆€◆

a. Tienhonderdse Middenweg 2, 4506 HS Cadzand
t. +31 117 391 968
w. minicamping10-100.nl

Camping De Wachtsluis (**31**) is surrounded by nature, close to dunes and beach. The owners have a vegetable farm, and one very sweet sheep who's really more of a pet. Woolly cuteness!

Less than 1 km from the beach and at your disposal during the summer season is their teahouse, Juffertje in het Groen - open for freshly baked bread, coffee, tea and cakes. Open from April to November. ◆€◆

a. Wachtsluis 1, 4525 ND Retranchement
t. +31 117 391 225
w. wachtsluis.nl

You know that feeling after spending the day at the beach, never ever wanting to go home? Well, if you choose to stay at one of the beach houses like **Panorama Huisje** (**32**) you won't have to leave. The front of the houses open up to sea, you'll have a panoramic view of beach and ocean. Imagine the sunset, and the stars at night, imagine waking up to an empty beach, imagine… ah… just imagine sleeping at the beach in your tiny house! The beach houses sleep up to 6 people - so not that tiny - and are built with sustainability in mind. Their design's inspired by shells and the old-fashioned beach wicker chairs. Closed in winter. ◆€€◆ ◆€€€◆

a. Strandcamping Groede, Zeeweg 1, 4503 PA Groede
t. +31 117 371 384
w. panoramahuisje.nl

HOLLAND

SURF

Both locals and Belgian-locals surf the breaks of Zeeland, and regularly returning Germans, as well as holidayers from all over. The most consistent spot here's Domburg, where you can expect crowds at times. But 'crowded' is relative in Zeeland, and besides, the vibe's easy-going and free from aggro. The level, however, may surprise you; as this small community of avid surfers find stoke in the sloppiest choppiest waves, on good days they shine like diamonds, shaped by dedicated surfing in all conditions.

The exposed NW-facing beach at **Ouddorp (I)** works best at lower tides with a small to large SW-W-NW-N (wind) swell. Ouddorp's known as a popular kite and windsurf spot. ♦ *All levels/sand/easy parking/restaurants/ camping/surf school.* ♦

Burgh Haamstede (II) is a W-facing beach that works at all tides with a small to large SW-W-NW-N (wind) swell. A bit of an isolated spot with some jetties, beware of currents. ♦ *All levels/sand/ easy parking/restaurants.* ♦

Domburg (III) works at all tides with all sizes SW-W-NW-N swell. Beware of currents and the (photogenic) pole jetties. And of course, being kind and respectful never hurt anybody, especially not visiting surfers at a break popular with the locals. ♦ *All levels/sand/paid parking/restaurants/campsites/surf school.* ♦

Dishoek (IV) works only at higher tides, with a large NW-W swell. Sheltered from strong N winds. As with Domburg; beware of currents, and watch out for those shifty pole jetties.

• Advanced levels/sand/easy parking/restaurants/campsites. •

You're as good as in Belgium when you get as far as **Cadzand (V)**. The NNW-facing beach has some jetties and works at all tides with a small to large SW-W-NW-N (wind) swell. Small harbour walls protect from NE and SW-W winds. You'll find predominantly kite and windsurfers here. • All levels/sand/easy parking/restaurants/campsites/surf school. •

Surf shop and school **Natural High (33)** offers surf and kite lessons, and rental of all gear. Situated at Landel Strand Resort, the brand new shop (the second of Natural High) has all essentials, clothing and accessories. Open all year.

a. Westerweg 26, 3253 LX Ouddorp
t. +31 187 723 927
w. natural-high.nl

SCHOOL RENTAL REPAIR

Surf Karavaan Ouddorp (34) offers surf lessons and rental, SUP lessons, beach yoga and longboarding (skate). Open from Easter to October.

a. Beach Het Flaauwe Werk 1, next to beach club C-side, 3253 LB Ouddorp
t. +31 683 085 020
w. surfkaravaan.nl

Surf shop and school **Sportshop Domburg (35)** has surf, skimboard and SUP lessons on offer, as well as rental and testing of gear. Open all year.

a. Strand Domburg 32 (Strand Noordduine), 4357 XZ Domburg
t. +31 118 584 795
w. sportshopdomburg.nl

Moio (36) at Cadzand's got surf, SUP, skimboard, kayak, powerkiting and blokarting on offer. After your session you can chill and unwind at their beach club. Open from May to October.

a. Vlamingpolderweg 3A, 4506 HZ Cadzand
t. +31 117 392 180
w. moio.nl

*To be, live, or act better takes action: I Love the Seaside teamed up with KEEN Footwear
to share stories of people who make a positive effort to make a change and/or inspire.*

Despite being a graduate of psychology, Suzanne van den Broek-Dietz (39) ended up working as a project manager in Amsterdam. Ten years in, she asked herself whether this was what she really wanted to do with her life. As she chatted with one of the boys at the farm rehabilitation centre where she volunteered, telling him about her most recent surf trip, he asked her the question that opened her eyes to what her next step should be: "Can't you teach us how to surf?" In 2014, the answer (a big YES - just in case you can't wait till the end to find out) became a reality, as Suzanne founded the Surf Project, an organisation that gives surfing lessons to children with Down syndrome, autism, and ADHD. Since then the project's expanded to four locations along the Dutch coast: Zandvoort, Ouddorp, Camperduin and Ter Heijde.

And the positive effects of surfing on the children are extraordinary: "One of the parents said that their child's disability seems to completely disappear when they're in the water. That was a tremendous compliment, as I didn't just want the project to be fun. The goal is to allow children to work on their confidence and to grow as a person. They're tough children engaging in an amazing sport - children who are incredibly proud of themselves. You can see it in their eyes when they receive their diploma at the end of the course. What they learn during the surfing lessons, they benefit from at home, at school, in their interactions with friends - it influences their whole being."

Putting her idea into action has given Suzanne the sense of fulfilment she was seeking: "The Surf Project is part of our family. It never feels like work, which is an experience I haven't had before. I was searching for something new, something worthy of recognition. Apart from volunteering at the farm rehabilitation centre, I wasn't doing anything with my degree in psychology. In hindsight, these phases of my life were a necessary step towards realising what really is fun and meaningful. I don't care about a full bank account. The more you earn, the more you want. Seeing the impact the Surf Project has on people is a lot more valuable to me."

*Suzanne currently lives in Haarlem with her husband Jurjen and their two sons Luuk (5) and Tom (3).
Want further info on the Surf Project or get involved?* **w.** surfproject.nl / intlsurftherapy.org

Together we rise.

SURFRIDER
FOUNDATION EUROPE

HOLLAND COAST

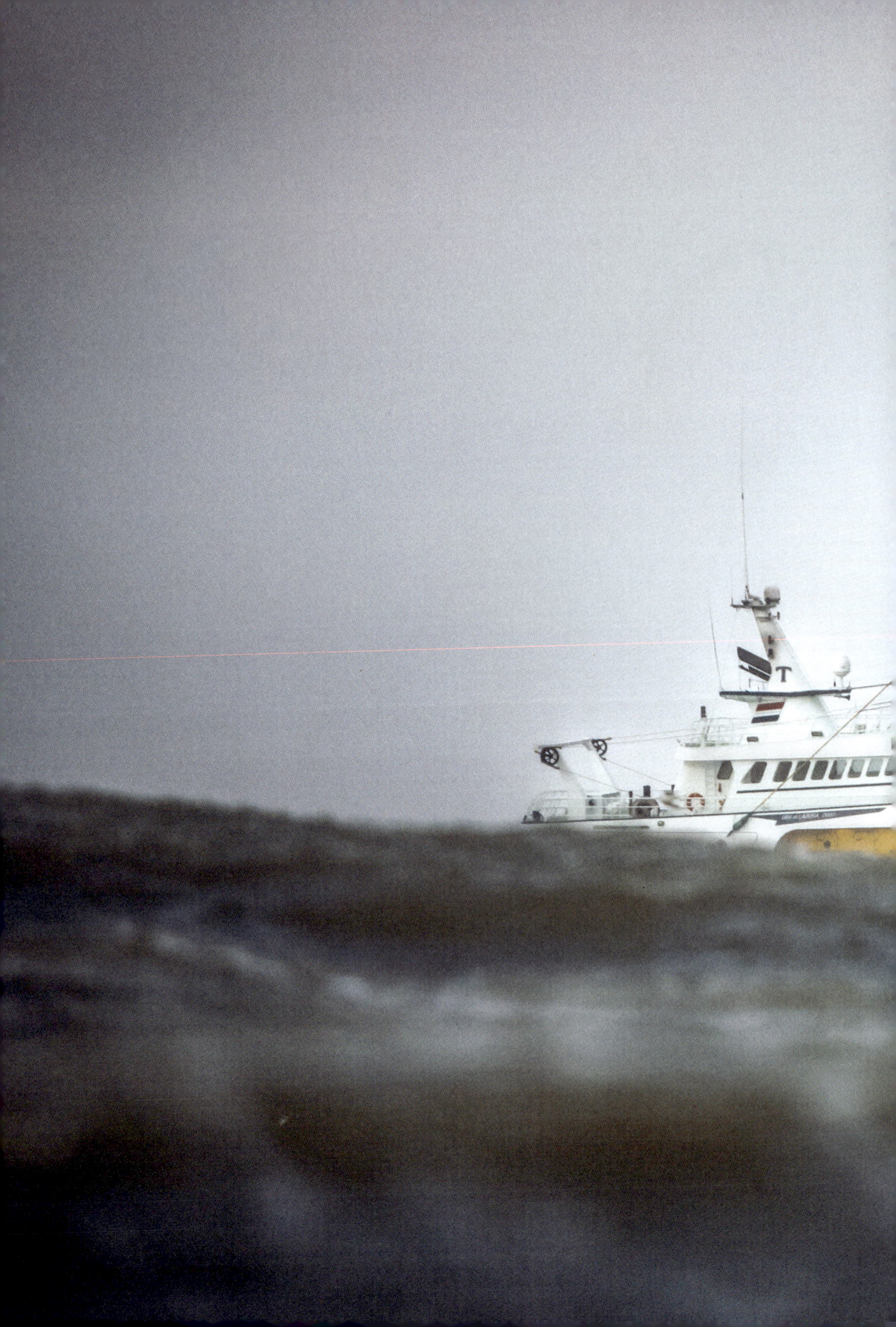

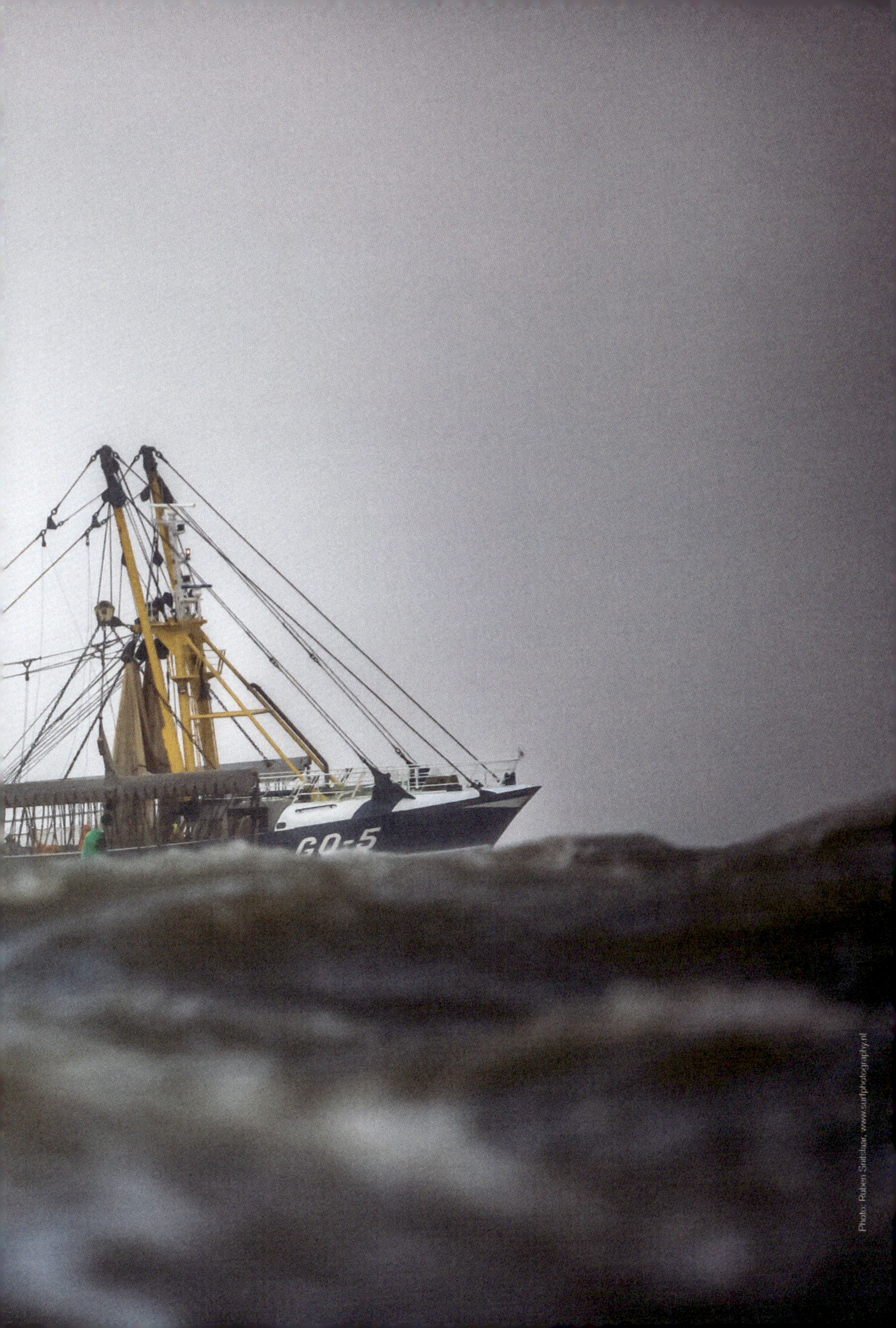

Photo: Ruben Smitshaar, www.surfphotography.nl

Belgium

BELGIUM

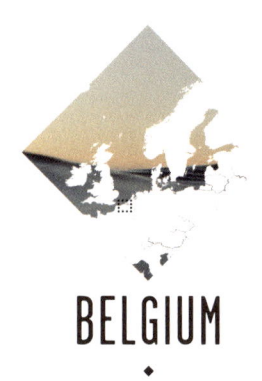

With just over 65 km of coastline, Belgium's not exactly known for the scope of its seaside, and its image suffers from blandness. Adding to the inconspicuous status is the massive use of concrete at the seaside resorts. Although their beaches are wide, white and endlessly sprawling, most sea view is blocked from sight by dull flats and soulless buildings. The first impression can be off-putting, which doesn't inspire you to explore.

But here's the thing: explore anyway! And look beyond what you see on the surface - it's the little things that are grand in their own way. Like the coastal tram, connecting coastal towns between the Dutch and French borders - the country may be small but they've got the longest tramline in the world. Gonna get on it?

And then there's the GR 5A coastal route, a 60 km hiking route along the Belgian seaside, from De Haan to De Panne. At Oostende you can take a free ferry across the harbour from the East Bank to the centre (West Bank). At the East Bank you'll find the area surrounding Fort Napoleon (built in 1813 by the French Emperor) still a bit of no man's land, extraordinary in a country like Belgium where every piece of land has been, or 'has to be' used for human needs, for commercial or whatever purposes. In the near future the whole area around Fort Napoleon is going to change, and we have high hopes it won't change for the worse, since parts of the terrain are earmarked to be given back to nature. That's a pretty big deal that could make for a big step towards a pretty city!

SURFER-TRAVELLER TYPE BELGIUM

◆

You're into nostalgia and love your fries to be Flemish, not French. You don't mind timing your surf sessions, or wait a bit for better circumstances. You like your bars to stay open till crazy-o-clock, because they don't have a legally mandated closing time, and you can't get enough of Tintin. Concrete doesn't bother you too much because you can see beyond the surface.

WORDS AND CONCEPTS THAT MIGHT COME IN HANDY

◆

Adding '*ke*' to words - You're probably aware that Belgium's divided into the Flemish region, Flanders, where Dutch is the common language, and the Brussels-Capital and Walloon regions, where mainly French is spoken. Since we're obviously just dealing with the coast, we're staying in West Flanders, the Dutch-speaking portion. Doesn't really make it easier, does it? Well, just add *–ke* to the end of every word or name you try to pronounce and you're close to being a local!

Amai! - Used frequently to express anything from surprise to disappointment, from utter despair to beyond relief. The closest English equivalent would be 'Wow!'

Zwerfauto - Literally a stray car, used for campervans.

Goedemorgen - Good morning. Belgians are generally a bit more formal (or some would say modest) than their Dutch neighbours. Save *Hi!* or *Hoi!* for your second encounter.

FOOD FACTS

VLAAMSE FRIETEN

We just can't get enough of it. Although commonly known as French fries, the Flemish fries rule! They're king! Usually served at a 'friet kot', in a paper cornet filled to the brim with big thick, crispy fries, topped with rich mayonnaise. Perfection!

WAFELS

The rectangular Belgium waffles are light on the inside, crisp on the outside and utterly irresistible. Best served piping hot and topped with powdered sugar. If they're fresh, as they should be, you won't need strawberries or cream. So don't buy them packaged, get them at their finest from a street vendor.

BEERS

Beer tradition goes way back in Belgium and they don't need to hipsterise their brands and blends by adding the word 'micro' before 'brewery', or 'craft' before 'beer'. Their love for beer is stronger than pursuing a fashionable status. It's not uncommon for a small-scale brewery that comes up with a tasty ale to want to share it, thus outsourcing it to a bigger brewery. Almost all bars and pubs have a dizzying choice of malts, lagers, stouts and beery allsorts.

A BIT ON SURF IN BELGIUM

◆

The first surfer spotted in Belgian waters was most likely the young man who was sent off to the USA by his parents for being a bit of a trouble-maker, later returned with a surfboard and tried his luck in the North Sea. No one knew what he was doing, and he was told off by the police on more than one occasion. The bigger stoke, however, started in the 1970s, mostly with windsurfers beginning to surf on windless days.

Nowadays, some breaks in Belgium can be crowded, much to the disbelief of many, especially those not familiar with the North Sea potential. Most surf clubs serve as surf schools, also for non-members.

So when and where is your best bet for consistent surf in Belgium? Blankenberge and Oostende have the advantage, because of the harbour walls giving wind protection. But in the end it comes down to perfect timing, wind and swell direction, and a great hearty wave of luck. As in 'wind's dropped'! When it comes to suits, neoprene's necessary even on hot summer days: you'll be ok with a 3/2 in summer, 4/3 in late spring and autumn, full everything you can get your body into along with your 5/4/3 in winter.

Need convincing and want a glimpse of North Sea beauty in Belgium? Check the wonderful work of Belgian photographer Wouter Struijf at **w.** wouterstruyf.com

KNOKKE-HEIST
(I)

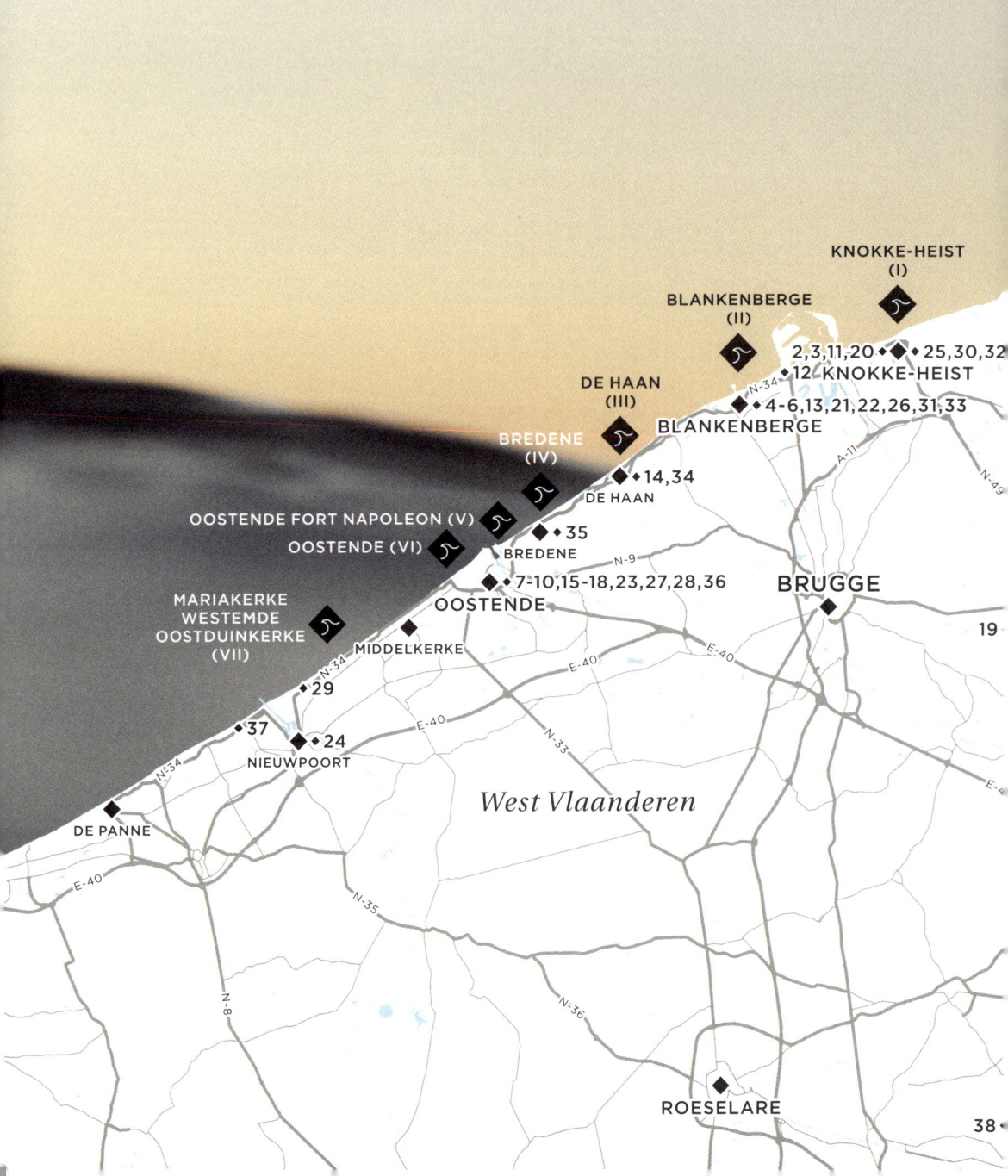

BLANKENBERGE
(II)

♦ 2,3,11,20   ♦ 25,30,32
12   KNOKKE-HEIST

DE HAAN
(III)

♦ 4-6,13,21,22,26,31,33
BLANKENBERGE

BREDENE
(IV)

♦ 14,34
DE HAAN

OOSTENDE FORT NAPOLEON (V)

♦ 35
OOSTENDE (VI)   BREDENE

♦ 7-10,15-18,23,27,28,36
OOSTENDE

BRUGGE

MARIAKERKE
WESTEMDE
OOSTDUINKERKE
(VII)

MIDDELKERKE

♦ 29

♦ 37   ♦ 24
NIEUWPOORT

West Vlaanderen

♦ DE PANNE

♦ ROESELARE

38

WEST VLAANDEREN

What were we thinking…" was our thought, on first impressions, when we began to travel the Belgian coast. We doubted our decision to add it to the Northwest guide. Because to begin with, exploring the seaside resorts, surf breaks and all else in between seemed disappointing. But, first impressions can be deceiving. And although Belgium's seaside isn't exactly prize-winningly beautiful - far from it - it's the charm of the nostalgie, the power of people trying to make some of none, or create poetry and dreams in the midst of a concrete world, that made us see through it. For us, the search for little nuggets of gold was all part of the adventure of unravelling that first layer of ugliness. Trust us, there's underlying beauty to be found.

TRAVEL INFO

There's small, smaller, and België, Belgium. Everything's a skip-hop car, train or bus ride away, if traffic's not a mischief-maker.

BY AIR

International and budget flights fly to/from Zaventem/Brussels.

w. brusselsairport.nl

BY TRAIN/BUS

Public transport for Flanders can be checked and planned at:

w. delijn.be

BY TRAM

Best thing ever, public transport-wise, is the Kust Tram, the coastal tram. Taking you from Knokke-Heist to De Panne down south in a 2-hour tram ride along the seaside. This route's been used for 130 years - nostalgie all the way!

w. dekusttram.be

IN AND AROUND OOSTENDE

Oostende is our best example for not judging a book by its cover. To make the most of it, don't waste time pondering on the whole lot of concrete and badly planned buildings, just open yourself up to what's right about the place. The wide beaches, the long boulevard, and all these tiny details to be found on the remaining old buildings, the art deco houses and quaint eateries and cafés, the many street-art paintings. People of Oostende even united in an organisation called 'Dement Oostende' (demented Oostende), to try and stop the demolition of old buildings and houses, and stimulate renovation. By handing out nominations and a prize for the best initiative to renovate, they hope to encourage more individuals to consider doing just that. Walking along the boulevard, check out the changing expositions at the colonnade. And, did you know Marvin Gaye resided in Oostende, of all places, and it's said he even wrote his classic 'Sexual Healing' here? Learn all about it and ask the tourist office about the guided Marvin Gaye 'Midnight Love Tour'!

Tourist office at Monacoplein 2, 8400 Oostende, and Zeedijk-Knokke 660, 8300 Knokke-Heist.

TO DO

Love anything fifties and sixties? Make sure to check out **Retro Sur Mer**, a vintage seaside festival held every year on the last weekend of July. Think old-timers, rockabilly, beauty boudoirs, vintage market and dance classes.

- **a.** Rotonde, Graaf Jansdijk 18, 8420 Wenduine
- **t.** +32 486 107 047
- **fb.** Retro sur Mer

Zwin Natuur Park (**1**) doesn't do borders. The large nature reserve that's part Holland and part Belgium is referred to as the international airport for birds. All sorts of species fly in and out, stay on a bit or make it their home. At low tide you can cross from one country to the other at the creek separating both at Retranchement (Holland) and Knokke (Belgium). There are numerous observation huts throughout the park, and if you're not looking up at birds, try searching the grounds for ancient, black shark teeth, for sure you'll dig up some! Open all year.

- **a.** Graaf Léon Lippensdreef 8, 8300 Knokke-Heist
- **t.** + 32 5060 7086
- **w.** zwin.be

Having both a lakeside and a wakeside, water sports club **Lakeside Paradise** (**2**) has all sorts of water and board activities. At the lakeside you can SUP, kayak and windsurf, at the wakeside you can choose water skiing, wakeboarding or wakeskating using a cable. The club's got a pro shop and a restaurant to visit before, after and in between sessions. Open all year (in winter only weekends).

- **a.** Duinenwater 41, 8300 Knokke-Heist
- **t.** +32 5060 6035
- **w.** lakesideparadise.be

It's men's talk only, traditional shaving, hot towels, and smart haircuts at **Barbier Tom** (**3**). With over 20 years of experience with shaving, cutting, brushing and sorts you'll be in safe hands at this barber. You do however need to be of the man species. Open all year.

a. Van Bunnenlaan 10, 8300 Knokke-Heist
t. +32 9251 5115
w. barbiertom.be

Blankenberge Skate Park (4) is a concrete skate park with all sorts of obstacles.

a. J. Guilinipad, 8370 Blankenberge

Piers are a pretty rare sight on continental Europe's coastline, which makes this one, and the fact that it was the first of them, rather special. The **Pier of Blankenberge (5)** was built in 1933, followed by the close-second pier in Scheveningen, Holland. And then they seemed to only pop up on islands apart from the odd one that appeared much further afield. Besides being an iconic sight at the beach of Blankenberge, you'll find an exhibition room, auditorium and several restaurants, here, at the pier, that's open all year.

a. Zeedijk 261, 8370 Blankenberge
t. +32 5043 3750
w. belgiumpier.be

We love Belgium for treasuring the old and nostalgic, especially when all else around them is built out of concrete. At **De Lustige Velodroom (6)** you can choose from dozens of 'zotte fietskes', crazy little bicycles, to pedal rounds on their wooden track, with a view of the equally quirky white-washed beach huts. This attraction's been around since 1933 and is pretty unique, to say the least. Open from April to September.

a. Zeedijk 171, 8370 Blankenberge
t. +32 496 257 254
w. delustigevelodroom.be

Jump, bounce, fly, loop-de-loop on the trampolines, or, try a bit of aerial time at the Aerial Yoga, or Antigravity Yoga hammocks at **Hangtime (7)**. Their hangout serves delicious homemade lemonade, healthy snacks, and a choice of coffees and teas. Open all year.

a. Fortstraat 128b, 8400 Oostende
t. +32 5930 2653
w. hangtime.be

Find outdoor skate park **De Velodroom (8)** in Oostende and indoor skate park **De Veiling 2.0 (9)** in Mariakerke. Regular workshops, films and contests are held at De Veiling. Open all year.

a. Iependreef, 8400 Oostende (De Velodroom)
a. Longchamplaan 29, 8400 Mariakerke / Oostende (De Veiling 2.0)
t. +32 5951 0176
fb. Skatepark de Veiling

At open-air museum **Atlantikwall Raversyde (10)**, on the outskirts of Oostende, you'll find an almost intact part of the infamous German defence system, built during WWII. There's a 2-kilometre network of open and underground tunnels and walkways, connecting some 60 constructions, amidst a protected dune reserve. At the bunkers and trenches you'll see a recreated version of the interiors, as it was in WWII. Open all year.

a. Nieuwpoortsesteenweg 636, 8400 Oostende
t. +32 5970 2285
w. raversyde.be

EAT/DRINK/HANG OUT
◆

Get a bit of Californian vibe at **Surfers Paradise (11)**, the large surf bar at the northern end of Knokke-Heist's beach. Stylishly done up with lots of wood, handmade tables resembling old skool boards, and lots of loungarabilia on their terrace such as hammocks, beanbags and a jacuzzi. Perfect spot for sundowners, morning coffees, midday breaks and pre or post surf snacks. Open daily from April to September, from October to March only at weekends. ◆€◆ ◆€€◆

a. Zeedijk-Het Zoute 0, 8300 Knokke-Heist
t. +32 5061 5960
w. surfersparadise.be

At the harbour of Zeebrugge you'll find **'t Werftje (12)**, the oldest café along the coast of Zeebrugge. Have a little taste of what they create with all sorts of North Sea delicacies. Open all year. ♦€€♦

a. Werfkaai 29, 8380 Zeebrugge
t. +32 497 553 010
w. twerftje.be

The lovely **Silversand (13)** tearoom used to be only slightly bigger than this guide, but its popularity grew bigger hence so did its seating. Now there are terraces, and more room, and they can serve a lot more happy customers. Although you'll still see a line for the tasty typical Belgian waffles - which are as big as this guide! Open all year. ♦€♦

a. Zeedijk 89-90-91, 8370 Blankenberge
t. +32 5041 4650
w. silversand.be

Family run **IJsbar Rene (14)** serves artisanal and biological ice-cream. According to ice-cream maker and owner Peter, who runs this ice parlour with his wife Anne, you can choose organic and biological vegetables and all sorts of food, so why not do the same with your ice-cream? Besides making a conscious choice, you'll get an iceliciously tasty treat. Open from Easter to September. ♦€♦

a. Leopoldlaan 22, 8420 De Haan
t. +32 5923 5453
w. ijsbarrene.be

Treat yourself - and your travel companion - to some delectable home-brewed coffee or a choice of teas at coffee roastery and café **De familie Jansen kaffiebar (15)**. They brew up all sorts of variations and creations with coffee and cream, and serve cakes and salads. Your companion will love you (even more) afterwards. ♦€€♦

a. Kapucijnenstraat, 8400 Oostende
t. +32 471 015 436
fb. De familie Jansen kaffiebar

Wow. A whole bar dedicated to bagels! At **Sanseveria (16)** you'll have a choice of them, and salads and quiches, or sweets. Besides an ode to bagels, Sanseveria celebrates the art of decoration and renovation. Set in a former jeweller's they've done this place up with style and taste. Good place to meet locals, having their morning coffee, breakfast or lunch. Open all year. ♦€♦ ♦€€♦

a. Wittenonnenstraat 36, 8400 Oostende
t. +32 5941 1740
w. sanseveria.be

Before and after surf hangout **Frituur Franky (17)** boosts your appetite with 20 different sorts of hamburgers to choose from, vegetarian and vegan included. Served with artisanal Flemish frites (that's right, who'd want French fries when you can have the real deal!). Open all year. ♦€♦

a. Karel Janssenslaan 53, 8400 Oostende
t. +32 5941 2695
w. frituurfranky.be

Whether it's Sunday brunch, salad and sandwich lunch, a hot drink with cakes, late afternoon drinks or dinner, at **Jeanne Nieuwpoort (18)** it's all served with love. Run by young couple Bigel and Stijn who made their dream come through opening up this restaurant and bed and breakfast. Open from March to October. ♦€€♦

a. Kerkstraat 11, 8620 Nieuwpoort
t. +32 477 790 135
w. jeannenieuwpoort.be

SHOP

♦

You'll have to get to Antwerp to visit this shop, but that's not a bad thing. Antwerp's nice, cool, conspicuous, singular. And **Haven (19)** is all the above, with a surfy vibe and a lot of soul. In this beautiful shop you'll find their own and small, independent brands, boards, accessories, books, and beautiful photography - amongst others, work of one of the owners Wouter Struyf, who is a talented shooter. Check them out while in Antwerp, or better yet, make a detour anyway! Open all year.

a. Volkstraat 18, 2000 Antwerpen
t. +32 3298 8192
w. havensurf.com

Le Muzée de l'Amuzette (20) is a concept store, which means as much as you can use, but also buy the chair, table or even the cup you're holding. Find furniture, quirky presents, vintage items. They've a tranquil little courtyard to enjoy your drinks (cocktails!) or lunch, if you want to escape the buzz from Knokke's summer crowds. Open all year.

a. Albertlaan 25, 8300 Knokke
t. +32 5069 1244
w. lamuzette.be

The Breeze Boardshop (21) sells all surf, skate, snow essentials and the clothes and accessories to fit the look. Open all year.

a. Kerkstraat 119, 8370 Blankenberge
t. +32 5068 3696
w. thebreeze.be

Black Jack Skate Shop (22) is owned and run by a skater and it shows in their collection. Skating is at the core of the business, and in addition to a select choice of skate brands and streetwear they support young skate talent. Open all year.

a. Bakkersstraat 40, 8370 Blankenberge
t. +32 474 946 518
w. blackjackshop.be

Oostende's well-stocked local surf shop **Steve's Skateshop (23)** is the place to find out all you need to know about Belgium's surf spots, scene, or gossip. Owner Steve's been around for a while, so he knows a thing or two about boards, leashes, suits and all else you might need a little expert help with. Open all year.

a. Alfons Pieterslaan 93, 8400 Oostende
t. +32 5950 9264
fb. Steves Skateshop

The **Nomad Lifestyle Shop (24)** is one of those places you walk past, walk back, go in and probably won't ever leave empty-handed. Mostly sustainable and carefully selected home décor items, jewellery and bags; often with a story, usually only available in small numbers. And the good news is, it's all pretty affordable. Open all year.

a. Langestraat 95, 8620 Nieuwpoort
t. +32 5859 8010
fb. Nomad Lifestyle Shop

SLEEP

♦

Lakeside Paradise Sleep Inn (25) is a one-of-a-kind youth hostel in that it's situated amidst nature and close to the city. So a perfect spot if you want it all. All rooms are inspired by the best surf spots around the world, the lounge is stylishly decorated with lots of wood, sheepskin, and floor to ceiling windows opening up to the lake. There are shared rooms sleeping from 4 to 12 persons. Open all year. ♦€♦

a. Duinenwater 41, 8300 Knokke-Heist
t. +32 5060 6035
w. lakesideparadise.be/sleep-inn

Bonanza 1 (26) is a friendly family campsite, nothing too special but ideally positioned near beach, village, and nature reserve. Open from April to September. ♦€♦

a. Zeebruggelaan 137, 8370 Blankenberge
t. +32 5041 6658
w. bonanza1.be

Campervans can stay the night at **Servicepunt Urbano Motorhomes (27)**. Not the best place, since it's close to the road and near an airport runway, but, it's a legal place to spend the night in your van. And, who knows, you might need something from their well-stocked campervan shop. Open all year.

a. Torhoutsesteenweg 581, 8400 Oostende
t. +32 5955 4000

Sanseveria B&B (28) is located in a stylishly decorated manor house in Oostende. The welcoming owner (yep, the same one from the bagel shop) gladly helps you find all the right places in the city and beyond to eat, drink and shop. Open all year. ♦€€♦

a. Frère Orbanstraat 43, 8400 Oostende
t. +32 5941 1740
w. sanseveria.be

Campervans can park and stay at **Camperpark Westende (29)**, next to Camping Westende, and use all facilities of the campsite. Open all year. ♦€♦

a. Heidestraat 18, 8434 Westende
t. +32 5823 3254
w. camperparkwestende.be

SURF

For such a small stretch of coast there are a surprising number of options. Maybe not world class, but if your timing coincides with the right tide and swell direction, you may be able to get your surf buzz. It's usually windswell, as with most of the coast around these parts, with the occasional groundswell. The majority of beaches are also popular kite and windsurfing spots. Be aware of strong currents at all breaks.

The backdrop of **Knokke-Heist (I)** gets prettier towards the north. The NNW-facing beach works at all tides with a small to big W-NW-N-NE swell. At Heist a long harbour wall gives protection from SW-W winds. ◆ *All levels/sand/difficult paid parking/restaurants/surf club.* ◆

Blankenberge (II) works best at lower tides with a small to big W-NW-N-NE swell. A large harbour wall at Zeebrugge protects from NE winds, and a smaller wall 'Oosterstaketsel' gives some protection from SW-W winds. The pier at Blankenberge provides a nice set-up for photos… ◆ *All levels/sand/difficult paid parking/restaurants/surf club.* ◆

The NW-facing exposed breaks at **De Haan (III)** (one of the nicest seaside towns along the coast) and **Bredene (IV)** work at all tides with a small to big W-NW-N-NE swell. Bredene has some jetties. ◆ *All levels/sand/easy parking/restaurants/campsites/surf club.* ◆

The never-ending stretch of beach at **Oostende Fort Napoleon (V)** is backed by dunes, and a long harbour wall protects from SW-W winds. Works at all tides with a small to big W-NW-N-NE swell. Expect crowds. ◆ *All levels/sand/easy parking/restaurant.* ◆

SCHOOL RENTAL REPAIR

Oostende (VI), south of the harbour, works at all tides with a small to big W-NW-N-NE swell. The harbour wall here protects from N-NE winds. ◆ *All levels/sand/difficult paid parking/restaurant/surf club.* ◆

Exposed NW-facing **Mariakerke / Westende / Oostduinkerke (VII)** work at all tides with a small to big W-NW-N-NE swell. Some jetties. ◆ *All levels/sand/easy parking/restaurant/surf club.* ◆

Surfers Paradise (30) offers kite, windsurf, SUP and surf lessons, rental of boards and gear, showers, and a restaurant in Californian style. Open daily from April to September, from October to March only at weekends.

a. Zeedijk-Het Zoute 0,
8300 Knokke-Heist
t. +32 5061 5960
w. surfersparadise.be

The **O'Neill Beachclub (31)** offers surf and SUP lessons and rentals. Their large beach club serves as a relaxed hangout. Open every day from Easter to October.

a. Zeedijk 245, 8370 Blankenberge
t. +32 5069 4313
w. oneillbeachclub.com

At **Anemos Beachclub (32)** you can choose a lot of active options, besides surf and SUP lessons, there's blokarting, kite-buggy, wakeboarding and sea kayaking, a bouldering area, skate ramp and slacklines. And a restaurant to indulge in advance of or after your active fun. Open every day from Easter to October.

a. Anemonenlaan, 8301 Knokke-Heist
t. +31 5051 0078
w. anemos.be

Flow and Soul (33) is shaper and renowned glasser Angelo de Meulenaere (also known as Angke - there's that

BELGIUM

'Ke' we were telling you about). His smart and smooth craft's so well respected around the world that shapers from all over ask him to come over to do their glassing work (think Ryan Lovelace, the Campbell brothers). Angelo shapes custom resin tinted boards in alternative shapes, and does repairs as well.

a. Kustlaan 174 A, 8380 Zeebrugge
t. + 32 495 892 198
w. flowandsoul.be

Watersport and beachclub **Windhaan** (**34**) have all kinds of water sports on offer, surf, SUP, catamaran sailing, kayaking, beach sailing, kite and windsurfing. At their tastefully decorated beach club you can shower, hang out and have a snack and drink. Open all year.

a. Zeedijk-De Haan 50, 8421 De Haan
t. +32 5944 1624
w. windhaan.be

If you become a member for the day at **Twins Club** (**35**) you can use the showers and other facilities. They offer surf lessons, surf camps and coaching and SUP yoga. Open from Easter to October.

a. Strandpost 1, 8450 Bredene
t. +31 5932 0313
w. twinsclub.be

Craftsman Oscar from **Surfer's Hell** (**36**) repairs and fixes your dings, and makes unique, classic-style custom boards, adapted to surf the north sea waves. Open all year.

a. 8400 Oostende
t. +32 487 175 884
w. surfershell.be

Surfclub Windekind (**37**) sits in a big wooden clubhouse, offering rental and lessons for surf, SUP, kite and windsurfing. Open from Easter to October.

a. Zuidenwindhelling 1,
   8670 Oostduinkerke
t. +32 5823 1919
w. surfclub-windekind.be

Not quite near the waves, but run with passion for ocean sports, **Freestyle Shop Waterloo** (**38**), offers all that watermen and waterwomen could wish for. Find surf and SUP gear, ocean lifestyle fashion, accessories, books, and yoga apparel. Open all year. .

a. 87 Chaussée de Bruxelles,
   1410 Waterloo (near Brussels)
t. +32 2354 3808
w. freestyle-shop.be

c-skins

c-skins.com

SEASIDE LOCALS: MARIJKE VAN BIERVLIET EN GIJS VANHEE

◆

Although they met in Belgium's quaint historic town Mechelen, landlocked and working steady jobs, Marijke and Gijs' shared passion for travelling and the ocean - among many other things - took them on the road shortly after their first kiss.

> *"Travelling slowly gives us the opportunity to accept the road as a destination on its own."*

They're still travelling, and living, in a beautiful 1987 Mercedes 508. Their garden stretching as far as the van can take them, usually alongside the ocean. "Bit by bit we enhanced our tiny rolling home and hit the road for good in December 2015." Since then they've travelled Norway, Sweden, Denmark, Germany, Holland, Belgium, Wales, Scotland, France, Spain, Portugal, Sardinia, Morocco, and all roads in between, taking them there. Artist and illustrator Gijs grew up in Mechelen. His urge to draw developed from a young age. His work is shown at several expositions and he makes huge wall paintings on commission. He's one of those creative souls, making constructions and finding solutions for whatever surfaces, no matter what the material; which comes in handy, living in a van. The only thing distracting him from his creativity, he says, is the ocean and being in the water with his longboard. It humbles him: "The way water and waves move, never the same, the power of nature and the knowledge that a wave you've ridden comes from a swell born miles away gives a feeling of huge respect." Photographer Marijke was born in South Africa but her family moved back to Belgium a few years after she was born. Both cultures added to her curious and adventurous nature. As a teenager she happily explored forests and cities with her camera. It's her medium, enabling her to look at life in a different way. For Gijs, she makes the perfect travel companion: "Her camera's stuck to her hands. Besides that Marijke finds joy in many other things. From paragliding to trail running, singing, playing the guitar, studying or working as a massage therapist."

Travelling and living in a van made them confront the habit of being in control. "We used to take life way too seriously, on the scale of succeeding and career-wise, worrying about long-term plans. Major problems of full-time living in a van can be stupid things like finding a toilet, or a quiet place to sleep. For us, it made the big ambition stuff a bit overrated. So many unexpected things happen while travelling, and things never turn out the way you imagined. Our van moves slow. We're forced to travel at a maximum cruise speed of 85 km/h. Travelling slow gives us the opportunity to be in places where we'd never have been, and to accept the road as a destination on its own."

Marijke and Gijs travel with a vague plan and according to their mood or sudden events. There's always a small chance to meet them on the road. Meanwhile, you can check them out at:

w. gijsvanhee.be / **w.** marijkevanbiervliet.com / **ig.** Gijs Vanhee and Changement Decor

BELGIUM

Read more about Gijs and Marijke at:
w. ilovetheseaside.com/stories

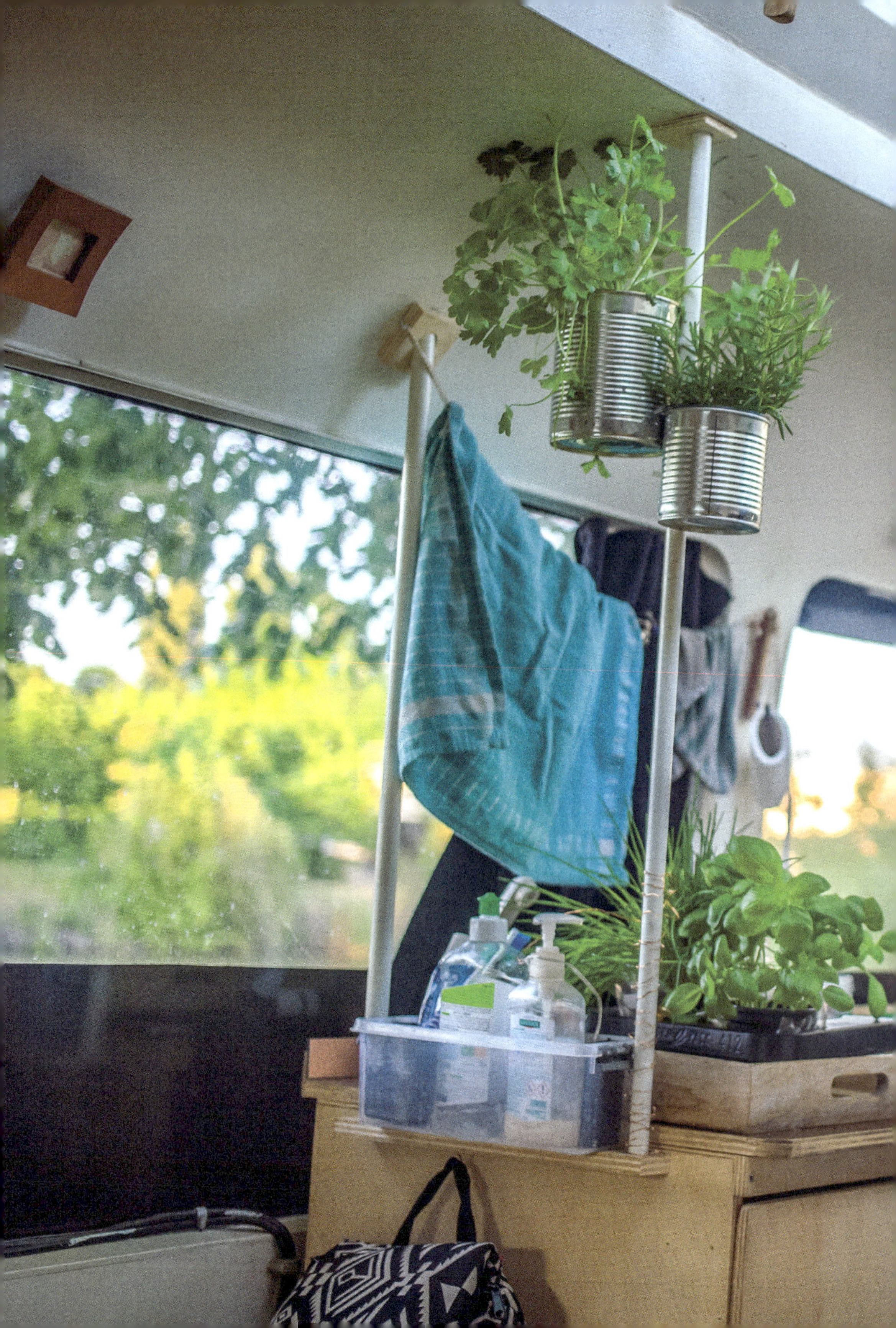

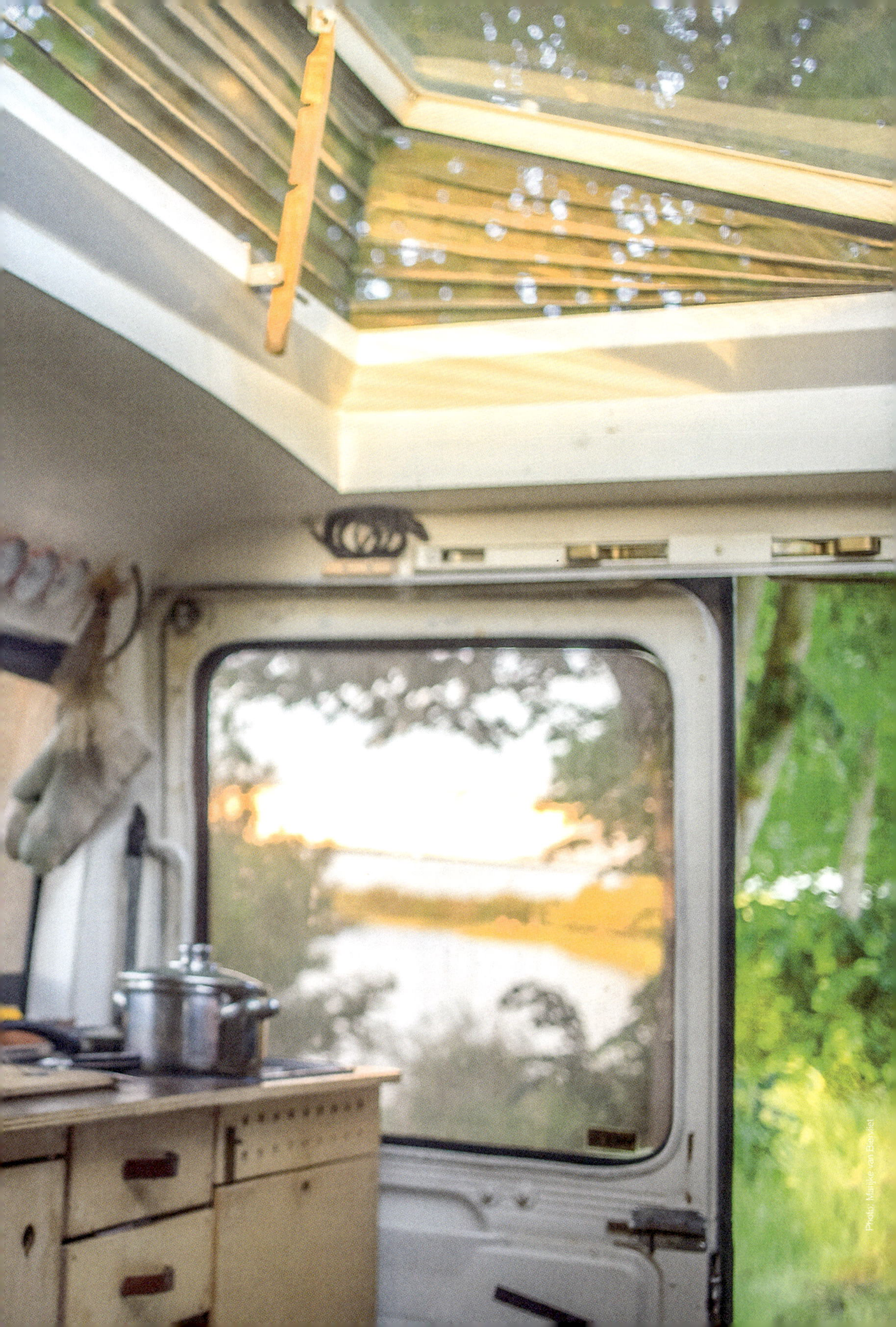

France

NORMANDY

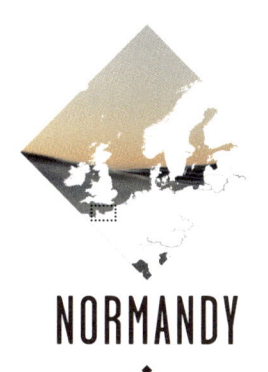

Our guide ends here in Normandy. The first edition, I Love the Seaside - The Surf & Travel Guide to Southwest Europe, begins in Brittany. So if you're the lucky owner of both editions, you're able to keep on travelling with us, from Norway all the way down to the south of Portugal and Spain!

Previously divided into Upper and Lower Normandy, Normandy's now one region. It's helpful for us, however, to split the coast into two parts. The northern stretch, between Le Tréport and Le Havre, offers astounding bays and cliffs along the Côte d'Albâtre.

The Côte d'Albâtre (Alabaster Coast) begins at Le Tréport and greets the waves of the English Channel with its steep chalk-white cliffs and sea-made rock formations all the way to Le Havre. Colourful houses dotted on the shore seem like toys next to the great pillars and arches that are carved out of the cliffs, and the dissolved rock gives a milky-white colour to the water which makes all even more fantasy-like.

Heading west, a completely different feeling from Honfleur in the direction of the Cotentin peninsula, with clusters of chic seaside towns and lovely bays. Then at the peninsula we reunite with a wild beauty; marshlands and dunes set on another (possibly the most of all?) rugged section of French coast.

SURFER-TRAVELLER TYPE NORMANDY

◆

You're totally into strong-smelling cheese and can see all kinds of animals in rock formations, besides elephants. You like your surfing playfield to be clean, a chance to get a tête-a-tête with dolphins, pitch your tent in a farmers' field, and just can't get enough of oysters, small harbours and woodwork houses.

WORDS AND CONCEPTS THAT MIGHT COME IN HANDY

◆

Bonjour! Bonsoir! - Bonjour can be used all day, around dinner time you start saying bonsoir.

Comme d'habitude - As usual, the same as always. Used in your new fav café where you always order the same. Or arriving at a spot at the wrong tide. As always.

Il n'y a pas un chat! - Arriving at the spot on time and seeing no one's out!

Qu'est-ce que tu bouines? - What's up? What are you up to? The verb bouiner is originally from Normandy and is the equivalent to not being or doing anything particularly productive.

Marée haute, marée basse - High tide, low tide. Extremely handy to know in these regions.

FOOD FACTS

CIDER

Ah, French and food, how very creative and foremost, economical they are when it comes to using each and every bit of the product. There's cow's cheek and pig's stomach, known as local delicacies, but they just didn't bring up the appetite in us… So we stuck with what we really loved, their cider! The countryside's dotted with apple orchards, picked for making scrumptious calvados, apple brandy, and cider.

CREAMY CHEESE

With so many vaches qui rit, smiling cows, it's pretty obvious there'll be cheese made from their milk at some point. Especially creamy cheese, those Normandy chefs love it creamy. If, in general, the word 'Normande' is added to any dish, it means it's creamy! Camembert and Boursin being the most renowned, or the delicious Pont l'Evêque.

A BIT ON SURF IN NORMANDY

♦

There's no doubt about the fact that surfing in France started in Biarritz in the late 1950s, and moved north to Vendée and Brittany some years later, but nobody seems to know when exactly the first surfers were seen in Normandy. They're there now, that's for sure!

Normandy's easily accessible for surfers from Paris, Belgium and Holland, who can check charts and take a short escape without having to book tickets or drive for days. Although some of the breaks in Normandy suffer crowds, it's still the southern areas of France that steal the limelight when it comes to fame and, let's face it, consistency. Which in the end is not a bad thing; saving Normandy's breaks from (yet another) surf camp invasion and still having that attraction of hope (p p please let the wind drop) and surprise (forecast said no, but look, waves say yay!).

So what's your best bet on consistent surf in Normandy? The long stretches of beach from Siouville-Hague and Le Rozel along the Cotentin peninsula are facing west, so receive almost all available swell. There are peaks to choose from, parking's easy and the vibe's pretty good most of the time. If you're keen on a breath-taking backdrop of steep white chalk cliffs, and weird rock formations, head for Yport and Étretat.

As for your tenue-d'eau: in the summer to early autumn months a 3/2 will do just fine. Late autumn and late spring a 4/3 and probably some boots keep you warm enough, whereas winter requires the full 5/4/3 hooded, booted and gloved version of yourself.

WISSANT
(I)

CAP GRIS-NEZ
(II)

WIMEREUX
(III)

LE TRÉPO

DIEPPE

YPORT
(IV)   FÉCAMP
ÉTRETAT   ◆2,5 ◆ ◆1,3,4,12,13,18,20
(V)
L'ANSE DU BRICK   ◆7,21
(VII)   YPORT
BARFLEUR   ◆6,8-11,14,16,17,19,22
◆43-45,51,59 ◆◆56   ÉTRETAT
SIOUVILLE   ◆41,42,57,58,60   LE HAVRE
(VIII)   CHERBOURG   TROUVILLE   ROUEN
          ◆52,53,61,68,69   (VI)   ◆23
         SIOUVILLE ◆38-40,50,55   HONFLEUR
LE ROZEL   ST VAAST   ST AUBIN   ◆24,25,67
(IX)   ◆54,62,63,70   ◆29   DEAUVILLE/
         ◆46,47 ◆26,27,30-37   TROUVILLE
                         ◆28
                      BAYEUX CAEN

                                Normandy

                ◆71

GRANVILLE
(X)   ◆GRANVILLE

ST MALO ◆48,49,64,65
      LE MONT ST MICHEL

NORMANDY

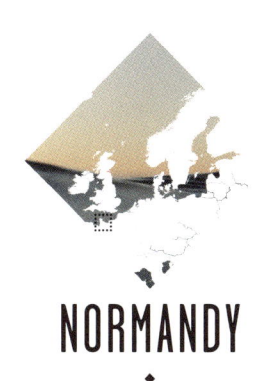

While sitting on the cliffs of Étretat, looking at the beach below, baguette and camembert in hand, a feeling of serenity takes hold. Freedom! The feeling that you can go wherever you want, do whatever tickles your fancy. Lush green surroundings, pure nature, and everything looking a little more rugged than your usual sandwich spot.

And how better to embrace that feeling than to think about the inextricable link between this region, especially its coastline, and the Second World War. It's hard not to imagine times past as you take in the bunkers and broken tanks, monuments and memorials, and the seemingly endless rows of soldiers' graves; all are poignant reminders of the D-Day Landings and the ensuing battle to liberate Europe. All are testament to the strength of people in general; and the people of this region in particular, who live with constant reminders of war all around, and yet rather than feel haunted by them… remember how it feels to be free. Vive la Liberté!

TRAVEL INFO

The obvious choice is to take your car, campervan, (or caravan or motorhome) to Normandy. They remain the most practical options if you want to be free to explore all the nooks and crannies of this captivating corner of the continent. Or get on your bike. If you can combine the two, even better!

BY TRAIN

From Saint-Lazare station in Paris, you can take an intercity service to Caen (2 hrs) and then another train from Caen to Cherbourg (1,5 hrs).

w. oui.sncf

BY BUS

Bus services in the region are operated by Transbus.

w. transbus.org

Public transport info, including operations, timetables, routes etc.

w. commentjyvais.fr

IN AND AROUND DIEPPE

Le Tréport gives a great indication of what to expect from Normandy's coastal towns, though they're by no means the same, each with its own distinct je ne sais quoi. Cruising alongside the river towards the harbour, you'll stumble upon a little lighthouse that sets a jolly mood with its charactful demeanour; it seems to be welcoming new arrivals, bidding farewell to those setting sail, sitting cheerfully looking out to sea. The atmosphere is exactly that; fishermen patiently staring at fishing rods on the wooden pier, tourists taking selfies, and the cafés setting out their menus to announce the specials of the day. During the Belle Époque, this coast was flooded with affluent visitors, artists and royals, especially from Paris and London. The seaside was absolutely en vogue, and Dieppe was the place to mingle. Until the end of the 1930s, when 'ordinary people' discovered the place, and the elite soireed southward to Deauville and Trouville. The Dieppe of today, with medieval church and centuries-old chateau alongside war memorials, a wide boulevard along its pebbly beach, several harbours and a grand marina, is better known as the first of France's fishing ports for scallops. And you'll find plenty of those on the menus.

Tourist office at Pont Jehan Ango, 76200 Dieppe.

TO DO

Thanks to a hundred kilometres of marked hiking routes and the Véloroute du Littoral bike routes along the shore, a favourable option is to spend your holiday **biking and hiking**. Pick a starting point anywhere along the coast and you're on your way to a great tour already - whether it's a long hike in sturdy shoes or a quick climb from the beach to the top of the cliffs for lunch with a 'littoraly' mindblowing view.

The **coastal path (1)** between Dieppe and Fécamp passes through a number of little villages, such as the bijou Sotteville-sur-Mer and Veules-des-Roses, offering cutesy little bays. Alternatively, opt for the somewhat speedier D925, which takes you wandering by estates, fields, and a farm here and there. Towards Fécamp, the route descends into a valley between two cliffs then back up a bit to **Cap Fagnet (2)**.

Here breathtaking views of Fécamp and the coast and ocean beyond make the climb worth the effort. Walk around the fortifications of a Gallic castle, visit a chapel dedicated to seafarers, or stop in for a well-deserved drink at the hotel. There's a small wooden bar if you're in need of a quick snack before you continue on.

Tourism Office at Quai Sadi Carnot, 76400 Fécamp.

After all your cliffpath hiking, perhaps get an invigorating foot massage or a relaxing Ayurvedic massage at **Tapovan** (**3**) - an oriental oasis offering massage and yoga classes. The resort's in a forest close to the cliffs of Caux, within walking distance of Petites Dalles beaches. If you get a taste for being pampered, you can spend a whole week on an Ayurvedic retreat.

a. Route d'Anneville,
   76540 Sassetot-le-Mauconduit
t. +33 235 292 021
w. tapovan.com

Pete the Monkey Festival (**4**) in Saint-Aubin-sur-Mer has got to be one of Europe's best summer festivals. A small-scale festival, colourful and trés cool, just a stone's throw from the beach, with a family feeling during the day and then lively up yourself in the evening. DJs and dance, theatre, workshops, food trucks, and live music on three stages. The artists play a variety of rock, pop, reggae, and folk, and most hail from France or the UK (Saint-Aubin lies directly facing the hip music scene of Brighton) and are generally unknown to the wider public. The festival's getting busier each year and organisers are keen to keep it small, so get your tickets well in advance. You can camp on site, there's a special camping area for families. And good to know: a percentage of proceeds supports a monkey sanctuary in Bolivia. Not sure who Pete is though... find out and let us know? The three-day festival takes places every year in mid-July.

w. petethemonkeyfestival.com

Woody Park (**5**) is a treetop adventure park with scavenger hunts, inflatables, paintball, silly Olympics (for adult/stag do kinda parties) and - perhaps best of all - you can spend the night in a tent that's hanging from a tree! Open daily from April to September (and in French school holiday periods between October and March).

a. 198 Avenue du Maréchal de Lattre de Tassigny, 76400 Fécamp
t. +33 235 108 483
w. woody-park.com

You can book a private hike or join a group with **Natterra's** (**6**) nature guides. Hikes take about two hours and are easy to do, which makes them suitable for children, too. The guide introduces you to the surroundings of Étretat and tells you everything there is to know about the geology, flora and fauna of the area.

a. 29 Route de la Plaine,
   76280 La Poterie-Cap d'Antifer
t. +33 235 282 157 / 682 778 755
w. natterra.fr

We suspect we're not the only ones from whom **Yport** (**7**) has stolen hearts. A cutesy village with a dainty little bay, entirely surrounded by cliffs on top of which grazing sheep seem blissfully unaware of the 100-metre tall cliff face only a few steps away. Milky-white water highlights colourful fishing boats dotting the pebble beach, and striped wooden beach huts behind them offer chips, crêpes, and ice-cream. There's also the option to rent a bike or - even better - borrow a book from the library. You'll find hiking paths across the cliffs all the way to Étretat, or to Fécamp.

Just to the west of Yport lies **Étretat** (**8**), another dreamy tiny town. Famous for its bow-shaped cliffside, which looks like an elephant trunk dipping into the water, you'll spot that easily on the west side of the bay - no 'hidden eye' type illusion so no straining to see it. It's a popular tourist spot, so don't expect a sleepy hideaway. If you want some solitary time with a killer view, take a bit of a hike-climb up to walk around the headland, there are walkways from the boulevard in the centre-ville.

A favourite way to inspect the thirsty elephant is to take a SUP tour with **Aloha Étretat** (**9**), along the rocky coves out to the 'Aguille'- the spot protruding from the water next to the trunk (**t.** +33 609 012 230). **Sailing club Voiles et Galets** (**10**) offers sailing classes in catamarans or 'optimists', small sailboats. Both can be found on the beach. Open from April to mid-November.

w. voilesetgalets.com

Looking for some adrenaline-boosting activity in Étretat: hang out in adventure park for all ages, **Parc Étretat Aventure** (**11**), they've got parcours through treetops, ziplining, and covered climbing walls for all levels. You can also stay overnight in simple chalets or hang for real in their 10 metre high tree huts! Open all year, opening hours reduced between October and April.

a. Le Chateau du Bois, 1632 Route de Gonneville, 76790 Les Loges
t. +33 235 298 445
w. etretat-aventure.fr

EAT/DRINK/HANG OUT
◆

Just west of Dieppe along the river Veules lies the small village Veules-les-Roses. British couple, David and Marilyn Eva, created the perfect combination of gallery and tea garden here: **Atelier 2** (**12**). The tea garden's reminiscent of the south of England, with green grass and rose bushes, tea served in proper teacups, scones and delicious tarts. While the setting feels English, it wasn't really intentional and, except for the British tea, whatever you indulge in has been made using ingredients from local farmers and businesses; something that's very important to Marilyn. If you happen to be around in winter, Marilyn uses the quiet months to share some British dishes in her cooking classes! Open whenever the weather allows it in spring, summer, and autumn. ◆€€◆

a. 2 Rue du Bouloir, 76980 Veules-les-Roses
t. +33 235 970 795 / 638 212 737
w. atelier2veules.com

Esta'frites (**13**) is just what everybody needs around the corner from their place. What a lovely chip shop! Located on the boulevard of Veulettes-sur-Mer, drop in to be wowed by the home-made food. Potatoes are locally sourced; peeled, cut, and cooked on site before they go in the fryer. Fresh sauces are prepared daily, with thyme, basil, camembert, ooh la la! The brochettes (skewers) are prepared with organic vegetables and pork from pigs that have been fed on a natural diet. The wines and ciders are organic too, and they brew their own beer! In summer, the owners organise small concerts outside. Open from April to September. ◆€◆

a. 2 Rue du Pont Rouge, 76450 Veulettes-sur-Mer
t. +33 610 895 033
w. estafrites.com

If you're after leisurely ambience rather than a fast-food dash, tea salon **La Dame au Chapeau** (**14**) offers tea, hot chocolate, cake, soup, and 'gourmet lunch' with a bay view or on the terrace. Take your time, enjoy the jolly backdrop of eclectic objects: paintings, pots, mirrors. There's something to marvel at both inside and outside. Open from Thursday to Sunday, closed during winter. ◆€◆

a. 3 Rue du Clos Masure, 76790 Bénouville
t. +33 6 76 824 999
w. ladameauchapeau.com

EAT/DRINK/HANG OUT

◆

While the region may not have the hippest shops, you'll find a variety of local, artisanal or just nice, old-fashioned products at the following addresses:

Le Tréport has a **covered fish market** (**15**), and even if you don't go there to buy fish, it makes for a pleasant nosey if you're curious about what the sea provides for this region. Open year round.

- **a.** Place de la Poissonnerie,
  76470 Le Tréport

Le Vieux Marche (**16**), in the centre of Étretat, is located in a renovated 19th-century timber building that's beautifully typical of the region. Inside, you'll find two floors full of everything a tourist's heart desires: cast-iron patio chairs, iron Pernod advertisements, striped jumpers and postcards, among other stuff. The building itself is a lot more interesting than the shopping. An added bonus is the open-air vintage market, held every Thursday around Le Vieux Marche.

- **a.** Place du Marechal Foch, 76790 Étretat

La Mer a Boire (**17**) is your spot for tasty products from the region. Tinned fish, jam, cider, calvados, products made from seaweed, coarse sea salt, biscuits, as well as herbs, sauces, and cookbooks, so you can give your home-cooked food a special French twist.

- **a.** 1 Place du General de Gaulle,
  76790 Étretat
- **w.** mer-a-boire.com

SLEEP

◆

Villa Argonne (**18**) consists of four lovely cottages in a large garden, each with its own distinctive character, warm and natural but far from twee. Their colours, tall ceilings and large windows give all a light and airy feel. There's a spa consisting of hot tub with massage jets, a sauna and a hammam. Guests are welcome to use the bikes provided. ◆€€€◆

- **a.** 64 Route d'Offranville,
  76860 Ouville-la-Rivière
- **t.** +33 698 819 265
- **w.** gite-spa-normandie.fr/
  homepage-villa-argonne

If bricks and stones don't float your boat, check out the houseboats of **Au Fil de l'Eau** (**19**)! Luxurious huts drifting on a river in a green valley, not far from the sea. The houses each have a creative name, such as 'Je n'suis pas du matin' or 'La terre est ronde pour ceux qui s'aiment'. You can rent them for a romantic trip for two, but also with 16 of your best friends. Get in a rowing boat in the morning or fish from your patio. Open year round. ◆€€€◆

- **a.** 691 Rue Cauchoise, 76400 Colleville
- **t.** + 33 607 965 995
- **w.** giteaufildeleau.fr

You won't have any issue finding places to camp in this region, which is the cheapest way to spend the night after all. We've chosen a couple of spots for their cosy close to the sea character or simply because they're *très sympa*.

Campervans (**20**) can park for the night at Plage Ouest in Saint-Valery-en-Caux, close to the lighthouse. The spots are narrow and therefore not suitable for large vehicles, but it has all the facilities you need, the baker drops by in the morning, and you're right by the sea. ◆€◆

- **a.** Quai d'Aval, Plage Ouest,
  76460 Saint-Valery-en-Caux

Campsite **Le Rivage** (**21**) in Yport boasts views of the sea and the cliffs. Apart from the camping spots, you can rent mobile homes and two gîtes. Open from April to early November. ◆€◆ ◆€€◆

- **a.** Rue André Toutain, RD 211,
  76111 Yport
- **t.** +33 235 273 378
- **w.** camping-lerivage.com

If you want to sleep in a real Mongolian yurt, a tipi, or in an authentic Normand guesthouse, **Yourte Étretat** (**22**) is the right place for you. Outside, you can pet Serge and Moumoute, the llama and the sheep, and inside, you can warm up by the fireplace or laze in the comfortable beds. Well maintained, with an original design. The yurt and tipi are available for rent in July and August, the chambre d'hôtes is open year round. And the owners are proud to tell you that Eva Longoria has previously stayed in the yurt! ◆€€◆

- **a.** 141 Impasse de la Haye d'Etigue,
  76790 Les Loges
- **t.** +33 620 746 315
- **w.** yourte-etretat.com

IN AND AROUND THE D-DAY BEACHES

Via the Pont de Normandie, you'll cross the Seine estuary. That alone is worth the trip. The more than two kilometre-long suspension bridge links Le Havre with Honfleur. At its highest point, it's 60 metres above the Seine. (You can park your car by the tollbooth and walk a bit on the bridge). Honfleur, the first port after the bridge, appears to be one of the most painted towns of Normandy. From there, you can access a beautiful coastal path to Trouville-sur-Mer and Deauville, two towns on the Touque estuary. Separated only by the water, the two towns actually look like one big town, as they reflect each others' atmosphere and architecture. Deauville is the prettier sister, while Trouville is a little more easy-going, featuring some very jolie streets behind the boulevard along the river. Further southwest: marvellous sand beaches, some of them surrounded by dunes, while others are situated right by a rock formation or at the foot of a village. Looking at how peaceful the coast is now, it's hard to imagine those days of battle, though a multitude of monuments, museums, and cemeteries commemorate the lives lost and freedom gained. This sense of commemoration is also reflected in the names of the local beaches, such as Omaha, Utah, and Juno Beach - code names used by the Allied Forces as they prepared for the D-Day Landings.

TO DO

Honfleur (23) is a beautiful and very touristy town you can walk through in no time, where a break for a coffee or wine on the terrace can easily cost half your day's budget. The town does, however, have a lovely holiday atmosphere even on a cool autumn day. Take a walk around the harbour, along the timbered houses and small squares. For those familiar with, or interested in, the composer and pianist Eric Satie, there's a small museum dedicated to him (a. 76 Boulevard Charles V) that's worth a visit. The audio guided tour tells you everything about his life with music, stories, and jokes.

Tourism office at Quai Lepaulmier, 14600 Honfleur.

Deauville (24) has always been favoured by the rich and famous. Its golf courses, horseracing, and annual film festival make sure it stays popular with high society. At the beginning of the 20th century, most coastal towns were still dominated by affluent ladies in corsets and long dresses hiding under large parasols, but in Deauville, in 1913, a young lady from Paris changed the ways of seaside fashion for good. Designer Gabrielle Chanel, also known as Coco - already popular with the beau monde and the young Parisian elite - opened a boutique shop in the town and brought her well-known sporty, somewhat androgynous, and nonchalant style to the coast; striped jumper, trousers, short hair. "I gave the female body back its freedom", she stated herself. It comes as no surprise that Deauville rivals the designer shops of

Paris or London. If you're in the mood to shop, but Vuitton, Chanel, and Dior are one step too far, there are two shopping streets you may want to try: Rue Desiré-le-Hoc and Rue Eugène Colas.

Trouville (25), on the other side of the water, is secretly our favourite. It's more laidback, with a cluttered street here and there, and inviting bars along the river. But you should make up your own mind, park the car by the river, and explore both towns. Don't forget to check out the station close to the bridge, a tremendous building from 1863!

You'd have a hard time visiting all of them, but there's one war memorial and cemetery we want to recommend.

The **Normandy American Cemetery (26)** will give you a vivid idea of just how serious and vast the D-Day operations were. It's not necessarily the cemetery itself - even though it's quite a haunting scene to see hundreds of crosses arranged in straight lines. The visitors' centre with its objects, stories, photos, and films will show you the hell, but also the heroes who ultimately led the Allied Forces to victory. It will also allow you to draw a direct comparison to other war zones and the impact war has on people and their surroundings.

a. 14710 Colleville-sur-Mer
 (clearly signposted)
w. abmc.gov

If you want to see the beaches from a different perspective, you can go (tandem) paragliding with **Elementair (27)**. No experience required, an instructor accompanies you.

a. 40 Quai du Baron Gérard,
 14520 Port-en-Bessin
t. +33 687 291 502
w. parapente-normandie.com

Get lost in a cornfield, get caught in a gigantic safety net, zipline, or rock-climb in the open air at the **Bayeux Aventure (28)** farm. Open from April to September.

a. Ferme de Rabodange, 14400 Cussy
t. +33 624 111 816
w. bayeux-aventure.fr

EAT/DRINK/HANG OUT

There are so many good fish restaurants and small brasseries with such a tasty variety of recipes on the menu that it's best to just pick whichever restaurant looks appealing to you (or has the nicest terrace). A very small selection:

On the boulevard of Saint-Aubin-sur-Mer you'll find several restaurants with terraces right by the water. **Le Charleston (29)** is just a bit more special than the rest, thanks to its crazy interior. The place is nicely decorated with a number of French retro objects. ◆€€◆

- **a.** 4 Digue Favreau, Rue Gambetta, 14750 Saint-Aubin-sur-Mer
- **t.** + 33 231 97 26 66
- **fb.** Le Charleston

La Barak'a (30) is a simple restaurant offering good food at a sensible price. It's a stone's throw away from the beach and you can easily park your car there. ◆€€◆ ◆€€€◆

- **a.** 3 Route du Debarquement, 14960 Saint-Come-de-Fresne
- **t.** +33 231 211 570
- **fb.** La Barak'a

SHOP

Salon de thé and boutique **La Compagnie Ordinaire de la Mer (31)** is somewhat a pop-up shop, run by the same couple who own Les Filles du Bord de Mer (see Sleep). Seeing as that means they don't have the time to be in the shop every day, they opted for a pop-up concept. We hope you'll happen to be around when the shop is open because it really is a beautiful one: decorative interior design items, often made by designers from the region, books, and toys. In the courtyard, they serve tea, coffee, and brunch, and sometimes they organise unexpected events, such as a restaurant night with a special chef, or they open the shop on a bank holiday or for an extra business day and invite artists and musicians. Open on Sundays, during holidays, and sometimes upon request.

- **a.** 6 Rue de Bayeux, 14520 Port en Bessin
- **t.** +33 777 222 470
- **w.** compagnie-mer.com

SLEEP

Lodgings in this region are charming but pricey, which is why camping is a great alternative. **Camping Les Bas Carreaux (32)** is a small-scale, affordable campsite with all necessary facilities. A baker comes by every morning delivering warm baguettes and croissants. Open from May to September. ◆€◆

- **a.** 20 Rue du Général Ezanno, 14117 Arromanches les Bains
- **t.** +33 688 332 496
- **w.** campinglesbascarreaux.com

Campervans (33) can park for free (even overnight) in Longues-sur-Mer. You'll have a phenomenal view from the rocks, and it's a quiet spot (with a battalion of cannons behind it). There are no facilities.

- **a.** Rue de la Mer, 14400 Longues sur Mer

The owners of pop-up shop La Compagnie Ordinaire de la Mer bring you eight tastefully designed lodgings, **Les Filles du Bord de Mer (34)**, right by the sea in the fishing village of Port-en-Bessin, A fantastic place to stay, even if just to get inspiration for a redo of your interior. The design follows a seaside theme and is rustic, yet light and bright. Four of the homes are right by the sea, the other four flats are in the village with a view of the harbour. Suitable for families or couples. Open year round except for January. ◆€€◆ ◆€€€◆

- **a.** Port-en-Bessin Huppain
- **t.** +33 777 222 470
- **w.** lesfillesduborddemer.com

Glamping **La Ferme de la Folivraie** (**35**) offers fully equipped tents. The ferme is a small organic farm with animals such as goats, sheep, donkeys, rabbits, and turkeys that potter around the tents and love to be petted. There are also calves you're allowed to feed. The tents are within walking distance of the beach. Open from April to November. ◆€€◆

a. Ferme de La Folivraie, 14710 Louvières
t. +33 141 310 800
w. unlitaupre.fr/destination/ferme-de-la-folivraie

If you want to camp on a real farm, **Ferme de Rouge Fosse** (**36**) is your spot. A relaxing and quiet campsite with a view of the fields and all the facilities you need. Open year round. ◆€◆

a. D514, 14710 Englesqueville-la-Percée
t. +33 672 051 530

Museum-hotel **Spirit of 1944** (**37**) is a bit of a crazy place, but definitely a special one. Want to sleeping in a museum full of World War II paraphernalia? Surrounded by newspapers, posters, and with music by Glenn Miller in the background, you'll find the hotel has no intention of romanticising the war, but to mimic the atmosphere of the 1940s. Open year round. ◆€€◆

a. Le Lieu Besnard, 14230 La Cambe
t. +33 231 510 752
w. spiritof1944.fr

FRANCE

IN AND AROUND COTENTIN

Cotentin is the peninsula northwest of the landing beaches. The landscape and coast are rougher and greener than the rest of Normandy's, and large parts of it are in the nature reserve Du Marais de Cotentin et du Bessin. Dominated by marshland, rivers and forests, the area's particularly popular among migratory birds in September, which use it as a safe stopover on their way south. The waters of the bay of Veys, in the north, are home to spoonbills, cranes, and cormorants. Interested in birds? Bring your binoculars! Unlike other rural areas in France, here the young people don't seem to move away, and some even return after their studies elsewhere. It's a wealthy region: tourism, agriculture, a large wharf, and two nuclear reactors keep unemployment low. Tourism's a relatively new source of income as the peninsula used to be hard to reach via the marshes, and you won't find the chic resort vibe of Deauville. The rich list here consists of the local specialities: cider, calvados, and oysters! The apples and pears for the first two are locally sourced, and the oyster culture along the coast keeps growing year by year.

P.S. From the coast you can see the Îles de la Manche (Channel Islands), the phone masts of which can confuse your phone - don't be surprised if your network welcomes you to Jersey or Guernsey - you're still en France!

TO DO

For quite some time, people kept telling us to go eat oysters in **Saint-Vaast-la-Hougue (38)**. We finally did and we can now tell you, hand on heart: go check out the delicious oysters of Saint-Vaast! There may not be a vast difference in taste compared to other places with oysters on their menu, but the tableau of foggy pier, screeching seagulls, fishing port, and wooden boats being repaired at the wharf is rather magical. Near the harbour, you'll find the island of **Tahitou (39)**, which is accessible on foot at low tide. Put on your hiking boots and bring your binoculars, there are lots of sea birds to observe. In case it's too late to walk back, you can hop on the amphibious vehicle that connects the island to the mainland. Every Saturday there's a market in the centre of Saint-Vaast.

Tourism office at 1 Place General de Gaulle, 50550 Saint-Vaast-la-Hougue.

From Saint-Vaast, you can reach **Valognes (40)** by travelling inland for just 15 minutes. A town also referred to as the Versailles of Normandy, thanks to its 18th century manors and villas whose gardens are just as stylish as those of Versailles.

Cherbourg (41) is the largest town of the region, so if you want to go shopping or have a night out, it's where you'll want to be. There's nothing wrong with its centre, but don't expect to be overwhelmed by its beauty or what it has to offer. With regards to tourist attractions, **Cité de la Mer (42)** could be a nice outing, particularly for children. There are numerous aquariums, as well as La Redoutable, one of the largest submarines in the world that's open to visitors.

a. Gare Maritime Transatlantique, 50100 Cherbourg-Octeville
t. +33 233 202 669
w. citedelamer.com

You'll most likely be following a section of the **Route de Caps** (**43**) towards the north-western cape without paying much attention to the road signs, but you can expect a couple of oh's and ah's on the way nonetheless. The route will take you along the capes of the peninsula and so it doesn't exactly follow the coast, but you're never far away from it either and will be able to take in all aspects of the landscape: medieval villages, farms, rock walls, immense cliffs, and lush hills.

If you keep following the Route de Caps, you'll automatically go through **Port Racine** (**44**). You'll have gone past it before you know it, as this is the smallest port in France.

A bit further, at the cape's outermost point, you'll reach **Cap de la Hague** (**45**). Make sure to get out of your car here, put on your hiking boots or grab your mountain bike. Countless paths take you around the cape, a bit inland, or along the shoreline.

One of the prettiest towns of the region is **Barneville-Carteret** (**46**), full of Belle Époque villas, and beautiful beaches where you'll find old-fashioned white-blue beach huts along Plage La Potinière as a living reminder of the first-ever beach holidays in the 19th century. The small village of **Portbail** (**47**) lies just south of Barneville-Carteret. If anything deserves to be called picturesque, it's this town.

Mont Saint-Michel (**48**) is without a doubt the best-known attraction on the Atlantic coast. This doesn't mean you shouldn't go - even though you'll likely be surrounded by busloads of tourists. In olden days the abbey was only accessible at low tide, nowadays there's an elevated causeway between the island and the mainland. Try to visit Mont Saint-Michel in autumn, or even winter on a clear sky day, and ideally head there way too early in the morning. If you're lucky you could be one of few early birds walking through the narrow streets, while racing up the many steps to enjoy the fabulous views of land and sea before the minions pour in the gates. Open year round.

a. Abbaye du Mont Saint-Michel, BP 22, 50170 Le Mont-Saint-Michel
t. +33 233 601 430
w. ot-montsaintmichel.com

Want to learn more about the ins and outs of Mont Saint-Michel and the surrounding nature? Join the passionate young guides of **Traversee Baie Nature** (**49**). Tours available year round.

- **a.** Abbaye du Mont Saint-Michel, BP 22, 50170 Le Mont-Saint-Michel
- **t.** +33 664 285 440
- **w.** traversee-baie-nature.fr

EAT/DRINK/HANG OUT
◆

One of the nicest beach bars is **Le Goeland 1951** (**50**). Built as an extension to a bunker, it comes with a rather austere yet beachy interior with a lot of wood. It has regular live music events and parties, and the menu offers cocktails, salads and burgers. Open from June to September, but occasionally off-season too, provided the weather is nice.

- **a.** 82 Route du Phare / Jonville Strand, 50760 Réville
- **t.** +33 972 839 407
- **fb.** Le Goeland 1951

Go for a drink at **Auberge des Grottes** (**51**), mostly for the view of the Channel Islands, Cap de la Hague, the lighthouse of Goury and of course the ocean. You'll find the restaurant on top of one of Europe's largest cliffs (128 m tall). ◆€◆ ◆€€◆

- **a.** Le Nez de Jobourg, 50440 Jobourg
- **t.** +33 233 527 144
- **w.** aubergedesgrottes.com

Crêperie **Le Manoir du Valciot** (**52**) in Siouville-Hague is located in a 16th century manor house and serves delicious pancakes, both sweet and savoury. Just what you need after a day on the beach. Open year round, weekends only from November to April. If you're still looking for a place to sleep: their chambres d'hôtes are located right next door. ◆€◆ ◆€€◆

- **a.** 14 Chemin des Costils, 50340 Siouville-Hague
- **t.** +33 233 529 315
- **fb.** Manoir Du Valciot Siouville

Brasserie le Baligan (**53**) awaits with its surf-themed décor and servings of fresh chips, tasty home-made hamburgers and daily specials. Regular music events. Open year round. ◆€◆ ◆€€◆

- **a.** 3/4 Place des Tamaris, 50340 Siouville
- **t.** + 33 233 010 645
- **fb.** Le Baligan

Restaurant **Le Sauve Qui Pleut** (**54**) is located next to the car park of Plage Sciotot, with a nice view of the bay, and of surfers coming and going to check the waves. With a pleasant atmosphere and friendly staff, it's a great place to enjoy a coffee on the terrace. Open year round, only for lunch and at weekends from November to April. ◆€€◆

- **a.** 1 Route du Fort, 50340 Les Pieux
- **t.** +33 233 943 385
- **fb.** le sauve qui pleut

SHOP
◆

La Biscuiterie de Quinéville (**55**) is a tea salon and confectioner, as well as selling special tarts and cakes. The selection is so good you'll have a hard time choosing.

- **a.** 6 Rue du Port Sinope, 50310 Quinéville
- **t.** +33 233 406 851
- **w.** biscuiterie-quineville.com

SLEEP
◆

Campsite **La Ferme du Bord de Mer** (**56**) lies, as the name suggests, right by the sea. A quiet spot with a relaxed atmosphere, minimal decor and perhaps even a tad dated, but that may just define its charm. Open from May to September, mobile homes for rent from April to November. ◆€◆

- **a.** 43 Route du Val de Saire, 50760 Gatteville-le-Phare
- **t.** +33 233 540 177
- **w.** camping-gatteville.fr

Gite des Deux Caps (57) is a beautiful farmhouse made of stone in Carneville, on the northern point of Cotentin, between Barfleur and Cherbourg. The farmhouse has four guestrooms to rent, and a detached house with its own kitchen. From the large garden you'll enjoy the view of the green valley, and from the upper rooms you'll have a sea view. ♦€€♦

a. 2 La Brasserie, 50330 Carneville
t. +33 233 541 381 / 612 283 619
w. gitedesdeuxcaps.com

Anse du Brick (58) is a terraced campsite so you always get sea views and there's a walkway to give direct beach access. It's a family-friendly site with a water park, a heated and covered pool and a waterslide (good luck getting your kids to the beach). It also offers homes with sea views. Open from April to September. ♦€€♦

a. 18 Anse du Brick,
   50330 Maupertus-sur-Mer
t. +33 233 543 357
w. anse-du-brick.com

If you need a couple more days to discover Cap de la Hague, **Du Hâble (59)** is your ideal campsite: small, quiet, friendly, and conveniently located. Open from April to September. ♦€♦

a. 4 Route de la Hague,
   50440 Omonville-la-Rogue
t. +33 233 528 615
w. omonvillelarogue.fr/tourisme/
   camping-municipal

There are lots of options for **campervans** to find a nice safe spot without having to go to a campsite. Check out the following car parks:

Next to the **lighthouse of Fermanville (60)** (Cap Levi), you can park up for free overnight and enjoy the view. A bit before it, there is another van park for € 5. Neither option has any facilities. Open year round.

On the grass patch of the official campsite by **Plage de Tamarisses (61)** in Siouville-Hague. All facilities available. Open year round. ♦€♦

a. Avenue des Peupliers,
   50340 Siouville-Hague

Another nice campervan spot is close to the beach of **Sciotot (62)**. It has toilet facilities as well as showers (in summer) and there's a beach hut. No other facilities.

a. Plage de Sciotot, 50340 Les Pieux

Campsite **Le Ranch (63)** is the perfect spot for sustainable camping, behind the long beach of Rozel. The site aims to actively reduce its water and energy consumption and asks guests to do the same. Open from April to September. ♦€♦ ♦€€♦

a. La Mielle, 50340 Le Rozel
t. +33 233 100 710
w. camping-leranch.com

Not far from Mont Saint-Michel, you'll find the campsite **la Bidonnière (64)**. Surrounded by fields and offering prime views of the abbey, it comes with all facilities, including showers and wifi. Free shuttle to the World Heritage Site and there's a friendly baker dropping by with warm fresh goodies in the mornings. Open all year. ♦€♦

a. 5 Route de la Rive, 50170 Ardevon
t. +33 625 553 070
w. campingcar.ardevivre.fr

La Ferme de la Moricière (65), an organic farm with views of Mont Saint-Michel, is on one of the seven hills of Sartilly, from which pilgrims used to descend to the abbey. Surrounded by the lush green of the large site, you can stay in a spacious and fully equipped tent, including woodstove and toilet. You'll also get to witness life on a cattle farm from up close - from milking cows to feeding chickens, pigs and goats. Open from April to November. ♦€€♦

a. La Ferme de la Moricière, 50530 Sartilly
t. +33 141 310 800
w. unlitaupre.fr/destination/
   la-ferme-de-la-moriciere

SURF

♦

Where most of this guide's surf destinations are along the North Sea coast, except the north of Norway, in Normandy we're back to the Atlantic. Normandy doesn't receive as much, or as consistent, surf as its southern provinces, but it has beaches, bays and reefs facing from N-NW-W to SW. Some exposed, some sheltered, receiving both wind and ground swell. So, many options in all sorts of circumstances, and still slightly under the radar from the masses.

Wissant (I) is a NW-facing long stretch of white sand beach. Works best at higher tide with a small to big swell from almost toutes directions SW-W-NW-N-NE. Beware of currents, can be crowded, surfers from north, especially Holland, will drive down if forecasts are good. Also a popular kite and windsurf spot. ♦ *All levels/sand/difficult parking/restaurants/camping.* ♦

Cap Gris-Nez (II) is sheltered from strong SW-W winds. Works best at mid-tide with a big SW-W-NW-N swell. Beware of currents and rips.
♦ *Advanced level/rocks/easy parking/restaurant/camping.* ♦

West-facing reefbreak **Wimereux (III)** works at higher tides with a medium to big SW-W-NW swell. Beware of currents, this spot can be crowded, with locals as well as regular Belgian and Dutch surfers. ♦ *Intermediate and advanced level/rocks/easy parking.* ♦

Beautiful **Yport (IV)** is a small, sheltered NNW-facing reefbreak. Works best on upcoming tide with SW-W-NW-N swell. ♦ *Intermediate and advanced levels/rocks/easy parking, except in summer/restaurants.* ♦

SCHOOL RENTAL REPAIR

Étretat (V) is another beauty of a sheltered bay. The WNW-facing reefbreak next to L'Aiguille Creuse works best at mid-tide with a medium to big SW-W-NW-N swell. Beware of currents, and when it's on, it'll be crowded. As a local surf school owner advised us: "Arrive with the smile". Be humble and wait your turn. ◆ *All levels/rocks/difficult paid parking/toilets/restaurants.* ◆

Trouville (VI) is small NW-facing bay that works on all tides with a W-NW-N swell. Beware of currents, can get crowded. ◆ *All levels/sand/difficult and paid parking/restaurants/surf school.* ◆

L'Anse du Brick (VII) is a small NW-facing beach with some rocks. Works best at lower tides with a medium to big W-NW-N swell. Can be crowded. ◆ *All levels/sand and rocks/easy parking/restaurant/camping.* ◆

The long exposed west-facing stretch of beach at **Siouville (VIII)** works best on upcoming tide with a small to big SW-W-NW swell. Lots of peaks to choose from. Beware of currents. Popular with kite and windsurfers. ◆ *All levels/sand/easy parking/toilets/restaurants/camping/surf school.* ◆

West-facing **Le Rozel (IX)** is another long stretch of exposed white sand beach. Works at all tides with a small to big SW-W-NW swell. Beware of currents. ◆ *All levels/sand/easy parking/toilets/restaurants/camping.* ◆

Surf and board shop **Airwave (66)** has surf, SUP, kite and windsurf gear, boards and essentials. Open all year.

- **a.** 1 Rue du Machicoulis, 62200 Boulogne-sur-Mer
- **t.** +33 321 306 389
- **w.** airwave-shop.com

North Shore Surf School (67) and Casual Store offer surf and SUP lessons and rentals. They organise SUP tours through the canals of Trouville-sur-Mer. Open from Easter to October.

- **a.** Promenade Savignac Les Planches, 14360 Trouville-sur-Mer (school)
- **a.** 377 Rue des Feugrais, 14360 Trouville-sur-Mer (shop)
- **t.** +33 649 527 901
- **w.** northshore-school.com

Kriss Custom (68) is a shaper of longboards and retro fish. The shop sells all surf, SUP, wave-ski and kite gear and essentials. Open all year.

- **a.** Les Houguettes, 50340 Siouville-Hague
- **t.** +33 233 930 106
- **w.** krisscustom.com

Cotentin Surf Club and School (69) is the organiser of national surf competitions and your go-to place for all information on surf, spots, tides in the area. They've got surf and SUP lessons and rentals on offer. Open from April to October.

- **a.** 14 Boulevard Ferdinand Deveaud, 50340 Siouville-Hague
- **t.** +33 233 413 958
- **w.** cotentinsurfclub.com

Find all sorts of surf, street and lifestyle apparel, surf and skate gear, at the small shop of **Habits et Vous (70)**.

- **a.** 10 Bis Rue Centrale, 50340 Les Pieux
- **t.** +33 233 020 875
- **fb.** habits et vous

Mézoya Surfshop (71) has got everything for your surf, SUP, skate, kite and windsurf needs.

- **a.** 102 Avenue du Passous, 50230 Agon-Coutainville
- **t.** +33 233 170 050
- **fb.** Mézoya Surfshop

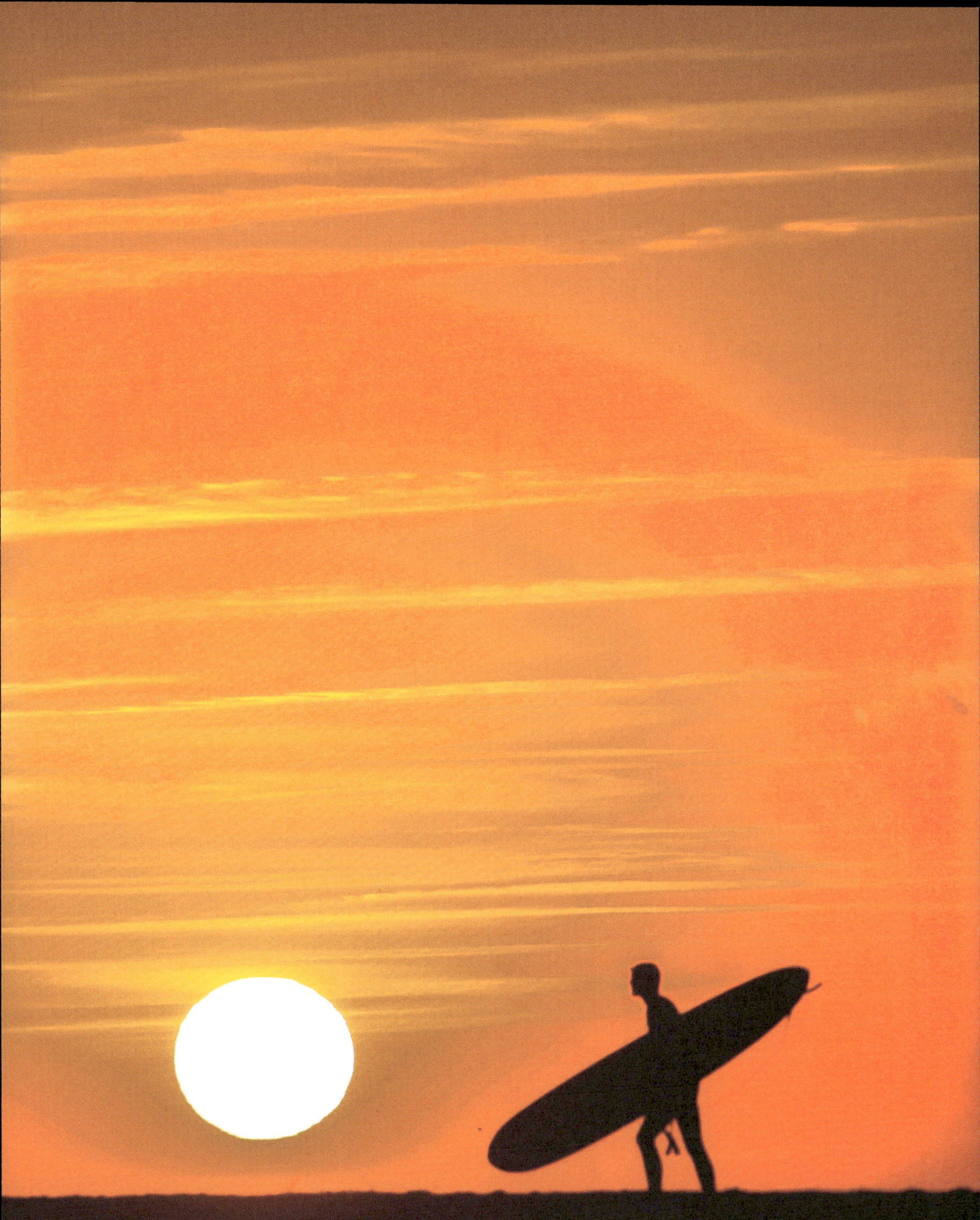

I LOVE THE SEASIDE

THERE'S MORE I LOVE THE SEASIDE!

Check out our online shop for I Love the Seaside travel essentials. We're talking sexy Seaside enamel mugs, super thermos flasks, snuggly soft beach towels and... car fresheners (that smell strongly like pine but look great in photos - they're actually free, go see for yourself). We're adding more all the time!

ilovetheseaside.com/shop

THANK YOU!

Oops, we did it again. A completely new edition (and adventure!) of I Love the Seaside. Made with love and a few sleepless nights, but mostly love. And, as with our first edition, the crucial and indispensable help of many. With our first Southwest Europe edition we set things in motion; inspiring travellers, and a continuation of creating seaside guides. We can't thank you enough, dear readers, supporters and partners, that we can do just so! We hope to meet you, either in a next edition or on social media (#iloveseaside), but preferably in the ocean.
Let us know you're out there, share your story, photo or wave. Stay stoked!

Big up, cheers and thank you to all supporters of our crowdfund campaign, friends and family for your faith. And of course Maaike, Kolja, Ravi, Bonzer & Django, Bom & Gail, Marinus, Melchior, Frank van Leeuwen, Ocean Republic, Nomads Valerie & Tim, Nordic Surfers Magazine, Artic Campers, Unstad Artic Surf, Hattvika Lodge, Arthur Pantalian Veines, Caroline Simensen & Zac Ifield, Anna Bergman, Mathieu Turries, Tim Wendrich, Harmen Piekema, Danny Bastiaanse, Wouter Struyf, Protest, C-Skins, Creatures, the Green Chef Jehtro van Luijk.

I Love the Seaside
Wassenaarsestraat 110
2586 AR Scheveningen
The Netherlands

t. +31 6 53 178 129
e. info@iloveseaside.com
w. iloveseaside.com
ig. iloveseaside
fb. iloveseaside

ISBN 978 90 825 0796 6
NUR 512
Second edition Summer 2019

Printed in the EU by Real Concepts,
w. realconcepts.nl
Paper from responsible sources.

Concept & text: zee-inkt.nl
Art direction & graphic design: re-act.nl
Copyediting: gailbennie.com
Merchandise: sourxing.com
Photography:
northseajuice.eu, melchior-photography.com

Want to sell our beautiful guides in your shop?
e. gj@iloveseaside.com

Cover & inside cover photos:
Melchior van Nigtevecht

BONZER & DJANGO

BRAND NEW HEAD & CHIEF
OF EXPLORING & WAGGISHNESS

All rights reserved.
No part of this guide (or publication) may be reproduced in any forms or by any means, stored in a retrieval system, or transmitted, in any form or by any means, electronic, graphic, photocopying, mechanical, recording, or otherwise without the permission of the publishers and copyright owners.

I Love the Seaside and the I Love the Seaside logo are registered trademarks of I Love the Seaside.

Feedback.
This guide has been compiled with the utmost care and attention to detail, however, details may change. Travellers should be aware that recommended providers and services may move, alter provisions or services, prices or opening times.

Having said that: we'd love your help! Please let us know about your experiences, share your knowledge, opinions, tips and insights - email us: info@iloveseaside.com.

Independent.
To clarify, we would like to assure you that none of the recommendations listed in our guide have paid by any means for entry in this guide.

I Love the Seaside is not liable for any injury or inconvenience however caused, or any inaccuracies in the text

Please note.
Maps are solely indicators of locations, they are not intended to be used as road maps.
© OpenStreetMap.org

ABOUT US

ALEXANDRA GOSSINK

WRITER, EDITOR & CONCEPT

Never really needs a break from travelling as a journalist, writing stories, surfing and walking the dogs. Likes her life to be healthy and happy.

GEERT-JAN MIDDELKOOP

PRODUCTION, SALES & DISTRIBUTION

Seaside explorer since childhood. Manages to do a lot of trade and business between sessions. When he's not on a surf trip in his campervan, he's planning one.

DIM ROOKER

GRAPHIC DESIGNER & CONCEPT

Gets his inspiration from the ocean. Besides designing and working on concepts for brands, books and websites at his harbour office, he loves to take his family on van-adventures and his sons surfing.

GAIL BENNIE

CO-WRITER, PROOFREADER & COPYEDITOR

Ocean-loving wordbird longboarder. Currently on a stopover in Jersey, Channel Islands, while planning long trips north and south. Never far from the sea.

MARINUS JORIS

PHOTOGRAPHER

Enjoys surf in and out of the water, camera in hand. Able to capture atmosphere and mood like no other.

MELCHIOR VAN NIGTEVECHT

PHOTOGRAPHER

Waterperson. Loves to ride waves with anything from hand board to log. Shoots surf and lifestyle pictures for magazines and stock.

#ILOVETHESEASIDE

*Share your I Love the Seaside stories! Check our website to
be inspired about your future travels, find new places to surf,
shop, eat, drink or hang out. Buy your travel essentials
or even book your next holiday...*

facebook.com/iloveseaside
instagram.com/iloveseaside

ilovetheseaside.com